INTEREST GROUP
POLITICS

INTEREST GROUP POLITICS

Fifth Edition

Edited by
Allan J. Cigler
Burdett A. Loomis
University of Kansas

A Division of Congressional Quarterly Inc.
Washington, D.C.

Copyright © 1998 Congressional Quarterly Inc.
1414 22nd Street, N.W., Washington, D.C. 20037

Printed in the United States of America

Cover design: Todd Kiraly, Westbound Publications

Chapter 5 adapted from Constance Ewing Cook, *Lobbying for Higher Education: How Colleges and Universities Influence Federal Policy* (Nashville, Tenn.: Vanderbilt University Press, 1998). Reprinted with the permission of the publisher.

Library of Congress Cataloging-in-Publication Data

Interest group politics / edited by Allan J. Cigler,
    Burdett A. Loomis. — 5th ed.
        p.   cm.
    Includes bibliographical references and index.
    ISBN 1-56802-159-3
    1. Pressure groups—United States. I. Cigler, Allan J., 1943– .
II. Loomis, Burdett A., 1945– .
JK1118.I565   1998
322.4'3'0973—dc21

98-30202

Contents

Preface

The study of interest groups remains something of a stepchild in American politics. Although the late Mancur Olson—to whom we dedicate this volume—did unquestionably revolutionize the way we think about interest groups with the 1965 publication of *The Logic of Collective Action*, the field has scarcely leapt toward new understandings of the role of membership groups, campaign contributions, lobbying strategies, or (especially) the overall impact of interests on policy outcomes. At the same time, organized interests have grown in number and apparent strength. The related growth of public interest groups and corporate involvement has defined much of the politics of the past thirty years.

Since 1983, five editions of this book have tracked the evolution of interest group politics in the United States. First examining the proliferation of groups (and how they overcame the obstacles outlined by Olson), we have turned more recently to focus on interests within the policy-making process and how they react to the great complexity and uncertainty of this process. In the fifth edition, as in all the previous volumes, we have learned a great deal from our contributors. The continuing insights of Bill Browne, for example, have helped define the relationships between interests and decision makers. Jim Guth, John Green, and their collaborators have provided, over time, solid data and sound analyses at the intersection of religion and politics. And Robert Salisbury has proven a consistently interesting and important voice as he explores facets of the lobbying–interest group connection that he first considered more than thirty years ago examining group entrepreneurs. Our debts are huge to all who have contributed, and our thanks inadequate.

If the theme of the past two volumes has been the search for certainty, this edition observes that such certainty is very difficult, perhaps impossible, to achieve, particularly in light of the increasing politicization of communication that surrounds both electoral politics and policy making. One might legitimately question whether we have any business being surprised by such a trend; after all, elections and policy making are inherently political phenomena. We see the level of political communication rising, often sponsored by particular interests who are dedicated, even desperate, to get their messages across. And they are willing to spend large sums to press their points, whether in the pages of the *Washington Post* or the halls of Congress. In turn, these are salad days for lobbyists, consultants, and public relations firms (often housed at the same K Street addresses in downtown Washington). In the end, we interpret contemporary interest group politics as different, certainly in degree and possibly in kind, from what we depicted in the first edition of this book. Are we in a "hyperpolitics" era? Are moneyed interests more and more advantaged? As noted in Chapter 18, we think so, but the evidence is scarcely conclusive. Whether we persuade the reader on this point or not, we do hope that this collection contributes to the further understanding of organized interests by students and scholars alike.

Our profound thanks go to CQ Press, which has supported our efforts with understanding and good humor (essential when dealing with two clowns). Brenda Carter has understood the nature of the book and has consistently made it better. Gwenda Larsen and Julie Rovesti have also been great, and we truly appreciate the long-standing support of David Tarr. Debbie Hardin was an excellent copy editor. Beth Cigler and Michel Loomis have, as always, offered their unique combination of support and critique. All in all, it's almost fun.

Allan J. Cigler
Burdett A. Loomis

Contributors

Brian Anderson is a lecturer of political science at Pennsylvania State University—University Park. His research interests include group resources, lobbying, and policy making.

Frank R. Baumgartner is a professor of political science at Texas A&M University. His previous books include *Basic Interests: The Importance of Groups in Politics and in Political Science*, with Beth L. Leech (1998), and *Agendas and Instability in American Politics*, with Bryan Jones (1993). His current research focuses on policy making and agenda setting in the postwar period.

William P. Browne is a professor of political science at Central Michigan University. His research interest is the process of public policy making. Most of his publications have been about interest groups or agricultural policy. His most recent book is *Groups, Interests, and U.S. Public Policy* (1998).

Allan J. Cigler is Chancellor's Club Teaching Professor of Political Science at the University of Kansas. He received his doctorate from Indiana University. His research focuses on parties and interest groups, and particularly on the interrelationship between the two mediating institutions.

Lauretta Conklin is a doctoral candidate at Washington University in St. Louis. Her current research focuses on the impact of informal norms and structural incentives on economic organization in immigrant communities.

M. Margaret Conway is a professor of political science at the University of Florida—Gainesville. She has written several books on political participation, political parties, and women and politics. She has also published a number of articles in academic journals.

Constance E. Cook is an associate professor of higher education at the Center for the Study of Higher and Postsecondary Education at the University of Michigan. She is the author of *Lobbying for Higher Education: How Colleges and Universities Influence Federal Policy* (1998), on which the chapter in this book is based. She currently serves as director of the Center for Research on Learning and Teaching at the University of Michigan.

William Frasure is a professor of government at Connecticut College. He received his doctorate from Johns Hopkins University. His research interests include Congress, public administration, lobbying, political parties and interest groups, and public policy.

Joanne Connor Green is an assistant professor of political science at Texas Christian University. Her research interests include the dynamics of open-seat elections for the U.S. House of Representatives, with special attention devoted to the impact of gender and money in elections and the political process.

John C. Green is director of the Ray Bliss Institute of Applied Politics and is a professor of political science at the University of Akron. He has written extensively on the topics of religion and politics, campaign finance, and political parties.

James L. Guth is a professor of political science at Furman University. A student of interest groups and social movements, his most recent books and articles have examined the politics of religious organizations and activists. He is currently engaged in a long-term study of the impact of religious factors on voting behavior.

Paul S. Herrnson is a professor of government and politics at the University of Maryland—College Park. He is the author of *Congressional Elections: Campaigning at Home and in Washington*, 2d ed. (1998) and *Party Campaigning in the 1980s* (1988) and coeditor of several volumes. He has written numerous articles on Congress, campaign finance, political parties, and elections, and has served as an American Political Science Association Congressional Fellow and as a congressional aide.

Paul E. Johnson is an associate professor of political science at the University of Kansas. His research on interest groups has been published in a number of academic journals. He is currently working on computer models of the way interest group organizers contact prospective members.

Lyman A. Kellstedt is a professor of political science at Wheaton College. He is the author and coauthor of numerous articles and books on religion and politics. His current research involves a reinterpretation of the role of religion in American politics and an examination of the role of contemporary religious activists.

Beth L. Leech is a doctoral candidate in the Department of Political Science at Texas A&M University. She is the coauthor, with Frank M. Baumgartner, of *Basic Interests: The Importance of Groups in Politics and in Political Science* (1998) and an article about interest group lobbying in the *American Journal of Political Science*. Her research interests include the roles of interest groups and the news media in policy formation.

Burdett A. Loomis is a professor of political science and director of the Robert J. Dole Institute of Public Service and Public Policy at the University of Kansas. He received his doctorate from the University of Wisconsin. His research interests include legislatures, political careers, interest groups, and policy making.

Anthony J. Nownes is an assistant professor of political science at the University of Tennessee. His research interests focus on public interest groups and group formation.

Kelly Patterson is an associate professor of political science at Brigham Young University. He is the author of *Political Parties and the Maintenance of Liberal Democracy* (1996). His teaching and research interests include political parties, campaigns and elections, and theories of American politics.

Andrew Rich is a doctoral candidate in political science at Yale University. His research interests focus on the interaction of ideas and interests in the policy-making process and the role of nongovernmental actors in policy making. He is completing a dissertation about the proliferation of think tanks and the politicization of the ideas and expertise made available by them in the policy-making process.

Robert H. Salisbury is a Professor Emeritus at Washington University. He has written extensively on interest groups in theory and practice.

Ronald G. Shaiko is an associate professor of government and academic director of the Lobbying Institute at American University. He was awarded the William A. Steiger Congressional Fellowship by the American Political Science Association for 1993–1994. He was awarded a Democracy Fellowship by the United States Agency for International Development in December 1997. He will be serving USAID in the Center for Democracy and Governance through May 1999.

Corwin E. Smidt is director of the Paul B. Henry Institute for the Study of Christianity and Politics and is a professor of political science at Calvin College. His research interests focus primarily on the relationship between religion and politics, and he is the author and editor of many books and articles on the subject.

John Tierney is an associate professor of political science at Boston College. He received his doctorate from Harvard University. His research interests include public policy, political origins and parties, and public administration.

Eric M. Uslaner is a professor of government and politics at the University of Maryland—College Park. In 1981–1982 he was a Fulbright professor of American studies at the Hebrew University in Jerusalem. His research interests focus on Congress, elections, civic engagement, and Canadian politics.

R. Kent Weaver is a Senior Fellow in the Governmental Studies Program at the Brookings Institution. His research interests include social policy, comparative political institutions, and the influence of policy research and policy research institutions on the policy-making process. He received his doctorate in political science from Harvard University in 1982.

Laura R. Woliver is an associate professor of political science in the Department of Government and International Studies at the University of South Carolina—Columbia. She is the author of *From Outrage to Action: The Politics of Grass-roots Dissent* (1993) and numerous articles and book chapters on women's rights, civil rights, grassroots dissent, social movements, and reproductive politics.

1

Introduction: The Changing Nature of Interest Group Politics

Burdett A. Loomis and Allan J. Cigler

From James Madison to Madison Avenue, political interests have played a central role in American politics. But this great continuity in our political experience has been matched by the ambivalence with which citizens, politicians, and scholars have approached interest groups. James Madison's warnings on the dangers of faction echo in the rhetoric of reformers ranging from Populists and Progressives near the turn of the century to the so-called public-interest advocates of today.

If organized special interests are nothing new in American politics, can today's group politics nevertheless be seen as having undergone some fundamental changes? Acknowledging that many important, continuing trends do exist, we seek to place in perspective a broad series of changes in the nature of modern interest group politics. Among the most substantial of these developments are:

1. A great proliferation of interest groups since the early 1960s
2. A centralization of group headquarters in Washington, D.C., rather than in New York City or elsewhere
3. Major technological developments in information processing that promote more sophisticated, more timely, and more specialized communications strategies, such as grassroots lobbying
4. The rise of single-issue groups
5. Changes in campaign finance laws (1971, 1974) and the ensuing growth of political action committees (PACs), and more recently, the growth of independent campaign expenditures by some interests
6. The increased formal penetration of political and economic interests into the bureaucracy (advisory committees), the presidency (White House group representatives), and the Congress (caucuses of members)
7. The continuing decline of political parties' abilities to perform key electoral and policy-related activities
8. The increased number, activity, and visibility of public-interest groups, such as Common Cause and the Ralph Nader-inspired public interest research organizations

9. The growth of activity and impact by institutions, including corporations, universities, state and local governments, and foreign interests
10. A continuing rise in the amount and sophistication of group activity in state capitals, especially given the devolution of some federal programs and substantial increases in state budgets.

All these developments have their antecedents in previous eras of American political life; there is little that is genuinely new under the interest group sun. Political action committees have replaced (or complemented) other forms of special interest campaign financing. Group-generated mail directed at Congress has existed as a tactic since at least the early 1900s.[1] Many organizations have long been centered in Washington, members of Congress traditionally have represented local interests, and so on.

At the same time, however, the level of group activity, coupled with growing numbers of organized interests, distinguishes contemporary group politics from the politics of earlier eras. Current trends of group involvement lend credence to the fears of scholars such as political scientist Theodore Lowi and economist Mancur Olson, who view interest-based politics as contributing to governmental stalemate and reduced accountability.[2] If accurate, these analyses point to a fundamentally different role for interest groups than those suggested by Madison and later group theorists.

Only during the past thirty years, in the wake of Olson's path-breaking research, have scholars begun to examine realistically why people join and become active in groups.[3] It is by no means self-evident that citizens should naturally become group members—quite the contrary in most instances. We are faced, then, with the paradoxical and complex question of why groups have proliferated, as they certainly have, when usually it is economically unwise for individuals to join them.

Interest Groups in American Politics

Practical politicians and scholars alike generally have concurred that interest groups (also known as *factions, organized interests, pressure groups,* and *special interests)* are natural phenomena in a democratic regime—that is, individuals will band together to protect their interests.[4] In Madison's words, "The causes of faction . . . are sown in the nature of man," but controversy continues as to whether groups and group politics are benign or malignant forces in American politics. "By a faction," Madison wrote, "I understand a number of citizens, whether amounting to a majority or minority of the whole, who are united and actuated by some common impulse of passion, or of interest, adverse to the rights of other citizens, or to the permanent and aggregate interests of the community."[5]

Although Madison rejected the remedy of direct controls over factions as "worse than the disease," he saw the need to limit their negative effects by promoting competition among them and by devising an elaborate system of procedural "checks and balances" to reduce the potential power of any single, strong group, whether that group represented a majority or minority position.

Hostility toward interest groups became more virulent in industrialized America, where the great concentrations of power that developed far outstripped anything Madison might have imagined. After the turn of the century many Progressives railed at various monopolistic "trusts" and intimate connections between interests and corrupt politicians. Later, in 1935, Hugo Black, then a senator (and later a Supreme Court justice), painted a grim picture of group malevolence: "Contrary to tradition, against the public morals, and hostile to good government, the lobby has reached such a position of power that it threatens government itself. Its size, its power, its capacity for evil, its greed, trickery, deception and fraud condemn it to the death it deserves."[6]

Similar suspicions are expressed today, especially in light of the substantial growth of PACs since the adoption of campaign reform amendments in 1974. PAC contributions to congressional candidates rose from less than $23 million in 1975–1976 to $430 million in the 1995–1996 election cycle, which amounted to roughly one-third of the House candidates' campaign funds and one-fifth of their Senate counterparts. Still, the number of PACs has leveled off at about 4,000, only a fraction of which are major players in electoral politics. Reformers in and out of Congress have sought to limit purported PAC influence, but as of 1998 legislators could not agree on major changes in laws regulating campaign spending or group activity. PACs continue to be an attractive target for reformers. One typical expression of dismay comes from Common Cause, the self-styled public interest lobby:

> The Special Interest State is a system in which interest groups dominate the making of government policy. These interests legitimately concentrate on pursuing their own immediate—usually economic—agendas, but in so doing they pay little attention to the impact of their agendas on the nation as a whole.[7]

Despite the considerable popular distrust of interest group politics, political scientists and other observers often have viewed groups in a much more positive light. This perspective also draws on Madison's *Federalist* writings, but it is tied more closely to the growth of the modern state. Political science scholars such as Arthur Bentley, circa 1910, and David Truman, forty years later, placed groups at the heart of politics and policy making in a complex, large, and increasingly specialized governmental system. The interest group becomes an element of continuity in a changing political world. Truman noted the "multiplicity of co-ordinate or nearly co-ordinate points of access to governmental decisions" and concluded that "the significance of these many points of access and of the complicated texture of relationships among them is great. This diversity assures various ways for interest groups to participate in the formation of policy, and this variety is a flexible, stabilizing element."[8]

Derived from Truman's work, and that of other group-oriented scholars, is the notion of the pluralist state in which competition among interests, in and out of government, will produce policies roughly responsive to public desires, and no single set of interests will dominate. As one student of group politics summarized,

> Pluralist theory assumes that within the public arena there will be countervailing centers of power within governmental institutions and among outsiders. Competition is implicit in the notion that groups, as surrogates for individuals, will produce products representing the diversity of opinions that might have been possible in the individual decision days of democratic Athens.[9]

In many ways the pluralist vision of American politics corresponds to the basic realities of policy making and the distribution of policy outcomes, but a host of scholars, politicians, and other observers have roundly criticized this perspective. Two broad (although sometimes contradictory) critiques have special merit.

The first critique argues that some interests systematically lose in the policy process; others habitually win. Without endorsing the contentions of elite theorists that a small number of interests and individuals conspire together to dominate societal policies, one can make a strong case that those interests with more resources (money, access, information, and so forth) usually will obtain better results than those that possess fewer assets and employ them less effectively. The numerically small, cohesive, well-heeled defense industry, for example, does well year in and year out in the policy-making process;[10] marginal farmers and the urban poor produce a much less successful track record. Based on the continuing unequal results, critics of the pluralist model argue that interests are still represented unevenly and unfairly.

A second important line of criticism generally agrees that inequality of results remains an important aspect of group politics. But this perspective, most forcefully set out by Theodore Lowi, sees interests as generally succeeding in their goals of influencing government—to the point that the government itself, in one form or another, provides a measure of protection to almost all societal interests. Everyone thus retains some vested interest in the structure of government and array of public policies. This does not mean that all interests obtain just what they desire from governmental policies; rather, all interests get at least some rewards. From this point of view the tobacco industry surely wishes to see its crop subsidies maintained, but the small farmer and the urban poor also have pet programs, such as guaranteed loans and food stamps, which they seek to protect.

Lowi has labeled the proliferation of groups and their growing access to government "interest-group liberalism," and he has argued that this phenomenon is pathological for a democratic government:

> Interest-group liberal solutions to the problem of power [who will exercise it] provide the system with stability by spreading a *sense* of representation at the expense of genuine flexibility, at the expense of democratic forms, and ultimately at the expense of legitimacy.[11]

Interest group liberalism is pluralism, but it is *sponsored* pluralism, and the government is the chief sponsor. On the surface, it appears that the *unequal results* and *interest-group liberalism* critiques of pluralism are at odds. Reconciliation, however, is relatively straightforward. Lowi does not suggest that all interests are effectively represented. Rather, there exists in many instances only the appearance of representation. Political scientist Murray Edelman pointed out that a single set of policies can provide two related types of rewards: tangible benefits for the few and symbolic reassurances for the many.[12] Such a combination encourages groups to form, become active, and claim success.

The Climate for Group Proliferation

Substantial cleavages among a society's citizens are essential for interest group development. American culture and the constitutional arrangements of the U.S. government have encouraged the emergence of multiple political interests. In the pre-Revolutionary period, sharp conflicts existed between commercial and landed interests, debtor and creditor classes, coastal residents and those in the hinterlands, and citizens with either Tory or Whig political preferences. As the new nation developed, its vastness, characterized by geographical regions varying in climate, economic potential, culture, and tradition, contributed to a great heterogeneity. Open immigration policies further led to a diverse cultural mix with a wide variety of racial, ethnic, and religious backgrounds represented among the populace. Symbolically, the notion of the United States as a "melting pot," emphasizing group assimilation, has received much attention, but a more appropriate image may be a "tossed salad."[13]

The Constitution also contributes to a favorable environment for group development. Guarantees of free speech, association, and the right to petition the government for redress of grievances are basic to group formation. Because political organization often parallels government structure, federalism and the separation of powers—principles embodied in the Constitution—have greatly influenced the existence of large numbers of interest groups in the United States.

The decentralized political power structure in the United States allows important decisions to be made at the national, state, or local levels. Within each level of government there are multiple points of access. For example, business-related policies such as taxes are acted on at each level, and interest groups may affect these policies in the legislative, executive, or judicial arenas. In the case of federated organizations such as the U.S. Chamber of Commerce, state and local affiliates often act independently of the national organization. Numerous business organizations thus focus on the varied channels of access.

In addition, the decentralized political parties found in the United States are less unified and disciplined than parties in many other nations. The resulting power vacuum in the decision-making process offers great potential for alternative political organizations such as interest groups to influence policy. Even in an era of strong legislative parties (mid-1980s on), many opportunities for influence remain.

Finally, American cultural values may well encourage group development. As Alexis de Tocqueville observed in the 1830s, values such as individualism and the need for personal achievement underlie the propensity of citizens to join groups. Moreover, the number of access points—local, state, and national—contributes to Americans' strong sense of political efficacy when compared to that expressed by citizens of other nations.[14] Not only do Americans see themselves as joiners, but they actually tend to belong to more political groups than do people of other countries.[15]

Theories of Group Development

A climate favorable to group proliferation does little to explain how interests are organized. Whatever interests are latent in society and however favorable the context for group development may be, groups do not arise spontaneously. Farmers and a landed interest existed long before farm organizations first appeared; laborers and craftsmen were on the job before the formation of unions. In a simple society, even though distinct interests exist, there is little need for interest group formation. Farmers have no political or economic reason to organize when they work only for their families. In the early history of the country before the industrial revolution, workers were craftsmen, often laboring in small family enterprises. Broad-based political organizations were not needed, although local guilds often existed to train apprentices and to protect jobs.

David Truman has suggested that increasing societal complexity, characterized by economic specialization and social differentiation, is fundamental to group proliferation.[16] In addition, technological changes and the increasing interdependence of economic sectors often create new interests and redefine old ones. Salisbury's discussion of American farming is instructive:

> The full-scale commercialization of agriculture, beginning largely with the Civil War, led to the differentiation of farmers into specialized interests, each increasingly different from the next. . . . The interdependence which accompanied the specialization process meant potential

conflicts of interests or values both across the bargaining encounter and among the competing farmers themselves as each struggled to secure his own position.[17]

Many political scientists assume that an expansion of the interest group universe is a natural consequence of growing societal complexity. According to Truman, however, group formation "tends to occur in waves" and is greater in some periods than in others.[18] Groups organize politically when the existing order is disturbed and certain interests are, in turn, helped or hurt.

It is not surprising, then, that economic interests develop both to improve their position and to protect existing advantages. For example, the National Association of Manufacturers (NAM) originally was created to further the expansion of business opportunities in foreign trade, but it became a more powerful organization largely in response to the rise of organized labor.[19] Mobilization of business interests since the 1960s often has resulted from threats posed by consumer advocates and environmentalists, as well as requirements imposed by the steadily growing role of the federal government.

Disturbances that act to trigger group formation need not be strictly economic or technological. Wars, for example, place extreme burdens on draft-age men. Thus, organized resistance to U.S. defense policy arose during the Vietnam era. Likewise, broad societal changes may disturb the status quo. The origin of the Ku Klux Klan, for example, was based on the fear that increased numbers of ethnic and racial minorities threatened white, Christian America.

Truman's theory of group proliferation suggests that the interest group universe is inherently unstable. Groups formed from an imbalance of interests in one area induce a subsequent disequilibrium, which acts as a catalyst for individuals to form groups as counterweights to the new perceptions of inequity. Group politics thus is characterized by successive waves of mobilization and countermobilization. The liberalism of one era may prompt the resurgence of conservative groups in the next. Similarly, periods of business domination often are followed by eras of reform-group ascendancy. In the 1990s, health care reform proposals have raised the stakes for almost all segments of society. Interest group politicking has reached historic proportions, as would-be reformers, the medical community, and business interests have sought to influence the direction of change in line with their own preferences.

Personal Motivations and Group Formation

Central to theories of group proliferation are the pluralist notions that elements of society possess common needs and share a group identity or consciousness, and that these are sufficient conditions for the formation of effective political organizations. Although the perception of common needs may be necessary for political organization, whether it is sufficient for group formation and effectiveness is open to question. Historical evidence documents many instances in which groups have not emerged spontaneously even when circumstances such as poverty or discrimination would seem, in retrospect, to have required it.

Mancur Olson effectively challenged many pluralist tenets in *The Logic of Collective Action,* first published in 1965. Basing his analysis on a model of the "rational economic man," Olson posited that even individuals who have common interests are not inclined to join organizations that attempt to address their concerns. The major barrier to group participation is the "free-rider" problem: "rational" individuals choose not to bear the participation costs (time, membership) because they can enjoy the group benefits (such as favorable legislation) whether or not they join. Groups that pursue "collective" benefits, which accrue to all members of a class or segment of society regardless of membership status, will have great difficulty forming and surviving. According to Olson, it would be economically irrational for individual farmers to join a group seeking higher farm prices when benefits from price increases would be enjoyed by all farmers, even those who contribute nothing to the group. Similarly, it would be irrational for an individual consumer to become part of organized attempts to lower consumer prices, when all consumers, members or not, would reap the benefits. The free-rider problem is especially serious for large groups because the larger the group the less likely an individual will perceive his or her contribution as having any impact on group success.

For Olson, a key to group formation—and especially group survival—is the provision of "selective" benefits. These rewards—for example, travel discounts, informative publications, and cheap insurance—go only to members. Organizations in the best positions to offer such benefits are those initially formed for some nonpolitical purpose and that ordinarily provide material benefits to their clientele. In the case of unions, for example, membership may be a condition of employment. For farmers, the American Farm Bureau Federation (AFBF) offers inexpensive insurance, which induces individuals to join even if they disagree with AFBF goals. In professional circles, membership in professional societies may be a prerequisite for occupational advancement and opportunity.

Olson's notions have sparked several extensions of the rational man model, and a reasonably coherent body of incentive theory literature now exists.[20] Incentive theorists view individuals as rational decision makers interested in making the most of their time and money by choosing to participate in those groups that offer benefits greater than or equal to the costs they incur by participation.

Three types of benefits are available. Olson, an economist, emphasized *material* benefits—tangible rewards of participation, such as income or services that have monetary value. *Solidary* incentives—the socially derived, intangible rewards created by the act of association, such as fun, camaraderie, status, or prestige—also are significant. Finally, *expressive* (also known as *purposive*) rewards—those derived from advancing a particular cause or ideology—clearly are important in explaining individual actions.[21] Groups formed on both sides of issues such as abortion or gun control illustrate the strength of such expressive incentives.

The examination of group members' motivations, and in particular the focus on nonmaterial incentives, allows for some reconciliation between the traditional group theorists' expectations of group development and the recent rational-actor studies, which emphasize the barriers to group formation. Nonmaterial incentives, such as fellowship and self-satisfaction, may encourage the proliferation of highly politicized groups and, according to Terry Moe, "have the potential for producing a more dynamic group context in which politics, political preferences, and group goals are more centrally determining factors than in material associations, linking political considerations more directly to associational size, structure, and internal processes."[22] Indeed, pure political benefits may attract potential members as well, and even collective benefits can prove decisive in inducing individuals to join large groups. Like elected officials, groups may find it possible to take credit for widely approved government actions, such as higher farm prices, stronger environmental regulations, or the protection of Social Security.[23]

Finally, several recent studies indicate that the free-rider problem may not be quite the obstacle to participation that it was once thought to be, especially in an affluent society. Albert Hirschman, for example, has argued that the costs and benefits of group activity are not always clear; in fact, some costs of participation for some individuals, such as time and effort expended, might be regarded as benefits in terms of personal satisfaction by others.[24] Other researchers have questioned whether individuals even engage in rational, cost-benefit thinking as they make membership decisions. Michael McCann noted that "there seems to be a general threshold level of involvement below which free rider calculations pose few inhibitions for . . . commitment from moderately affluent citizen supporters."[25] In short, there is increasing evidence that in the modern era individuals may join and participate in groups for reasons beyond narrow economic self-interest or the availability of selective benefits.[26]

Contemporary Interest Group Politics

Several notable developments mark the modern age of interest group politics. Of primary importance is the large and growing number of active groups and other interests. The data here are sketchy, but one major study found that most current groups came into existence after World War II and that group formation has accelerated substantially since the early 1960s.[27] Also since the 1960s groups have increasingly directed their attention toward the center of power in Washington, D.C., as the scope of federal policy making has grown, and groups seeking influence have determined to "hunt where the ducks are." As a result, the 1960s and 1970s marked a veritable explosion in the number of groups lobbying in Washington.

A second key change is evident in the composition of the interest group universe. Beginning in the late 1950s political participation patterns underwent some significant transformations. Conventional activities such as voting declined, and political parties, the traditional aggregators and articulators of mass interests, became weaker. Yet at all levels of government, evidence of citizen involvement has been apparent, often in the form of new or revived groups. Particularly impressive has been the growth of citizens' groups—those organized around an idea or cause (at times a single issue) with no occupational basis for membership. Fully 30 percent of such groups have formed since 1975, and in 1980 they made up more than one-fifth of all groups represented in Washington.[28]

In fact, a participation revolution has occurred in the country as many citizens have become active in an ever-increasing number of protest groups, citizens' organizations, and special interest groups. These groups often comprise issue-oriented activists or individuals who seek collective material benefits. The free-rider problem has proven not to be an insurmountable barrier to group formation, and many new interest groups do not use selective material benefits to gain support. Still, since the late 1970s, the number of these groups has remained relatively stable, and they have become well-established in representing the positions of consumers, environmentalists, and other public interest organizations.[29]

Third, government itself has had a profound effect on the growth and activity of interest groups. Early in this century, workers found organizing difficult because business and industry used government-backed injunctions to prevent strikes. By the 1930s, however, with the prohibition of injunctions in private labor disputes and the rights of collective bargaining established, most governmental actions directly promoted the growth of labor unions. In recent years changes in the campaign finance laws have led to an explosion in the number of PACs, especially among business, industry, and issue-oriented groups. Laws facilitating group formation certainly have contributed to group proliferation, but government policy in a broader sense has been equally responsible.

Fourth, not only has the number of membership groups grown in recent decades, but a similar expansion has occurred in the political activity of many other interests such as individual corporations, universities, churches, governmental units, foundations, and think tanks.[30] Historically, most of these interests have been satisfied with representation by trade or professional associations. Since the mid-1960s, however, many have chosen to employ their own Washington representatives. Between 1961 and 1982, for example, the number of corporations with Washington offices increased tenfold.[31] The chief beneficiaries of this trend are

Washington-based lawyers, lobbyists, and public relations firms. The number of attorneys in the nation's capital, taken as a rough indicator of lobbyist strength, tripled between 1973 and 1983, and the growth of public relations firms was dramatic. The lobbying community of the 1990s is large, increasingly diverse, and part of the expansion of policy domain participation, whether in agriculture, the environment, or industrial development. Overall, political scientist James Thurber has calculated that, as of the early 1990s, 91,000 lobbyists and people associated with lobbying were employed in the Washington, D.C., area.[32] As of 1993, the *Encyclopedia of Associations* listed approximately 23,000 organizations, up more than 50 percent since 1980 and almost 400 percent since 1955.[33]

Governmental Growth

Since the 1930s the federal government has become an increasingly active and important spur to group formation. A major aim of the New Deal was to use government as an agent in balancing the relationship between contending forces in society, particularly industry and labor. One goal was to create greater equality of opportunity, including the "guarantee of identical liberties to all individuals, especially with regard to their pursuit of economic success."[34] For example, the Wagner Act (1935), which established collective bargaining rights, attempted to equalize workers' rights with those of their employers. Some New Deal programs did have real redistributive qualities, but most, even Social Security, sought only to ensure minimum standards of citizen welfare. Workers were clearly better off, but "the kind of redistribution that took priority in the public philosophy of the New Deal was not of wealth, but a redistribution of power."[35]

The expansion of federal programs accelerated between 1960 and 1980; since then, costs have continued to increase, despite resistance to new programs. In what political scientist Hugh Heclo termed an "Age of Improvement," the federal budget has grown rapidly (from nearly $100 billion in 1961 to $1.7 trillion in 1998) and has widened the sweep of federal regulations.[36] Lyndon Johnson's Great Society—a multitude of federal initiatives in education, welfare, health care, civil rights, housing, and urban affairs—created a new array of federal responsibilities and program beneficiaries. The growth of many of these programs has continued, although that growth was slowed markedly by the Reagan and Bush administrations, as well as by the Republican capture of Congress in 1994. In the 1970s the federal government further expanded its activities in the areas of consumer affairs, environmental protection, and energy regulation. It also redefined some policies, such as affirmative action, to seek greater equality of results.

Many of the government policies adopted early in the Age of Improvement did not result from interest group activity by potential beneficiaries. Several targeted groups, such as the poor, were not effectively organized in the period of policy development. Initiatives typically came from elected officials responding to a variety of private and public sources, such as task forces composed of academics and policy professionals.[37]

The proliferation of government activities led to a mushrooming of groups around the affected policy areas. Newly enacted programs provided benefit packages that served to encourage interest group formation. Consider group activity in the field of policy toward the aging. The radical Townsend Movement, based on age grievances, received much attention during the 1930s, but organized political activity focused on age-based concerns had virtually no influence in national politics. Social Security legislation won approval without the involvement of age-based interest groups. Four decades later, by 1978, roughly $112 billion (approximately 24 percent of total federal expenditures) went to the elderly population, and it was projected that in fifty years the outlay would amount to 40 percent of the total budget.[38] By the early 1990s, however, the elderly population already received one-third of federal outlays, and long-term projections had been revised upward. The existence of such massive benefits has spawned a variety of special interest groups and has encouraged other organizations, often formed for nonpolitical reasons, to redirect their attention to the politics of the aging.

Across policy areas two types of groups develop in response to governmental policy initiatives: *recipients* and *service deliverers*. In the sector devoted to policies affecting elderly individuals, recipient groups are mass-based organizations concerned with protecting—and if possible expanding—old-age benefits. The largest of these groups—indeed, the largest voluntary association represented in Washington—is the American Association of Retired Persons (AARP).

The AARP is well over twice the size of the AFL-CIO and, after the Roman Catholic Church, is the nation's largest organization. In 1998 it counted thirty-three million members, an increase of twenty-three million in twenty years.[39] Approximately one-half of Americans aged fifty or older, or one-fifth of all voters, belong to the group, in part because membership is cheap—$8 per year. Much of the organization's revenue is derived from advertising in its bimonthly magazine, *Modern Maturity*. The organization's headquarters in Washington has its own zip code, a legislative/policy staff of 165; 28 registered, in-house lobbyists; and more than 1,200 staff members in the field. Charles Peters, the editor of *Washington Monthly*, observed that the "AARP is becoming the most dangerous lobby in America," given its vigorous defense of the elderly population's interests.[40] At the same time, because the AARP represents such a wide array of elderly individuals, it is often cautious and slow in its actions.

Federal program growth also has generated substantial growth among service delivery groups. In the health care sector, for example, these range from professional associations of doctors and nurses to hospital groups to the insurance industry to suppliers of drugs and medical equipment. Not only is there enhanced group activity, but hundreds of individual corporations have strengthened their lobbying capacities by opening Washington offices or hiring professional representatives from the capital's many lobbying firms.[41]

Federal government policy toward the aging is probably typical of the tendency to "greatly increase the incentives for groups to form around the differential effects of these policies, each refusing to allow any other group to speak in its name."[42] The complexity of government decision making increases under such conditions, and priorities are hard to set. Particularly troublesome for decision makers concerned with national policy is the role played by service delivery groups. In the area of aging, some groups are largely organizational middlemen concerned with their status as vendors for the elderly population. The trade associations, for example, are most interested in the conditions surrounding the payment of funds to elderly individuals. The major concern of the Gerontological Society, an organization of professionals, is to obtain funds for research on problems of elderly individuals.

Middleman organizations do not usually evaluate government programs according to the criteria used by recipient groups; rather, what is important to them is the relationship between the program and the well-being of their organizations. Because many service delivery groups offer their members vitally important selective material incentives (financial advantages and job opportunities), they are usually far better organized than most recipient groups (the elderly population in this case, the AARP notwithstanding). As a result, they sometimes speak for the recipients. This is particularly true when recipient groups represent disadvantaged people, such as poor or mentally ill peoples.

Middleman groups have accounted for a large share of total group growth since 1960, and many of them are state and local government organizations. Since the late 1950s the federal government has grown in expenditures and regulations more than in personnel. Employment in the federal government has risen only 20 percent since 1955, whereas that of states and localities has climbed more than 250 percent. Contemporary federal activism largely involves overseeing and regulating state and local governmental units, which seek funding for a wide range of purposes. The intergovernmental lobby, composed of such groups as the National League of Cities, the International City Manager Association, the National Association of Counties, the National Governors' Association, and the U.S. Conference of Mayors, has grown to become one of the most important in Washington. In addition, many local officials such as transportation or public works directors are represented by groups, and even single cities and state boards of regents have established Washington offices.

Not only do public policies contribute to group proliferation, but government often directly intervenes in group creation. This is not an entirely new activity. In the early twentieth century, relevant government officials in the agriculture and commerce departments encouraged the formation of the American Farm Bureau Federation and the U.S. Chamber of Commerce, respectively. Since the 1960s the federal government has been especially active in providing start-up funds and in sponsoring groups. One study found that government agencies have concentrated on sponsoring organizations of public service professions:

> Federal agencies have an interest in encouraging coordination among the elements of these complex service delivery systems and in improving the diffusion of new ideas and techniques. Groups like the American Public Transit Association or the American Council on Education . . . serve as centers of professional development and informal channels for administrative coordination in an otherwise unwieldy governmental system.[43]

Government sponsorship also helps explain the recent rise of citizens' groups. Most federal domestic legislation has included provisions requiring some citizen participation, which has spurred the development of various citizen action groups, including grassroots neighborhood associations, environmental action councils, legal defense coalitions, health care organizations, and senior citizens' groups. Such group sponsorship evolved for two reasons:

> First, there is the ever-present danger that administrative agencies may exceed or abuse their discretionary power. In this sense, the regulators need regulating. Although legislatures have responsibility for doing this . . . the administrative bureaucracy has grown too large for them to monitor. Therefore, citizen participation has developed as an alternative means of monitoring government agencies. Second, government agencies are not entirely comfortable with their discretionary power. . . . [T]o reduce the potential of unpopular or questionable decisions, agencies frequently use citizen participation as a means for improving, justifying, and developing support for their decisions.[44]

Participation by citizens' groups thus has two often inconsistent missions: to oversee an agency and to act as an advocate for the groups' programs.

Government funding of citizens' groups takes numerous forms. Several federal agencies—including the Federal Trade Commission (FTC), Food and Drug Administration (FDA), and Environmental Protection Agency (EPA)—have reimbursed groups for participation in agency proceedings.[45] At other times the government makes available seed money or outright grants. Interest group scholar Jack Walker found that 89 percent of citizens' groups received outside funding in their initial stages of development.[46] Not all the money was from federal sources, but much did come from government grants or contracts. Government can take away as well as give, however, and the Reagan administration made a major effort to "defund" interests on the political Left, especially citizens' groups. But once established, groups have strong instincts for survival. Indeed, the Reagan administration provided an attractive target for many citizens' groups in their recruiting efforts. This dance of defunding took place again, in 1995, after Republicans won control of the House of Representatives in the 1994 elections.

Citizens' groups, numbering in the thousands, continually confront the free-rider problem because they are largely concerned with collective goods and rarely can offer the selective material incentives so important for expanding and maintaining membership. With government funding, however, the development of a stable group membership is not crucial. Increasingly, groups have appeared that are essentially staff organizations with little or no membership base. In the world of interest group politics, overall resources are often more important than the mere number of members.

Government policies contribute to group formation in many *unintended* ways as well. Policy failures can impel groups to form, as happened with the rise of the American Agriculture Movement in the wake of the Nixon administration's grain export policies. An important factor in the establishment of the Moral Majority was the perceived harassment of church-run schools by government officials. As for abortion, the 1973 Supreme Court decision in *Roe v. Wade* played a major role in right-to-life group mobilization, as did the 1989 *Webster* decision in the growth of pro-choice groups. Even the *lack* of federal funding can play a role. The rise in the incidence of prostate cancer, coupled with a modest budget for research, helped lead to the formation of the National Prostate Cancer Coalition. This group has pressed the government to increase funding on prostate cancer toward levels that are spent on AIDs and breast cancer, given that the three diseases kill about the same number of individuals each year.

Finally, the expansion of government activity itself often *inadvertently* contributes to group development and the resulting complexity of politics. Here a rather obscure example is instructive: the development of the Bass Anglers Sportsman Society (yes, the acronym is BASS). It all began with the Army Corps of Engineers, which dammed enough southern and midwestern streams to create a host of lakes, thereby providing an inviting habitat for largemouth bass. Anglers arrived in droves to catch their limits, and the fishing industry responded by creating expensive boats filled with specialized and esoteric equipment. The number and affluence of bass aficionados did not escape the attention of Ray Scott, an enterprising soul who began BASS in 1967. In the early 1990s, with its membership approaching one million (up from 400,000 in 1982), BASS remained privately organized, offering its members selective benefits such as a slick magazine filled with tips on how to catch their favorite fish, packages of lures and line in return for joining or renewing their memberships, instant information about fishing hot spots, and boat owners' insurance. BASS also provided a number of solidary benefits, such as the camaraderie of fishing with fellow members in specially sanctioned fishing tournaments and the vicarious excitement of fishing with "BASS pros" whose financial livelihood revolved around competitive tournament fishing. The organization is an excellent example of Robert Salisbury's exchange-theory approach to interest groups, because it provides benefits to both members and organizers in a "mutually satisfactory exchange."[47]

In fact, "members" may be a misnomer, in that the nominal members have no effective role in group decision making. In 1993 a federal district judge dismissed a $75 million suit filed against Scott by some BASS members. The judge reasoned that the organization was and always had been a for-profit corporation; its "members" thus had no standing to sue.

Although Scott sold the organization to a private corporation in 1986 (the ultimate expression of entrepreneurial success), he remains active in much of its work and writes a column for the monthly publication, *BassMaster*. Never denying that the organization was anything but a profit-making entity, Scott stated, "Every time I see one of those BASS stickers I get a lump, right in my wallet."[48]

Like most groups, BASS did not originate as a political organization, and, for the most part, it remains an organization for fishermen. Yet BASS has entered politics. *BassMaster* has published political commentary, and in 1980, 1988, and 1992 endorsed George Bush for president. It also has called for easing travel restrictions to Cuba, where world-record catches may lurk.

Most groups claim that access is their major goal within the lobbying process, and here BASS has succeeded beyond its wildest dreams. President Bush has been a life member of BASS since 1978 and has claimed that *BassMaster* is his favorite magazine. Scott has used his relationship with Bush to lobby for a number of goals of the fishing community in general and BASS in particular. In March 1989 Scott visited the White House and, during a horseshoe match with President Bush, indicated his concern about rumors that the Office of Management and Budget (OMB) planned to limit the disbursement of $100 million in trust funds for various fishery-management projects. The next morning Bush informed Scott that "all of *our* monies are secure from OMB or anyone else."[49]

Scott and BASS have increased their political activities in other ways as well. The group now sponsors VOTE (Voice of the Environment), which lobbies on water quality issues, and the group has filed class-action lawsuits on behalf of fishermen against environmental polluters. Although the organization can point to a number of conservation and environmental activities, it is distrusted by much of the mainstream environmental movement. BASS's connections to the boating industry often put it at odds with groups seeking to preserve a pristine natural environment or elite angling organizations whose members fish for trout in free-flowing streams rather than for the bass that swim behind federally funded dams.

Indeed, regardless of the entrepreneurial skills of Scott, there would probably be no BASS if it were not for the federal government and the Army Corps of Engineers. (Moreover, there would be far fewer large-mouth bass.) Fifty years of dam building by the Corps and the U.S. Bureau of Reclamation have altered the nature of fish populations. Damming of rivers and streams has reduced the quality of fishing for cold-water species such as trout and pike and has enhanced the habitat for largemouth bass, a game fish that can tolerate the warmer waters and mud bottoms of man-made lakes. Finally, because many of these lakes are located close to cities, the government has made bass fishing accessible to a large number of anglers.

From angling to air traffic control, the federal government has affected, and sometimes dominated, group formation. Governmental activity does not, however, exist in a vacuum, and many other forces have contributed to group proliferation, often in concert with increased public sector involvement.

The Decline of Political Parties

In a diverse political culture characterized by divided power, political parties emerged early in our history as instruments to structure conflict and facilitate mass participation. Parties function as intermediaries between the public and formal government institutions, as they reduce and combine citizen demands into a manageable number of issues and enable the system to focus on the society's most important problems.

The party performs its mediating function primarily through coalition building—"the process of constructing majorities from the broad sentiments and interests that can be found to bridge the narrower needs and hopes of separate individuals and communities."[50] The New Deal coalition, forged in the 1930s, illustrates how this works. Socioeconomic divisions dominated politics from the 1930s through the 1960s. Less affluent citizens tended to support government provisions for social and economic security and the regulation of private enterprise. Those economically better off usually took the opposite position. The Democratic coalition, by and large, represented disadvantaged urban workers, Catholics, Jews, Italians, eastern Europeans, and African Americans. On a variety of issues, southerners joined the coalition, along with a smattering of academics and urban liberals. The Republicans were concentrated in the rural and suburban areas outside the South; the party was made up of established ethnic groups, businesspeople, and farmers; it was largely Protestant. Party organizations dominated electoral politics through the New Deal period, and interest group influence was felt primarily through the party apparatus.

Patterns of partisan conflict are never permanent, however, and since the 1940s various social forces have contributed to the creation of new interests and the redefinition of older ones. This has destroyed the New Deal coalition without putting a new partisan structure in its place and has provided opportunities for the creation of large numbers of political groups—many that are narrowly focused and opposed to the bargaining and compromise patterns of coalition politics.

Taken as a whole, the changes of recent decades reflect the societal transformation that scholars have labeled the "postindustrial society." Postindustrial society is centered on several interrelated developments:

> [A]ffluence, advanced technological development, the central importance of knowledge, national communication processes, the growing prominence and independence of the culture, new occupational structures, and with them new life styles and expectations, which is to say new social classes and new centers of power.[51]

At the base is the role of affluence. Between 1947 and 1972 median family income doubled, even after controlling for the effects of inflation. During that same period the percentage of families earning $10,000 and more, in constant dollars, grew from 15 percent to 60 percent of the population.[52] A large proportion of the population thus enjoys substantial discretionary income and has moved beyond subsistence concerns.

The consequences of spreading abundance did not reduce conflict, as some observers had predicted.[53] Instead, conflict heightened, because affluence increased dissatisfaction by contributing to a "mentality of demand, a vastly expanded set of expectations concerning what is one's due, a diminished tolerance of conditions less than ideal."[54] By the 1960s the democratizing impact of affluence had become apparent, as an extraordinary number of people enrolled in institutions of higher education. It is not surprising, then, that the government was under tremendous pressure to satisfy expectations, and it too contributed to increasing demands both in rhetoric and through many of its own Age of Improvement initiatives.

With the rise in individual expectations, class divisions and conflicts did not disappear, but they were drastically transformed. Political parties scholar Walter Dean Burnham noted that the New Deal's class structure changed, and by the late 1960s the industrial class pattern of upper-, middle-, and working class had been "supplanted by one which is relevant to a system dominated by advanced postindustrial technology."[55] At the top of the new class structure was a "professional-managerial-technical elite . . . closely connected with the university and research centers and significant parts of it have been drawn—both out of ideology and interest—to the federal government's social activism."[56] This growing group tended to be cosmopolitan and more socially permissive than the rest of society. The spread of affluence in postindustrial society was uneven, however, and certain groups were disadvantaged by the changes. At the bottom of the new class structure were the victims of changes, those "whose economic functions had been undermined or terminated by the technical revolution of the past generation . . . people, black and white, who tend to be in hard core poverty areas."[57] The focus of the War on Poverty was to be on this class.

The traditional political party system found it difficult to deal effectively with citizens' high expectations and a changing class structure. The economic, ethnic, and ideological positions that had developed during the New Deal became less relevant to parties, elections, and voter preferences. The strains were particularly evident among working-class Democrats. New Deal policies had been particularly beneficial to the white working class, enabling that group to earn incomes and adopt lifestyles that resembled those of the middle-class. And although Age of Improvement policies initiated by Democratic politicians often benefited minorities, many white workers viewed these policies as attempts to aid lower-class blacks at the expense of whites. By the late 1960s the white working class had taken on trappings of the middle-class and conservatism, both economically and culturally.

At the same time, such New Deal divisions as ethnicity also had lost their cutting edge because of social and geographic mobility. One analyst observed in 1973,

> It does not seem inaccurate to portray the current situation as one in which the basic coalitions and many of the political symbols and relationships, which were developed around one set of political issues and problems, are confronted with new issues and new cleavages for which these traditional relationships and associations are not particularly relevant. Given these conditions, the widespread confusion, frustration, and mistrust are not surprising.[58]

Various conditions led to the party system's inability to adapt to the changing societal divisions by *realigning*—building coalitions of groups to address new concerns. For example, consider the difficulty of coalition building around the kinds of issues that have emerged over the past fifteen or twenty years.

Valence issues—general evaluations of the goodness or badness of the times—have become important, especially when related to the cost of living. Yet most such issues do not divide the country politically. Everyone is against inflation and crime. A second set of increasingly important issues are those that are highly emotional, cultural, or moral in character, such as abortion, euthanasia, AIDS, the death penalty, and drug laws. These subjects divide the electorate but elicit intense feelings from only a relatively few citizens. Opinion on such issues often is unrelated to traditional group identifications. Moreover, public opinion is generally disorganized or in disarray—that is, opinions often are unrelated or weakly related to one another on major issues, further retarding efforts to build coalitions.

There is some question about whether parties retain the capacity to shape political debate even on issues that lend themselves to coalition building. Although the decline of political parties began well before the 1960s, the weakening of the party organization has accelerated in the postindustrial age. The emergence of a highly educated electorate, less dependent on party as an electoral cue, has produced a body of citizens that seeks out independent sources of information. Technological developments—such as television, computer-based direct mail, and political polling—have enabled candidates to virtually bypass political parties in their quest for public office. The rise of political consultants has reduced even further the need for party expertise in running for office. The recruitment function of parties also has been largely lost to the mass media, as journalists now "act out the part of talent scouts, conveying the judgment that some contenders are promising, while dismissing others as of no real talent."[59]

Evidence does suggest that parties are finally starting to adapt to this new political environment, but party organizations no longer dominate the electoral process. In an era of candidate-centered politics, parties are less mobilizers of a diverse electorate than service vendors to ambitious individual candidates. The weakness of political parties has helped to create a vacuum in electoral politics since 1960, and in recent years interest groups have moved aggressively to fill it. Indeed, in the 1996 election many interests bypassed the parties—and even the candidates' organizations—to advertise directly on behalf of particular candidates, all the while articulating their own positions on key issues such as Medicare and term limits.

The Growth of Interest Groups

Although it may be premature to formulate a theory that accounts for spurts of growth,[60] we can identify several factors fundamental to group proliferation in contemporary politics. Rapid social and economic changes, powerful catalysts for group formation, have developed new interests (for example, the recreation industry) and redefined traditional ones (for example, higher education). The spread of affluence and education, coupled with advanced communication technologies, further contributes to the translation of interests into formal group organizations. Postindustrial changes have generated a large number of new interests, particularly among occupational and professional groups in the scientific and technological arenas. For instance, genetic engineering associations have sprung up in the wake of recent DNA discoveries, to say nothing of the growing clout and sophistication of the computer industry, from Microsoft's Bill Gates on down.

Perhaps more important, postindustrial changes have altered the pattern of conflict in society and created an intensely emotional setting in which groups rise or fall in status. Ascending groups, such as members of the new professional–managerial–technical elite, have both benefited from and supported government activism; they represent the new cultural liberalism, politically cosmopolitan and socially permissive. At the same time, rising expectations and feelings of entitlement have increased pressures on government by aspiring groups and the disadvantaged. The 1960s and early 1970s witnessed wave after wave of group mobilization based on causes ranging from civil rights to women's issues to the environment to consumer protection.

Abrupt changes and alterations in status, however, threaten many citizens. Middle America, perceiving itself as downwardly mobile, has grown alienated from the social, economic, and cultural dominance of the postindustrial elites, on one hand, and resentful of government attempts to aid minorities and other aspiring groups, on the other. The conditions of a modern, technologically based culture also are disturbing to more traditional elements in society. Industrialization and urbanization can uproot people, cutting them loose from familiar life patterns and values and depriving them of meaningful personal associations. Fundamentalist elements feel threatened by various technological advances (such as use of fetal tissue for medical research) as well as by the more general secular liberalism and moral permissiveness of contemporary life. In the 1990s, the growth of the Christian Coalition, both nationally and locally, has profoundly affected both electoral and legislative politics by mobilizing citizens and activists. In addition, the growth of bureaucracy, in and out of government, antagonizes everyone at one time or another.

Postindustrial threats are felt by elites as well. The nuclear arms race and its potential for mass destruction fostered the revived peace movement of the 1980s and its goal of a freeze on nuclear weapons. In addition, the excesses and errors of technology, such as oil spills and toxic waste disposal, have led to group formation among some of the most advantaged and ascending elements of society.

Illustrating the possibilities is the growth since the mid-1980s of the animal rights movement. Although traditional animal protection organizations such as the Humane Society have existed for decades, the past fifteen years have "spawned a colorful menagerie of pro-animal offspring" such as People for Ethical Treatment of Animals (PETA), Progressive Animal Welfare Society (PAWS), Committee to Abolish Sport Hunting (CASH), and the Animal Rights Network (ARN). Reminiscent of the 1960s, there is even the Animal Liberation Front, an extremist group that engages in direct actions that sometimes include violence.[61] Membership in the organizations that make up the animal rights movement has increased rapidly; founded in 1980, PETA grew from 20,000 in 1984 to 250,000 in 1988 and 370,000 by 1994.[62] One estimate places the number of animal rights organizations at 400, representing approximately ten million members.[63]

One major goal of these groups is to stop, or greatly retard, scientific experimentation on animals. Using a mix of protest, lobbying, and litigation, the movement has contributed to the closing of several animal labs, including the Defense Department's Wound Laboratory and a University of Pennsylvania facility involved in research on head injuries. In 1988 Trans-Species, a recent addition to the animal rights movement, forced the Cornell University Medical College to give up a $600,000 grant, which left unfinished a fourteen-year research project in which cats were fed barbiturates.[64]

As the most visible of the animal rights groups, PETA embarked on an intensive campaign in the early 1990s to influence children's attitudes and values toward society's treatment of animals. Using a seven-foot mascot, Chris P. Carrot, to spread its message, PETA organizers have sought to visit public schools throughout the Midwest. Although some of their message is noncontroversial (for example, children should eat their vegetables), they also argue aggressively against consuming meat. Chris P. Carrot thus carries a placard stating, "Eat your veggies, not your friends." More prosaically, PETA produces publications denouncing hunting, trapping, and other practices that abuse animals; PETA's *Kids Can Save Animals* even encourages students to

> call the toll-free numbers of department stores to protest furs and animal-test cosmetics, to call sponsors and object to rodeos, circulate petitions for "violence-free" schools that do not use frog corpses for biology lab, and to boycott zoos and aquariums, and marine parks.[65]

It is not surprising that threats to those involved in activities that PETA protests have spawned countermobilizations, as, for instance, in the growth of an anti–animal rights movement. In the forefront of such actions are organizations that support hunting as a sport. They must contend with a public that has become increasingly hostile to hunting; a 1993 survey reported that 54 percent of Americans were opposed to hunting, with the youngest respondents (ages 18 to 29) expressing the most negative sentiments.[66] In addition, farm and medical groups have mobilized against the animal rights movements, and a number of new organizations have been formed. Such groups range from the incurably ill for Animal Research (iiFAR), representing those who hope for medical breakthroughs in biomedical research, to the Foundation for Animal Health, organized by the American Medical Association in hopes of diverting funds away from animal rights groups.

The most visible group in the animal rights countermobilization, Putting People First (PPF), claimed more than 35,000 members and one hundred local chapters within one year of its formation. As well as its individual members, PPF counted hunting clubs, trapping associations, rodeos, zoos, circuses, veterinary hospitals, kennels/stables, and carriage horse companies among its membership. Taking a page from animal rights' public relations activities, PPF has begun a Hunters for the Hungry campaign that has provided 160,000 pounds of venison to economically disadvantaged families in the South. To PPF, the animal rights movement has declared war on much of America and is "seeking to destroy a way of life—to tell us we can no longer believe in the Judeo-Christian principles this country was founded on. They insist every form of life is equal: humans and dogs and slugs and cockroaches." PPF leaders see the organization as speaking for "the average American who eats meat and drinks milk, benefits from medical research, wears leather, wool, and fur, hunts and fishes, and owns a pet and goes to the zoo."[67]

The intensity of conflict between the animal rights advocates and their opponents typifies the deep cultural divisions of the postindustrial era. Similar differences affect many other key issues, from gun control to education (school choice) to immigration policy. Moreover, many of these conflicts do not lend themselves to compromise, whether because of vast policy differences or group leaders' desire to keep "hot" issues alive as a way to increase membership.

Although postindustrial conflicts generate the issues for group development, the spread of affluence also systematically contributes to group formation and maintenance. In fact, affluence creates a large potential for "checkbook" membership. Issue-based groups have done especially well. Membership in such groups as PETA and Common Cause might once have been considered a luxury, but the growth in discretionary income has placed the cost of modest dues within the reach of most citizens. For a $15 to $25 membership fee, people can make an "expressive" statement without incurring other organizational obligations. Increasing education also has been a factor in that "organizations become more numerous as ideas become more important."[68]

Reform groups and citizens' groups depend heavily on the educated, suburban–urban, white middle-class for their membership and financial base. A Common Cause poll, for example, found that members' mean family income was $17,000 above the national average and that 43 percent of members had an advanced degree.[69] Animal rights groups display a similar membership profile, although they are disproportionately composed of college-educated, urban, professional women.[70] Other expressive groups, including those on the political Right, have been aided as well by the increased wealth of constituents and the community activism that result from education and occupational advancement.

Groups can overcome the free-rider problem by finding a sponsor who will support the organization and reduce its reliance on membership contributions. During the 1960s and 1970s private sources (often foundations) backed various groups. Jeffrey Berry's 1977 study of eighty-three public interest organizations found that at least one-third received more than half of their funds from private foundations, and one in ten received more than 90 percent of its operating expenses from such sources.[71] Jack

Walker's 1981 study of Washington-based interest groups confirmed many of Berry's earlier findings, indicating that foundation support and individual grants provide 30 percent of all citizens' group funding.[72] Such patterns produce many staff organizations with no members, raising major questions about the representativeness of the new interest group universe. Finally, groups themselves can sponsor other groups. The National Council of Senior Citizens (NCSC), for example, was founded by the AFL-CIO, which helped recruit members from the ranks of organized labor and still pays part of NCSC's expenses.

Patrons often are more than just passive sponsors who respond to group requests for funds. In many instances, group mobilization comes from the top down, rather than the reverse. The patron—whether an individual such as General Motors' heir Stewart Mott or the peripatetic conservative Richard Mellon Scaife, an institution, another group, or a government entity—may serve as the initiator of group development, to the point of seeking entrepreneurs and providing a forum for group pronouncements.

Postindustrial affluence and the spread of education also have contributed to group formation and maintenance through the development of a large pool of potential group organizers. This group tends to be young, well educated, and from the middle-class, caught up in a movement for change and inspired by ideas or doctrine. The 1960s was a period of opportunity for entrepreneurs, as college enrollments skyrocketed and powerful forces such as civil rights and the antiwar movement contributed to an idea orientation in both education and politics. Communications-based professions—from religion to law to university teaching—attracted social activists, many of whom became involved in the formation of groups. The government itself became a major source of what James Q. Wilson called "organizing cadres." Government employees of the local Community Action Agencies of the War on Poverty and numerous VISTA volunteers were active in the formation of voluntary associations, some created to oppose government actions.[73]

Compounding the effects of the growing number of increasingly active groups are changes in what organizations can do, largely as a result of contemporary technology. On a grand scale, technological change produces new interests, such as cable television and the silicon chip industry, which organize to protect themselves as interests historically have done. Beyond this, communications breakthroughs make group politics much more visible than in the past. Civil rights activists in the South understood this, as did many protesters against the Vietnam War. Of equal importance, however, is the fact that much of what contemporary interest groups do derives directly from developments in information-related technology. Many group activities, whether fund-raising or grassroots lobbying or sampling members' opinions, rely heavily on computer-based operations that can target and send messages and process the responses.

Although satellite television links and survey research are important tools, the technology of direct mail has had by far the greatest impact on interest group politics. With a minimum initial investment and a reasonably good list of potential contributors, any individual can become a group entrepreneur. These activists literally create organizations, often based on emotion-laden appeals about specific issues, from Sarah Brady's Handgun Control to Randall Terry's Operation Rescue.[74] To the extent that an entrepreneur can attract members and continue to pay the costs of direct mail, he or she can claim—with substantial legitimacy—to articulate the organization's positions on the issues, positions probably defined initially by the entrepreneur.

In addition to helping entrepreneurs develop organizations that require few (if any) active members, information technology also allows many organizations to exert considerable pressure on elected officials. The Washington-based interests increasingly are turning to grassroots techniques to influence legislators. Indeed, after the mid-1980s these tactics had become the norm in many lobbying efforts, to the point that they were sometimes discounted as routine and "manufactured" by groups and consultants.

Communications technology is widely available but expensive. In the health care debate, most mobilized opinion has come from the best-financed interests, such as insurance companies, the drug industry, and the medical profession. Money remains the mother's milk of politics. Indeed, one of the major impacts of technology may be to inflate the costs of political action, whether for candidates engaged in increasingly expensive election campaigns or in public lobbying efforts that employ specifically targeted advertisements and highly sophisticated grassroots efforts.

Group Impact on Policy and Process

Assessing the policy impact of interest group actions has never been an easy task. We may, however, gain some insights by looking at two different levels of analysis: a broad, societal overview and a middle-range search for relatively specific patterns of influence (for example, the role of direct mail or PAC funding). Considering impact at the level of individual lobbying efforts is also possible, but here even the best work relies heavily on nuance and individualistic explanations.

Although the public at large often views lobbying and special interest campaigning with distrust, political scientists have not produced much evidence to support this perspective. Academic studies of interest groups have demonstrated few conclusive links between campaign or lobbying efforts and actual patterns of influence. *This does not mean that such patterns or individual instances do not exist.* Rather, the question of determining impact is exceedingly difficult to answer. The difficulty is, in fact, compounded by groups' claims of impact and decision makers' equally vociferous claims of freedom from any outside influence.

The major studies of lobbying in the 1960s generated a most benign view of this activity. Lester Milbrath, in his portrait of Washington lobbyists, painted a Boy Scout-like picture, depicting them as patient contributors to the policy-making process.[75] Rarely stepping over the limits of propriety, lobbyists had only a marginal impact at best. Similarly, Raymond Bauer, Ithiel de Sola Pool, and Lewis Dexter's lengthy analysis of foreign trade policy, published in 1963, found the business community to be largely incapable of influencing Congress in its lobbying attempts.[76] Given the many internal divisions within the private sector over trade matters, this was not an ideal issue to illustrate business cooperation, but the research stood as the central work on lobbying for more than a decade—ironically, in the very period when groups proliferated and became more sophisticated in their tactics. Lewis Dexter, in his 1969 treatment of Washington representatives as an emerging professional group, suggested that lobbyists would play an increasingly important role in complex policy making, but he provided few details.[77]

The picture of benevolent lobbyists who seek to engender trust and convey information, although accurate in a limited way, does not provide a complete account of the options open to any interest group that seeks to exert influence. Lyndon Johnson's long-term relationship with the Texas-based construction firm of Brown & Root illustrates the depth of some ties between private interests and public officeholders. The Washington representative for Brown & Root claimed that he never went to Capitol Hill for any legislative help because "people would resent political influence."[78] But Johnson, first as a representative and later as a senator, systematically dealt directly with the top management (the Brown family) and aided the firm by passing along crucial information and watching over key government-sponsored construction projects.

> [The Johnson–Brown & Root link] was, indeed, a partnership, the campaign contributions, the congressional look-out, the contracts, the appropriations, the telegrams, the investment advice, the gifts and the hunts and the free airplane rides—it was an alliance of mutual reinforcement between a politician and a corporation. If Lyndon was Brown & Root's kept politician, Brown & Root was Lyndon's kept corporation. Whether he concluded that they were public-spirited partners or corrupt ones, "political allies" or cooperating predators, in its dimensions and its implications for the structure of society, their arrangement was a new phenomenon on its way to becoming the new pattern for American society.[79]

In the 1980s and 1990s, one could legitimately substitute Senator Bob Dole's name for Johnson's and that of agribusiness giant Archer Daniels Midland for Brown & Root; the basic set of linkages were very similar.

Any number of events, such as the 1980s savings and loan scandal, demonstrate that legislators can be easily approached with unethical and illegal propositions; such access is one price of an open system. In addition, the growth of interest representation has raised long-term questions about the ethics of former government officials acting as lobbyists. Despite some modest reforms, many executive-branch officials, members of Congress, and high-level bureaucrats leave office and eventually return to lobby their friends and associates who have remained. Access is still important, and its price is often high.

Contemporary Practices

Modern lobbying emphasizes information, often on complex and difficult subjects. Determining actual influence is, as one lobbyist noted, "like finding a black cat in the coal bin at midnight,"[80] but we can make some assessments about the overall impact of group proliferation and increased activity.

First, more groups are engaged in more forms of lobbying than ever before—both classic forms, such as offering legislative testimony, and newer forms, such as mounting computer-based direct mail campaigns to stir up grassroots support.[81] As the number of new groups rises and existing groups become more active, the pressure on decision makers—especially legislators—mounts at a corresponding rate. Thus, a second general point can be made: Congressional reforms that opened up the legislative process during the 1970s have provided a much larger number of access points for today's lobbyists. Most committee (and subcommittee) sessions, including the mark-ups at which legislation is written, remain open to the public, as do many conference committee meetings. More roll-call votes are taken, and congressional floor action is televised. Thus, interests can monitor the performance of individual members of Congress as never before. This does nothing, however, to facilitate disinterested decision making or foster graceful compromises on most issues.

In fact, monitoring the legions of Washington policy actors has become the central activity of many groups. As Robert Salisbury has observed, "Before [organized interests] can advocate a policy, they must determine what position they wish to embrace. Before they do this, they must find out not only what technical policy analysis can tell them but what relevant others, inside and outside the government, are thinking and planning."[82] Given the volume of policy making, just keeping up can represent a major undertaking.

The government itself has encouraged many interests to organize and articulate their demands. The rise of group activity thus leads us to another level of analysis: the impact of contemporary interest group politics on society. Harking back to Lowi's description of interest group liberalism, we see the eventual result to be an immobilized society, trapped by its willingness to allow interests to help fashion self-serving policies that embody no firm criteria of success or failure. For example, even in the midst of the savings and loan debacle, the government continued to offer guarantees to various sectors, based not on future promise but on past bargains and continuing pressures.

The notion advanced by Olson that some such group-related stagnation affects all stable democracies makes the prognosis all the more serious. In summary form, Olson argued that the longer societies are politically stable, the more interest groups they develop; the more interest groups they develop, the worse they work economically.[83] The United Automobile Workers' protectionist leanings, the American Medical Association's fight against intervention by the Federal Trade Commission into physicians' business affairs, and the insurance industry's successful prevention of FTC investigations all illustrate the possible linkage between self-centered group action and poor economic performance—that is, higher automobile prices, doctors' fees, and insurance premiums for no better product or service.[84]

In particular, the politics of Social Security demonstrate the difficulties posed by a highly mobilized, highly representative set of interests. Virtually everyone agrees that the Social Security system requires serious reform; at the same time, many groups of elderly citizens (with the AARP among the most moderate) have resisted changes that might reduce their benefits over time. In the end, the Social Security system will have to be restructured to maintain its viability, but particular interests pose serious obstacles to pursuing the more general welfare of society as a whole.

Conclusion

The ultimate consequences of the growing number of groups, their expanding activities both in Washington and in state capitals, and the growth of citizens' groups remain unclear. From one perspective, such changes have made politics more representative than ever before. Although most occupation-based groups traditionally have been well organized in American politics, many other interests have not. Population groupings such as African Americans, Hispanics, and women have mobilized since the 1950s and 1960s; even animals and the unborn are well represented in the interest group arena, as is the broader "public interest," however defined.

Broadening the base of interest group participation may have truly opened up the political process, thus curbing the influence of special interests. For example, agricultural policy making in the postwar era was almost exclusively the prerogative of a tight "iron triangle" composed of congressional committee and subcommittee members from farm states, government officials representing the agriculture bureaucracy, and major agriculture groups such as the American Farm Bureau. Activity in the

1970s by consumer and environmental interest groups changed agricultural politics, making it more visible and lengthening the agenda to consider such questions as how farm subsidies affect consumer purchasing power and how various fertilizers, herbicides, and pesticides affect public health.

From another perspective, more interest groups and more openness do not necessarily mean better policies or ones that genuinely represent the national interest. "Sunshine" and more participants may generate greater complexity and too many demands for decision makers to process effectively. Moreover, the content of demands may be ambiguous and priorities difficult to set.

Finally, elected leaders may find it practically impossible to build the kinds of political coalitions necessary to govern effectively, especially in an era of divided government.

This second perspective suggests that the American constitutional system is extraordinarily susceptible to the excesses of minority faction— in an ironic way a potential victim of the Madisonian solution of dealing with the tyranny of the majority. Decentralized government, especially one that wields considerable power, provides no adequate controls over the excessive demands of special interest politics. Decision makers feel obliged to respond to many of these demands, and "the cumulative effect of this pressure has been the relentless and extraordinary rise of government spending and inflationary deficits, as well as the frustration of efforts to enact effective national policies on most major issues."[85]

In sum, the problem of contemporary interest group politics is one of representation. For particular interests, especially those that are well defined and adequately funded, the government is responsive to the issues of their greatest concern. But representation is not just a matter of responding to specific interests or citizens; the government also must respond to the collective needs of a society, and here the success of individual interests reduces the possibility of overall responsiveness. The very vibrancy and success of contemporary groups contribute to a society that finds it increasingly difficult to formulate solutions to complex policy questions.

Notes

1. Kay Lehman Schlozman and John T. Tierney, "More of the Same: Washington Pressure Group Activity in a Decade of Change," *Journal of Politics* 45 (May 1983): 351–377. For an earlier era, see Margaret S. Thompson, *The Spider's Web* (Ithaca: Cornell University Press, 1985).
2. Theodore J. Lowi, *The End of Liberalism*, 2d ed. (New York: Norton, 1979); and Mancur Olson, *The Rise and Decline of Nations* (New Haven, Conn.: Yale University Press, 1982).
3. Mancur Olson, *The Logic of Collective Action* (Cambridge, Mass.: Harvard University Press, 1971); Robert Salisbury, "An Exchange Theory of Interest Groups,"

Midwest Journal of Political Science 13 (February 1969): 1–32; and Terry M. Moe, *The Organization of Interests* (Chicago: University of Chicago Press, 1980).

4. David Truman's widely used definition of interest groups is "any group that, on the basis of one or more shared attitudes, makes certain claims upon other groups in the society for the establishment, maintenance or enhancement of forms of behavior that are implied by the shared attitudes." Truman, *The Governmental Process*, 2d ed. (New York: Knopf, 1971).

5. James Madison, "Federalist 10," in *The Federalist Papers*, 2d ed., ed. Roy P. Fairfield (Baltimore: Johns Hopkins University Press, 1981), 16.

6. L. Harmon Ziegler and Wayne Peak, *Interest Groups in American Society*, 2d ed. (Englewood Cliffs, N.J.: Prentice-Hall, 1972), 35.

7. Common Cause, *The Government Subsidy Squeeze* (Washington, D.C.: Author, 1980), 11.

8. Truman, *Governmental Process*, 519.

9. Carole Greenwald, *Group Power* (New York: Praeger, 1977), 305.

10. Leslie Wayne, "800-Pound Guests at the Pentagon," *New York Times*, March 15, 1998, section 5, p. 3.

11. Lowi, *End of Liberalism*, 62.

12. Murray Edelman, *The Politics of Symbolic Action* (Chicago: Markham Press, 1971).

13. Theodore J. Lowi, *Incomplete Conquest: Governing America* (New York: Holt, Rinehart & Winston, 1976), 47.

14. Gabriel Almond and Sidney Verba, *The Civic Culture* (Boston: Little, Brown, 1963), chaps. 8 and 10.

15. Ibid., 246–247.

16. Truman, *Governmental Process*, 57.

17. Salisbury, "Exchange Theory of Interest Groups," 3–4.

18. Truman, *Governmental Process*, 59.

19. James Q. Wilson, *Political Organizations* (New York: Basic Books, 1973), 154.

20. Major works include Olson, *The Logic of Collective Action;* Peter Clark and James Q. Wilson, "Incentive Systems: A Theory of Organizations," *Administrative Science Quarterly* 6 (September 1961): 126–166; Wilson, *Political Organizations;* Terry Moe, "A Calculus of Group Membership," *American Journal of Political Science* 24 (November 1980): 593–632; and Moe, *Organization of Interests*. The notion of group organizers as political entrepreneurs is best represented by Salisbury, "Exchange Theory of Interest Groups," 1–15.

21. See Clark and Wilson, "Incentive Systems," 129–166; and Wilson, *Political Organizations*, 30–51. In recent years researchers have preferred the term *expressive* to *purposive*, because, as Salisbury notes, the term *purposive* includes what we call collective material benefits. *Material, solidary,* and *expressive* would seem to be mutually exclusive conceptual categories. See Salisbury, "Exchange Theory of Interest Groups," 16–17.

22. Moe, *Organization of Interests*, 144.

23. John Mark Hansen, "The Political Economy of Group Membership," *American Political Science Review* 79 (March 1985): 79–96.

24. Albert O. Hirschman, *Shifting Involvements* (Princeton, N.J.: Princeton University Press, 1982).

25. Michael W. McCann, "Public Interest Liberalism and the Modern Regulatory State," *Polity* 21 (Winter 1988): 385.

26. See, for example, R. Kenneth Godwin and R. C. Mitchell, "Rational Models, Collective Goods, and Non-Electoral Political Behavior," *Western Political Quarterly* 35 (June 1982): 161–180; and Larry Rothenberg, "Choosing among Public Interest Groups: Membership, Activism and Retention in Political Organizations," *American Political Science Review* 82 (December 1988): 1129–1152.

27. Jack L. Walker, "The Origins and Maintenance of Interest Groups in America," *American Political Science Review* 77 (June 1983): 390–406; for a conservative critique of this trend, see James T. Bennett and Thomas Di Lorenzo, *Destroying Democracy* (Washington, D.C.: Cato Institute, 1986). See also many of the articles in *The Politics of Interests*, ed. Mark P. Petracca (Boulder, Colo.: Westview, 1992).

28. Walker, "Origins and Maintenance of Interest Groups," 16.

29. Robert H. Salisbury, "Interest Representation and the Dominance of Institutions," *American Political Science Review* 78 (March 1984): 64–77.

30. See Jeffery Berry, "The Power of Citizen Groups," unpublished manuscript.

31. Gregory Colgate, ed., *National Trade and Professional Associations of the United States 1982* (Washington, D.C.: Columbia Books, 1984).

32. Cited in Kevin Phillips, *Arrogant Capital* (Boston: Back Bay/Little, Brown, 1995), 43.

33. Jonathan Rauch, *Democlerosis* (New York: Times Books, 1994), 39.

34. Samuel H. Beer, "In Search of a New Public Philosophy," in *The New American Political System*, ed. Anthony King (Washington, D.C.: American Enterprise Institute, 1978), 12.

35. Ibid., 10.

36. Hugh Heclo, "Issue Networks and the Executive Establishment," in *New American Political System*, ed. King, 89.

37. Beer, "In Search of a New Public Philosophy," 16.

38. Allan J. Cigler and Cheryl Swanson, "Politics and Older Americans," in *The Dynamics of Aging*, ed. Forrest J. Berghorn, Donna E. Schafer, and Associates (Boulder, Colo.: Westview Press, 1981), 171.

39. The AARP offers free memberships to spouses, which artificially enlarges its ranks, but it remains—by any count—a huge group.

40. See John Tierney, "Old Money, New Power," *New York Times Magazine*, October 23, 1988; and "The Big Gray Money Machine," *Newsweek*, August 15, 1988.

41. Tierney, "Old Money, New Power."

42. Heclo, "Issue Networks and the Executive Establishment," 96.

43. Walker, "Origins and Maintenance of Interest Groups," 401.

44. Stuart Langton, "Citizen Participation in America: Current Reflections on the State of the Art," in *Citizen Participation in America*, ed. Stuart Langton (Lexington, Mass.: Lexington Books, 1978), 7.

45. Ibid., 4.

46. Walker, "Origins and Maintenance of Interest Groups," 398.

47. Salisbury, "Exchange Theory of Interest Groups," 25.

48. Quoted in Ted Williams, "River Retrieval," *Fly Rod and Reel* 15 (January/February 1994): 17.

49. Ray Scott, "Presidential Promises," *BassMaster*, May 1989, 7 (emphasis added).

50. David S. Broder, "Introduction," in *Emerging Coalitions in American Politics*, ed. Seymour Martin Lipset (San Francisco: Institute for Contemporary Studies, 1978), 3.

51. Everett Carll Ladd, Jr., with Charles D. Hadley, *Transformations of the American Party System*, 2d ed. (New York: Norton, 1978), 182.

52. Ibid., 196.

53. See, for example, Daniel Bell, *The End of Ideology* (New York: Free Press, 1960).

54. Ladd and Hadley, *Transformations of the American Party System*, 203.

55. Walter Dean Burnham, *Critical Elections and the Mainsprings of American Politics* (New York: Norton, 1970), 139.

56. Ibid.

57. Ibid.

58. Richard E. Dawson, *Public Opinion and Contemporary Disarray* (New York: Harper and Row, 1973), 194.

59. Everett Carll Ladd, *Where Have All the Voters Gone?* 2d ed. (New York: Norton, 1982).
60. But see Virginia Gray and David Lowery, *The Population Ecology of Interest Representation* (Ann Arbor: University of Michigan Press, 1996).
61. Kevin Kasowski, "Showdown on the Hunting Ground," *Outdoor America* 51 (Winter 1986): 9.
62. Sarah Lyall, "Scientist Gives up Grant to Do Research on Cats," *New York Times*, November 21, 1988, A12.
63. Lauristan R. King and Kimberly Stephens, "Politics and the Animal Rights Movement" (Paper delivered at the annual meeting of the Southern Political Science Association, Tampa, Florida, 1991).
64. Lyall, "Scientist Gives Up Grant."
65. John Balzar, quoted in Kit Harrison, "Animal 'Rightists' Target Children," *Sports Afield* 211 (June 1994): 12.
66. "Americans Divided on Animal Rights," *Los Angeles Times*, December 17, 1993. This national survey of 1,612 adults also found that 50 percent opposed the wearing of fur.
67. Phil McCombs, "Attack of the Omnivore," *Washington Post*, March 27, 1992, B1, B4.
68. Wilson, *Political Organizations*, 201.
69. Andrew S. McFarland, *Common Cause* (Chatham, N.J.: Chatham House, 1984), 48–49.
70. King and Stephens, "Politics and the Animal Rights Movement," 15.
71. Jeffrey M. Berry, *Lobbying for the People* (Princeton, N.J.: Princeton University Press, 1977), 72.
72. Walker, "Origins and Maintenance of Interest Groups," 400.
73. Wilson, *Political Organizations*, 203.
74. Sarah Brady, wife of former White House press secretary James Brady, organized Handgun Control after her husband was wounded in John Hinckley's 1981 attack on Ronald Reagan. Randall Terry formed Operation Rescue, which seeks to shut down abortion clinics through direct action (for example, blocking entrances), after concluding that other prolife groups were not effective in halting abortions.
75. Lester Milbrath, *The Washington Lobbyists* (Chicago: Rand-McNally, 1963).
76. Raymond Bauer, Ithiel de Sola Pool, and Lewis Dexter, *American Business and Public Policy* (New York: Atherton Press, 1963).
77. Lewis A. Dexter, *How Organizations Are Represented in Washington* (Indianapolis, Ind.: Bobbs-Merrill, 1969), chap. 9.
78. See Ronnie Dugger, *The Politician* (New York: Norton, 1982), 273; and Robert A. Caro, *The Years of Lyndon Johnson: The Path to Power and the Years of Lyndon Johnson: Means of Ascent* (New York: Knopf, 1982 and 1990, respectively).
79. Dugger, *Politician*, 286.
80. Quoted in "A New Era: Groups and the Grass Roots," by Burdett A. Loomis, in *Interest Group Politics*, 2d ed., ed. Allan J. Cigler and Burdett A. Loomis (Washington, D.C.: CQ Press, 1983), 184.
81. Schlozman and Tierney, "Washington Pressure Group Activity," 18.
82. Robert H. Salisbury, "The Paradox of Interest Groups in Washington—More Groups and Less Clout," in *The New American Political System*, 2d ed., ed. Anthony King (Washington, D.C.: American Enterprise Institute, 1990), 225–226.
83. For an expansion of this argument, see Rausch, *Democlerosis*.
84. Robert J. Samuelson's description in *National Journal*, September 25, 1982, 1642.
85. Everett Carll Ladd, "How to Tame the Special Interest Groups," *Fortune* (October 1980): 6.

I. GROUP FORMATION AND MEMBERSHIP

2

Interest Group Recruiting:
Finding Members and Keeping Them

Paul E. Johnson

The contemporary environmental movement is composed of a diverse set of groups, ranging from mass-based organizations with broad political agendas such as the Sierra Club, to much smaller organizations focusing on narrow interests, such as the International Crane Foundation or the Bluebird Society. Regardless of size and focus, all groups share the imperative of finding resources to start and maintain their organization and to underwrite their political activities. Resources can come from a variety of places, including foundations, corporations, or other patrons. But for most groups the acquisition of resources means developing a strategy for attracting and retaining members, often in competition with the efforts of other environmental groups.

In this chapter, Paul Johnson analyzes data from a survey of environmental organizations directed toward understanding membership recruitment tactics of such groups. He finds that direct mail is the most important tactic for contacting potential members and encouraging them to join. Groups offer a variety of selective benefits to potential recruits, and the success of organizations often depends on their ability to "differentiate themselves by the quality of their selective incentives and the nature of their collective appeal."

In Johnson's view, although interest in environmental issues creates an opportunity for environmental groups, it is recruiting activity, not the collective good itself, that best explains group membership. This is because "people who have an interest in a collective good do not tend to be 'self-starters' who seek out and join groups. Instead they must be sought out, pursued, enticed, and persuaded." The most successful groups are those with well planned, comprehensive strategies for membership recruitment.

This research was sponsored by a grant from the University of Kansas General Research Fund. Special thanks to Chris Elmore for his research assistance.

Do you know someone who belongs to the Sierra Club? It has more
than 500,000 members, so there is a good chance that you might.
The Sierra Club has a broad political agenda, but is known mostly for efforts to protect forests and wilderness areas. If they are not in Sierra,
maybe your friends are more interested in wildlife. Perhaps one of them
belongs to the World Wildlife Fund? The panda bear is their famous logo,
but they actually have wide-ranging interests in the protection of animal
habitat. And they have about 800,000 members. Perhaps you know someone who belongs to the National Wildlife Federation (NWF)? If you include about five million children enrolled in its Ranger Rick Club, the
NWF has 6.2 million members. Maybe you know people who are concerned about protecting land from pollution and development? Ask if
they belong to the Nature Conservancy. That is an organization with
600,000 members that seeks to protect land from development by buying
it and controlling its use.

The number of environmental interest groups is truly staggering. It
is difficult to find a policy issue arena that has spawned a larger and more
diverse set of interest organizations. There are 189 nonoccupational
membership organizations listed in the *Encyclopedia of Associations* under
the categories of ecology, conservation, and the environment.[1] There are
organizations with titles and logos to suggest that they want to protect
rivers, lakes, oceans, air, wilderness, national parks, and all varieties of
animals. They range from the most general sort of organization to the
most specific. The organizations with relatively broad agendas, such as
the Sierra Club, coexist with animal-specific organizations like the Save
the Manatee Club. Even someone with a relatively specific wildlife interest, such as birds, might be bewildered by the array of organizations
from which to choose. The most general is the Audubon Society, which
was founded in 1905 and named in honor of John Audubon, a famous
artist and student of birds. Its membership is about 600,000. If someone
likes ducks, they can join a 650,000 member organization called Ducks
Unlimited. Many of the members of Ducks Unlimited are sportspersons,
who seek to preserve wetland habitats for hunting purposes. People with
more specific bird interests can surely find an organization to suit them.
Consider the Purple Martin Conservation Association, the American
Loon Fund, Pheasants Forever, the National Wild Turkey Federation,
the International Crane Foundation, or the Bluebird Society. The variety is not limited to bird interests. People who want to protect wild animals, such as wolves and bears, can join the Defenders of Wildlife, which
has about 85,000 members. Someone who wants to protect the habitat of
gorillas can join the Digit Fund. There are organizations to protect wild
mustangs, beavers, wolves, whales, and numerous other species. There
is even an organization for bugs! The Xerces Society, an interest group
with about 30,000 members, is dedicated to the study and protection of
insects.

These organizations are often collectively referred to as "the Environmental Movement." Although many of these organizations are long-standing, they are referred to as a *movement* because their political involvement significantly increased in the 1960s. Where organizations once did hands on work to conserve habitats, their leaders came to focus an increasing amount of attention on politics (at both the state and national levels). In the 1960s, increasing levels of public concern about tainted water and air went hand in hand with more vigorous efforts by organized groups to change the plans of legislators, judges, and executive officials.[2] Many long-standing organizations, which had previously seen a limited role in politics, came to see lobbying and political action as a central aspect of their activity. Consider as an example the Sierra Club, which was founded in 1892.[3] For most of this century, it remained a small organization of activists, sponsoring wilderness trips and educational activities. Its political activities were rather limited, focusing on protection of particular canyons or valleys in the western states. In 1950, it had fewer than 7,000 members; it did not form a regional branch office until 1961. The club's political activities drew more attention in the 1960s, and its membership grew to 39,000 by the end of the decade. Still, its political arm was only a shadow of what it would become. The club's litigation department, the Legal Defense Fund, was founded in 1971. In 1976, Sierra started to get involved in election politics, endorsing candidates on the basis of their environmental stances. The decision to become a mass-based organization, to recruit members through the mass media or the mail, led to tremendous growth in the organization's budget and membership. Sierra, like other growing organizations, increased the size and professional quality of its full-time staff. By 1980, Sierra had 182,000 members, and by 1988 it counted 440,000 as members.

The story is the same for many of the large, well-known organizations. For the Audubon Society, for example, the 1960s brought an increasingly important political agenda and more aggressive membership recruiting. It is interesting to note that not all organizations experienced the same expansion. The Izaak Walton League (IWL), formed in 1922, had 54,000 members in 1970 and in the 1990s its membership was stable in the low 50,000s. The IWL, unlike Sierra or Audubon, did not embark on direct-mail campaigns to build its membership base. Some organizations have been on a veritable roller-coaster. Consider Greenpeace, which was founded in 1971. Greenpeace members hit the news headlines with direct actions to block nuclear tests and whale hunting, and their membership grew at a phenomenal pace. By 1991, Greenpeace was one of the largest environmental organizations, with a membership of 1.2 million. The membership has fallen just as swiftly, however. In 1997, it reported there were 400,000 members in the United States.

Such ups and downs depend in a significant way on the strategy and volume of organizational recruitment. The variables that help us to understand why some organizations grow while others shrink are often inside the organization itself. In particular, they are inside the recruiting department. Membership levels reflect the willingness to expend resources to contact prospective members and the ability to offer them something that they want in return for their dues payment. To a significant extent, one must study these organizations as businesses that contact prospective clients and nurture their "brand name loyalty." As political scientist Terry Moe observed, the group organizer's situation

> is analogous to that of the business firm whose products are virtually unknown to the consuming public. In order to sell his products—and thus in order to enlist new group members and retain old ones—he must somehow contact customers, inform them of the benefits he has to offer, and establish the terms of exchange.[4]

Group organizers incur the costs of contacting nonmembers in the hope that some of them will be moved to join. Although there is no doubt that rising interest in environmental issues created an opportunity for organizational growth, organizational action was necessary to exploit that opportunity. The conclusion is that the ups and downs of organizational membership reflect not only changes in public opinion, but also changes in the volume and strategy of recruiting.

Environmental Organizations and the Logic of Collective Action

Environmental organizations are an interesting set for study because they exemplify variety in virtually every respect. Some are highly specialized, and others are generalists. Some are highly professionalized in their staffing and recruiting activities, and others are not. Some have increased their membership bases, and some have shrunk. They are also academically interesting because they provide an ideal testing ground for ideas about the so-called collective action problem that has animated political science research for thirty years.

As Cigler and Loomis explained in Chapter 1 of this volume, there have been competing theories of interest group membership. The old group theory, associated with David Truman's *The Governmental Process*,[5] held that interest organizations form because people seek to contribute to a shared objective, a collective good. When people share a political impulse, an organization forms to advance that point of view. Mancur Olson's *The Logic of Collective Action*[6] shattered that way of thinking about membership organizations. Olson argued that people are not generally inclined to work together to achieve shared objectives because of the collective action problem. The collective action problem applies to a group of people who share a common goal and would like to have an organization form to represent their collective interest. The benefits of political action are typically laws, which apply to everyone, whether or not they lobby for them. A law forbidding air pollution creates fresh air for members and nonmembers alike. As such, it is a collective good, something from which noncontributors cannot be excluded. Because people realize they can enjoy the benefit of the law without contributing, they are tempted to "free ride" on the efforts of others. (As explained in Chapter 1, a *free-rider* is someone who agrees with a cause—or reaps the benefits of its success—but does not contribute to its accomplishment.)

If each individual's contribution has an impact on the amount of collective good provided for the whole group, then rational individuals might pitch in. Olson suspected that in all but the smallest groups, this is not the case. In large groups, individuals are unlikely to be able to perceive the impact of their contribution. Olson argued that, as a result, some points of view that are widely held are not represented by interest organizations.

One solution to the problem of collective action is to rely on a *major donor*. In Olson's terminology, a set of people is *privileged* if there is someone who is willing and able to provide the collective good for them. When students are assigned to work together on a project, teachers often observe that one student who is preoccupied with her or his shared grade will do almost all of the work. There is a famous story about Howard Hughes, who bought a television station in Las Vegas because he wanted to watch movies on late-night television. The station manager had refused to broadcast after 11:00 P.M., so Hughes bought the station! His satisfaction from the collective good—the broadcast signal—was so strong that he paid $3.8 million for the station. The fact that all of the other people in Las Vegas could enjoy the signal as well did not deter him—nor, presumably, did it motivate him.[7]

It is somewhat difficult to find interest organizations that are privileged groups in that sense. H. Ross Perot's financial support for United We Stand may be as close as we are going to get. Even in that case, the role of the major donor is to defray the costs born by the other members of the organization, not to single-handedly provide a collective good. Many organizations do in fact receive resources from foundations, corporations, or the government, and thus their members are not taxed as heavily as they might be.[8] Subsidies make it possible for organizations to provide services that they can not afford to finance with the dues they collect from members.[9]

When a set of people is not privileged, Olson argued that either the collective need goes unmet or that the collective good is provided as a by-product of other organizational activities. Olson's by-product theory of interest groups emphasized the use of *selective incentives* to attract members and supplement resources gathered from other sources. A selective incentive is a members-only benefit. Organizations sell things that people want, and then use the profits to pay for collective goods that people may (or may not!) also want, but are unwilling to pay for. Olson argued that entities such as labor unions, the American Farm Bureau Federation, and the American Medical Association are able to sell people something that they need (respectively, jobs, farming advice, and medical licensing). Those organizations in turn became politically powerful because their leaders divert some of their profits to pay for political action. The ultimate modern example of such an organization is the American Association of Retired Persons (AARP). The AARP, which had fewer than one million members in 1959, has seen its membership swell to more than 34 million. The AARP sells a magazine and offers discounts on insurance, medicine, and travel, and uses a portion of its profit to pay for a large lobbying department. Olson said that political action is a by-product in the sense that it is not motivating individuals to join the organization, but they receive the collective good anyway.

For the examples that he supplied, Olson's by-product theory seemed to work rather well. However, critics were quick to point out its weaknesses, both logical and factual. Three logical shortcomings seem particularly important. First, as Russell Hardin argued, "Although [the theory] can make sense of contributions to an ongoing political organization, it does not seem to explain how it is that many groups come to be organized in the first place."[10] Hardin provided examples of organizations that formed even though they did not sell selective benefits from the outset. Second, if someone could make a profit selling something, why would they spend it on a collective good?[11] Why wouldn't they take a trip to the Bahamas or pocket the money instead? Third, why wouldn't competitors be willing to undercut the group's price for the selective incentive? If an organization can sell insurance for $20 per month, and then divert $2 per month into political action, it seems that a new business might form to sell the insurance for $19 and thereby take away the organization's members.

To these logical problems, we can add one important factual shortcoming of Olson's logic: Many groups exist even though they do not offer irresistible material ("tangible") selective incentives. Jack Walker's survey of interest organizations found that only a relatively small proportion offered tangible members-only rewards. Walker doubted that material selective incentives are the explanation for membership in public interest groups and observed that "collective benefits have a more potent attraction than Olson understood."[12] It is hard to avoid the fact that some people participate in organizations even though they derive no particular personal benefit. People who are united to protest the death penalty, for example, do not belong because they are trying to save their own lives or get access to discount insurance.

The best approach to deal with these problems is an enriched version of Robert H. Salisbury's exchange theory of interest group politics. The exchange theory does not clash with Olson's major point of emphasis, the free-rider problem. Rather, it offers more detail about the way that the problem may be overcome. Salisbury described the relationship between an organizer (whom he called the *entrepreneur*) and members as an "exchange relationship," one in which leaders seek to amass a following and cultivate resources. He noted the shortcoming that the benefits offered by Olson's organizations were typically material benefits. To that category, he added two new kinds of selective benefits: *expressive* and *solidary*. An expressive benefit is a feeling of personal satisfaction that results from donating and thereby expressing a personal point of view. An expressive benefit is a selective benefit in the sense that a person cannot feel they have expressed themselves unless they join the organization. Perhaps only a small fraction of the people who agree with a political cause will also feel a need to contribute in order to express themselves. A solidary benefit is satisfaction that results from togetherness and feelings of acceptance that people get from joining an organization.[13]

Salisbury argued that organizations that offer tangible benefits may recruit more successfully and have higher rates of membership retention than organizations based on expressive and solidary benefits. Material benefits are, however, costly and not feasible for many organizations. Many of the so-called citizen's groups have neither the resources nor the administrative hierarchy required to mass market material selective incentives. As a result, these organizations try to market meager material benefits along with expressive and selective incentives.

Organizations that offer only expressive benefits often experience a high rate of membership turnover. Part of this turnover is a result of the learning experiences of the members themselves. Citizens are typically uninformed about the kinds of organizations that they might join. When they are invited to join, they may have only sparse facts about the organization's activities. In what Larry Rothenberg calls "experiential search," they join and often quit.[14] Another significant factor is the fact that, for many people, the expressive joy of membership is fleeting. People tend to feel that they have "done their part" by joining, or perhaps they are distracted by other activities (and uses for their money). Although an organization finds it inexpensive to recruit a person by offering him or her a chance to "speak his or her mind," the person who is recruited also finds it rather painless to quit. As a result, maintaining a membership organization is like running on a treadmill, and the larger the organization is, the faster the treadmill turns.

Environmentalism and the Free-Rider Problem

Although the scholars who specialize in environmental attitudes do not discuss the logic of collective action as such, there is no doubt that they are aware of the problem. Many studies have found widespread and rising levels of concern for the environment, but that proenvironmental attitudes are not necessarily accompanied by proenvironmental behavior.[15] A relatively small number of people with strong collective concerns follow through on those attitudes by taking individual action. Scott and Willits observed that two decades of studies have found that "although people express a relatively high level of concern about the environment, they engage in few environmentally oriented behaviors."[16] Citing the breadth of methodologies, they emphasized that there is "a real disparity between words and deeds,"[17] which is not simply an artifact of question wording or measurement error.

Even though the free-rider problem is widespread, it has been overcome by a number of organizations in the environmental arena. In order to find out more about these organizations, a mail survey was conducted. The survey was sent to all environmental, ecology, and conservation organizations listed in the *Encyclopedia of Associations*. The questionnaire included a mixture of open-ended and fill-in-the-blank questions that attempt to elicit information about how a group is organized to recruit and maintain membership, including data about means of communication that are used to contact nonmembers and the benefits that are offered. A cover sheet describing the general purpose of the study, along with an assurance of confidentiality, was sent to each group on the list. After the first wave of answers was received, the groups who did not respond were contacted on the telephone and invited to do so. Additional copies of the survey were mailed out. Those mail surveys were followed up by telephone interviews that explored the questions in greater depth. Insights into the logic of recruiting in an information-sparse environment are offered.[18]

The sample included organizations of many different sorts, ranging from the most general environmental interest to groups that are interested in particular species. There are groups interested in protecting inanimate objects such as soil, rivers, oceans, and lakes. There are also groups that are interested in protecting forests, trees, and plants. Almost all respondents requested that their confidentiality be protected, so a list of their names cannot be provided.

The average number of members per group is 48,712. This average is based on a badly skewed distribution. Most of the organizations that answered are small. Thirty-eight of them—about 70 percent of respondents—have fewer than 25,000 members. There are eleven medium-sized groups of membership from 25,001 to 100,000. There are six large groups with more than 100,000 members; two of them have more than 500,000.

The Costs and Benefits of Membership

The goal of the recruitment process is to convince people that the benefits of membership exceed the costs. The costs of the groups whose members answered the survey are uniformly moderate; the average dues rate is $23.50.

In return for their payment, what are members offered? The survey included a laundry list of possibilities. The responses are summarized in Table 2-1. In the category of material benefits, most striking is the fact that fifty-eight of sixty-one groups provide a periodical publication as a part of their membership package. Three-quarters of all groups offer access to group-oriented items, such as t-shirts. More than one-fourth provide access to a discount credit card. One-third of the groups offer access to wilderness outings, which might be classified either as a material or a solidary benefit. A number of groups offer other kinds of benefits, such as affinity long-distance telephone service or a special frequent flyer program. Thirteen of fifty-eight groups offer a premium for first-time members, such as a calendar, book, mug, totebag, fannypack, backpack, book, or t-shirt.

The Audubon Society is an example of an organization that offers the full array of selective incentives. Depending on which particular version of the direct-mail package is delivered, a new member is offered either a free Audubon backpack or windbreaker with the society's emblem. New members have to pay only $20 in the first year—a discount of $15. The glossy pamphlet explains that each member gets the "award-winning" Audubon magazine, along with a "great deal more." Members

Table 2-1   Selective Benefits Offered by Environmental Organizations

Selective benefit	Count	Percentage
Journal, newsletter, or magazine	58	95
Opportunity to purchase life or medical insurance at discount rates	2	3
Access to a special credit card	17	28
Opportunity to participate in wilderness outings	18	30
Opportunity to join in grassroots efforts to affect legislation	23	38
Opportunity to participate in meetings that determine the organization's political strategy	13	21
Opportunity to participate in meetings that change the group's bylaws or organizational structure	13	21
Opportunity to purchase group-related items, such as calendars, t-shirts, and bumper stickers	44	72

$N = 61.$

have "unique purchase opportunities," access to Audubon nature trails, wildlife sanctuaries, and exotic vacation packages, and membership in a local chapter. The local chapter offers a chance to "meet people who share your interests." The benefits offered by the Nature Conservancy are almost identical. New members can join for less than half of the regular fee. They get a magazine, 10-percent discount on purchases from the Nature Company, a state chapter newsletter, and exclusive invitations to special social events and field trips.

The Audubon also offers members a chance to "make a difference" by joining an activist network that provides a monthly news journal on environmental issues. This service can be viewed as a selective incentive if we suppose that people want to get involved, but many are too busy or confused to find out how. Group membership is thus a "cost-saving information cue," akin to membership in a political party. More than one-third of the organizations in the sample organize grassroots political campaigns and offer members the opportunity to participate. It is interesting to note that only one-fifth of the groups offer members a chance to participate in political strategizing or in meetings about the organizational future of the group. On the basis of this fact, one might doubt that Rothenberg's observations about citizen participation in Common Cause[19] will generalize to the environmental arena.

A number of organizations volunteered in the open-ended section of the questionnaire that another benefit of membership is the opportunity to participate in an adopt-an-animal program. These benefits appeal to the individual's inclination to provide a collective good for the benefit of all people. The International Wildlife Coalition (IWC), for example, administers the Whale Adoption Project. The IWC keeps records on whales and assigns them names. For $20, one can adopt a whale in the wild by choosing its name from a list. It then becomes "their whale." A person who adopts a whale receives a personalized whale adoption certificate, a photo of the whale, a four-color migration map, a decal, and a subscription to *Whalewatch*, an IWC newsletter. Adopt-an-animal programs fit within the Olsonian perspective because they make a person believe that his or her personal impact is significant. (Recall the story of Howard Hughes and the television station: If one person cares enough to provide the collective good, there is nothing irrational about doing so.) The fact that the same whale is adopted by several, perhaps thousands, of others is obscured in the direct-mail package. The donor is made to feel that his donation is providing for the welfare of one whale (even though the direct-mail literature clearly explains that the money is being used to support marine research and other IWC activities).

How important are these benefits to the people who join? The survey put the following question to the group leaders: "Do you feel that members expect something tangible in return for their contributions?" Forty of the group respondents, representing 73 percent of those who answered the question, said "yes." The division of the sample on that question, I believe, represents a broader philosophical–methodological disagreement that divides activists within the environmental arena. Some groups regard recruitment as a business. People are offered a magazine subscription or other benefits in return for their membership. Other group leaders, who tend to be volunteers, do not strive for that professionalized model of an organization. Instead, they want to view their organization as a spontaneous "bubbling up" of public sentiment and they deride the larger groups whose managers seek to be more professional and businesslike. This division is one of the major themes of Donald Snow's *Inside the Environmental Movement: Meeting the Leadership Challenge*,[20] a study of group management sponsored by The Conservation Fund. It is interesting to note that the organizations that are the largest, as we shall see, tend to be the ones with a more business-like attitude.

The Chicken and the Egg: Big Organizations and Direct-Mail Advertising

The cost of membership in an environmental interest organization is typically low. The benefits are also mild. These are ripe conditions for high levels of turnover in membership. Among the forty-three organizations that were willing to report their retention rates of members, the average retention rate is 70 percent. That means that an average organization must replace 30 percent of its members every year just to maintain itself. The 70-percent retention rate may seem low, but consider this: Among first-year recruits, the retention rate is typically much lower. One recruiter with whom I discussed this asserted, on the basis of her experience in three different organizations, that fewer than 50 percent of first-year recruits will renew. Among those who do renew, the chances that they will sign up again gradually increase. The overall retention rate climbs as the organization accumulates long-standing members, whose loyalty is balanced against the undependability of new members.

Because of the pressure to add new members, it is vital for an organization to communicate its message to prospective members. The survey asked respondents how they "make people aware of the group and encourage them to join." In particular, did they contact potential members through the mass media (apart from organizational newsletters and publications), door-to-door canvasing, direct-mail advertising, activities coordinated with commercial enterprises, and on-line computer networks (either of the general sort, such as Compuserve, or more narrowly, the Econet)? The results of this question are shown in Table 2-2.

The most widely used method of contacting people is the mass media, but this should be interpreted with some care. Follow-up questions asked if the groups were *buying* time on television or in print media. Only one group reported that it had bought television time, and thirteen

Table 2-2   How Organizations Contact Prospects

Method of contact	Count	Percentage of respondents
Mass media	37	61[a]
Door to door	0	0.0[a]
Direct mail	32	53[b]
Coordinated with commercial	26	44[c]
On-line computer networks	19	33[d]

[a] $N = 61$
[b] $N = 60$
[c] $N = 59$
[d] $N = 58$

had advertised in the print media. Hence, although thirty-five groups indicated they used the mass media, a large portion of those groups were attempting to use free media—in other words, public service announcements or coverage in the news. Several group respondents have informed me that, at some times in the past, they have advertised for members by purchasing time–space in the mass media, but that those efforts were deemed too expensive.

The survey found no groups who use door-to-door canvasing as a way of recruiting members. Most of us know, of course, that at least one group *does* go door to door. The survey results indicate that this approach is not in widespread use.

The survey found more than one-third of the groups use an on-line computer network. The rapid development of the World Wide Web (WWW) has outdated these results, however. At the time that the survey was conducted, the groups who responded affirmatively were mainly referring to bulletin boards for active group members. In the time since the survey first went out, a myriad of WWW pages have appeared. People who wander in the Web can find information and recruitment-oriented homepages for organizations such as Audubon, Sierra Club, National Resources Defense Council, International Wildlife Coalition, Save the Manatee Club, Defenders of Wildlife, and others. These Web pages were created after the mail survey started. One indication of the rapid pace of development in this form of communication is that one respondent returned the mail survey in April 1995 indicating that the group did not communicate with prospective members through the Internet. In July 1995, I spoke to that person on the telephone and she was surprised that I had not yet visited the organization's Web page. Group respondents indicate that the recruiting impact of these Web pages is not expected to be significant in the short term.

Direct-mail efforts are at the forefront of recruitment activities for many organizations. More than half of the groups who responded use direct-mail advertising. As shown in Table 2-3, larger organizations are significantly more likely to use direct-mail advertising. Only among the smallest organizations do we not find a majority of organizations using direct-mail advertising. Six of the seven largest organizations use direct mail. There are a number of possible explanations and the direction of causality is difficult to pin down. On the one hand, it may be that large organizations are more inclined to use direct-mail campaigns because they have more resources at their disposal and they can take advantage of economies of scale in purchase of supplies and lists of names. On the other hand, it may be that organizations that choose to use direct mail grow more quickly than other organizations. There is probably some truth in both of these explanations and the topic is explored in greater depth later.

For the organizations that use direct mail, two very interesting pieces of information are available. Respondents were asked how many non-members they contact each year and what percentage of those contacted respond by contributing to the group. It appears that organizations are sending out massive numbers of advertisements. The sheer magnitude of the direct-mail process is staggering. In total, the twenty-eight organizations who reported their direct-mail activities contacted 17,370,000 non-members collectively. The unweighted average of the number of pieces of direct sent per current member is 8.7. Especially among small organizations, there are gross variations, with some sending more than twenty pieces of mail per member and others send significantly less than ten.

The average of the response rates is 3.13 percent, which seems low to the uninitiated but is higher than the 1- to 2-percent rates frequently cited in the literature.[21] The number in this study is on the high side because there are a few small organizations—ones that send out a small number of pieces of mail—who report double-digit return rates. There are nine organizations with more than 25,000 members who were willing to report their response rates. Among them, the average is 2.3 percent. The average response rate among the largest organizations (three organizations with more than 100,000 members) is 1.7. Some respondents re-

Table 2-3   Group Size (in thousands)

		0–4.9	5–24.9	25.0–99.9	100.0 and up
"Does your organization use direct mail advertising to contact potential members?"	No	56%	33.3%	45.5%	14.3%
	Yes	44%	66.7%	54.5%	85.7%
Number of organizations polled		25	12	11	7

fused to reveal response rates, citing proprietary rights and magazine advertising policy, so these estimates of response rates are not based on the large sample that one might like.

These figures about the magnitude of direct-mail advertising match up in an interesting way against our facts about membership turnover. The mathematics of group membership indicate that a group's membership at a given time will reflect a blend of new and old members.[22] Suppose an organization is able to renew only 40 percent of its new members each year. Among the ones who remain, the retention rate goes up over the following years, so that by the fourth or fifth year the (admittedly small) cohort of members is also highly loyal. The rate of membership turnover drops over time, so in the long run the organization has to replace about 28 percent of its members in order to keep a stable membership level. If the response rate is 3 percent, then the organization should send about 9.3 pieces of mail to nonmembers for each existing member. The observed average response rates and recruitment rates square with this calculation: The average organization recruits to cover its membership losses. Some organizations grow because they recruit at a higher volume or somehow increase their response rates, whereas others shrink because they do not.

Direct-Mail Advertising: A Deeper Exploration

Because direct-mail advertising is the way that many of the largest organizations are contacting the bulk of their prospective members, some follow-up questions are in order. Why are there differences in the number of pieces of mail for similar-sized organizations? How do these organizations develop direct-mail packages? How do they decide which benefits to offer? To understand more about an organization's choice of a fund-raising strategy, follow-up telephone interviews were conducted with fifteen who currently or in the past used direct-mail advertising. The main focus was to find out more about the factors that affect an organization's decision to use direct-mail advertising and how they go about it.

Before delving into details, it is important to introduce a little direct-mail jargon. Direct mail may offer a *front-end premium*, such as wildlife stationary or personalized address labels, in the envelope that invites a person to join. The front-end premium is a "free sample" used to captivate the interest of the consumer. The best front-end premium I have ever received came with a membership invitation from the World Wildlife Fund. They provided four beautiful color postcards showing Siberian Tigers. The National Wildlife Federation is known to provide return address labels to some prospects, whereas the Environmental Defense Fund has on occasion provided a free color calendar. There is often also the offer of a *back-end premium*, which is something that first-time members receive in addition to their regular membership benefits. The back-end premium is typically a new-members-only benefit, as in the Audubon backpack.

Taken together, the organization's benefits, the write-up of its activities, the color of the paper or envelope all form the *package* that is presented through the mail. This mix of ingredients is chosen carefully to balance organizational cost against the recruiting power of the package. The group's most successful direct-mail package, including the style of the envelope, the letter, and the premiums, is often referred to as a *control mail package*.

The control mail package is typically subjected to experimentation and testing. Organizations send the control package to most of the people on the mailing list, but they will also have test packages that offer a different incentive package. If a test package succeeds, its strengths are added to the control. As one organizational administrator explained in a telephone interview, "Every little piece in the package affects the response rate. . . . I don't just do these things without testing it. . . . So I test every time I roll out more mail quantity, I look at the elements that could affect response. So what becomes my 'continuation,' or 'control' package, is the product of head-to-head testing. . . . Everything is done on the basis of a cost-benefit analysis." This should be qualified because some respondents admit that they have, perhaps unwisely, not experimented very much in the past and respondents in some small organizations say they cannot afford to do any experimentation at all.

Organizations are very secretive about the results of their experiments. Many of the respondents absolutely refused to discuss the details, citing the strict codes of privacy. Most respondents admitted that the package does make a difference, and one went so far as to break down the components of the package. Omitting the premiums in one test, for example, resulted in a "marked decrease in response." That group currently offers a number of front-end premiums and a back-end premium as well. "With all the little doodads [front-end premiums] and the [back-end premium], on a recent test we ran at a 1.7 percent response rate. I expect that will decrease as we increase the number of pieces we are mailing, so I expect it will end up around 1.5. If I took the [back-end premium] out, my response rate would drop from anywhere to 1.06 to 1.25, probably." Without the front-end premiums, the response rate would be 1 percent or lower. An attractive back-end premium can work, then, under the right conditions. One other respondent, who refused to provide details, confirmed the scale of these results. The inclusion of a back-end premium "dramatically lifts the response . . . 25 to 50 percent."

The back-end premiums are the typical material selective incentives that Olson described. Olson's critics were quick to point out that competing businesses could sell the selective incentive directly to the member, without the surcharge that pays for the collective effort, and the group would be out-competed. One group with whom I spoke, in fact, indicated that their efforts to market back-end premiums were not success-ful. That group, a general environmental group, said its mail response rate is 0.75 percent. When asked why premiums are not offered, the respon-dent said, "It's because we are above that sort of crass, materialistic thing. No, I'm sorry, I'm joking. It's because it doesn't work for us. If it worked, we would do it." To help understand why incentives work for some or-ganizations and not for others, I have developed a hypothesis. A group that wants to market a calendar, totebag, or mug must compete in the market against retailers such as Wal-Mart. If people can buy the same thing for less at the store, the group will not be successful. To gain a com-petitive advantage, a group can tie its product to the group's name and collective-interest orientation. For some people, it is worth a little more money to have a totebag with a group's emblem and a screen of an ani-mal. The group's mastery of the collective issues related to habitat and animal welfare can likewise be channeled into the marketing of back-end premiums such as coffee mugs and calendars. Organizations that have no reputation of expertise in the protection of a particular animal will have difficulty in marketing products because they do not have the obvious as-sociation in the public mind from which to make their sales pitch.

Even if the organization can put together a nice direct-mail package, the organization faces another problem: Where will they get a list of names? If an organization wants to send out two or three million pieces of mail, the only feasible way to collect those names is by trading with other organizations or renting names through a list broker. A list broker will tell the group which lists are available and will obtain permission from the owners of the list if access is desired. When organizations report that their response rates are between 0.5 and 2 percent they are usually referring to lists obtained in that way. In virtually every case, a group loses money in the first year on a recruitment effort using brokered lists. The cost of con-tacting the ninety-eight people who do not join outweighs the revenue gained from the two people who do join.

The smallest organizations are inclined to say that the cost of a mail campaign aimed at those generally available lists is too great. In the mail survey, many wrote comments such as, "No longer using this method. Not cost effective with blind contacts." Others added, "Direct mail is too expensive for us compared with the results obtained," "No money," "Limited resources," "Too expensive. I'd like to if we had the money." These conclusions may be reached after considerable debate; they are not cut and dried. One membership director said, "As you know, prospect mailing is a money loser in the immediate response, being that our board is heavily into making money, they continuously decline my request to do prospect mailing."

Some organizations will go ahead with a direct-mail campaign, even if they know it will not pay for itself right away. To justify doing so, they take an investment perspective. Several respondents used the term *life-*

time value of a member. If a group mails 10,000 pieces at $.35 each, at a 1-percent rate of response the organization spends $35 dollars to recruit each individual member. If the member pays $25 in the first year, the group not only loses money on the acquisition but also ends up providing the benefits of the group for free during that first year. But organizations expect between 30 and 50 percent of first-year members to renew, and the renewal rate climbs over the following years. "So what you are doing is looking at the cumulative value over time of those hundred members. In the end, you have 10 'really good' members," as one veteran recruiter said. "It is like any sort of capital investment. You put your money in and it comes out eventually, over time. . . . You know, it's fairly simple, and a lot more secure than a lot of the kinds of investments that people make all the time . . . like the stock market and that kind of stuff."

Not all organizations are losing money on direct-mail prospecting, however. Use of a specialized list can reduce the number of nonjoiners who are contacted. If a group can narrow the mailing universe to focus on the most likely respondents, then the response rate can be significantly enhanced. For example, there are conservation organizations that have the principal aim of protecting habitat for use by hunters. Those organizations can obtain the names of people who own licenses to hunt the particular animal around which the group is organized. A mailing to people who have already paid a state fee for a license is more likely to find people who are willing to pay to join a group as well. As one membership director told me, "People will spend a disproportionate share of their income on their hobby." Using demographic research, one such group claims that they target people much more precisely than other conservation organizations. That group obtains a very high response rate of 2.5 percent, and when asked why, the director of membership replied gruffly, "We're smarter. . . . Most of the organizations probably don't have as much experience in database marketing as we do. . . . We watch our market segments and we test. We do a lot more segmentation than other folks."

Nonhunting organizations also have access to special kinds of lists, but such access is highly idiosyncratic. One animal-specific group maintains an in-house list of 70,000 people who have responded to package inserts in commercial products or their own catalogs that feature products for the care of that animal. Another medium-sized general conservation organization reported a response rate of 5 percent. That response rate is obtained in a list compiled by a magazine publishing group with which the group is affiliated. The response rate was high because the group had "special access that other organizations don't," in the words of the group's marketing manager. Seeking to grow beyond that list, the organization has sampled from lists of other environmental groups, a path referred to as *outside acquisition*. "Our [outside acquisition] efforts resulted in response rates around 2 percent, somewhere between 1.5 and 2.5 percent. . . . Which is not working for us. . . . We are constantly testing using different approaches, different positioning and different packaging. . . . The high rates like 2.2 are for the 'address label package,' that compares with .8 or 1.2 percent for a package without address labels." That group will not signif-icantly expand its advertising to the broader lists until they develop a package that ensures a response rate well above 2 percent.

These harsh realities mean that building a membership organization is far from easy. Some organizations remain small because they lack ac-cess to specialized mailing lists. Some organizations remain small if their decision makers are conservative, unwilling to risk precious funds on a campaign to expand the membership of the organization. Among organi-zations that choose to use direct mail, there are some significant differ-ences in the volume of direct-mail activity. If they were recruiting to re-place losses, they would be contacting about eight or ten prospects for each current member. In Figure 2-1, a scatterplot of the number of pieces of mail against organizational size is shown. As one might expect, the larger organizations send more mail, but there are some significant differ-ences in the volume of mail for organizations of any given size.

When asking organizations about the procedure that they use to de-cide on the number of pieces of mail, there were a number of answers. Or-ganizations that expect to lose money must treat direct mail as a capital investment and reconcile it with the rest of their budget. If the organiza-

Figure 2-1   Volume of Direct-Mail Recruiting

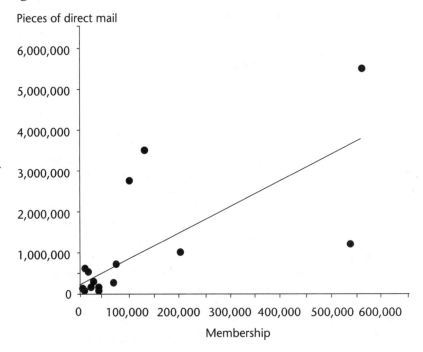

Pieces of direct mail

tion places a heavy emphasis on expanding its membership base, it will send significantly more pieces than an organization that wants only to maintain its existing membership level. These goals, of course, must accommodate other organizational activity. When asked how much mail it sends, a general environmental organization's membership director said, "The organization's budget decides, basically." The president of a small ecosystem-oriented group said, "It's just what we can afford." Another added, "In terms of acquisition mail, we mail what we can afford to mail. We know what it costs us to bring in a member, we know we lose money to bring people in, it is an investment program." Group directors set the advertising budget with the expectation that the investment will be repaid in the second or third year of membership.

Fluctuations in the budget—either on the revenue or expenditure side—can significantly affect the direct-mail campaigns of such organizations. The ups and downs of direct-mail advertising volume are seen clearly in an organization such as the Mountain Lion Foundation (whose executive director Mark Palmer was kind enough to make this data available). That organization, which has about 25,000 active members, seeks to preserve the habitat of mountain lions and prevent hunting of them, mainly in California. A member who pays $35 can receive a book or calendar in addition to regular membership benefits. The response rate is about 1.3 percent, at which the organization nearly breaks even in the first year of a direct-mail campaign. Nevertheless, the rate of direct-mail activity varies considerably. In 1993, the organization sent out 30,000 pieces. In 1994, the total number was 140,000, and in 1995 it expects the total will be 300,000. There may be a significant cutback in the next year, however. "We would like to send out more; the problem is 'will we have enough cash up front?' It looks like we will have to mount another ballot campaign on mountain lion hunting in California. The sportsmen organizations have been able to get the state legislature to move a ballot measure. . . . It looks like we are facing that for next March. Because of that, we are going to be cutting back as much as we can in expenses for the Foundation and the question is, 'will we have enough cash flow to put out additional recruitment mailing?' which given the publicity should be very lucrative, but at the same time it ties up a lot of cash we might need to dig into."

Direct-mail fund-raising is viewed as a residual budget category only when the response rate is low. If a group can mail at a high response rate, it need not take the long-term investment perspective. The number of pieces of mail may be limited only by the size of the high quality mailing list. As one membership director put it, "It is what we think the market will bear at a certain return on investment." Another said the ability to break even in the first year brings organizational considerations into the decision-making process. "A lot of our acquisition is on a break-even basis. It is not an investment for us to acquire new members. We have a certain amount of attrition . . . and we have a certain amount of desired growth, and based on our response rate we have to mail that number of pieces to maintain our membership level and growth rate." One group that is just beginning to use a small mailing list said, "We don't like to do anything that would not have that piece pay for itself. I understand 'life-time value of a member' and 'associated revenues from each member-ship' but we operate quite a bit differently. We won't sell lists or do any-thing like that."

Implicit in all of these approaches is the idea that only a limited num-ber of people can be solicited profitably. Many organizations, especially the smaller ones, are conservative, reluctant to take risks with scarce bud-getary resources. One animal-specific group said that it tested the market last year by mailing 80,000 pieces to a list of names drawn from many en-vironmental organizations. It then selected the most productive lists (re-sponse rate above 2 percent), "and decided to send 30,000 pieces to names drawn from those lists." That group expects to come close to breaking even in the first year, but is keeping the volume down just in case.

Most organizations that use direct mail use it reluctantly and wish they had a better way. As one staff member said, "We know how many new people we have to bring in each year. A large percentage are from di-rect mail. We are trying to get away from mailing so many pieces, but right now it is the most cost-effective way to bring in new members." An-other added, "I don't really like direct mail. . . . I feel it's very costly, and not that effective. . . . But it can grow your membership." Organizations like these are either experimenting with or using methods other than di-rect mail to create mailing lists. As noted previously, in 1995, many orga-nizations jumped with both feet into the Internet, hoping that someday it might be a significant source of members.

Some organizations that have made effective use of direct mail in the past are no longer doing so. The president of the 200,000-member Inter-national Wildlife Coalition, Daniel J. Morast, said that although in 1994 his organization sent out more than one million pieces of mail, it would probably not send any in the recruiting season from fall 1995 through spring 1996. The cost-benefit ratio is the reason.

> This year we . . . probably won't do any acquisition mail, any standard direct mail. We'll try to do other forms of promotion to capture names. Because the response rate is so low, direct mail has gotten so expen-sive. We'd rather not invest that much money into new mailings, and try to use other forms.

The IWC, for example, is aligned with a company that sells whale adop-tion kits in stores, and the kits include an IWC membership. It also en-courages existing members to give whale adoptions as gifts to friends and family during the holidays. The same strategy has worked very well for the Save the Manatee Club, which has discontinued direct mail and has instead encouraged its members to make a holiday gift of membership in the Adopt-a-Manatee program.

Collective Goods, Expressive Benefits, and Competitive Recruitment

What is the relationship between the collective goods that these organizations seek to advance and the selective incentives that they offer? In his by-product theory, Olson argued that the two would often be completely separate entities. The two need not be completely separate, however. In the previous section, it was noted that organizations may have their best chance of competing with ordinary retail outlets if they link their selective incentives to their collective cause. Some people, perhaps as many as 0.5 percent of the recipients of direct mail, may be willing to buy a totebag, mug, backpack, calendar, or coffee-table book if it is linked to such a cause. By choosing to focus their collective action and marketing effort on a particular creature, the group is able to convert a mundane item into something for which people are willing to pay. A group's identification with a collective good creates demand for certain kinds of selective incentives it may offer.

The relationship between the collective identification of the group and its selective incentives arose in answers to questions about competition among organizations in the recruitment process. Group respondents were asked if they felt their group was in competition for members and, if so, how do they differentiate themselves. In their answers to these questions, there are indications that organizations are marketing selective incentives related to their collective goods and using a particular sort of brand name appeal to attract people. Because I cannot reveal the identity of the respondents, I will not include the names of the specific creatures in the analysis. Instead, the generic term "animal X" will be inserted to conceal the identities of the respondents.

When asked "Do you feel your organization competes for members with other environmental organizations?" 61 percent of people who responded (thirty-four of fifty-six) said "yes." When asked "How so?" and "What are the distinguishing features of your organization that appeal to prospective members?" people made a number of interesting comments. On a general level, organizations are competing for the time, attention, and money that are finite. One respondent who answered "yes" wrote simply that "there are limited environmental dollars." Another added, "There are only so many people with an interest and with the financial ability." General-purpose organizations have a problem because their titles and purposes seem indistinguishable to prospective members. One group leader wrote, "Yes, to a small degree. Most people do not see the difference, or do not distinguish one environmental group from another. Therefore, they feel that if they contribute to one organization it's as good as any other." Most group leaders would probably agree that they are competing for scarce disposable income, partly because they are trading (or selling each other) mailing lists. As one group leader wrote, "Most of our members come from direct mail, and potential members receive it from many environmental organizations. They are forced to choose between them."

The competitive strategies of the organizations varied according to their stated *raison d'être*. The more general environmental organizations compete on the basis of their publications and their brand name. One wrote that his group is distinguished by "the magazine, name recognition, and identification with [a group of animals]." One group leader of a medium-sized group explained that, during tough times, they compete with a broad array of organizations for support simply because people do not see differences among organizations. However, that group is distinguished by the following factors.

1. We take on hard fights with an arsenal that includes lawsuits if necessary.
2. We have a proven track record of success in such battles.
3. [Our Journal] is a very good magazine of serious interest.
4. We are not extremists.

A small group with a general environmental orientation is distinguished because, "We have a strong Hill presence and we arm grassroots organizations with the tools to affect local and national legislation." In that small group, most people who are members can actually get involved and experience these services firsthand.

Among specific-animal organizations there was a most interesting division of opinion on the question of competition for members. Many specific-animal groups said that they were not competing for members because there were no other organizations interested in their particular animal. One such person described his group's distinction bluntly: "Unique—only organization dedicated solely to [animal X]." Others made comments such as, "We specialize in protecting [animal X]," or "No. We are a single-mission group and we have a unique, solid niche. No other group competes with us." Another wrote, "We are small and different enough." The distinguishing feature of the group is "Our personality. They visit and like our smallness. Also the adopt-a-[animal X] program. They get a lot of attention, plus the chance to meet their [animal X]."

Other specific-animal group leaders did recognize the fact that they were competing for the attention of donors with other organizations, and yet they felt that their specificity protected them. A group whose title includes animal X commented, "More groups are popping up everywhere. Everybody wants money. Most people who join don't have a huge disposable income." That group, she felt, was distinguished because "We only work on [animal category]-related issues." Another respondent wrote, "Because we are a single-species advocacy group, we compete with other marine environmental groups." However, the respondent went on to argue that his group is distinguished because, "We are a single-species advocacy group." Another said his group did "occasionally" compete for members, but added "we are the only group that does what we do." "[We are] highly focused on one animal and its habitat," wrote another. Some respondents held out the simple idea that their animals are popular and attract adherents to the group. Along those lines, when asked about competition, one wrote, "Yes. Obviously. Although there are people who *just* love [animal X]." One admitted his group was in competition because it "use[s] the same enviro mailing list pie," but "we adopt out live [animal Xs]" and "we challenge abuses of commercial wildlife exploitation." One animal group said the distinguishing feature was his group's "Focus on charismatic megafauna, like [animal X]. . . . We are successful, bold, don't compromise. Issues are easy to understand. We have good staff, support of prominent people, etc."

In two cases, respondents volunteered that they were competing with another organization head-to-head. One wrote, "Yes, there is another national group promoting [animal X] that has a periodical." That group, she claimed, is distinguished because, "Our publication is printed in color and is more scientific than the other group." The opposing group did not answer the survey. Another group claimed there were "copy cat" groups who even used the name of the animal in the title of their group to try to confuse prospective donors.

The foregoing comments indicate that prospective members are seen quite differently by the different kinds of organizations. The general organizations tend to see nonmembers as people with an undefined interest in the environment who may not be able to distinguish the organizations. From that perspective, a group's major objective is to activate people, to catch their interest and persuade them that their interest in the environment can be satisfied by that particular group. On the other hand, the specific-animal organizations see nonmembers as people who may have an interest in a particular kind of animal but are waiting to be made aware of the group's activities. The common response "we are the only animal X group" indicates that the identification with animal X is thought to be a significant factor in recruiting. I suspect that these representatives of specific-animal groups are wrong; all of these groups are probably recruiting from the same pool of people who are (1) environmentally concerned and (2) inclined to join groups. This is certainly one area in which a survey of the general public would help.

The activities of organizations that pursue the collective good can influence recruiting in other ways. Conservation organizations with a prohunting focus provide a different set of benefits to members. Their magazines and information are not geared simply to protect habitat but to enhance the sportsperson's enjoyment of it. People who oppose hunting find these materials repellent and do not choose to purchase a membership, but the people who like hunting may find them useful. Groups oriented to sportspersons have also been very successful in marketing solidary incentives. These groups ask local volunteers to organize banquets. Current members seek out new members, who pay for the price of membership with the single check that pays for the expense of the banquet. People who like to hunt a particular kind of animal are often eager to make acquaintance of others who like to do the same, and so the banquets have been great fund-raising and member-recruiting devices.

Discussion

How does this research help us to better understand the important questions of politics, particularly about representation? Whereas Mancur Olson argued that the free-rider problem created systematic distortions in political representation, particularly where diffuse collective interests are concerned, the evidence points in a different direction. Some organizations are able to mobilize members, and the mobilization process may depend in an important way on the organization's mastery of a public policy issue. Some kinds of organizations, particularly the ones that can sell beautiful calendars or backpacks with logos, are able to mobilize a significant number of people who support their causes. On the other hand, many organizations remain small, even though they may speak for collective interests that are widely held. They are unable or unwilling to market themselves to build a membership base. As a result, the link is not tight between the number of citizens with a given interest and the number of people who belong to an interest group that works for that collective interest.

Some organizations grow because they recruit aggressively, whereas others that might espouse more popular collective causes wither for lack of effective recruitment and leadership. Whenever I read in the newspaper that membership in some organization has taken a nosedive, I always wonder if the cause is a fall-off in public interest or a change in recruiting strategy. In 1997, newspaper articles appeared about the decline of membership in Greenpeace, which had crested at about 1.2 million in 1991. The conventional wisdom seemed to be that Greenpeace had somehow taken the wrong stances in politics, or that it had lost its "freshness." A look at the recruiting activities tells another story. Greenpeace grew aggressively through the 1980s with a high-volume direct-mail advertising campaign. Its membership swell was almost exclusively driven by direct-mail advertising at a volume far above the norm.[23] Christopher Bosso, for example, noted that in 1990, Greenpeace sent out forty-eight million pieces of mail. [24] For a base of one million existing members, this rate—forty-eight pieces of mail per current member—is grossly in excess of the number needed to maintain the organization's membership. Greenpeace never experienced the membership-stabilizing effect of maturity because it kept recruiting ever larger cohorts of new (high-turnover) members. In the following years, according to Bosso, Greenpeace leaders decided to try to get off the direct-mail treadmill, significantly reducing direct-mail volume. The change produced an almost immediate contraction in membership, which in turn set off cutbacks in staff and recruiting activity.[25]

One of the large general environmental organizations in this study suffered a relatively abrupt loss of membership in the early 1990s. Membership has grown back to the original level and I was curious to know how the staff would explain the fluctuation. Was it economic recession or a fall-off in interest in environmental questions? The staff reported that it was nothing of the kind. "We had mismanagement in the membership department, it was internal problems. . . . [They] rolled out with a direct mail campaign, a new control, without testing it, and it was not too successful, and then used it again in another campaign. . . . They stopped doing renewal telemarketing and they . . . cut the last two efforts of the renewal series plus two renewal wraps on the magazines that were sent out." The ups and downs of organizations are typically more complicated than the usual view that changes in public interests drive membership levels.

Conclusion

First, direct-mail advertising is the most important method of contacting nonmembers and encouraging them to join environmental organizations. All but the smallest organizations tend to use direct-mail recruitment, despite the fact that a very high volume of mail is required to compensate for low response rates. Some organizations avoid the worst expenses of direct-mail campaigns because they have access to special membership lists. Organizations that lack such access may be unwilling to bear the high cost of direct-mail advertising. Some organizations have turned away from that method of recruitment, even though they know their membership levels are likely to shrink.

Second, organizations offer a variety of selective incentives that they hope will interest prospective members, and three-quarters of group respondents feel that members expect something tangible in return for their membership fees. Many of these selective benefits are tied to the organization's collective role. That tie, emphasized by organizational logos or emblems on backpacks, jackets, totebags, or coffee cups, means that the organization's reputation as a servant of a collective interest can enhance the value of its selective incentives. Interest in magazines, nature catalogs, and other group-related items is driven by the substantive content of the group's collective activities.

Third, environmental organizations are competing for members. Even though proenvironment attitudes are widespread through the population, the willingness to join an organization is considerably less widespread. Some people with a general, unrefined interest in the environment might join the first organization that contacts them, whether it is the World Wildlife Fund, the Purple Martin Conservation Association, or the Save the Manatee Club. It may be that organizations are seldom compared head to head, because people are seldom contacted by two organizations at the same moment. Still, the organizational leaders feel that they are trying to differentiate and distinguish themselves. Among the more discerning prospects, organizations attempt to differentiate themselves by the quality of their selective incentives and the nature of their appeal. General multipurpose organizations exist, especially when it comes to Washington politics. But they tend to market themselves as specialists. The Audubon Society is a general organization with an interest in wildlife habitat, but in its marketing material, it looks to be mainly about birds.

Collective interests do not explain group membership—recruiting activity does. This is the case because people who have an interest in a collective good do not tend to be "self-starters" who seek out and join groups. Instead they must be sought out, pursued, enticed, and persuaded. A widespread collective interest, a belief that rivers should be clean or that forests should not be razed, does not generate an interest group. Rather, to understand the groups that exist, one must understand that there are organizers and recruiting strategies whose efforts must somehow interact with the attitudinal basis of support in the community.

Notes

1. Peggy Daniels and Carol Schwartz, *Encyclopedia of Associations, '96* (Detroit, Mich.: Gale Research, 1995).
2. Robert C. Mitchell, Angela G. Mertig, and Riley E. Dunlap, "Twenty Years of Environmental Mobilization: Trends among National Environmental Organizations," in *American Environmentalism: The U.S. Environmental Movement, 1970–1990*, ed. Riley E. Dunlap and Angela G. Mertig (Philadelphia: Taylor and Francis, 1993), 11–26.
3. Tom Turner, *Sierra Club: 100 Years of Protecting Nature* (New York: Harry N. Abrams, 1991).
4. Terry Moe, *The Organization of Interests* (Chicago: University of Chicago Press, 1980), 39.
5. David Truman, *The Governmental Process: Political Interests and Public Opinion* (New York: Alfred A. Knopf, 1951).
6. Mancur Olson, Jr., *The Logic of Collective Action* (Cambridge, Mass: Harvard University Press, 1965).
7. Russell Hardin, *Collective Action* (Baltimore: Johns Hopkins University Press, 1982), 42.
8. Jack L. Walker, "The Origins and Maintenance of Interest Groups in America," *American Political Science Review* 77 (June 1983): 390–406.
9. Allan J. Cigler and Anthony J. Nownes, "Public Interest Entrepreneurs and Group Patrons," in *Interest Group Politics*, 4th ed., ed. Allan J. Cigler and Burdett A. Loomis (Washington, D.C.: CQ Press, 1995), 77–98.
10. Hardin, *Collective Action*, 34.

11. Norman Frohlich and Joe A. Oppenheimer "I Get by with a Little Help from My Friends," *World Politics* 23 (October, 1970): 119.

12. Jack Walker, *Mobilizing Interest Groups in America: Patrons, Professions, and Social Movements* (Ann Arbor: University of Michigan Press, 1991), 85. See also David Marsh, "On Joining Interest Groups: An Empirical Consideration of the Works of Mancur Olson," *British Journal of Political Science* 6 (1976): 257–272; Robert Cameron Mitchell, "National Environmental Lobbies and the Apparent Illogic of Collective Action," in *Collective Decision Making*, ed. Clifford Russell (Baltimore: Johns Hopkins University Press, 1979), 88; Kenneth Godwin and Robert C. Mitchell, "Rational Models, Collective Goods, and Non-electoral Political Behavior," *Western Politics Quarterly* 35 (1982): 161–180; Allan J. Cigler and John Mark Hansen, "Group Formation through Protest: The American Agriculture Movement," in *Interest Group Politics*, ed. Allan J. Cigler and Burdett A. Loomis (Washington, D.C.: CQ Press, 1983); John Mark Hansen, "The Political Economy of Group Membership," *American Political Science Review* 79 (1985): 79–96; Lawrence Rothenberg, *Linking Citizens to Government: Interest Group Politics at Common Cause* (New York: Cambridge University Press, 1992).

13. Robert H. Salisbury, "An Exchange Theory of Interest Groups," *Midwest Journal of Political Science* 13 (February 1969): 1–32. See also Peter B. Clark and James Q. Wilson, "Incentive Systems: A Theory of Organizations," *Administrative Science Quarterly* 6 (1969): 129–166.

14. Lawrence S. Rothenberg, "Organizational Maintenance and the Retention Decision in Groups," *American Political Science Review* 82 (1988): 1129–1152.

15. Susan E. Howell and Shirley B. Laska, "The Changing Face of the Environmental Coalition," *Environment and Behavior* 24 (1992): 134–144; Paul C. Stern, Thomas Deitz, and Linda Kalof, "Value Orientations, Gender, and Environmental Concern," *Environment and Behavior* 25 (1993): 322–348; R. E. Dunlap and K. D. Van Liere, "The New Environmental Paradigm: A Proposed Measuring Instrument and Preliminary Results," *Journal of Environmental Education* 9 (1978): 10–19; R. E. Dunlap, "Public Opinion in the 1980s: Clear Consensus, Ambiguous Commitment," *Environment* 33 (1991): 10–37; K. D. Van Liere and R. E. Dunlap, "The Social Bases of Environmental Concern," *Public Opinion Quarterly* 44 (1980): 181–197.

16. David Scott and Fern K. Willits, "Environmental Attitudes and Behavior: A Pennsylvania Survey," *Environment and Behavior* 26 (1994): 239–260.

17. Ibid., 255.

18. A total of seventy-three organizations sent the survey back, but twelve of them did not provide answers to more than one or two questions. There was one piece of antiacademic hate mail and several group leaders said they did not have time to answer the questions or that they did not think they were a membership group in the sense that the questions implied. Excluding those from consideration, there are sixty-one valid and relatively complete surveys. Some questions were left blank, apparently the result of the fact that the numbers for which we asked were either not easily accessible or were considered confidential.

19. Lawrence S. Rothenberg, *Linking Citizens to Government: Interest Group Politics at Common Cause* (New York: Cambridge University Press, 1992).

20. Donald Snow, *Inside the Environmental Movement: Meeting the Leadership Challenge* (Washington, D.C.: Island Press, 1992).

21. Kenneth R. Godwin, *One Billion Dollars of Influence* (Chatham, N.J.: Chatham House, 1988).

22. These calculations are discussed in Paul E. Johnson, "A Sieve Model of Interest Group Recruitment" (Paper delivered at the annual meeting of the American Political Science Association, Washington D.C., August 29, 1997).

23. Ronald G. Shaiko, "Greenpeace USA: Something Old, New, Borrowed," *Annals of American Academy of Political Science* 528 (1993): 88–100.
24. Christopher J. Bosso, "The Color of Money: Environmental Groups and the Pathologies of Fund Raising," in *Interest Group Politics*, 4th ed., ed. Allan J. Cigler and Burdett A. Loomis (Washington, D.C.: CQ Press, 1995), 101–130.
25. Emily Gurnon, "Greenpeace Loses Ground in the U.S., Plans Major Cuts," *Washington Times*, August 27, 1997, 18.

3

Corporate Philanthropy in a Political Fishbowl: Perils and Possibilities

Anthony J. Nownes and Allan J. Cigler

Corporate giving to nonprofit and public interest organizations has emerged in recent years as a controversial political activity, both for the corporations involved as well as the recipient groups. Tobacco company contributions to groups such as the American Civil Liberties Union (ACLU) and a number of women's and AIDS activist organizations have raised concerns among those on the political Left concerning the effect on the independence of such recipient groups. Those on the political Right have been upset by corporate support for organized interests such as Planned Parenthood and the Humane Society of the United States. In some cases, companies have been boycotted because of their philanthropic decisions.

In this chapter, Anthony Nownes and Allan Cigler trace the development of the politicalization of corporate giving, then report the results of a series of in-depth interviews with officials in charge of corporate philanthropy. Their aim is to uncover how corporate giving priorities are set, how specific recipient groups are chosen, and whether or not corporate giving is viewed as a tool for political influence.

They find that altruism and, increasingly, business interests, are the primary motivating forces behind most corporate giving. Political considerations are ever present, however, as firms must make sure their contributions do not rile either shareholders or the general public. Although corporate giving programs are not political tools in most instances, Cigler and Nownes believe the contemporary corporate economic environment, with its emphasis on efficiency and competitiveness, may eventually lead to more politically strategic philanthropy by business concerns.

In the interim between the end of World War II and the mid-1960s individual American corporations were largely disengaged from national politics.[1] Few corporations had a permanent Washington presence. Lobbying was typically done by peak associations representing multiple corporations, such as the American Petroleum Institute, or business umbrella organizations, such as the National Association of Manufacturers. Legal restrictions on corporate political contributions limited the role of companies in elections. Corporations still did well in the policy process. Public opinion toward business was quite favorable.[2] A conservative, probusiness coalition of southern Democrats and Republicans ruled Congress, and opposition to corporate interests, with the exception of organized labor, was not well mobilized. Corporate America, in an age of unprecedented growth and domination of world markets, had little need to devote much attention to government affairs.

The political environment for business changed markedly starting during the Johnson administration. Public confidence in business eroded, at least in part as a result of a number of business scandals and widely publicized corporate abuses of power.[3] The election of a liberal Congress in 1964 altered the political agenda; especially troublesome in the decade following was the expansion of regulatory activity in the hands of various government agencies. The period witnessed the rise of a number of public interest lobbies ranging from consumer advocates to aggressive environmental groups, many of which directly challenged business practices.

Business political mobilization occurred in the face of the threat.[4] The number of trade associations and business coalitions grew, but so did a more active role for individual corporations. By the 1990s, it was commonplace for large American corporations to have a Washington office and to engage in lobbying activity directly. A number of corporations are now actively involved in advocacy advertising and grassroots lobbying. Contributing to political campaigns through corporate PACs and underwriting certain political party activities through soft money contributions is widespread.

In this chapter, we focus on an important but less well-known business activity: corporate giving programs to nonprofit organizations, including public interest groups. By the mid-1990s corporations were contributing nearly $7.5 billion to such organizations, more than 1 percent of their pretax profits.[5] Such funds have become an important part of public interest group budgets.[6] By supporting some types of groups to the exclusion of others, corporate patronage has potential implications for the nature of public interest representation. And for the corporation, operating in today's morally charged political environment, political controversy sometimes follows even the best of intentions.

The Politicalization of Corporate Giving

The United States has a long history of philanthropy, but corporate giving to political groups is of rather recent vintage. Gifts have traditionally been made by individuals not companies, and businesspeople who did target causes typically chose charities unrelated to their main business interests (for example, bankers tended to support the arts, industrialists gave to children's organizations, and so on).[7] The little corporate money that was given tended to go to mainline umbrella charities such as Community Chests. The prevailing ethic was that "the business of business was making money, not giving it away."[8]

The pattern of corporate giving began to change in the late 1960s and early 1970s, as business felt pressure to demonstrate its social responsibility. In-house foundations were established in many corporations. Companies such as Dayton Hudson, Levi Strauss, and Cummins Engine received positive press attention for giving as much as 5 percent (the maximum allowed by law at the time for tax deductibility purposes) of their pretax profits to public interest and other nonprofit organizations.[9] Most corporate contributions went to fund services, but a growing amount targeted a number of controversial advocacy interests, ranging from civil rights organizing to voter registration drives targeted at minorities.

Corporate giving patterns underwent further change during the Reagan years. The Economic Recovery Tax Act of 1981 enabled corporations to deduct up to 10 percent of taxable income each year. Cuts in social program expenditures, coupled with Reagan's call for the private sector to assume an active social role, contributed to major increases in corporate giving.

But by the late 1980s and early 1990s the economic climate had again changed, as the nation entered a prolonged recession. Foreign competition was eroding corporate profits, and it was clear that the American hegemony in a number of world markets no longer existed. Some companies had begun to rethink their giving programs. A few, such as the Scott Paper Company, eliminated their corporate giving programs altogether.[10]

Competitive efficiency, often through downsizing, became the order of the day. Corporate executives came under pressure to view giving less as charity and more as a strategic investment, directly related to their businesses. Such giving often had political as well as business implications. For example, insurance companies, concerned with rising medical claims; pharmaceutical companies, interested in the market for AIDS drugs; and fashion companies, with a large percentage of gay men and lesbians in their workforce, became involved in supporting AIDS organizations such as the American Foundation for AIDS Research, which aggressively sought government funds.[11] And the relationship between Philip Morris and the American Civil Liberties Union (ACLU) seemed more than coincidence: Soon after receiving funds the ACLU took up the cause of "smokers rights."[12]

Corporate giving programs came under increased scrutiny from the general public and various "cause" groups. For example, in the late 1980s and early 1990s companies that donated to Planned Parenthood, a leading abortion rights advocacy organization, found themselves in the midst of a public relations nightmare. Even though corporations defended their giving by saying their grants were specifically aimed at reducing teenage pregnancies, a number were targeted by prolife groups, which organized letter-writing and calling campaigns directed at corporate executives. Among the companies singled out for negative publicity were corporate giants AT&T and J.C. Penney.[13]

The period also witnessed a number of consumer boycotts by groups on the political Right. For example, the Christian Action Council (CAC), a coalition of twenty-four prolife organizations, launched a boycott of forty-three corporations that were targeted for their financial support of such groups as the National Organization for Women Legal Defense Fund and the Children's Defense Fund. At the head of the boycott list was American Express, which was highlighted with the slogan, "Leave Home Without It."[14] In the face of boycott pressures many corporations discontinued their support for such groups. As a Gannett Foundation spokesperson, in the face of pressure over Planned Parenthood contributions, noted, "No CEO is comfortable with letters saying: 'You're murdering babies.' "[15]

By the early 1990s it was becoming clear that American corporations were living in a fishbowl in which the political implications of even their philanthropic activities were under intense scrutiny. A widely circulated study of corporate giving by a conservative think tank, the Capital Research Center, chastised many corporations for supporting public interest organizations, especially those that lobbied against business interests in Congress.[16] Suddenly, what had been the sleepy business of corporate philanthropy was no longer so sleepy.

The Basics of Corporate Giving

The nature of corporate giving is both encouraged and constrained by the nation's very complex tax laws. Like individuals, corporations are not restricted from making contributions of any amount to any group. But in order to deduct the gift from taxable income, a firm must contribute to "public charities"—501(c)(3) organizations in the tax code. Most public interest groups (including think tanks) are considered 501(c)(3) groups or have 501(c)(3) affiliates (for example, foundations). Though no tax-deductible corporate support directly funds lobbying efforts, 501(c)(3) organizations are permitted to use a proportion of their budgets for "advocacy" and "education" purposes, including grassroots organizing.[17]

Corporations can support nonprofit organizations either through direct giving or through company-sponsored foundations. Each form has its advantages. On one hand, direct contributions are attractive because they do not require public disclosure. Giving through a foundation has additional tax advantages, however. Unlike private foundations, corporate foundations do not usually have endowments; companies typically fund foundations through periodic gifts. As a consequence some firms have the ability to make exceptionally large contributions through their foundations in years when the corporate tax rate is high (lowering their taxes as a consequence), and are able to "smooth the flow of gifts by ensuring that total gifts remain high."[18] The firm may deduct the total of its direct and foundation gifts to charities in a given year up to a maximum of 10 percent of taxable income. Roughly 1,600 corporations have foundations, and among the largest corporations both direct and corporate giving is common.

In practice, the amount given by corporate interests varies according to the health of the business climate, decreasing in periods of low profitability and increasing during good economic times. The bulk of corporate funding supports services such as education, the arts, social services, and health care. The largest contributions go to education (93 percent of all gifts over $1 million in 1991), and gifts to federated programs such as the United Way garner roughly one-eighth of all corporate contributions.[19]

Nevertheless, corporate America is an important source of funds for nonprofit groups. One organization that studied corporate giving, the Capital Research Center, a Washington-based think tank, estimated that in 1992, in the midst of a recession that had depressed corporate giving, public affairs research organizations received more than $200 million.[20] The precise figure is difficult to verify because direct contributions do not have to be divulged to the public. Moreover, it is often a struggle to assign a dollar value to in-kind gifts of goods and services.[21] Research on public interest group budgets indicates that corporate contributions make up about 4 percent of operating funds, though amounts can be much higher for certain groups.[22]

As we shall see from the study to be presented, most contributions are relatively modest. But some are not. The National Association for the Advancement of Colored People (NAACP) and its legal defense fund and the National Urban League receive more than $1.5 million a year from corporations. Groups such as the Nature Conservancy, the Audubon Society, Ducks Unlimited, Children's Defense Fund, the National Wildlife Federation, the Izaak Walton League, the B'nai B'rith Anti-Defamation League, and the Free Congress Foundation, just to name a few, typically receive high, six-figure contributions from the corporate sector each year. Funds for conservative organizations seem to be increasing. The American Enterprise Institute, a conservative Washington think tank, typically receives more than $1.5 million from corporate sponsors annually. The Heritage Foundation garners more than $500,000.[23]

The Study

The actual process by which corporations decide to give to nonprofit and public interest organizations has been largely unexplored by political scientists and other social scientists. Researchers have tended to look at corporate contributions from the perspective of the public interest group involved, especially the role of such funding in starting and maintaining such groups.

Our study focuses on the giver rather than the receiver—the corporation as a political actor. The concern is with discerning the broad outlines of the corporate giving process and how it fits into broader corporate political goals and strategies. Data for our analysis were derived from interviews with a number of individuals responsible for the giving programs of a diverse group of large American corporations.

Our starting point was a list of ninety individuals highlighted in the 1994 annual edition of *Corporate Foundation Profiles*.[24] Fifty of the ninety were contacted and twenty-seven agreed to participate in the study. The interviews were extensive and varied from roughly forty minutes to two and a half hours, the average being nearly one and a half hours. Most responses came from a set of structured, open-ended questions. Respondents typically were asked to respond to questions in general terms and then to give examples from their own experience. Because we were dealing with representatives of publicly traded, high-profile companies, we believed that only by promising anonymity would we get the kind of candid information were seeking on sensitive financial matters. Most of those interviewed were employed by Fortune 500 corporations, recognizable names in such industry sectors as international oil, rails, insurance, pharmaceutical, and consumer products. None of the comments quoted were made for direct attribution.

The Findings

Organizing to Give

Our data make it clear that although our sample companies vary in terms of corporate culture and commitment to philanthropy, foundation and direct giving programs are often "bare bones" operations within the corporation. Almost to a person, our respondents complained about their lack of resources and staff. Our quantitative data seem to validate their complaints. The average staff size of our sample corporate foundations was seven; twenty of the twenty-seven foundations had between two and ten staff members. One respondent told us: "I may be looking at a few thousand grants and I maybe have two people helping me . . . it's insane." Another noted, "We don't have the number of program officers (staff members who research grant recipients, scrutinize grant applications, etc.) that most private foundations have."

Because they lack extensive staff, foundation executives, most of whom also head direct-giving programs, rely on others within the corporation. Our data show that although corporate giving is usually coordinated at a company's national headquarters, the bulk of dollar allocation decisions are "farmed out" to specific company operating departments or units. Although many of the funding executives have the final word on all patronage decisions, in practice they often defer to other company personnel. One respondent explained it this way:

> One of the things you have to realize about corporate giving is that a lot of the money we give away is directed by our employees. We have employees spread out all over the country . . . the world really. And what we do is allocate a certain amount to each of our operating units. And they allocate the money to certain departments within the operating units.

Another told us: "Let's say we give $10 million. We let the ten different operating units each determine what to do with at least some of the money."

The corporate giving process is most often decentralized and fragmented. Even when decision making is centralized formally, the process in practice is not. One respondent, who admitted that he had virtual veto power over any decision, explained,

> Believe it or not, there are close to 100 people involved in the giving process. Here is how it works. I am the funnel—everything comes through me. First, I have to make a determination. Number one, I ask is the organization within our operating territory? If the group is in a community where we have no employees we are not interested. Number two, do they fit in our well-defined areas of interest. If the answer to both of these questions is yes, we look at their application and ask for other information [including] their IRS determination letter [which confirms they are eligible for tax deductible support], a list of their other corporate supporters, and a list of their board of directors. After I make a determination [about eligibility] then I take it to the committee.

The committee this respondent refers to is a corporate contributions committee. All twenty-seven of our respondents told us that although they had few staff resources, gifts were overseen by a committee consisting of corporate executives and other company personnel. Such committees allow executives and employees to communicate with one another, as well as those who make final funding decisions.

The formal arrangements for corporate giving, however, can belie great differences among corporate cultures. We found that some of the corporate foundations operated very much like private foundations, essentially autonomous units with little real oversight by other corporate officials, where the foundation director was the final authority. Others were separate units in name only, and in a number of cases the corporate CEO reviewed and had a final veto of all contributions over a certain amount (usually $5,000 and above).

Why Support Nonprofits? Mixed Motives

Why do corporations support nonprofits? Our interviews suggested a mix of altruism and economic self-interest with strategic political considerations of relatively minor importance. Not one of our respondents mentioned political motivations when talking about top giving priorities. Although all respondents agreed that they gave "because it was the right thing to do," they also made it clear the corporate "bottom line" was always a consideration. One respondent noted, "You bet we think about the 'bottom line.' If the company has a positive public image, it's likely to be more successful. People are more likely to buy the product, and customers have a good feeling about us." Twenty-three of our twenty-seven respondents mentioned "good public relations" as a motivation for corporate giving. There was also a widespread belief among respondents that *doing good* and *doing well* were not mutually exclusive goals. One respondent put it this way:

> Everyone here wants the company to do well. If the company does poorly, we all lose our jobs. But my job is very different than many of my colleagues. What I do has little or nothing to do with making money. I am trying my damnedest to support worthy causes. Obviously, the company thinks it is in their long-term best interest to support these causes. But to tell the truth, how this (grant making) might affect the corporation's bottom line is seldom mentioned at our meetings.

Forms of Corporate Largess

To get an idea of what types of groups attracted corporate support, we analyzed the data on contribution recipients found in the annual reports of our sample foundations. As Table 3-1 indicates, the vast majority of corporate patronage accrues to noncontroversial, nonpolitical organizations of a service nature. On average, our sample foundations give only 6 percent of their yearly grants to public interest advocacy groups and think tanks. The other 94 percent goes to educational institutions, social service organizations, arts organizations, and health care providers and researchers.

Three types of public interest organizations appear most attractive to corporate funders: (1) minority rights groups such as the National Urban League and the NAACP; (2) mainstream environmental groups such as the National Wildlife Federation, the Nature Conservancy, and the

Table 3-1 Corporate Foundation Donations to Nonprofit Groups

Recipient type	Average percentage
Education institutions	41
Social service organizations	24
Health care providers and researchers	15
Arts organizations (museums, ballets)	12
Public interest groups/think tanks	6
Other	2

Audubon Society; and (3) conservative think tanks such as the Heritage Foundation and the American Enterprise Institute. Our best estimates suggest that together these three categories account for roughly two-thirds of corporate foundation grants to public interest groups among our sample foundations. The only organization that consistently turns up in foundation annual reports, but does not fit into any of these categories, is the Children's Defense Fund.

Most corporate support (more than 75 percent in our sample) for nonprofits comes in the form of grants, of which there are three types: *capital grants* fund building projects, *program grants* fund specific programs or projects, and *general operating grants* are unrestricted in use. Most corporate grants (more than 80 percent) are program grants, which means that support comes "with strings attached." However, most of our respondents agreed that typically such restrictions are not excessively limiting. One respondent explained it this way: "Our average grant runs about $5,000, and seldom are [they] above $20,000. It just doesn't make sense to put a lot of restrictions on that little money." Another respondent told us: "We don't like people telling us what to do with our money, so we don't tell people what to do with theirs." The single most common restriction is the one required by federal law: Group recipients are required to sign a form indicating that no corporate money is to be used directly on political activity.

If our sample of corporations is any indication, most corporate grants are generally quite small. Few grants are larger than $5,000; grants of more than $100,000 are highly unusual. According to our respondents, the provision of in-kind goods to nonprofits is becoming more prevalent. All twenty-seven of our respondents said they have provided some sort of in-kind support during the past year. Typical in-kind gifts included outmoded computers, used furniture, and old copy machines. As far as in-kind services, some corporate personnel work as volunteers for nonprofit groups. For example, a company accountant may "do a group's books" gratis, a CEO may sit on a nonprofit board, and an employee may participate in a group fund-raising venture. Our respondents agreed that in-kind gifts and services virtually always accrue to nonpolitical organizations such as local chapters of the United Way.

Respondents mentioned two other forms of corporate support. Seven respondents reported providing cause-related marketing support, which involves a partnership between a firm and a nonprofit in which the group receives support for the use of its name for marketing purposes. A good example is Johnson and Johnson's efforts to market the pain-killer Tylenol in conjunction with an endorsement by the Arthritis Foundation (which received a "gift" from the company). Several respondents noted that this form of support was becoming more common. In addition, all twenty-seven respondents noted that they provided matching gifts. However, twenty-five of twenty-seven respondents pointed out that their companies did not match contributions to politically active organizations; the bulk of matching funds went to educational institutions, especially colleges and universities.

Choosing Beneficiaries

Companies tend to adopt overarching priorities that guide their specific philanthropic activities. Without exception, all of the companies in our sample focused on a very small number of priority areas. A number told us that contributions to federated groups such as the United Way had been decreasing in recent years. Among the most prominently mentioned were early childhood education, child safety, health care, and violence prevention.

Although one respondent told us that the focus area was chosen by the CEO, most companies typically choose their priorities through periodic reviews, in which they query a range of executives, employees, community leaders, and nonprofit personnel. As one respondent put it: "Reviews provide us with information about what needs are out there." The same respondent told us how her foundation conducted its review.

> Right now we are doing a priority review. I have been sitting in on some of these meetings. We will present what we find to the board. [My] staff is there [at the meetings], the CEO, his administrative assistant, and a couple of program officers. Each one of these people interviewed employees within the corporation. We also contacted outside organizations and interviewed people within those organizations and asked them what issues they thought were important. We also hired some consultants—people who gave us some information about what the local community thought were important things for us to be doing.

Two criteria appear to guide the selection of broad priorities: safety and need. All twenty-seven respondents said they looked first to safety—making sure the issue "will not come back to haunt the company." As one foundation director noted, "Why offend people? It's just bad business. Safeness is one way we chose [the issue supported]." Safety is why the arts, education, and health care attract so much corporate support; no one is adamantly opposed to museums, plays, education, or good health.

The perception of community need is an overriding concern as well. One respondent told us his primary goal in setting priorities was to see "what issue . . . needs the most attention." He continued, "We will probably hire consultants . . . people who will go out into the community and get a feeling for what is going on out there." Another noted, "We are genuinely concerned with what's happening in our communities. We want to put the money where it's needed."

After determining priority areas to target, specific beneficiaries are chosen. For many companies their geographic area of operation is paramount. Proctor and Gamble, with headquarters in Cincinnati, gives mostly to Cincinnati-based groups. First Interstate Bank of California does not support groups outside of California, and Fireman's Fund Insurance (headquartered in San Francisco) provided money almost exclusively to groups in the Bay area. Of our twenty-seven sample foundations, twelve do not fund organizations removed from their company's major area(s) of operation, and all of the others indicated they give "top priority" to local organizations. One respondent justified local giving as follows: "Employees are such a big part of determining where our money goes that they naturally tend to want to support groups in their own communities."

However, according to a number of our respondents, a group's link to the business of the corporation increasingly is a major criteria for support. The director of a pharmaceutical in-house foundation, in charge of $33 million in direct and foundation giving to nonprofits, explained it this way:

> Insulin and humilin are two of our biggest products. So we support the American Diabetes Foundation. I have only been here a couple of years, but I've noticed that in the past we have made that gift from the direct-giving program instead of the foundation. But I think trends in corporate philanthropy are that more and more companies are aligning themselves with organizations in line with the business.

The Conservative Nature of Corporate Giving

Clearly, the bulk of corporate giving has few obvious political implications. Nonetheless, it is not uncommon for corporate patrons to find themselves seriously considering grant applications from politically active groups. For example, if a corporation wishes to support programs for ethnic minorities, it almost always receives proposals from organizations that are active in politics. If a company decides to focus on the environment, AIDS, housing, or hunger, it will probably find itself involved with advocacy groups, occasionally on different sides of an issue.

"Political groups," one respondent told us, "are not automatically 'blackballed.' . . . If a [political group] has a non-political program we like, we'll go ahead and support it. You have heard this before, but it's true; we support programs not groups." This view was shared by virtually all our respondents.

Often corporations take cues from other corporations when deciding which groups to support. Several respondents noted that among the first items scrutinized in a grant application is the list of other corporate sponsors. One respondent explained it this way: "When groups come to us . . . we generally check to see who else is supporting them. Unless we see that there are other companies aboard we usually stay away." Substantial support from other corporations, several respondents noted, signals need, safety, and reliability. One respondent told us: "We figure that if the XYZ Company is supporting the group it's probably OK." Another respondent noted that if a group "already has one or more corporate sponsors it is most likely not 'anti-business' or 'anti-establishment.' "

Because corporate patrons sometimes support advocacy groups, they are careful to consider the political implications of their giving decisions. "Avoiding problems is always a priority," as one respondent put it. What constitutes a problem? One respondent replied, "Anything that reflects badly on the company." Another noted that "there are two constituencies we are concerned with—our shareholders and our customers. Shareholders are important . . . because they may see a 'bad grant' as an indicator that the company has bad judgement." In describing AT&T's well-publicized debacle over its support for Planned Parenthood, one respondent noted, "Even shareholders who did not oppose abortion or didn't care about abortion were upset . . . wondering why the company would become involved with something like that." Customer opinion is also crucial. AT&T's problems, one respondent pointed out, "were not all that bad" until customers got involved: "Customers began complaining and started to switch phone companies . . . they did not want their money supporting an abortion group."

Well-known and well-traveled horror stories notwithstanding, several factors help minimize the politicization of corporate giving and the breeding of problems. Besides the preference for supporting nonpolitical groups or groups few find offensive, supporting local organizations mitigates against problems. Thus, even when companies do support groups such as Planned Parenthood or the NAACP—groups that have explicit political agendas with which some people may disagree—the money is contributed locally. As one respondent pointed out, giving money to the local NAACP is "safe because the local chapter does very little in the way of politics . . . most of their work is in education and service provision." Even local Planned Parenthoods, one of our respondents noted, are not seen by most people as political organizations, but rather as local groups providing health care services and education. "The local group had little connection with the national," she told us, "and focused on teen pregnancy, pre-natal care . . . none of which were controversial."

Internal corporate communication can also cut down on potential problems. One respondent noted, "We make sure that the contributions committee is broad enough. This way we are fairly aware of which groups to align with and which to stay away from." Several respondents noted that they commonly "check groups out" with public affairs personnel—people who have experience in politics. Fourteen of our twenty-seven respondents reported they worked in the same division as public affairs–government relations personnel. For example, one foundation director told us:

> We will touch bases with government affairs and they are certainly aware of what we're doing. And if anything remotely becomes a government relations issue we check with them. For example, we have a

community health care program. And we once had a check presented in Little Rock and Jocelyn Elders [the controversial former surgeon general of the United States] showed up. We would have to clear that with the government affairs people.

Part of the difficulty funders face is determining what exactly is a "political group." As one respondent noted,

> Well, would you define the American Diabetes Association as a political group? What's interesting is that we typically restrict our grants to groups like that . . . it must strictly be used for a public awareness campaign. The National Mental Health Association, for example, we would fund them to help destigmatize mental illness as a disease . . . not directed at the government. They are all public awareness campaigns.

Dealing with the Unexpected: Controversy and Politics

Despite their caution and best intentions, corporations still sometimes find themselves in a political controversy because of their giving decisions. All but one of our foundation directors acknowledged they had "been burned" at some point in the past. It is ironic to note that our interviews also revealed that companies actually spent the least time checking out the grants that have the most potential to create problems. Because grants with political implications are such a small part of a foundation's overall budget, such grants typically merit little attention.

As one foundation director noted, corporate patrons use a mix of "police patrol" and "fire alarm" methods in overseeing their giving program. Although corporate funders investigate groups before supporting them, some organizations simply do not raise concerns until a grant is made. We found a number of cases where corporate funders displayed a political naivete that betrayed their best efforts to avoid problematic decisions. One respondent, for example, told us that her company—a consumer products company that used animals in product testing—angered shareholders with its support for the local Humane Society, which used funds for animal shelter purposes. She related that her foundation did not support the Humane Society of the United States, a national group opposed to using animals in such research, and was puzzled by the fact that some shareholders would equate support for the local Humane Society with support for the national group's proanimal rights agenda. "They are two totally separate things," she told us, "I just don't understand why people can't see that." Similar naivete was found with some of our respondents when discussing support for Planned Parenthood.

Ten of our respondents told us they had supported Planned Parenthood at some point. But only two, when looking back on their support, told us they "should have seen problems coming." One respondent explained,

I guess I don't get it . . . why people would complain. What happened is that we were giving to the local group here. We got into it originally to fund a program for educating prepubescent women and [this] was really fine information. And to this day I don't think many people would get upset about it except that it had their [Planned Parenthood's] name attached to it.

A number of our respondents reflected frustration with either shareholders' or the public's inability to make a distinction between local affiliates and national organizations or between groups and specific programs. One respondent told us of the great anger she experienced when faced with a shareholder who called to complain about the company's support for the Nature Conservancy, a group the shareholder felt was "too liberal" for the company. "I told him," the respondent explained, "that the Nature Conservancy did good work, they buy land, they don't work against us. But he just wouldn't listen."

How do companies respond when such problems arise? Although all respondents acknowledged that shareholder and public complaints are taken seriously, they also claimed that it was rare for corporate giving policies to be altered in the face of criticism. As one respondent explained, "We won't give in to some fringe element out there." "We don't tow anybody's line," another respondent told us. Another, exasperated about some bad publicity her company had received recently about her company's support for an environmental group, explained, "I will not give [the complainers] the satisfaction . . . we support who we want . . . period."

Respondents' exhortations to the contrary, it is clear that external pressure *does* affect giving programs. One respondent, who told us that his firm would never bow to public pressure, indicated that his company did stop its support of Planned Parenthood in the wake of bad publicity. When asked about the contradiction, he explained less than convincingly: "We stopped the program because it didn't make sense any more. I am sure if they [Planned Parenthood] could have come up with a program we like we would have continued to support them. But it was time for us to move on." It did not surprise us that none of the twenty-seven sample companies currently supported Planned Parenthood!

Implications for Public Interest Group Representation

Much has been written concerning the role of patron funding on the composition of the public interest group universe. Such funding is particularly important to new and fledgling groups.[25] Our findings suggest that unlike the case with private foundations, in which ideology may be a dominant motive, there are a number of factors that lessen corporate influence on public interest group representation, especially when it involves "seed money" for new groups.

At base, the corporate giving process is inherently reactive rather than proactive. As one foundation manager put it, "Yeah, we're reactive. Every now and then they we'll start something up . . . but usually we just sit back and let the proposals roll in." Although fourteen of the twenty-seven respondents told us they had provided organizational "seed money," all also agreed such support was rare. And not one respondent admitted to providing seed money for the creation of a politically active, public interest group.

Corporate reactivity is also demonstrated by the tendency for corporate patrons to support only those groups that attract other corporate money. One respondent told us: "Not only do we hardly ever seek out groups to support, but when groups come to us—which is almost always—we generally check to see who else is supporting them. Unless we see that there are other companies on board we usually stay away." Another respondent put it even more bluntly: "We just don't like to be on the 'cutting edge.' That's not how we operate here. We are not unusual in that respect."

Nor do most companies see giving to new public interest groups as an effective political tool. As one respondent noted, "Why would we go out of our way to start a new [public interest] group that lobbies for us when we have our own lobbyists?" Seeking to co-opt unfriendly public interest groups is also seen as fruitless. Co-optation is "not realistic" and "next to impossible" because most public interest groups are "paranoid about it," noted one respondent. The same respondent, an employee of a large energy corporation, related a story that demonstrated his point.

> You may have read that we have an unsatisfactory relationship with [a certain] community because of a plant we have in that area. But I had a lady call me once from a group down in that area and ask me if we could consider something if she sent it to us. It was a proposal. So I said I certainly would. And the next day a fellow called me and told me that he did not want anything from a company like us. He was a person who believed strongly that we were polluting the area with all kinds of noxious chemicals and radioactive elements and ruining the quality of life and he just didn't want to take money from us. He told me, "I won't even give you the pleasure of looking over my proposal."

Finally, another factor that lessens corporate impact on the nature of public interest group representation is the tendency for corporate patrons to attach conditions to their support.[26] Virtually all corporate support for politically active groups is earmarked for specific nonpolitical goals. As one respondent put it: "That money is not used for [politics] and is [given] to serve other goals . . . good publicity, community goodwill, things like that." Another respondent noted, "Even when we do support groups that are politically engaged, it [the money] is not for politics. It is for other programs and practices."

Think Tanks: An Example of Strategic Political Giving

It would be naive, of course, to accept the notion that corporations neither support public interest groups for political reasons nor attempt to alter group agendas. Our data suggest that one type of corporate giving is at least partially designed to overtly serve political goals: support for conservative think tanks.[27] Such support, we found, typically began not at the urging of corporate officials with responsibility for giving programs but at the instigation of other corporate officials more directly involved in political influence. One respondent explained it this way: "The support we give to [conservative think tanks] is requested by the national affairs unit in Washington. It's a small part of our budget. But they are familiar with what's going on and they make requests like that all the time." Another respondent told a similar story: "It's almost always the people at state or federal government affairs that request the money [for think tanks]. They get to submit things every year for the budget like everyone else and sometimes those types of political groups get on their list." For at least some firms, support for think tanks is a well-thought out part of the corporation's political strategy.

> We support some of the think tanks. That is really the responsibility of the people in national government relations. We have always been reluctant to get involved in that, but because today Congress may any day make a law that absolutely drives us out of business, we must be involved. And they [the government relations staff] pretty well have found a group of think tanks that they think are doing good work. We defer to them on these issues. I would imagine these are not what we would call the most liberal think tanks. Brookings is probably the most liberal we support. . . . We keep the records, we write the checks . . . but the evaluation of whether or not they should continue, we rely on the people in government relations.

It appears that corporate support for think tanks did not consciously begin as part of some grand scheme to strategically serve corporate political goals. Rather, for the companies we talked to, it was the result of a decentralized process that explicitly avoided adopting political goals for corporate giving initially, but over time the advantages of think tank giving became clear. For example, one respondent told us: "What began as a small pot of money we allocated for our public affairs [unit] became larger as we became convinced that supporting [conservative think tanks] was good for us. We began giving more and more, and now we give about $100,000 a year." When asked about how his firm became convinced that support for think tanks was worthwhile, he responded by noting, "We looked at some of their reports and they seemed to be doing good work."

Is there an explicit quid pro quo among corporate patrons and the think tanks they support as a consequence? Clearly conservative think tanks that depend heavily on corporate support (the Heritage Foundation

and the American Enterprise Institute, especially) tend to adopt probusiness positions on most issues. On the other hand, the independence of
think tanks argues against any simple interpretation. Several respondents
told us that think tanks—even those highly dependent on corporate support—were fiercely independent and resented any attempt by patrons to
alter their activities. One respondent related, "The people who work at
these places are pretty conservative anyway. We don't really affect what
they do or what they say." Another related a story to illustrate the inherent difficulty in counting on think tanks to serve a corporation's political
interest.

> Part of what we do is aerospace. Some time ago we were giving to the
> Heritage Foundation. But we had a falling out with them . . . over
> something they wrote which we didn't like. We had been giving them
> unrestricted general support. And they were going to do an article on a
> business that we're in—in fact [that] we're a leader in. And we thought
> we had a relationship with them through our Washington office—the
> people who made the grant request in the first place—that was such
> that if they ever fooled around in this field they would come and re-
> view it with us. Well they didn't and [what they] published was 180
> degrees from the position we were taking so our people got incensed
> and said, "forget it." I mean, we told them, "You didn't even give us a
> chance to respond and we believe firmly that you owed that to us." We
> cut them off for a few years.

This example illustrates the danger of using an agent—in this case a
think tank—to serve corporate political goals. One respondent acknowledged the principal-agent problem when he told us: "We can lobby on
our own behalf. We don't need some [public interest] group doing it for
us. We spend millions on public affairs, and hardly any of it goes to [pub-
lic interest] groups."

Conclusion

Despite well-publicized attempts by a number of corporations to
fund certain public interest groups for political reasons, our findings suggest that strategic political giving is not a high-priority motivation of corporate philanthropists. Genuine corporate altruism, increasingly coupled
with long-term business interests, remain the major motivations of corporate givers.

Indeed, if our findings are representative, when corporate philanthropy does have political ramifications, it typically represents an unfore-
seen consequence of a decision made for strictly nonpolitical reasons.
The process of corporate giving that we have described is designed to
avoid even the pretense of giving for political purposes. But safeguards in
the process—wide corporate input, a preference for local giving, a ten-

dency to fund projects not groups—sometimes break down in a highly charged political environment, where even a charity can become the center of political controversy.

It is ironic to note that as corporate givers face increasing pressure to balance altruistic and profit motivations, corporate philanthropy may become more overtly political. At the end of each of our interviews we asked respondents about trends in corporate giving. The findings are revealing. There was little doubt among most respondents that in an era of corporate downsizing and increasing business competition, those in charge of giving programs feel internal corporate pressure to defend their activities. As one foundation manager noted, "Everyone in the company is asking: 'How can we become more competitive?' Of course this is trickling down to us." Another noted, "The do-gooder kind of stuff is not holding weight in an environment where managers who were part of the production and revenue side are being cut back. The justification of the foundation has been and will continue to be put to the test." One respondent summed up the dominant outlook for corporate foundation personnel best when he said, "When belt-tightening is taking place we're the first place they look."

Largely as a result of such pressures, a number of our corporate funders indicated they were considering more explicit political giving. Support for conservative groups and think tanks, one respondent told us, is easier to justify to "bean counters" than support for schools and health care. Another respondent told us: "If we are going to support nonprofits we might as well support nonprofits that help us out . . . and these are usually conservative groups." This does not mean that nonpolitical giving will cease. Education, for example, will always attract corporate money because, as one respondent noted, "Education is important to every corporation in America . . . that is where we get our employees." It may mean, however, that conservative public interest groups and think tanks are likely to see an increase in corporate patronage in the future.

We suspect, for most corporations, philanthropy will never become a political influence tool on par with the arsenal of government relations activity and PAC–soft money giving that characterizes many of today's large business entities. In many, a wholesale restructuring of the giving process, going from a decentralized, local perspective, to one with central direction coordinated with the firm's other political activities, would meet with great internal resistance, as well as external disapproval. But at least for some among the corporations we examined, strategic political considerations are likely to become increasingly important in their giving decisions.

Notes

1. Graham Wilson, "American Business and Politics," in *Interest Group Politics*, 2d ed., ed. Allan J. Cigler and Burdett A. Loomis (Washington, D.C.: CQ Press, 1988), 221–235; Raymond Bauer, Ithiel de Sola Pool, and Lewis Anthony Dexter, *American Business and Public Policy* (New York: Atherton, 1968).

2. David Vogel, *Fluctuating Fortunes* (New York: Basic Books, 1989), 33.
3. Especially influential were criticisms leveled by various consumer advocates. See, for example, Ralph Nader, *Unsafe at Any Speed* (New York: Grossman, 1965).
4. Jeffrey M. Berry, *The Interest Group Society* (New York: Longman, 1997), 218–233; Vogel, *Fluctuating Fortunes*, 194–227. There was some evidence of business mobilization evident as early as the Kennedy years. See Cathie Jo Martin, "Business and the New Economic Activities: The Growth of Corporate Lobbies in the Sixties," *Polity* 27 (Fall 1994): 52–75.
5. Daniel Kadler, "The New World of Giving," *Time*, May 5, 1997, 63–64. The proportion of giving was actually greater prior to the late 1980s recession, approximating nearly 2 percent of pretax profits.
6. See, for example, Christopher J. Bosso, "The Color of Money: Environmental Groups and the Pathologies of Fund Raising," in *Interest Group Politics*, 4th ed., ed. Allan J. Cigler and Burdett Loomis (Washington, D.C.: CQ Press, 1995), 101–130.
7. Craig Smith, "The New Corporate Philanthropy," *Harvard Business Review* 72 (May–June 1994): 107.
8. David Dodson, "Corporate Support for Social Justice," in *Grantseekers Guide*, 3d ed., ed. Jill R. Shellow and Nancy C. Stella (Washington, D.C.: Network of Grantmakers, 1989), 51.
9. Ibid.
10. Kadler, "The New World of Giving," 64.
11. Smith, "The New Corporate Philanthropy," 106.
12. Morton Mintz, *Allies: The ACLU and the Tobacco Industry* (Washington, D.C.: Advocacy Institute, 1993).
13. See, for example, Barbara Tierney, "Planned Parenthood Didn't Plan on This," *Business Week*, July 3, 1989, 34. In the face of such pressure, both AT&T and J.C. Penney stopped contributing to Planned Parenthood at any level.
14. Kim Lawton, "Christian Action Council Announces Boycott," *Christianity Today*, September 1989, 72. See also Kenneth Sheets, "Products under Fire," *U.S. News and World Report*, April 16, 1990, 44.
15. Quoted in Tierney, "Planned Parenthood Didn't Plan on This," 34.
16. The Capital Research Center (CRC) was created in 1984 by conservative interests to monitor corporate and private foundation giving. The CRC is funded largely by private foundations, with the aim of preventing "foundations established by capitalists from being taken over by socialists." See Joel Bleifuss, "Building Plans," *In These Times*, July 10, 1995, 12.
17. Natalie J. Webb, "Tax and Government Policy Implications for Corporate Foundation Giving," *Non-Profit and Voluntary Sector Quarterly* 23 (1994): 42–46. See also Ronald Shaiko, "More Bang for the Buck," in *Interest Group Politics*, 3d ed., ed. Allan J. Cigler and Burdett Loomis (Washington, D.C.: CQ Press, 1990), 109–130.
18. Ibid., 47.
19. Barbara Clark O'Hare, "Good Deeds Are Good Business," *American Demographics* 12 (September 1991): 38–44.
20. Marvin Olasky, Daniel T. Oliver, and Stuart Nolan, *Patterns of Corporate Philanthropy* (Washington, D.C.: Capital Research Center, 1992).
21. There is also some evidence that in-kind giving instead of cash contributions is increasing. See Nelson Swartz, "Giving—and Getting Something Back," *Business Week*, August 28, 1995, 81.
22. Allan J. Cigler and Anthony J. Nownes, "Public Interest Entrepreneurs and Group Patrons," in *Interest Group Politics*, 4th ed., ed. Allan J. Cigler and Burdett A. Loomis (Washington, D.C.: CQ Press, 1995), 77–100.
23. Olasky, Oliver, and Nolan, *Patterns of Corporate Philanthropy*, 11.
24. *Corporate Foundation Profiles* (Washington, D.C.: Foundation Center, 1994).

25. Jack Walker, "The Origins and Maintenance of Interest Groups in America," *American Political Science Review* 77 (June 1983): 75–102; Anthony J. Nownes and Allan J. Cigler, "Public Interest Groups and the Road to Survival," *Polity* 27 (Spring 1995): 379–404.
26. In a couple of cases the corporation fund-raisers go even further in seeking accountability, making a large contribution contingent on the recipient group adding a corporation representative to their governing board. This was the exception rather than the rule, however; most companies have the policy that such a relationship would create a conflict of interest.
27. For a comprehensive study of the role of think tanks in American politics see David M. Ricci, *The Transformation of American Politics: The New Washington and the Rise of Think Tanks* (New Haven, Conn.: Yale University Press, 1993).

4

Taking Organization Seriously: The Structure of Interest Group Influence

Brian Anderson and Burdett A. Loomis

As with studies of legislatures, most analyses of lobbying focus on national-level politics. Both journalists and political scientists have detailed the growing sophistication of Washington-oriented, Washington-based lobbying. Part of this sophistication falls under the heading of grassroots lobbying, in which constituents are encouraged, often through enhanced communication capabilities (for example, 800 numbers, the Internet, faxes), to deliver pointed messages to their legislators. Groups such as the National Federation of Independent Business have gained influence as they have used their members as effective conduits of their organizations' information.

Not all organizations can activate a good number of their members (or even some of them) within the political process. Brian Anderson and Burdett Loomis look inside several groups to understand how organizational structure can facilitate or retard a group's influence, especially as it seeks to enlist its members in the Washington influence wars. If a group can identify potentially effective member-lobbyists from its ranks and get them in touch with Congress in a timely manner, it can place great pressure on a specifically targeted set of legislators. The fewer organizational obstacles to such communication, the more capacity a group has to mobilize its key members. At the same time, as devolution pushes more policy making to the states, those groups with strong, independent state affiliations (and some resistance to national direction) may prove the most effective in state-house lobbying.

The National Federation of Independent Business (NFIB) has been on a roll. Although it grew in strength throughout the 1980s and early 1990s, it has become one of the true success stories in the Washington lobbying community since the 1994 Republican takeover of Capitol Hill. In part this derives from the close relationship of ideological soulmates. As an aide to Sen. Christopher Bond (R-Mo.) observed, "The phone conversations between Sen. Bond and [NFIB president] Jack Faris are very brief. It's like: I agree with everything you say."[1] Still, the Republican majority has lots of new best friends and dozens of compatible conservative interests. What sets NFIB apart is its capacity to mobilize its grassroots supporters in downtowns, strip malls, and industrial parks across the country. Dan Danner, chief NFIB lobbyist, put it this way: "Politics here in Washington have fundamentally changed. Instead of listening to the chairman of their committee or the head of their party, as was the case years ago, what [members of Congress] listen to now are the grass roots—and that's what we're all about."[2]

Our argument is simple, yet often overlooked: The organizational structure of interest groups—and especially membership groups and trade associations—determines much of their impact in Washington (and also in state capitals).[3] Indeed, organizations have adapted to policy making in a multilevel, dynamic system, and such adaptations contribute to the politics of influence in a host of venues. In an era of policy devolution (at least as advertised), federated organizations may well offer advantages in the state by state politics of influence, but our focus remains, for the most part, on national policy making.

Multilevel Structure and Interest Representation

Interests often pursue representation in a federal system through multilevel organizational structure. A national group works with regional–state–local counterparts to monitor policy developments in the thousands of governmental venues in the country, anticipate which trends are likely to spread state by state or win adoption in Washington, and coordinate activities intended to effect favorable outcomes. Although success in these endeavors depends on ample resources and their effective use, there also needs to be good relations among the elements within the interest.

For Truman and the relatively few other scholars who have examined this issue, the position of the national organization in a multilevel structure boils down to how much control it can exercise over subnational entities.[4] In the end, the unitary structural form affords national groups greater control than the more common federated form.

In a unitary organization, members join one central group, which charters, staffs, and funds state offices, and then shape their agendas to provide grassroots pressure on congressional delegations for national-level issues. State issues are not normally considered a high priority. Truman and Hall identified a limited number of trade associations, such as the National Association of Manufacturers, as unitary, though today we regard this form to be the domain of citizen interests with individual memberships, such as Common Cause and Citizens for Reliable and Safe Highways. Still, some federations, such as the NFIB, allow for considerable centralized control—especially if national officials and staff can demonstrate their influence.

National groups must work hard to make the unitary form pay off. Although formal control is ensured by the charter, day-to-day control can only be secured through the maintenance of a consistent funding flow to the states and the credibility of national threats to withhold budget money or fire state staff. If money is tight, the interest faces the prospect of choosing which states are most important for its agenda—a worrisome task if the interest plans sweeping grassroots efforts or if policies on its agenda are being devolved. If national staff members sanction wayward or recalcitrant state staffers, they risk advertising internal rifts to competing interests and legislators and alienating other state coordinators wary of strong-arm tactics. Control in the unitary form comes at a price: The interest's flexibility is limited (in other words, not well-suited for action at state and local levels) and internal disagreements may break down the mechanisms of multilevel interest action.

Truman maintained that national groups have little control over their state counterparts if the latter antedate the former, if groups are organized along geographic rather than functional lines (geographic groups being more self-sufficient), and if the national staff have no vital resources they can hold over the heads of state staff.[5] All three conditions are found in federated structures, which sanctify state groups as "rival subcenters of power" within the interest. Federations are plentiful in the group universe, ranging from broad economic interests such as the NFIB and the AFL–CIO, to industry specific groups such as the American Trucking Associations (ATA) and the National Retail Federation (NRF). Citizen groups such as the American Automobile Association (AAA) take on a federated character as well, as do many intergovernmental associations.

The national groups usually have sizeable budgets and enjoy the advantage of an overhead view of state policy developments. Although these arrangements have the advantage over unitary interests of being able to sustain policy involvement in national and subnational issues, federations normally divide national and state group responsibilities clearly. Affiliates are content to have the central organization pursue a national agenda, provided it does not intrude on state turf. If a national group does get involved in state issues (without being invited to do so), affiliates naturally feel resentful, especially if the national staff uses media attention or commands an audience with high-ranking state government officials because of their Washington ties. State groups are often heard to complain that national interference in their affairs could ultimately jeopardize the federation.

The federal policy-making system is loaded with gray areas, where national and state policy responsibilities are blurred and where a proposed federal statute must be reconciled with varying codes of law, and varying attitudes, in the fifty states. In such situations, both the national and state groups may announce positions on the issue and find that disagreements prevail. Consider one AAA affiliate's view regarding California's auto emissions standards that exceeded those of the Clean Air Act amendments of 1990.

National is taking the environmental view on emissions standards. . . .
We say especially that the reformulated gas plan (part of the California
standards) would be very costly for drivers and that strict air quality
standards are unnecessary outside major cities. The issue is still up in
the air. . . . National has been passive to state resistance, but nothing
has been done to unify our views on the matter—mainly because this
is seen as a state matter. . . . I see the possibility of the issue "snow-
balling" state to state. National may be compelled to switch their view
if enough states are opposed to the California plan.

If the national organization hopes to win over affiliates on any matter, it must convince them ultimately that membership in the federation
is worthwhile. First, state groups must conclude that they have some say
in Washington affairs. Though all groups may not be represented on the
national board of directors, devoting some seats to affiliate officials ensures that a "Beltway mentality" will not prevail. Board membership
gives them some control over national staffing decisions, budget allotments, and decision making. However, state associations are primarily focused on developments in their individual state political environments,
so the ultimate worth of the federation is estimated in terms of how well
the relationship with the national group can further the affiliates' own
agendas.

Second, the national group can offer numerous services to state affiliates and, just as important, their memberships. In this way, state groups
behave rationally in the Olsonian sense: The exploitation of federation
resources (selective goods) becomes the incentive to comply with a national agenda (the collective good).[6] Information is clearly the currency
that builds cooperative group relations, and most national groups pride
themselves in serving as "information clearinghouses" for the federation.
The national staff typically produces a periodical journal or newsletter,
published regularly at weekly to quarterly intervals, that provides a
wealth of information on technologies, management and employee issues, finance, and an overview of policy developments around the country (with discussion of the impact on the interest). Although most policy
information is "old news" to state affiliates, it keeps members informed
and packages details in a way that lets these groups work with concise, coherent summaries rather than volumes of sometimes questionable information collected from scattered sources.

Affiliates get more useful and timely information through weekly,
even daily, mail, fax, or e-mail from national headquarters. Such communications include statistical reports, surveys, position papers, and policy
alerts and updates. State staff remark that these transmissions keep them
tied in to the grapevine, and although some affiliates feel mired in piles
of transmissions regarding peripheral issues,[7] state groups do get much information from the national office that aids their state-oriented lobbying
activity.

In addition, national organizations usually put on extensive conventions and conferences, often many times a year. These gatherings are mostly geared toward assisting the membership: A typical business convention will showcase new technologies, offer seminars on pressing issues, feature numerous awards ceremonies and social events, and so on. However, affiliate staffers often attend to interact with other federation officials, and some conventions even permit attendees to vote on resolutions offered by the national board. On a more informal level, national officers and professional staff can identify potential grassroots spokespersons for the organization, whom they can later bring to Washington.

Though national groups do not flatly ask for favors in return for their resources (most affiliates believe membership dues are adequate payment anyway), they commonly request that affiliates lend a grassroots angle to a national-level lobbying effort. As one state (Ohio) official noted,

> National will assist us with technical assistance, and they will lobby in Columbus on federal issues with the federal legislators that are back in their home districts. They'll come back and hit the congressman at his local office. We've just been doing it with [Rep. John] Kasich, who's here in Columbus. We had federal people in and not only lobbying but maybe a little protesting.

A successful grassroots campaign can provide an impressive thrust to the lobbying strategy: Competitors and legislators understand that autonomous state groups cannot be commanded to participate. Rather, they appear to offer honest support for the national group's policy stances.

Grassroots tactics are used selectively and usually involve a letter or telephone campaign. The national group cannot always expect an overwhelming response, because it can only *recommend* that affiliates participate. (A typical communication goes as follows: "We suggest that you contact your congressional delegation and make sure that it is aware that this policy could have a detrimental impact on the district's economy.") More compelling results can be attained by inviting certain affiliate officials (and members) to Washington to give testimony. National staff take care to target important committee members, bringing in affiliate officials—members from the chair's home district, for example. Occasionally the national group will fly all affiliate presidents and executive directors in to visit their congressional delegations at one time. These fly-ins are saved only for the most crucial issues, such as reauthorization of a major federal program.

Above all else, the national organization must be patient. It must provide effective resources to affiliates and build a reputation as a serious, reliable voice for the interests at the national level—all the while respecting the autonomy of state affiliates. Only then can it expect to employ its relationship with subnational affiliates to advance its own agenda.

Federal Impact on State Policy Making

State affiliates are the focus of interest representation in many federations, and it would appear that policy devolution would further weaken the position of national groups. Federations are ideally suited to address decentralized policy making: State affiliates have their own state-based members, budgets, and staff, and they attend almost exclusively to state policy issues. What would happen to the national groups? Washington-based staff would need even more patience as key policy decisions shifted from Congress to fifty state legislatures. Still, their services might well become even more valuable to affiliates on two counts.

First, high-stakes policy (for example, electric utility deregulation) made at the state level would require affiliates to prepare thoroughly for battle with competing interests and to present a convincing case within the policy debate. Thus, the role as information clearinghouse and the prospects of national group consultation and guidance would rise in importance. Indeed, for some federations the national groups might do less lobbying themselves and devote most of their energy to resource support. Second, with fifty autonomous affiliates acting on their own, the national group could become even more valuable as a forum for consensus building. Inconsistencies across state lines could wreak havoc for the policy goals of individual affiliates; the national staff could arbitrate and facilitate compromise to prevent state groups from working at cross-purposes.

An effort in this direction was seen with the National Automobile Dealers Association (NADA), which held meetings at its headquarters in the early 1990s for state affiliate officials to share information concerning the proposed adoption by northeastern states of California's strict vehicle emissions regulations. The NADA did not try to influence affiliate opinion; it merely gave them a meeting place and a chance to see how fellow affiliates perceived the policy proposal. Of particular importance was the attention given to the New York affiliate; other states learned how the policy was being debated in Albany (New York had done the most to adopt the regulations at that time) and which lobbying strategies appeared most productive.

Beyond this rather passive "meeting place" role, federations could devise compromise procedures for affiliate-versus-affiliate disputes, to be administered by the national group. It is unclear how much power the affiliates would be willing to grant the national group on this score, but devolution could well weaken the position of national groups in federations even further.

The American Trucking Associations: A Classic Federation

Created in 1933 by a number of state-level trucking groups, some of which dated to the turn of the century, the American Trucking Associations's national organization has perfected its role as information clearinghouse through the weekly publication of *Transport Topics*, which includes summaries of state-level developments in a section called "Stateline"; a generous flow of issue-specific information through mailings and faxes; numerous conferences addressing both business and legislative issues; and TranSat, a satellite television program series intended to keep members and staff up to date on the latest legal and legislative issues. The ATA also operates a research foundation with regional offices that develop databases and other valuable tools that enhance state associations' policy activities.

An ATA official summed up the national organization's relationship with state affiliates:

> There is a clear "line in the sand" with respect to state and national association policy responsibilities. But [the ATA] is sure to keep the states informed of national trends. If we see South Dakota impose a sales tax on service, we let everybody else know . . . It gives them a "heads up" that this type of issue is brewing.

Most ATA affiliates regard the national organization with a great deal of respect. The organization has been active at the national level on issues vital to trucking companies (for example, environmental regulations, highway safety) and has been able to muster grassroots support through letter-writing campaigns and fly-ins on such issues as highway authorization and NAFTA. As one state president noted,

> We follow mostly national's policies as set forth on specific issues . . . on speed [limits], [truck] size and weight, NAFTA, . . . because we don't have the expertise, the time or the knowledge to be able to sit down and converse and set policy and make policy decisions on things like NAFTA. What the hell do I know about trade with the Mexicans? I know nothing about it. I want to be able to know where the information is and get it.

On issues straddling the national–state "line in the sand," such as the California vehicle emissions regulations, the ATA has encouraged certain state associations to be "involved in the management and technical aspects" of the issue, inviting them to the national office and taking direction from their expertise and experience. Another state president summarized, "We greatly depend on ATA for information. ATA is the heart surgeon, [state affiliates] are the practitioners."

Organizational bylaws mandate that state affiliates can only participate in national issues "along lines suggested by the national association," and that national staffers can only become involved in a state-level issue "upon request of the state association."[8] In no way are state groups obligated to assist with national policy, or alter their position on state issues to be in line with the national group:

> We've had some interesting discussions in the association family about how obligated we are to do certain things for the ATA. . . . And the fact of the matter is that if it ever came to a hardcore vote . . . the state would pursue its own interests, because [the decision of the state board of directors is the final word for affiliate staff]. . . . I'm sure if I would, for whatever reason, advocate a sudden wholesale increase of the tax level on motor carriers nationally, there would be someone from ATA down to check, number one, my sanity, and to check what the hell we're talking about . . . and the impact it's going to have.

Conflict within the ATA does arise (for example, federal preemption of state-level trucking regulation), and the national organization has more leverage to persuade defiant affiliates if it advocates a view shared by a majority in the federation.

> Normally the rule [for national–state disagreement] is "may the best man win." I'm sure the ATA would attempt to change our view, but we wouldn't expect coercion since [our organization] is autonomous. A common end result is that we will simply agree to disagree, but the ATA makes it clear that they will not assist dissenters on an issue. The ATA always holds to the view of a majority of affiliates. (ATA affiliate interview)

The ATA national organization has to take care at every turn to minimize the tension found in a federation of very independent-minded affiliates. Agreement cannot be forced, but has to be patiently instilled through the dissemination of information and the garnering of consensus among at least a simple majority of affiliates. Ultimately, state affiliates extract numerous benefits from their relationship with the national association in that, as one official noted, "there's no way for ATA to strong-arm state groups." In the end, the national association must face real structural barriers in trying to employ the federation resources to serve its national agenda.

The AFL-CIO: A National Federation of Unions

The AFL-CIO employs a federated structure, mainly because of the autonomy of its many member trade unions. In many ways, however, the national–state relationships allow the federation to function as a unitary organization. Immediately following the 1955 merger between the American Federation of Labor and the Congress of Industrial Organizations, the new organization chartered entities in each state. These state AFL-CIOs serve state-based memberships (complete with their own budgets and an autonomous board of directors), yet are in a way bound to follow national staff directives on national issues. In fact, they can be sanctioned for recalcitrance. The AFL-CIO appears at times torn between its federated and unitary characteristics.

True to its federated form, the AFL-CIO national group acted as information clearinghouse to the state organizations. From the widely read *AFL-CIO News* to numerous faxes and mail packets related to specific policies, state affiliates felt very well connected to Washington, though some state leaders remarked that the bulk of the information was "excessive and repetitious." What distinguished this federation from those of business interests (for example, the ATA) was that many of these transmissions took the form of *policy directives on national issues.*

> National sends out issue information with a description of the issue, pro and con views, views of Congress, the president and the view of the national organization. This national view is made by presidents and CEOs of national unions in conference with the national AFL-CIO. . . . Since state organizations are chartered by national and subordinate to it, we have to follow the national position.

The impact of such directives promotes labor's grassroots clout. As one state official put it,

> National organization direction is usually rather generic in our case, because our congressional delegation votes over ninety percent correct as far as our issues are concerned. . . . Occasionally when we are at odds with the West Virginia delegation, the correspondence increases from our national office. They make sure we have the very basic arguments when we contact them, and when Congress is out of session and they're back in the states, [the national organization] encourage[s] us to contact them. We always follow their suggestions.

To an extent, the national organization can command affiliate participation in national policy matters. However, a state AFL-CIO answers to its own board as well, which keeps it focused for the most part on state-level issues. When the prospects for contradiction between national and state positions develop, national staffers have been alert to recognize when the affiliate's position is vital for its own individual interest. State AFL-CIO officials are not shy in protecting their own positions. Take, for example, the comments of two such individuals:

> The big national–Delaware disagreement was over striker replacement. National said, "None whatsoever." We said, "Yes, they could replace them, but they have to be Delaware residents." In a recent press strike Gannett was flying replacements up from other states. . . . National sent us a letter opposed to our position on replacements, but they left us alone, they accommodated our view.

> National is avowedly democratic. They understand that Maryland politics is Maryland's turf, but things are different at the national level. For example, Maryland is the only state with Hospital Services Cost Review, which allows poor people to go to any hospital. . . . National

supported a surtax which would wreck HSCR in Maryland, so we opposed it. "Words of concern" were exchanged with national, and we were able to get them to back off the idea.

Officially, the national organization can remove state affiliate staff over any significant disagreement. But in an interest consisting of numerous, widely varying labor unions, and at a time when the power of labor in Washington is constantly in question, to "shake up" operations in one state could demoralize or anger members elsewhere, threatening the viability of the interest. Sanctions available to the national AFL-CIO ordinarily go unused.

One additional feature of the AFL-CIO's multilevel character can be found in how it mobilizes the grassroots side of the labor movement. Business and trade associations bring affiliate officials to Washington to testify or participate in fly-ins to blanket Congress as part of an overall policy campaign. By comparison, the AFL-CIO both allows and encourages affiliates to exert pressure at the grassroots level, visiting members of Congress at their district offices or holding rallies (even for national-level issues) within the state. Moreover, in comparison to trade associations (for example, ATA), national unions devote more resources to political purposes. One labor official stated,

> The staffers help us more on politics than on legislation. [National] wants to coordinate election funding with our organization so we're all consistent across state and national races. . . . It's a big deal when [AFL-CIO's Committee on Political Education—COPE] comes into a state to help with voter turnout percentages. They come in and crunch numbers. . . . I feel it makes a difference. We've been getting about ten percent higher turnout. The [national] technicians tell you how to spend your money, how to craft different letters for different parts of the state.

The relative absence of multilevel group strategy on key issues, such as NAFTA, certainly did not go without notice. Some affiliates complained that the national organization was "too laid-back" in responding to what was considered labor's biggest policy challenge of the 1990s. No significant calls for affiliate participation in a national lobbying agenda went out from Washington. As a result, some state groups lobbied extensively at home. The Ohio affiliate operated a lengthy anti-NAFTA bus tour across the state, and the West Virginia group held statewide rallies, and others did nothing. Conversely, AFL-CIO affiliates were actively involved in the electoral "retaliation" of 1994, in which COPE reduced or withheld funding from Democratic legislators who had voted "the wrong way" on NAFTA.

The AFL-CIO can and does inform state affiliate activities on national issues, but the geographic diffusion of labor and its varied points of view encourage democracy within the federation. Affiliates thus retain substantial autonomy, leaving the national group in no greater control of the federation than most business associations are in control of theirs. National staffers must remain patient, allowing the quality of the resources they provide to convince state groups that cohesion is advantageous and that their participation in the national agenda has meaning. At the same time, with no competition in representing the labor community, the AFL-CIO remains the dominant national voice of the American labor movement.

The Nuanced Effect of Structure:
Small Business and the Retailers

John Motley, the top lobbyist for the National Retail Federation and a tough cookie, spoke wistfully of his erstwhile employer, the National Federation of Independent Business. With its tight organizational structure and ability to mobilize highly motivated, local voices, the NFIB has become one of the most influential organizations in national politics. A 1997 *Fortune* survey of 2,200 Washington insiders ranked the NFIB fourth overall in its Power 25 listing of most influential lobbies.[9] No other business organization came close, with such traditional kingpins as the National Association of Manufacturers and the U.S. Chamber of Commerce ranked thirteenth and fifteenth, respectively. Most astonishing, the Business Roundtable, which emphasizes direct contacts between major corporate CEOs and legislators, did not make the top twenty-five. As John Motley quoted one member of Congress, "I don't want to hear from CEOs. I want to hear from constituents." What the NFIB does so well is to make sure that the appropriate legislators hear from the appropriate constituents. Indeed, "the heart of the federation's strategy is simple":

> Step 1, decide which senators and representatives will be the swing votes on the committees charged with [the relevant] issues. Step 2, mobilize small-business owners who are influential in their states and districts and are willing to deliver a rock-hard message. Step 3, take the people from Step 2 and aim them at the people from Step 1.[10]

Still, any large organization such as the NFIB, with its 600,000 members, would see grassroots lobbying as a natural tactic. Why, then, is the NFIB so successful? The answer goes back to how organizational structure can help facilitate participation and bridge the national–local divide.

NFIB: A Federation with a Single Voice

At first glance, the NFIB looks like other federation, with structures that may delay—even prevent—rapid, effective action. Although the NFIB does have fifty state legislative offices, the crucial communications take place between the national organization and the individual member businesses. This happens in two related ways. First, the members regularly "cast yes or no votes on five current issues that ultimately establish the organization's legislative positions."[11] Although other organizations' lobbyists express skepticism about the framing of the questions, the NFIB can cite its data as it seeks legislative support and as it readies the second element of its communications strategy. The NFIB succeeds as well as any organized interest in mobilizing its members to contact particular members of Congress on specific issues.

Although the NFIB solicits volunteer grassroots lobbying activity from its members, the national staff and officials scout out potentially effective local members, whom they can ask to make the key telephone call to the personal friend, who just happens to be a member of Congress. Political scientist William Browne observed that legislators often "cultivate constituents" who have special expertise and judgment;[12] likewise, a national NFIB lobbyist noted that a major part of his job is to "cultivate" his own organization's members with the hope that he will reap some effective grassroots influence. Once identified, these individuals—a total of twenty or thirty thousand—stand ready to contact their respective legislators, giving a local twist to the well-honed information provided by national staff. The "federation" of small business is essentially a single, large, relatively homogeneous membership organization that can speak a single message, albeit in any number of regional dialects.

The NFIB uses a host of conventional techniques to communicate and exert influence, ranging from its young, aggressive corps of lobbyists on Capitol Hill to a growing political action committee.[13] And it can ordinarily speak with a single voice, given the relative similarity of its members. In the end, however, its capacity to act a lot like a unitary group—with the national staff communicating clearly and easily with well-prepared local "key contacts"—stands at the center of its strength as an effective organization.

The National Retail Federation: Structural Impediments

Unlike the NFIB, the National Retail Federation is rarely mentioned as one of the nation's most effective lobbying groups. Indeed, the reach of the NRF is impressive, as it "represents an industry which encompasses over 1.4 million U.S. retail establishments."[14] And those retailers are spread across the country, in every congressional district, much like the NFIB.

Two major problems confront the NRF as it seeks to wield the power in setting agendas and influencing legislators. First, it must mesh the interests of several different kinds of members, such as state and national associations, domestic retailers, and international retail firms. At the same time, a second kind of diversity affects internal operations: the great disparity among members in terms of firm size. More than half the domestic retail members have net sales of less that $1 million, whereas about 15 percent enjoy sales of $100 million or more. The local children's bookshop may have little in common with the new superstore book seller down the street. In fact, their interests may be completely at odds. Yet the NRF would (or at least could) represent them both. This contrasts sharply to the NFIB, whose members are all relatively modest operations, even as they represent myriad kinds of businesses.

The large size of many NRF members, such as Kmart and J.C. Penney, and the relative importance of state affiliates create two distinct organization challenges to the federation's effectiveness as a broad-based, constituent-oriented, grassroots lobbying force. As the NRF's Motley explained, in the NFIB, national lobbyists can communicate directly with their key contacts in a congressional district. But to employ the long reach of a major retailer, there is an additional step in the process. Motley observed, "I need to get my counterpart [inside the retail firm] to think the way I think. Then that person makes the call [to the manager of the local retail outlet]. This may reflect a single extra step, but the differences are great in the speed and clarity with which messages can be delivered."

In addition, the NFIB maintains extensive files on key contact personnel, complete with data on their personal ties to legislators, types of business, and important issues to these individuals. The small business owners seem comfortable with this sharing of information. Again, the retailers differ dramatically, in that they remain suspicious of surrendering some control of their capacity to communicate with their own employees. The inability of NRF to act quickly and directly imposes important limitations on its ability to lobby as quickly and coherently as the national organization would prefer. One nascent NRF plan would create a "totally secure warehouse for [member] data," where "all contacts would be stored." Armed with different companies' letterheads, the NRF could communicate directly with individuals stored in the database, who could then reach out to specific legislators.

Finally, but not insignificantly, we simply note the differences between the NFIB and the NRF in terms of their relations with state offices. The retailers include forty-nine state affiliates, each of which has its own members and staff; the NFIB's state operations are run by its own employees. Again, "federation" is in the NFIB's title, but it operates much more like a unitary enterprise. The NRF, conversely, must accommodate its affiliates, its diverse membership, and the independent operations of its large members. It is no wonder that the retailer's John Motley yearned to recast the NRF, at least for lobbying, more in the form of the NFIB.[15]

Conclusion

Across a number of cases, reported here and elsewhere,[16] national–state relations can vary widely, as can the relations between the national organization and particular (usually large) interests within the overall structure. Our first emphasis is simply to take organizational form seriously. It may not always make a difference, but it often does. Who controls decision-making authority? Who can contact local firms and key constituents for grassroots lobbying purposes? Who controls information?

Moreover, as the Congress discusses devolution of power to the states, and sometimes actually follows through on this discussion, multi-level structure becomes an increasingly important component of nation-wide lobbying efforts. Different structures may demonstrate distinct strengths as information is shared and as state-specific lobbying efforts go forward, at least loosely harnessed to similar national efforts. In addition, the lobbying structure can also be linked to electioneering–campaign finance decisions for many federations. As communications and the reach of government link local concerns to state and national issues, how interests are structured will prove impossible to ignore.

Notes

1. Quoted in David Hosansky, "Hill Feels the Big Clout of Small Business," *Congressional Quarterly Weekly Report*, January 10, 1998, 59.
2. Ibid.
3. Brian B. Anderson, *Interest Group Federations: A View from the States*, Ph.D. dissertation, Pennsylvania State University, 1997.
4. David B. Truman, *The Governmental Process* (New York: Knopf, 1951); Donald R. Hall, *Cooperative Lobbying* (Tucson: University of Arizona Press, 1969); Carol S. Greenwald, *Group Power: Lobbying and Public Policy* (New York, Praeger, 1977); Anderson, *Interest Group Federations*.
5. Truman, *The Governmental Process*, 119–129.
6. See Mancur Olson, *The Logic of Collective Action* (Cambridge, Mass.: Harvard University Press, 1965).
7. One common federation rule is that if information is important to one affiliate, the national organization will send it to all affiliates. National group officials avoid appearing to favor one affiliate over others. What might seem like inefficient resource transfer is actually a vital feature of multilevel interest maintenance.
8. "Spheres of Functions for ATA, State Associations and the Conferences," *American Trucking Associations* 1–2: 4.
9. Jeffrey Birnbaum, "Washington's Power 25," *Fortune*, December 8, 1997, 63.
10. Neil A. Lewis, "Lobby for Small Business Owners Puts Big Dent in Health Care Bill," *New York Times*, July 6, 1994, A1.
11. Kirk Victor, "Swing Time," *National Journal*, June 12, 1993, 1403.
12. William Browne, *Cultivating Congress* (Lawrence: University Press of Kansas, 1995).
13. On the lobbyists, see Louis Jacobson, "The Place to Go for Young Stars," *National Journal*, November 15, 1997, 2320–2321.
14. *National Retail Federation 1996 Annual Report*, introduction.
15. Motley eventually became frustrated with his NRF position and moved on to another group in 1998.
16. Brian Anderson, "The Fundamentals of Multi Level Interest Structure," unpublished paper; also, Anderson, *Interest Group Federations: A View from the States*.

5

The Washington Higher Education Community: Moving Beyond Lobbying 101

Constance E. Cook

In the pantheon of organized interests, higher education—both through its various associations and individual institutions—has prospered in the post-1945 era of sustained growth of government. An important reason for the success of higher education policy initiatives on Capitol Hill was the continuous Democratic control of the U.S. House of Representatives for the forty years following the election of 1954. The House Education and Labor Committee stood as one of the most liberal panels in the Congress, and the Appropriations Committee generally supported increased spending on higher education. Even if the linkages were not quite of the "iron triangle" variety (linking congressional committees to the bureaucracy to higher education interest groups), they were historically strong and sympathetic to the higher education community.

All this changed dramatically in 1994, when Republicans won control of the House for the first time in four decades. Suddenly, friendly staff members and supportive subcommittee chairs were replaced by Republicans who had long harbored suspicions of higher education spending. In this chapter, Constance Cook lays out how the higher education community responded to the Republican revolution by adapting its tactics and stepping up its lobbying efforts. Moving beyond their traditional inside strategies, the higher education associations adopted outside strategies, in large part because they were no longer insiders. In the short run, at least, the affected groups effectively presented their positions and avoided much of the damage that they had feared they might incur.

This chapter is based on a chapter from *Lobbying for Higher Education: How Colleges and Universities Influence Federal Policy* (Nashville, Tenn.: Vanderbilt University Press, Issues in Higher Education Series, 1998). Research for the book was funded by the Spencer Foundation, the W. K. Kellogg Foundation, and the University of Michigan Office of Research. The data presented, statements made, and views expressed are solely the responsibility of the author.

The sweep of the 1994 election brought in the first Republican congressional majority in forty years. Based on election year promises in the Contract with America, House Speaker Newt Gingrich (R-Ga.) led the campaign to balance the federal budget by cutting domestic spending. Republican plans included a reduction and restructuring of higher education funding, which looked like an easy target because no one expected colleges and universities to lobby effectively in response. As one observer put it, "Higher ed has always been 'Amateur Hour' in Washington." John Kasich (R-Ohio), chair of the House Budget Committee, expressed a similar sentiment, saying, "Higher education couldn't organize its way out of a paper bag."[1]

Kasich was proven wrong, and the 104th Congress (1995–1996) enacted legislation favorable to the higher education community. Congress preserved and even increased some funding for federal student aid and university-based research, and the higher education community made gains on a number of other issues as well. As one lobbyist proclaimed, "We won everything we ever dreamed of." By way of contrast, a Republican congressional staff member admitted, as the Congress adjourned, "Whatever revolutionary fervor [about higher education policy] we [Republicans] had is gone now." In fact, going into the 1996 election Republicans found their attempts to cut federal aid to higher education were a political liability, and candidates held press conferences to proclaim support for it. As an article in the *Chronicle of Higher Education* explained at the start of the next Congress, "Higher education is hot on Capitol Hill. More Americans cite education as their first concern than any other topic. Lawmakers of both parties know it's a can't-miss issue and scramble for a piece of it."[2] Most observers credited this change not only to President Bill Clinton's highly visible support for higher education but also to the lobbying done by Washington associations and other college and university representatives. For example, one prominent lobbyist said, "The effective work done by college leaders on Capitol Hill during the past year demonstrates that higher education can make a compelling case about the importance of this sprawling enterprise to the nation's well-being."[3]

This chapter describes new lobbying techniques the higher education community used successfully and contrasts them with those it relied on prior to the 104th Congress. Its changes demonstrate a policy community's reaction to policy turmoil—in other words, what it does more of, or differently, when faced with a dramatic change in congressional leadership. A *policy community*, in this usage, consists of individuals and groups outside of government that lobby on a particular public policy topic and consider each other's activities and positions as they plan their own.[4]

Methodology

The research for this chapter was both quantitative and qualitative in nature. The first stage involved survey data collection; the second stage involved exploratory field work and interviews. The quantitative data analysis was based on a 1994 mail survey of the presidents of colleges and universities,[5] which asked about their federal relations activities and opinions. There was a 62-percent response rate for the 2,524 institutions that received the survey.[6]

One of the survey topics was presidents' opinions of the six major presidentially based Washington associations. These associations are presidentially based in the sense that it is the presidents who serve as institutional representatives, and most American colleges and universities have memberships in one or more of these associations. The Big Six, as they are called, are the Association of American Universities (AAU); the American Association of Community Colleges (AACC); the American Association of State Colleges and Universities (AASCU); the National Association of Independent Colleges and Universities (NAICU); the National Association of State Universities and Land-Grant Colleges (NASULGC); and the American Council on Education (ACE), which serves as an umbrella association for the others.

The second, qualitative stage of the research involved telephone and face-to-face interviews in 1995–1996. The interviewees were a sample of college and university presidents who serve on the Big Six boards, the presidents and government relations officers of the Big Six and other Washington associations, and many of the people on Capitol Hill and in the executive branch identified by the higher education community as particularly influential in shaping the policies that affect it.[7] Both survey and interview data are cited in this chapter.

Traditional Higher Education Lobbying

Historically, the Washington higher education community lobbied reluctantly and poorly. Daniel Patrick Moynihan, then counselor to President Richard Nixon, was so exasperated during the debate over the 1972 Higher Education Act (HEA) that he called the higher education community "the worst lobby in Washington."[8] That was an era when many higher education leaders believed they should stay above the fray and considered *lobbying* a dirty word.

Over the twenty-five years since then, the community has gradually come to understand the necessity of fuller participation in the political process. Washington higher education associations have become increasingly numerous and active, and more campuses have sent their own representatives to Washington or hired lobbyists to represent them.[9] The community consists of not only the long established Big Six, but also specialized associations, campus representatives (some of whom have Washington offices), and hired guns (in other words, for-profit legal, consulting, and lobbying firms with which colleges and universities sometimes contract).

Most policy communities have experienced the same proliferation of Washington representatives as higher education. Schlozman and Tierney described the explosion of groups in Washington in the 1970s and 1980s, and interviewed lobbyists to find out whether "the massive increase in pressure activity" was accompanied by "an expanded use of various kinds of weapons in the organizational arsenal."[10] They reasoned that the previous decade had been a period of rapid change and, for many groups, a period of substantial political upheaval. As a consequence, they were interested in understanding how groups respond during periods of turmoil, and particularly whether they do more or behave differently than usual. Based on their data, they concluded that political turmoil leads to more political activity. However, they found that each type of group typically pursues the same lobbying techniques it used previously; they simply do more of the same.

An analysis of the higher education community's lobbying techniques prior to the 104th Congress show that although it used some techniques frequently, it tried others less frequently, or not at all. Higher education representatives typically used the same techniques most commonly used by other policy communities, such as testifying at hearings; contacting public officials directly; engaging in informal contacts with officials; presenting research results; sending letters; attempting to shape the implementation of policies; consulting with government officials to plan legislative strategy; inspiring letter-writing or telegram campaigns; shaping the government's agenda; and helping draft legislation, regulations, rules, and guidelines. Eighty-five percent or more of all types of Washington organizations use these same techniques (see Table 5-1), so the higher education community simply lobbied the way the largest number of other groups do and usually avoided other kinds of techniques. In other words, it took a cautious, low-key approach to lobbying.

Choice of lobbying strategies and tactics depends in part on a group's determination of what might work best, given who is currently in power.[11] If there is a change in the majority party in Congress, for example, it is possible that changes in lobbying techniques may also be appropriate. During the 104th Congress, the higher education community's approach to lobbying became increasingly varied and aggressive. It began using political advertising, protests and demonstrations, constituent contacts, grassroots lobbying, and coalition building to an extent it had not before. As the 1996 presidential election approached, it was emboldened to try, in addition, more electoral involvement.

What follows is an analysis of the higher education community's lobbying techniques in the 104th Congress, showing where its practices during the period of turmoil diverged from its historical approach. For the first time, the community moved beyond "Lobbying 101" and tried a more spirited, sophisticated approach to inform public officials about its needs and preferences.

Table 5-1   Use of Lobbying Techniques by All Types of Washington Organizations

Lobbying technique	Extent of use (percentage)
Testifying at hearings[a]	99
Contacting officials directly[a]	98
Informal contacts[a]	95
Presenting research results[a]	92
Sending letters to members[a]	92
Entering into coalitions with other organizations	90
Shaping implementation[a]	89
Planning legislative strategy[a]	85
Helping to draft legislation[a]	85
Inspiring letter-writing campaigns[a]	84
Having constituents contact	80
Mounting grassroots lobbying	80
Contributing financially to campaigns	58
Publicizing voting records	44
Running ads in the media	31
Contributing work or personnel to campaigns	24
Endorsing candidates	22
Engaging in protests	20

Source: List of lobbying techniques excerpted from Kay Lehman Schlozman and John T. Tierney, *Organized Interests and American Democracy* (New York: Harper and Row, 1986), 150.

[a]Major higher education lobbying techniques prior to 1995.

Political Advertising

Until 1995 the higher education community almost never chose to do political advertising. In that respect it was unusual because organizations have used political advertising campaigns throughout this century. Although some groups are constrained by high costs of electronic media, most believe that political advertising can influence public opinion and activate the public to communicate with policy makers. As Schlozman and Tierney pointed out, "The public can be a natural ally—and increasingly in this electronic age, a created ally."[12] Given the enormous number of people enrolled in higher education programs, employed by colleges and universities, or supportive of their objectives, political advertising could be a useful strategy.

When student financial aid was threatened in the early years of the Reagan administration, the higher education community experimented with political advertising, and then it did so again in 1995.[13] An ad hoc coalition called the Alliance to Save Student Aid was organized primarily by David Warren, president of NAICU, along with Robert Atwell, president of ACE, for the sole purpose of protecting existing levels of student aid. Thirty other higher education associations contributed funding. The lobbying of the Alliance to Save Student Aid differed substantially from previous efforts in that it was much more active and visible, with more wide-ranging tactics.

The Alliance began by hiring a Republican public relations firm to conduct polling and focus groups. The results showed more widespread support for student financial aid than the higher education community had anticipated. In fact, the polling revealed that public support for federal student aid was second only to public support for Social Security: 92 percent supported current funding levels for Social Security, and 89 percent supported current funding levels for student financial aid. However, focus groups showed that most parents and students did not understand that their financial aid, both loans and grants, usually came from the federal government.[14] Thus, it was clear that an education campaign would be necessary and the public was likely to be receptive to the message of higher education.

With that political intelligence in hand, the Alliance devised a media strategy, with press kits and press conferences, especially targeting the regional House Budget Committee hearings. The Alliance also created an 800 number to inform callers about the status of legislation and connect them with congressional offices for advocacy. In addition, the Alliance paid for newspaper ads and aired radio spots during drive time in the Washington area, as well as in the seven states of key House and Senate Budget Committee members. The Alliance also offered the media suggestions for op-ed pieces on student financial aid, and it characterized financial aid issues in simple terms, appropriate for sound bites, thereby generating substantial public awareness of the threat to student aid.

All these Alliance tactics were new for higher education. As one association vice president put it, "The Alliance has been a big change in strategy for higher education. In fact, there is a systemic change in the way we are doing business now."

There was a second higher education ad hoc group established for political advertising at the start of the 104th Congress. Known as the Science Coalition, its purpose was advocacy of university-based research in science and engineering, with special emphasis on medical research. The Coalition was created by eighteen major research universities, mostly private ones, with their senior government relations and public affairs officers taking the lead. Unlike the Alliance, the Coalition's budget was university funded rather than association funded. It included among its members not only universities, science and engineering societies, and other higher education groups, but also corporations, voluntary associations, and prominent scientists. By 1996 it had grown to more than 370 organizations, institutions, and individuals.[15]

Like the Alliance, the Coalition employed a consulting firm for polling and focus groups, and its Washington strategies were message development and media outreach. Its major 1995 achievement was an "advertorial"—a letter and newspaper ad titled "A Moment of Truth for America"—which advocated federal investment in university research. One version of the advertorial was signed by twenty-seven governors, both Republican and Democratic, and the other by fifteen corporate CEOs. Besides serving as a newspaper advertisement, it was used as a letter to all members of Congress. The Coalition also published a letter signed by sixty Nobel Prize winners expressing concern that budget cuts would hinder medical and scientific achievements. The Coalition took out advertisements in *Roll Call*, the Capitol Hill magazine, and organized forums on science and technology in the spring of 1996 for both the Democratic and Republican Policy Committees.[16]

The Republicans were sufficiently concerned about higher education's aggressive new techniques to threaten retribution. One congressional staff member said, "We will start investigating how much colleges are actually spending on political issues. We are going to find out just what it has cost them to pay for every ad and what every 800 number call has cost them. We intend to use this information against them when we need to. We are watching what they do. We know that the money they spend on advertising just means that tuition will be that much higher."

Nonetheless, those who led the ad hoc organizations felt the results would be worth the risks. As NAICU's president put it, "All this is new for higher education and higher education is in it for the long haul."[17]

Protests and Demonstrations

Protests are a lobbying technique used by a sizable number of citizen groups, and their purpose is to gain publicity for a cause. The protest is judged a success if media decide to cover it because that leads to more public understanding of the protesters' point of view. Media coverage usually provides the protesters with leverage in the policy-making process.[18]

The civil rights and Vietnam War protests of the 1960s began on college campuses and then spread beyond them. Given that student groups have long used civil disobedience on campus to pressure their institutions' administrators, it is surprising that they have so rarely organized protests and demonstrations in Washington to pressure public officials on higher education policy issues. Student groups often demonstrate to express opinions on issues unrelated to higher education, but prior to 1995, the only time that most observers remember protests about higher education policy (specifically, student aid) was during the early years of the Reagan administration.

In the 104th Congress, during the debate on student aid, there were two student organizations working regularly with other major higher education associations in the Alliance to Save Student Aid: namely, the United States Student Association (USSA) and the National Association for Graduate and Professional Students (NAGPS). As one higher education association president stated, "We have seen students (and their representative organizations) who are connecting with the associations for the first time." Another association leader said, "In the Alliance, the associations were the generals, but the students were the army. They were the ones who provided the numbers. They had the stories."

The activism of the student groups could be traced to the publicity given to congressional Republicans' plans to cut $18 billion out of the student aid budget. Usually students are largely unaware of the potential consequences as millions of dollars move into and out of various student aid programs. However, this time Speaker Gingrich and other congressional leaders were very vocal about their legislative plans, and the magnitude of the cuts got the students' attention—thanks in no small part to the leadership and resources provided by the major higher education associations.

The student groups took advantage of electronic message groups on the campuses and sent daily e-mail messages through the Internet. They mobilized students to conduct demonstrations, most often local in nature but sometimes on Capitol Hill, to protest the proposed cuts in student aid. Altogether there were four rallies during the 104th Congress at which students packed congressional committee sessions and buttonholed individual legislators. According to many association lobbyists, the spirited participation of the two student organizations in the Alliance to Save Student Aid was probably the single greatest influence on congressional policy decisions.

Constituent Contacts: College and University Presidents

Political scientists have long contended that members of Congress are motivated first and foremost to ensure their own reelection.[19] They do that most effectively by responding to the concerns of their constituents, so it is common for interest groups to bring influential constituents to Washington. Constituent pressures often replace interest group pressures as the major factor influencing congressional policy choices.[20]

College and university presidents have always come to Washington on behalf of their institutions, and their lobbying has often been effective. As a congressional staffer commented, "Members [of Congress] tend to trust and value visits and information from college presidents." In 1995–1996 the Washington associations tried to mobilize the presidents much more often than previously. As a higher education lobbyist explained, "Now we need to do less talking and have our members do more talking, and that has been a big difference since November [1994]." As a consequence, presidents for the first time were more visible on Capitol Hill than association personnel. Even before the arrival of the 104th Congress, it was evident that federal relations had taken on increasing importance for college and university presidents, but during that period association leaders said presidents were better informed and more active than they had been in the past. As one commented, "Presidents' level of interest, their attention span, and their turnout are all greater now."

Associations urged presidents to telephone legislators or write letters, e-mail, telegrams, or faxes, and they especially encouraged the presidents to make personal visits. They called on presidents from all sectors and types of higher education institutions, not just the elites. As one college president noted, "Members of Congress think that the elites don't really need federal help. Using [Harvard President] Rudenstine gets you in the door of a member of Congress but then he is not helpful in actually making the case for higher education [as a whole]." Fortunately for the higher education community, there are college and university presidents who are constituents of every member of Congress. The associations especially target for mobilization those presidents whose congressional delegations occupy leadership positions, and they are often asked to express the views of their colleagues. For example, the presidents of Kansas and Vermont institutions were especially important during the 104th Congress because of the influence Sens. Nancy Kassebaum (R-Kan.) and James Jeffords (R-Vt.) had on higher education policy making.

Association personnel talked about the careful calculus of determining when it is really important to activate the presidents, and how. As one of them put it, "You have to think about how many times you can go to the well and ask the presidents to contact members of Congress. You can only ask them so many times. They are busy people." During 1995–1996 it was clear that the Washington associations had to "go to the well" more than usual.

Grassroots Lobbying

Higher education institutions and associations have rarely mobilized their various constituencies for grassroots lobbying, which is usually defined as efforts by government relations people in Washington to involve the folks back home in contacting their legislators for the purpose of influencing policy making.[21] Grassroots organizing is a particularly resource-intensive activity for Washington offices, so they reserve this effort for times when their interests are most threatened.[22]

The potential number of people who could be marshaled for advocacy is huge. The higher education community includes not only college and university administrators, but also large numbers of faculty, students, alumni, trustees, and other constituencies such as parents of college students, community leaders who value their local institutions, and businesses that rely on higher education for job training. However, institutional administrators have often been reluctant to run the risk of involving others in lobbying and have even discouraged association personnel from contacting them because their own public policy views and institutional priorities may not be shared by these other higher education players. For example, students are unlikely to support university requests to state officials for tuition hikes, and faculty may not support university requests to Congress for indirect cost reimbursement for federally funded research projects.[23]

Most college and university faculty do relatively little lobbying. An association leader explained, "The university faculty are truly disconnected from federal relations. They have no awareness of how things work; in fact, they disdain the process. They actively remove themselves."[24] That is not true of all faculty members; some are heavily involved in politics. They may provide expert testimony on issues facing Congress, or spend their sabbaticals working on policy concerns in congressional offices, or even run for Congress themselves. However, such faculty members are rare. More numerous are the faculty who do lobbying on behalf of their own grants and projects. Although the percentage that lobbies is very small, it has grown in recent years as faculty have tried to generate or maintain funding for themselves and their departments. Faculty in the sciences have been particularly active, because they have the most at stake in terms of federal research dollars.

Faculty lobbying grew substantially during the 104th Congress, especially because of concern about proposed cuts in research funding. Disciplinary professional associations sent e-mail or newsletter action alerts to members, urging them to contact members of Congress at key points in the budget debates. The American Association of Medical Colleges (AAMC) helped bring together 130 medical and scientific societies (including hospital groups, physicians, and those in allied health fields), voluntary health groups, and academic and research organizations in the Ad Hoc Group for Medical Research Funding. Its objective was an increase in support for biomedical and behavioral research at the National Institutes of Health (NIH). Similarly, faculty and others in a variety of professional associations conducted lobbying efforts on behalf of the budget and programs of the National Science Foundation (NSF), especially through the Coalition for National Science Funding. The NSF Coalition comprises fifty-five organizations, including the American Physical Society, the American Mathematical Society, and the American Society of Cell Biology. They encouraged faculty to voice their support for NSF, and their call to action produced about 10,000 letters, telephone calls, and e-mail messages to Congress. Other coalitions were equally active in lobbying the 104th Congress. In many cases they were organized around specific research topics, such as oceanographic research, or for advocacy to specific agencies, such as the Departments of Defense or Energy.

It has been even more unusual for college and university administrators to ask their students to lobby, even though their sheer numbers (about 14.3 million in 1995–1996) could be powerful, and students, like faculty, could give dry policy debates a human face. Nor do the major associations typically involve student organizations. Although the spirited participation of USSA and NAGPS in the Alliance to Save Student Aid was credited with having a substantial impact on congressional policy decisions, the participation of these organizations in concert with other associations is uncharacteristic of higher education lobbying. The institutions students attend almost never inform and mobilize them for lobbying on aid or other issues.

Similarly, although most colleges and universities have their own boards of trustees, administrators rarely call on board members for participation in higher education advocacy. That generalization applies less often to community colleges because their trustees are mobilized by the Association of Community College Trustees (ACCT), which works closely with the American Association of Community Colleges (AACC). The same partnership does not operate for four-year institutions, even though the association that represents the trustees, the Association of Governing Boards (AGB), would be glad to have its 28,000 trustee members more engaged in higher education initiatives.[25] Nonetheless, with the exception of the Ad Hoc Tax Group's trustee network, major associations have usually refused to involve trustees in lobbying efforts. Although trustees are often well connected politically and could have easy access, presidents worry that they may have opinions that are unrepresentative of their own and those of the faculty. As a consequence, trustees are often a neglected resource.[26]

Although there are millions of college and university alumni, they too are rarely mobilized for federal lobbying.[27] It has even been unusual for the various higher education sectors to identify congressional staffers among their alumni and try to organize their assistance to serve institutional needs. The few institutions that have done so are mostly small liberal arts colleges, especially Jesuit institutions.

During the second session of the 104th Congress the Washington higher education community began to mobilize more of its constituents. NAICU decided to encourage its member institutions to activate the more influential college trustees,[28] and there was discussion about creating a database of alumni of private colleges and parents of students who attend those schools, for the purpose of mobilizing them in the future. Similarly, the Science Coalition announced its plan to expand the use of a *grasstops* strategy in which it more vigorously identified and mobilized key opinion leaders, including alumni, donors, trustees, parents, and others. It was evident by 1996 that grasstops and grassroots lobbying were becoming more commonly used for higher education constituencies.

Electoral Involvement

Occupationally based nonprofit communities typically try to avoid too close identification with either political party, especially at election time.[29] By contrast, many citizen groups, such as environmental and consumer groups, provide publicity for candidates' voting records and policy stands (often called *voter scorecards*), and they endorse candidates and contribute work or personnel to campaigns.[30]

To college and university presidents, partisanship seems risky. Presidents pointed out in interviews that their trustees and donors, as well as other constituents, are sensitive to partisan leanings and consider them inappropriate for a higher education institution. They noted that partisanship is likely to get a chief executive officer in trouble. Bornstein conducted a survey of private college and university presidents on their role in public policy issues and partisan politics. She found that 74 percent of them thought presidents should not be involved in partisan politics. Presidents say their biggest worries about political involvement are that it could offend diverse constituencies, have an adverse impact on fundraising, and incite a negative reaction from their trustees.[31]

During the 104th Congress bipartisanship was a real challenge for higher education leaders. On one issue after another they found themselves opposed to Republican congressional proposals and allied with the Clinton administration. President Clinton publicized higher education as a Democratic Party policy issue, and he courted the community by making the rounds of association annual meetings and sending cabinet secretaries as well. Nonetheless, the associations tried to avoid overt partisanship, such as voter scorecards or outright candidate endorsements.

At the start of the 1996 election year, higher education began to involve itself in electoral politics to an unprecedented extent, and it did so through spirited voter registration drives. Their purpose was to change the fact that in 1992 only slightly more than half (52.4 percent) of the 18- to 24-year-olds in the country had registered to vote, and of those registered, many fewer than half (42.8 percent) had actually voted.[32] NAICU's President David Warren and AASCU's President James Appleberry cochaired the National Voter Registration Project, made up of thirty-eight Washington associations. It took advantage of the Motor Voter Law, which was passed in 1993 to make voter registration easier. NAICU published a handbook that showed campuses how to set up voter registration drives; form steering committees of faculty, staff, students, and community representatives; and organize nonpartisan educational events, such as voter forums, to inform the campus about political issues and candidates.[33] There were other voter registration efforts as well, such as MTV's Rock the Vote campaign and those of the College Republicans, the College Democrats, and Youth Vote '96, a coalition of twenty youth groups (including USSA) concerned about issues such as the environment and consumer rights.

Altogether, there were voter registration activities of one sort or another on about three-quarters of the campuses. These efforts seemed to lead to the registration of more than one million 18- to 24-year-olds prior to the 1996 election.[34] Some student groups created voter scorecards, such as USSA, Campus Green Vote, and the U.S. Public Interest Research Group (USPIRG), but they did so independently, without the encouragement of the major higher education associations. As a result of all these uncoordinated and student-based efforts, the higher education community was more involved in electoral politics than ever before. Exit polls showed that President Clinton led overwhelmingly among voters for whom education was the primary concern, and the majority of college-age voters cast their votes for him.[35]

Coalitions: Standing and Ad Hoc

Coalitions are ubiquitous in Washington, especially because they are so effective at influencing public policy making. Coalition building is particularly helpful when there is strong organized opposition.[36] It is a strategy that does not depend on resources and, in fact, can result in savings.[37] It has many advantages, ranging from providing assistance for friends, to addressing member pressures for greater issue involvement, to gaining information from allies.[38]

The higher education community has always been good at creating internal standing coalitions, as evidenced by its Washington umbrella association, ACE, and the five other major higher education associations that represent various types of institutions. However, historically, higher education has had fairly limited alliances with other policy communities. As one public official put it, higher education has "talked only to itself."

During the 104th Congress, higher education became especially adept at building ad hoc coalitions. Their purpose is to deal with a current policy problem and then vanish when the threat subsides. As described previously, some or all of the major presidentially based associations joined with various student groups and many of the professional or disciplinary associations and others outside of academe to pursue advocacy jointly, as in the Alliance to Save Student Aid, the Science Coalition, the National Campus Voter Registration Project, and the groups lobbying for funding for specific federal agencies. 1995–1996 marked a period in which ad hoc coalitions became the norm for higher education lobbying.

These ad hoc coalitions in 1995–1996 were not unique; over the years higher education has had a long list of them. On student aid issues, especially before the advent of direct lending, there were coalitions between higher education and the banks and guarantee agencies. In regard to state funding issues, there have been coalitions with groups such as the National Governors' Association (NGA), the National Conference of State Legislators (NCSL), the State Higher Education Executive Officers (SHEEOs), and the Education Commission of the States (ECS). Higher education advocates have often aligned themselves with the Independent Sector coalition, an umbrella group for more than 800 nonprofit organizations, such as the Salvation Army, the YMCA, health groups, religious groups, and charities. There have also been periodic alliances between higher education associations and the environmental lobby and the children's lobby, such as the Children's Defense Fund. In addition, interviewees mentioned coalitions with unions such as the American Federation of State, City, and Municipal Employees (AFSCME), as well as ad hoc coalitions with utilities, veterans' groups, the arts, transportation, telecommunications, aerospace contractors, civil rights groups, and scientific professional societies.

In contrast to its relatively frequent use of ad hoc coalitions, higher education representatives have had fewer standing coalitions with external communities. The most permanent coalition partner for higher education has been the elementary–secondary education community. In fact, a key purpose of the twenty-five-year-old Committee for Education Funding (CEF) is to bring the two parts of the education community together. As one association official put it, "The purpose of CEF is [for higher education and K–12] to avoid hurting each other or offending each other." According to reports from policy makers, CEF is quite effective in that regard. The higher education community's standing alliances also extend to business and industry, with ACE's Business–Higher Education Forum being one of the best examples. The medical community has also maintained standing coalitions, such as Research America, a 10-year-old organization made up of academic and industry groups interested in biomedical research.

During the 104th Congress, higher education community leaders enlisted more allies than ever before. Many interviewees cited the Science Coalition's letter from major corporate leaders as an example of the kind of alliance with other sectors that should be brought to bear more often. At least for now, most of the higher education coalitions seem to be ad hoc in nature, but in time, ad hoc coalitions often take on permanence.

Political Action Committees

Although higher education representatives have begun lobbying more aggressively in most other respects, they have not embraced political action committees (PACs). The legitimization of PACs in the 1970s by federal laws and Supreme Court decisions made them a technique frequently used by other policy communities for gaining access to legislators. In fact, it is very unusual for a prosperous, sophisticated policy community *not* to use PACs as a regular part of its lobbying operation. Although it is partisan and ideological factors that lead to the spurious connection between money and voting,[39] nonetheless distribution of PAC money does correlate highly with access and sometimes with success on policy issues.[40] As a consequence, there has been an explosion of PACs, with several thousand of them providing campaign contributions to sympathetic candidates and helping friendly incumbent legislators to get reelected. PACs are typically used by corporations, trade associations, and labor unions, and less frequently by citizen groups.[41]

Higher education PACs are very unusual.[42] There are several states in which college and university personnel do belong to PACs,[43] but they are usually for state lawmakers. At the federal level, the only segment of the postsecondary community with PACs is the proprietary vocational school segment.

Members of Congress who serve on higher education committees know well that doing so will not win them the same funds for their next campaign that would come from involvement with other policy issues. One of them said she was told by congressional colleagues, "Don't work on higher ed issues because you won't get any campaign money." Another commented that he would have "gold stars on his forehead when [he] got to the pearly gates" thanks to all the effort he had expended on higher education in spite of the failure of colleges and universities to provide him with funds for his reelection campaigns. He dubbed the higher education community "the worst cheapskates in the political business" and noted that several key legislators friendly to higher education had been defeated over the years because of inadequate campaign coffers.[44] As a result, some members of Congress refuse to serve on committees dealing with higher education, or switch committees as soon as they have the flexibility to do so.

Survey responses show that college and university presidents are clear about their reluctance to form PACs. They continue to believe in the value of what one association president disparagingly called "self-inflicted laryngitis."[45] In response to a question about whether the Big Six should have PACs, the overwhelming response from the presidents was "no," and nearly 200 presidents took time to write in comments on the survey about why they do not want to create higher education PACs in Washington. Only one president wrote a comment favoring PACs.

Two-thirds of the presidents agreed that "forming a PAC would diminish higher education's special status, moving it from a public interest to a 'special interest.' " Several presidents commented on the apolitical nature of higher education, their dislike of hardball politics, and their lack of resources. For example, one asserted, "Higher education is not the National Rifle Association!"

Although PACs may provide access to public officeholders, higher education has access already. One official commented, "The presidents are unusually lucky. They get calls back easily from members of Congress. That is not true of most average citizens." The presidents agree they do not need PACs to get access and be successful. As one president put it, "We don't depend as much on the strategy of financial contributions to accomplish our policy objectives. We strategically try to substitute information and public support for money." Another president linked access to public officials with the legitimacy of the ideas he advanced and said, "If we can't convince without money, it must not be justifiable."

Conclusion

The story of higher education lobbying is the story of adaptability. Although the community used to do little lobbying, and usually with reluctance, in recent years higher education representatives have adopted many techniques commonly used by other interest groups. Their lobbying became especially intensive in 1995–1996, when the change in congressional leadership and policy objectives served as a wake-up call. Their activities support the finding that during periods of turmoil, interest groups are likely to do more lobbying than usual.[46]

Unlike the lobbying of other groups, higher education lobbying expanded not only in intensity but also in the array of techniques used; it was not just more of the same. Established groups do occasionally, though rarely, alter their preferred lobbying strategies—but they seldom do so without first having prolonged discussion and a series of policy failures.[47] Going into the 104th Congress, higher education had not suffered a series of policy failures, so the fact that the community altered its strategies anyway makes it unusual.

The higher education community moved beyond Lobbying 101 to try a more spirited, sophisticated approach. In addition to their usual techniques, higher education associations made more use of campus-based resources. They had more college and university presidents lobbying on Capitol Hill, which meant that association personnel were less often on the front lines. Student organizations used the Internet to mobilize their members for demonstrations and coordinate lobbying with the major associations. Most important, two major ad hoc organizations, the Alliance to Save Student Aid and the Science Coalition, both used polling and focus groups to gauge public opinion, and then did effective political advertising and grassroots mobilization. A multitude of other ad hoc coalitions also employed these and other lobbying tactics, including a massive voter registration drive on the nation's campuses. It was clear that a new higher education lobbying paradigm developed during the 104th Congress, because ad hoc coalitions and campus-based resources were used by the community to a greater extent than ever before.

As noted in Table 5-1, the higher education community's traditional techniques were the ones almost universally used by all kinds of interest groups. After examining all groups, Schlozman and Tierney then divided them into categories in order to compare the techniques of each type of group.[48] Among the groups were corporations and citizen groups, and the higher education community bears some resemblance to both. The community is occupationally based and organized around an economic interest, as are profit-sector corporations and the trade associations that represent them. However, higher education institutions and their associations are nonprofits, like citizen groups, and their spokespersons also believe they champion a public good, in the national interest. It is not surprising, therefore, that higher education representatives use some of the lobbying techniques of both corporations and citizen groups (see Table 5-2).

Profit-sector organizations typically lobby with *inside strategies.* For example, corporate trade associations more often help draft legislation and shape policy implementation.[49] These techniques depend on having substantial resources, such as a sizable staff, policy expertise, and access to influential constituents. Higher education representatives have begun to take better advantage of their resources, but their lobbying is still unlike the profit sector because they eschew the use of political action committees. They lack both the resources and the will to use PACs for federal lobbying.

In 1995–1996, as higher education representatives began experimenting with new lobbying techniques, they chose some that could be called *outside strategies*—in other words, ones that are more common to low-budget citizen groups[50] than to corporations. The outside strategies used

Table 5-2   Use of Lobbying Techniques by Corporations and Citizen Groups (in percentages)

Lobbying technique	Corporations	Citizen groups
Contacting officials directly[a]	100	100
Testifying at hearings[a]	98	100
Informal contacts[a]	98	96
Entering into coalitions with other organizations[b]	96	92
Presenting research results[a]	94	92
Shaping implementation[a]	90	92
Planning legislative strategy[a]	90	83
Contributing financially to campaigns	86	29
Sending letters to members[a]	85	86
Inspiring letter-writing campaigns[a]	83	83
Helping to draft legislation[a]	86	74
Mounting grassroots lobbying[b]	81	71
Having constituents contact[b]	77	58
Running ads in the media[b]	31	33
Publicizing voting records[c]	28	75
Contributing work or personnel to campaigns	14	33
Endorsing candidates	8	29
Engaging in protests[c]	0	25

Source: Excerpted from Kay Lehman Schlozman and John T. Tierney, *Organized Interests and American Democracy* (New York: Harper and Row, 1986), 431.

[a] Major higher education lobbying techniques prior to 1995.
[b] Additional higher education lobbying techniques in 1995–1996.
[c] Lobbying techniques used only by student groups in 1995–1996.

by colleges and universities included media ads and voter registration drives. Student groups, without higher education association coordination, used additional outside strategies, especially protests and demonstrations, and voter scorecards.

There is nothing inherently better or worse about the use of inside or outside strategies. They are simply tactics deemed to be most appropriate for an interest group's own history and characteristics, and most helpful for organizational maintenance.[51] They are also tactics most suited to the degree of conflict involved. The stakes are higher with outside tactics because, when misused, they can backfire.[52] Groups choose tactics they think will be most effective in influencing the group currently in power. In this case, the change from Democratic to Republican control of Congress meant that higher education representatives no longer felt like insiders, so their use of more outside strategies made sense, especially given the highly conflictual nature of their relationship with the Republican leadership.

Observers agree that higher education has come a long way since the days when it was considered the worst lobby in Washington. Prior to the 1994 election, one college president asserted, in response to a survey question about new lobbying techniques, "I do not wish to politicize our work." Another commented, "Education already has adequate priority in the government arena." Thanks to the wake-up call delivered by the 1994 election, most higher education leaders understand now that their work is already politicized and the future of colleges and universities is on the line. The Washington representatives of the higher education community responded energetically to the change in party leadership, using more varied and aggressive advocacy techniques. Contrary to Representative Kasich's expectations, during the 104th Congress higher education learned to "organize its way out of a paper bag."

Notes

1. Quoted in an interview with David Warren, president, National Association of Independent Colleges and Universities, Washington, D.C., June 15, 1995.
2. Stephen Burd, Patrick Healy, and Douglas Lederman, "One Day on Capitol Hill for Higher Education," *Chronicle of Higher Education,* April 25, 1997, A28–A31.
3. Terry Hartle, "The Specter of Budget Uncertainty," *Chronicle of Higher Education,* June 28, 1996, B1–B2.
4. Other terms for policy *community* are policy *domain* or *sector.* The study of interest group communities has been a fairly recent and important addition to the interest group literature. The most notable studies have been the following: On agriculture, health, labor, and energy, John P. Heinz, Edward O. Laumann, Robert H. Salisbury, and Robert L. Nelson, *The Hollow Core: Private Interest in National Policy Making* (Cambridge, Mass.: Harvard University Press, 1993); on energy and health, Edward O. Laumann and David Knoke, *The Organizational State: Social Choices and National Policy Domains* (Madison: University of Wisconsin Press, 1987); and on agriculture, William P. Browne, *Private Interests, Public Policy, and American Agriculture* (Lawrence: University Press of Kansas, 1988).

5. Surveys were sent to colleges and universities listed in the 1994 *HEP Higher Education Directory* (Falls Church, Va.: Higher Education Publications, 1994) that are not specialized institutions, such as theological seminaries or schools of music.
6. A majority of all types of institutions responded, including 78 percent of the research universities, 89 percent of the doctoral universities, 70 percent of the master's institutions, 61 percent of the baccalaureate colleges, and 51 percent of the associate of arts colleges.
7. Many of the 110 interviewees asked not to be identified by name, so names appear only for those who did not request anonymity and whose identity is important in understanding the significance of their remarks.
8. Lawrence E. Gladieux, "Appraising the Influence of the Educational Lobbies: The Case of Higher Education" in *The Changing Politics of Education: Prospects for the 1980s*, ed. Edith K. Mosher and Jennings L. Wagoner, Jr. (Berkeley, Calif.: Phi Delta Kappa/McCutcheon, 1978), 266.
9. With the exception of proprietary schools, all of postsecondary education is a nonprofit enterprise. As such it has 501(c)(3) status. That is also the case with all of the major higher education associations. This nonprofit status makes them tax exempt, and it also means that, according to the Internal Revenue Code, they cannot devote a substantial amount of their activities or resources to attempts to influence legislation. The Lobbying Disclosure Act defines *lobbying* as oral or written communications to high-level executive or legislative branch officials regarding the selection of federal officials or the formulation, modification, or adoption of federal legislation, regulations, and programs. Because this definition does not include education and information for policy makers, those activities are acceptable under the Code. In any case, the major higher education associations have many activities and services apart from federal relations.
10. Kay Lehman Schlozman and John T. Tierney, *Organized Interests and American Democracy* (New York: Harper and Row, 1986), 156–157. They interviewed 175 Washington representatives, concentrating on those from large, active, and affluent groups with Washington offices.
11. William P. Browne, "Variations in the Behavior and Style of State Lobbyists and Interest Groups," *Journal of Politics* 47 (May 1985): 450–468.
12. Schlozman and Tierney, *Organized Interests*, 396.
13. Its most noteworthy effort to do political advertising occurred in the early 1980s when the Reagan administration was trying to cut student aid and eliminate the newly created Department of Education. An ad hoc coalition was formed by NAICU and the Council for the Advancement and Support of Education (CASE), along with twenty-five other associations, in December 1981. The Action Committee for Higher Education (ACHE), as it was called, did intensive political advertising, with leadership from both government relations and public relations staff in the associations. Students were heavily involved in the lobbying effort as well. Because the Department of Education survived and Congress made no additional cuts in student aid, ACHE's efforts appear to have been effective. C. Brown, "The Role of the Government Relations Representative in the Efforts of Some National Higher Education Associations to Influence Federal Education Policy: A Case Study Analysis of the Action Committee for Higher Education" (Ph.D. diss., University of Maryland, College Park, 1985).
14. Alliance to Save Student Aid, *Stop the Raid on Student Aid: A Handbook for Organizers* (Washington, D.C.: National Association of Independent Colleges and Universities, 1995).
15. Jared Blank, "Science Coalition Works for University Research Funding," *The University Record*, September 17, 1996, 2.
16. Ibid.

17. Warren interview.
18. Jeffrey M. Berry, *Lobbying for the People* (Princeton, N.J.: Princeton University Press, 1977), 233.
19. An early book on this topic was David R. Mayhew, *Congress: The Electoral Connection* (New Haven, Conn.: Yale University Press, 1974).
20. William P. Browne, *Cultivating Congress: Constituents, Issues, and Agricultural Policymaking* (Lawrence: University Press of Kansas, 1995).
21. Schlozman and Tierney, *Organized Interests*, 185. Grassroots mobilization used to be the sole province of labor and citizen groups, but this is no longer the case. Corporations have learned to mobilize grassroots activism from the top down, out of their public affairs offices, using employees, suppliers, customers, and stockholders. Jack L. Walker, *Mobilizing Interest Groups in America: Patrons, Professions, and Social Movements* (Ann Arbor: University of Michigan Press, 1991), 51.
22. Diana Evans, "Lobbying the Committee: Interest Groups and the House Public Works and Transportation Committee," in *Interest Group Politics*, 3d ed., ed. Allan J. Cigler and Burdett A. Loomis (Washington, D.C.: CQ Press, 1990), 269.
23. Some faculty resent the high overhead rates their institutions charge the federal government, both because they do not understand where that money goes and also because they worry that their total funding request will be too high for their grant proposal to be competitive.
24. In "America's Professoriate: Politicized, Yet Apolitical," Russell Jacoby hypothesizes that some faculty have so politicized their approach to teaching their own disciplines that they already believe they "give at the office" and, therefore, do not have to devote their energies to practical politics. *(Chronicle of Higher Education,* April 12, 1996, B1–B2.)
25. Interview with Richard T. Ingram, president, Association of Governing Boards of Universities and Colleges, Washington, D.C., May 16, 1995.
26. E. M. Crawford, "The Role of Presidents and Trustees in Government Relations," *New Directions for Institutional Advancement* 12 (1981): 25–34.
27. On the state level, the University of California system has organized some of its prominent graduates for advocacy, and other institutions such as the University of Michigan have developed similar in-state networks. The University of Florida is one of the few institutions that organizes its alumni for federal lobbying.
28. The fact that many of the Christian colleges' boards of trustees include major Republican Party donors made that prospect especially attractive.
29. Heinz et al., *The Hollow Core*, 81.
30. Berry, *Lobbying for the People*, 238; Heinz et al., *The Hollow Core*, 81; Schlozman and Tierney, *Organized Interests*, 431.
31. Rita Bornstein, "Back in the Spotlight: The College President as Public Intellectual," *Education Record* 76 (Fall 1995): 57–62.
32. John DiBiaggio, "Getting the Next Generation of Voters to Go to the Polls," *Chronicle of Higher Education*, September 27, 1996, B5.
33. National Association of Independent Colleges and Universities, *Your Voice—Your Vote: The National Campus Voter Registration Project Organizing Handbook* (Washington, D.C.: Author, 1996).
34. Interview with Michael Combs, coordinator of Grassroots Development, National Association of Independent Colleges and Universities, Washington, D.C., November 14, 1996.
35. Jeff McMillan, "Clinton Won the College Vote, Polls Indicate," *Chronicle of Higher Education*, November 15, 1996, A39.
36. Schlozman and Tierney, *Organized Interests*, 279; Berry, *Lobbying for the People*, 187–194; Marie Hojnacki, "Interest Groups Decisions to Join Alliances or Work Alone," *American Journal of Political Science* 41 (January 1997): 61–87.
37. Berry, *Lobbying for the People*, 254–255.

38. William P. Browne, "Organized Interests and Their Issue Niches: A Search for Pluralism in a Policy Domain," *Journal of Politics* 52 (May 1990): 477–509.
39. John R. Wright, *Interest Groups and Congress: Lobbying, Contributions, and Influence* (Needham Heights, Mass.: Allyn & Bacon, 1996) 137; Diana Evans, "Lobbying in the Committee: Interest Groups and the House Public Works and Transportation Committee," in *Interest Group Politics*, 3d ed., ed. Allan J. Cigler and Burdett A. Loomis (Washington, D.C.: CQ Press, 1990), 272.
40. For example, Heinz et al., *The Hollow Core*, 349.
41. Schlozman and Tierney, *Organized Interests*, 431; Heinz et al., *The Hollow Core*, 81.
42. Because of their tax status, higher education institutions and most associations cannot participate or intervene in political campaigns on behalf of or in opposition to candidates, though individuals within those organizations have the same rights as any other citizens. For example, they can form PACs with their personal funds. Organizations can also adapt to the restrictions on their political activities by creating affiliated arms with 501(c)(6) status that are registered as lobbying organizations.
43. There are about two dozen higher education political action committees operating in at least six states, especially in Texas and Michigan. The PAC contributors range from university administrators and faculty to alumni and other local supporters. It appears that only one of the PACs, at Ferris State University, contributes to candidates for national office. Douglas Lederman, "Political Action Committees Help Lawmakers Who Help Universities," *Chronicle of Higher Education*, April 18, 1997, A29–A30.
44. For example, when Rep. John Brademas, one of higher education's best allies, lost his seat in the House in 1980, many observers noted that the domain's weak financial support for his reelection may have contributed to his loss. Michael O'Keefe, "Self-Inflicted Laryngitis," *Change* 17 (March/April 1985): 12; Robin Wilson, "Lobbyists and College Presidents Debate Need for Political Action Committee," *Chronicle of Higher Education*, November 11, 1987, A23–A25.
45. O'Keefe, "Self Inflicted Laryngitis," 11.
46. Schlozman and Tierney, *Organized Interests*, 388–389.
47. Thomas L. Gais and Jack L. Walker, "Pathways to Influence in American Politics," in *Mobilizing Interest Groups in America: Patrons, Professions, and Social Movements*, ed. Jack L. Walker (Ann Arbor: University of Michigan Press, 1991), 119.
48. Schlozman and Tierney, *Organized Interests*, 431.
49. Gais and Walker, "Pathways to Influence," 117–119.
50. Ibid.
51. Ibid., 120.
52. Evans, "Lobbying the Committee," 258–259.

6

The Political Firepower of the National Rifle Association

Kelly Patterson

Perhaps no single American interest group is regarded either with greater affection or disdain than the National Rifle Association (NRA). Founded more than a century ago, the NRA in the past three decades has evolved into a high-profile advocate for the rights of gun owners, opposing any attempt to compromise what the group leaders argue is the unrestricted right to bear arms as found in the Second Amendment to the U.S. Constitution. The NRA has been largely successful in its policy goals, despite the fact that public opinion over the period has supported much stricter gun controls.

In this chapter, Kelly Patterson examines the origin, development, and activities of the group from an organizational perspective. Over the past thirty years, the NRA has gone through a metamorphosis from mainly an organization for sportspersons into a comprehensive political organization, with a cadre of Washington lobbyists, a well funded PAC, a legal foundation, and grassroots political connections in every congressional district. The NRA is currently one of the largest membership groups in Washington, with a staff of 300, nearly three million members, and an annual budget of nearly $90 million.

Despite the success and size of the NRA, the evolution of the group has been stressful. Membership fluctuations have caused financial hardship, and the organization has been beset with factional difficulties because it must satisfy two types of members: the Second Amendment fundamentalists who resist any attempt to regulate firearms or ammunition and the shooters who join for sporting and shooting activities. The latter do not see some restrictions on the "right to bear arms" as unreasonable. The challenge for the NRA, according to Patterson, "will be to maintain its

The author would like to thank those who assisted with this chapter, including Tanya Metaksa, executive director of the NRA's Institute for Legislative Action, for her interview; Bernie Hoerr, director of the membership programs in the membership division of the NRA, for providing membership data; Edward J. Land, Jr., secretary of the NRA, for providing information about NRA charters; research assistants Carter Swift and Elizabeth Pipkin for their diligent work; and the Brigham Young University College of Family, Home, and Social Sciences for providing the resources that made this research possible.

commitment to a goal that generates enthusiasm (and contributions) from among its members while not alienating the moderate
elements that enlarge its membership base."

Single-interest groups capable of promoting one issue over a variety of
issues have become a prominent fixture in American politics. These
groups condense the emotional aspects of a given issue and vividly connect that issue to the life of the individual.[1] For a variety of reasons, the
number of these groups has increased dramatically in America, and the
effects of their proliferation can be seen throughout American politics.[2]
However, few single-interest groups have enjoyed the success and noto-
riety of the National Rifle Association (NRA).

The NRA defines what it means to be a condensational interest
group. Its stated goal and national reputation revolve around its ability to
promote and protect the rights of gun owners. Its ability to focus on the
achievement of its goal seems to be the envy of other interest groups.
Very few single-interest groups are as large, complex, and powerful as the
NRA. The magnitude of its operation, the size of its budget, and the intensity of its ideological commitment make the NRA a formidable force.
It participates in more than 10,000 campaigns in any given electoral cycle
and raises millions of dollars to disburse to candidates who are committed
to the goals of the organization.

Normally success does not come without a price. Organizations that
grow rapidly and win political battles become difficult to manage and create bitter enemies. The NRA is no exception. In the past decade the
NRA has suffered attacks from presidents (Republican and Democrat),
struggled through financial difficulties, and waged internecine battles
that have fractured the organization. How has the NRA come to this
point? Are these difficulties inevitable in any single-interest group that
grows to the size and prominence of the NRA? In this chapter I look at
the history and development of the NRA. I focus on the organization's
leadership, growth in membership, and campaign activities. I begin with
a brief discussion of its colorful history and the rise of its organization and
influence. In the next section I look at why individuals join the NRA and
the benefits that it provides to its members. I argue that a combination of
environmental and organizational factors led to the explosive growth in
membership. I analyze the organizational difficulties and controversies
currently swirling around the NRA and connect them to the decline in
membership. Finally, I examine the NRA's participation in numerous
campaign activities. Although the NRA can easily be characterized as a
single-interest group, it cannot avoid contradictions and controversies.
The NRA, like most large enterprises, faces numerous tradeoffs as it expends resources in pursuit of multiple, often conflicting, goals contained
in its charter.

History and Purpose

David Truman theorized that groups form to meet the needs of individuals in an increasingly complex society. This "disturbance" theory contends that groups form in response to changes in society and the economy.[3] Disturbances, such as war, recessions, or depressions, stimulate the creation of groups whose purpose is to restore the balance in society. In the wake of the Civil War, Union officers sought to find a remedy for the poor marksmanship and rifle skills exhibited by the Union throughout the conflict. The original charter of the NRA stated that, "The object for which [this organization] is formed is the improvement of its members in marksmanship, and to promote the introduction of the system of accuracy drill and rifle practice as part of the military drill of the National Guard of this and other states, and for those purposes to provide a suitable range or ranges in the vicinity of the City of New York."[4] Through proper training and facilities the NRA hoped to avert another poor performance by Union soldiers in the event of a future conflict.

The organization grew slowly until passage of the Militia Act of 1903. This act authorized creation of a National Board for the Promotion of Rifle Practice. One of the first acts of the board was the sale of surplus weapons and ammunition to rifle clubs around the United States. The sale of these weapons created potential members who could sustain the organization and help to fuel its growth.[5] Through the first half of this century the NRA grew modestly. It had no more than 300,000 members in the 1950s and was concerned primarily with serving the sporting needs of its members that it identified in the original charter.[6]

Although Truman's theory may explain the origin of groups, it fails to account for how groups evolve over time, prosper, or fail altogether. Robert Salisbury posited that groups prosper if the leadership makes a "profit" and provides a proper mix of incentives to its members.[7] Over time, the NRA built on the mandate in the original charter. Where it once provided only a range of "material" incentives to its members (access to ranges, gun training, etc.), the NRA gradually began to play an active role in efforts by the federal government to regulate firearms. In the 1930s Congress passed three main gun control acts. The Uniform Firearms Act of 1930 forbade the delivery of pistols to "convicts, drug addicts, habitual drunkards, incompetents, and minors under the age of 18." Karl T. Frederick, then president of the NRA, served as a special consultant with the Commission on Uniform State Laws to frame this act. The NRA also supported the National Firearms Act of 1934, which taxed and required registration of such firearms as machine guns, sawed-off rifles, and sawed-off shotguns, although some controversy existed surrounding Congress's definition of a machine gun. Finally, the NRA supported the Federal Firearms Act of 1938, which imposed regulations on interstate and foreign commerce in firearms and pistol ammunition and restricted the use of sawed-off shotguns and machine guns.[8] In all of these attempts at regulation, the NRA worked as an insider without the ideological zeal that characterizes today's organization.

The crucial moment for the organization came in 1968, when, in response to the assassinations of Martin Luther King, Jr., and Robert F. Kennedy, Congress passed the Gun Control Act of 1968. President Lyndon Johnson signed it into law on October 22, 1968, and it took effect on December 16, 1968, as Public Law Number 90-618. Congress combined two bills (H.R. 17735 and S. 3633) to make the law that prohibited unlicensed persons from buying, selling, or otherwise transferring rifles, shotguns, handguns, or ammunition outside of their home state or in any form of interstate commerce. Viewing these regulations as serious infringements on Second Amendment rights, the NRA opposed the act, but as a group of hunters and gun owners interested mainly in sport, it was ill-prepared for the rough-and-tumble world of politics. The NRA had less than a million members at the time and it was unable to prevent passage of the act. Indeed the passage of the act was viewed by many as a slap at the organization. To succeed in the future, the NRA needed to provide "purposive" incentives to its members, and this incentive came to be defined primarily around the constitutional right "to keep and bear arms." Such purposive incentives involve the achievement of ideological goals, and very few groups have been able to replicate the zeal and commitment of the NRA.

The expansion of the incentives offered by the NRA was reflected by changes made to the charter in July of 1977. The certificate of amendment to this charter states that one of the purposes of the NRA is "generally to encourage the lawful ownership and use of small arms by citizens of good repute; and to educate, promote, and further the right of the individual of good repute to keep and bear arms as a common law and constitutional right both of the individual citizen and of the collective militia." The grafting of this additional purpose on to the original goal of educating citizens and promoting firearm safety places the organization in a precarious position. Although the NRA can continue to try and fulfill its original purpose, the addition of a new mission can alter the mix of members in the group, making it easier for conflicts to occur. What happens when the portion of the membership dedicated to hunting and sport disagree with the single-minded pursuit of Second Amendment freedoms? Over the past decade the NRA has faced just such a dilemma.

Membership Has Its Privileges

The NRA is a full-service interest group. It attracts and retains a large and faithful membership through a range of benefits and plans. It services that membership with a gleaming new building in Fairfax, Virginia, and a full-time staff of about 300 individuals. The NRA appeals to two types of gun owners: sportspersons and Second Amendment funda-mentalists.[9] Tanya Metaksa, director of the Institute for Legislative Action (ILA), explained that the NRA changed in the late 1970s from a small, tightly knit group of people who were interested in target shooting and supporting the military to include more diverse interests.[10] In order to entice these various groups of gun owners to join the NRA, the organization offers a range of benefits that can be categorized into three types: material, solidary, and purposive.[11]

Material incentives involve actual goods, such as assistance with work or other financial opportunities. For example, the NRA has culti-vated a relationship with police departments by offering police training sessions that include Police and Security Firearm Training and Law En-forcement Instructor Certification, and as much as $25,000 in life insur-ance to the families of NRA member police officers killed feloniously in the line of duty. It also sponsors and trains shooters going to the Olympics and funds research on the causes of violent crime. It is fair to say that large numbers of individuals are connected to the organization through the kinds of opportunities the NRA makes available to any individual who can make a living working with or studying a firearm. The NRA also offers selective benefits that appeal to all of its members. These benefits include gun loss insurance; accidental death insurance; and car rental, hotel, and airline discounts.

Numerous opportunities exist for members to develop relationships with each other. These solidary incentives can make an otherwise large group seem more like a community, thereby providing the members with a social outlet. For the sportspersons, they offer such activities as safety and training programs and recreational and competitive shooting. Safety and training programs include Comprehensive Hunter Clinics, home firearms safety courses, beginner to advanced training for hunters and shooters, hobbyist and gunsmithing classes for gun collectors and design-ers, and an "Eddie Eagle" Gun Safety Education course for youth. For recreational and competitive shooting, the NRA's Competitions Division sanctions about 12,000 shooting tournaments each year and sponsors nu-merous national shooting championships. These include the Action Pis-tol Championship, Collegiate Shooting Championships, and the National Matches at Camp Perry. The NRA also sponsors the Charlton Heston Celebrity Shoot, the Bianchi Cup, and various other charitable shooting events.

The NRA also provides purposive benefits. A purposive benefit is the ideological satisfaction an individual receives from seeing the accom-plishment of the group's goals. Citizens concerned with Second Amend-ment rights join the NRA because they expect the organization to protect their rights to own guns. In the pursuit of this goal, the organization has attained a reputation for effectiveness and influence matched by few single-interest groups.

The dedication of the organization and its membership to this goal has earned the NRA a rather dubious reputation. Critics characterize the stance of the organization as fanatical and uncompromising. They "resist any gun controls on the fear that it will lead inexorably to confiscation of all guns owned by private citizens."[12] Some contend that the tactics and goals of the NRA have placed it out of step with its rank-and-file membership. Several recent incidents with celebrity members only underscore this tension. Former president George Bush resigned his membership in 1995 when an NRA fund-raising letter referred to federal agents as "jack-booted government thugs."[13] Rep. John Dingell, a long-time member of the NRA, left the NRA board in 1994 to protest some of its policies. And in 1993 Phoenix mayor Skip Rimsza decided not to renew his membership when the NRA actively opposed a city ordinance that keeps minors from carrying guns in public without the consent of their parents.[14] The final blow came in 1995 when Senate majority leader, soon to be presidential candidate, Robert Dole quipped that the association could stand "a little image repair job."[15] The NRA retaliated by refusing to endorse candidate Dole during the 1996 presidential election campaign.

It is the single-minded pursuit of its goal that allows the NRA to withstand a public opinion environment that seems to be hostile toward its all-or-nothing approach. Dependable and long-term trend data about American's preferences for stricter gun control are just not available, but the data that do exist tend to reveal widespread support for some kind of regulation of firearms.[16] The National Opinion Research Center/General Social Survey (NORC/GSS) indicates that since 1972 more than 70 percent of citizens have said that they would favor a law that would require a person to obtain a police permit before he or she could buy a gun.[17] Similar, if not higher, levels of support have been expressed for waiting periods before the purchase of a gun or for laws that would register all guns that are purchased.[18]

With the public increasingly willing to support gun control measures, the aggressive tactics and uncompromising positions of the NRA seem to have eroded its standing in public opinion polls. In 1989, 58 percent of the people asked said that they had a "very favorable" or "mostly favorable" opinion of the NRA. Six years later only 44 percent were willing to say that their opinion was "very favorable" or "mostly favorable" and 45 percent revealed that their opinion was "mostly unfavorable" or "very unfavorable."[19]

Despite its increasingly poor standing in public opinion polls, the NRA has experienced phenomenal growth over the past twenty years. Various theories seek to account for the growth or decline in the membership of interest groups. Some theories emphasize the benefits that members receive for the dues that they pay.[20] If members receive ample material benefits for the dues, then membership figures should remain stable and perhaps even increase. Other theories emphasize the policy environment in which the groups operate. If the policy environment is hostile toward the goals of the organization, then the threats should stimulate a growth in membership.[21] Single-interest groups routinely trumpet, if not exaggerate, the consequences of particular initiatives or policies to make appeals for new membership and to rally the faithful. Finally, some theories emphasize the economics of group membership. Recessions or increases in dues adversely affect membership because of the damage done to a member's or potential member's disposable income. When individuals have money to spend, they can spend it on interest groups; when economic difficulties arrive, such expenditures become hard to justify.

There are three problems that the NRA faces as an ideological organization in relation to membership dues. First, demand for ideological benefits is highly *income-elastic,* meaning that small fluctuations in income will result in large changes in how much individuals want what interest groups provide. If the economy is doing well and people are making more money, then they feel more able to back up their ideological beliefs through membership in ideological organizations. Second, demand for ideological benefits will be very *price-elastic,* meaning the organization will be sensitive to the level of dues. Third, demand for ideological benefits are *sensitive to changes in fashion.* When it is fashionable to belong to the NRA, membership will flourish. When members are viewed as extremists or radical, it becomes unfashionable to belong to the NRA. Under such circumstances, the recruiting and retaining of members becomes difficult.[22]

Which theory best accounts for the fluctuations and growth in the membership of the NRA? Since 1977 membership in the NRA has almost tripled (Figure 6-1). Such growth has occurred despite increases in dues and cutbacks in the benefits offered to members. Before 1977 a one-year membership in the NRA cost $10. Dues have steadily increased to the current level of $35 for a one-year membership (Table 6-1). In 1981 a membership in the NRA fetched a year's subscription to *The American Rifleman,* $300 in firearm insurance, $10,000 accidental death and dismemberment insurance, $300,000 worth of shooter's liability insurance, and an NRA cap.[23] The NRA has altered the benefit package through the years, eventually reducing and finally dropping the shooter's liability insurance (Table 6-2). The group still offers $10,000 in personal accident insurance and the NRA cap, but it has replaced the hunter's liability insurance with $1,000 worth of ArmsCare Firearm Insurance. The NRA modernized its benefit structure and now offers its members an NRA Visa card with no annual fee and a 40-percent discount on interstate moves of household goods. Some NRA officials have attributed the recent decline in membership to the increase in dues. In 1991, acting executive vice president Gary Anderson said "a $5 rise in annual dues to $25 in July of 1989 had a major effect on membership."[24]

Figure 6-1 NRA Membership, 1977–1996

Membership (in thousands)

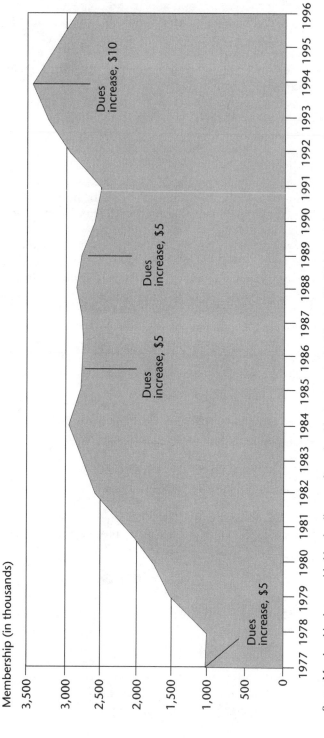

Source: Membership data provided by the director of membership programs in the Membership Division of the NRA, and membership dues in *American Rifle-man* 1977, 1986, 1989, 1994.

Table 6-1   Changes in NRA Membership Dues

Membership	Before 1977	Oct. 31, 1977	April 1, 1986	July 1, 1989	July 1, 1994
One year	$ 10	$ 15	$ 20	$ 25	$ 35
Two years	19	27	a	a	a
Three years	27	40	55	68	90
Five years	42	60	85	100	140
Life	200	300	500	500	750

Source: American Rifleman 1977, 1986, 1989, 1994.

[a] Two-year memberships not available in these years.

Another theory contends that membership fluctuates according to the threats experienced by the group.[25] Current executive vice president Wayne LaPierre claimed that the growth in membership since 1991 can be traced to the hostility of the Clinton administration toward gun owners. LaPierre stated that "people respond when there's a threat. I think Clinton is mobilizing gun owners at record rates."[26] Highly visible and controversial pieces of legislation such as the Brady Bill have the distinct capacity to mobilize members who will most likely view the act as a threat. Some argue that in the wake of its passage, membership in the NRA increased dramatically.[27] There does seem to be some indirect evidence for this position. After the passage of the Gun Control Act of 1968 and the Omnibus Crime Control and Safe Streets Act of 1968, the NRA began its metamorphosis from mainly a sporting organization into a politically motivated giant. The leaders of the organization first looked at the failures of its past and hoped to make up for lost ground in its efforts to reverse components of the congressional acts of the late 1960s. A large percentage of bills presented to Congress during the 1970s dealt with the repeal of different aspects of the Gun Control Act of 1968. From 1977 to 1984 the membership of the NRA steadily increased from 1,059,682 to 2,924,488 (Figure 6-1).[28] During this period of time, around 200 bills were presented to Congress that dealt with the issue of gun control.[29]

The NRA is an organization that relies on people's expectations of certain political benefits. People have a notion of what the benefits provided by the NRA are worth to them. They also have an idea of the likelihood that those benefits will not be provided if they do not cooperate through membership in the organization. When threats occur to gun ownership, individuals begin to discover that they may not receive the benefits provided by the NRA. Individuals who may have been disposed to free-ride are motivated to join the organization. This argument maintains that people's risk attitudes change when the threat becomes too great. Normally risk-averse, people are slow to invest their money in any ideo-

Table 6-2   NRA Membership Benefits, 1981–1997

Year	Benefits
1981	Year subscription to *American Rifleman* or *American Hunter* $300 firearms insurance $10,000 accidental death and dismemberment insurance $300,000 to $1,000,000 shooter's liability insurance NRA cap
1983	Year subscription to *American Rifleman* or *American Hunter* $300 firearms insurance $10,000 accidental death and dismemberment insurance $100,000 shooter's liability insurance NRA cap
1985	Year subscription to *American Rifleman* or *American Hunter* $300 firearms insurance $100,000 hunting liability insurance $10,000 accidental death and dismemberment insurance Pocket pal 3″ lockback knife or NRA cap
1987	Year subscription to *American Rifleman* or *American Hunter* $600 gun theft insurance $10,000 accidental death and dismemberment insurance Discounts for Hertz car rentals NRA window decal NRA cap Sportsman's bonus book with discounts and rebates
1989	Year subscription to *American Rifleman* or *American Hunter* $600 gun theft insurance $10,000 accidental death and dismemberment insurance Discounts for Hertz car rentals NRA window decal NRA cap
1991	Year subscription to *American Rifleman* or *American Hunter* $600 gun theft insurance $10,000 accidental death and dismemberment insurance Law enforcement insurance benefits for officers NRA window decal NRA cap
1997	Year subscription to *American Rifleman* or *American Hunter* $10,000 in personal accident insurance $1,000 in ArmsCare firearm insurance A no-annual-fee NRA VISA card 40% discount on interstate moves of household goods NRA window decal NRA cap

Source: American Rifleman 1981, 1983, 1985, 1987, 1989, 1991, 1997.

logical organization such as the NRA. Faced with such large potential risks as the regulation of firearms, people become risk-seeking.[30] Threats increase awareness of the collective benefits of group membership. Political benefits that avoid losses are considered more important than political benefits that promise gains. From this perspective, leaders of ideological interest groups tend to emphasize threats over prospects in their campaigns for membership.[31]

During the years 1984 to 1991 growth in membership stagnated and hovered near the 2,700,000 mark, reaching a low of 2,516,908 in 1991 (Figure 6-1). During these same years approximately one hundred bills were presented to each Congress. Most of these bills seemed to deal with attempts to repeal various aspects of gun control legislation that had been enacted in the past. The focus of Congress and of the country no longer seemed to revolve around gun control issues. The lack of some external threat, shown by the decline in the number of bills seeking to regulate firearms and the presence of a Republican in the White House, probably contributed to the stall in membership growth.

Beginning with the Brady Bill in 1990 the number of gun control bills before Congress began to increase. Gun control once again became a hot topic in Washington and around the nation. With this increase in gun control bills and the election of a pro–gun control president in 1992, the membership of the NRA soared. Increasing from its low of 2,516,908 in 1991, membership reached 3,454,430 in 1994 (Figure 6-1). The NRA also began to more actively campaign against certain pieces of legislation in its monthly magazines, the *American Rifleman* and the *American Hunter*. The NRA's political renaissance during the period leading up to the congressional elections of 1994 convinced old members to renew their memberships and attracted new members to the organization.

In the 1994 congressional races, 138 of 186 candidates endorsed by the NRA won their elections.[32] This success seemed to affect the membership of the NRA, giving off the impression that the battle had been won and membership was no longer crucial. The Republicans became the majority party in both chambers of Congress and were certainly poised to lead the fight against a pro–gun control White House. After the 1994 elections, membership dropped from 3,454,430 to 2,843,637. This loss of members for the NRA was most likely magnified by the $10 increase in the one-year membership dues.

These fluctuations in membership seriously affect the budget of the NRA because the largest source of revenue is membership dues. The NRA gains its revenues from five main sources: membership dues (55 percent), contributions (15 percent), advertising in its magazines (9 percent), interest and dividends (9 percent), and other sources (13 percent).[33] Despite the drop in membership, the budget of the NRA increased from $50 million in 1990 to $86.9 million in 1996, the last year for which figures are available.[34]

So although unfavorable pieces of legislation and attacks on the group provide the grist for membership drives, groups must have the financial resources to package the threats to potential members and to alert current members that renewal is critical. The NRA must print the materials and mail the kits to prospective members, and such membership drives, even in the face of threats from external sources, are not cheap. Over the past few years the NRA has invested heavily in membership drives. Only about 25 percent of memberships are renewed, and renewals for new members are running at less than 20 percent. According to former NRA leaders and outside analysts, it costs the group an average of $46 to recruit a new member.[35] The NRA also attracts members through brief promotions with certain manufacturers of hunting and shooting equipment. The NRA had such a relationship with Leupold Inc., which sells rifle scopes and binoculars. For a limited time before March 31, 1993, Leupold offered a free one-year membership with the purchase of a Leupold product. Five thousand one-year NRA memberships were renewed or begun through this promotion.[36]

Membership drives, clout in state and national legislatures, and educational activities cost money. Some individuals contend that the large amounts of money invested in political activities mortgaged the future of the organization. In 1991 the NRA ran a deficit of $9 million. The deficit more than tripled to $30 million in 1992.[37] Seeking to erase the deficits, the group initiated a vigorous fund-raising campaign in 1993. LaPierre headed this campaign, which consisted of surveying members and using the results to raise dues. These internal NRA polls found that 93 percent of the members wanted the NRA to spend money on efforts to defeat gun bans in Congress and to keep guns and ammunition from being taxed and regulated out of existence. The surveys also found that 99.8 percent of membership felt that the Second Amendment was facing its worst threat ever. The survey showed that 99.2 percent of membership felt that increased radio and television advertising was needed and, astonishingly, that 96.1 percent of the membership agreed with the need to increase dues.[38] These efforts ultimately helped the NRA to continue its vigorous and generous support of candidates who believed in the aims of the organization.

It is ironic that Republicans winning control of the House of Representatives in 1994 negatively affected fund-raising and only compounded the groups' financial difficulties. NRA members generally had the feeling that they had won the elections. Metaksa stated that when people think they have won, they do not need to do any more. She has argued that losing is better to preserve the vitality of issue advocacy.[39] The financial problems were compounded once again by slowdowns in fund-raising efforts in 1995. The organization did not raise money as vigorously in 1995 as it did in 1993. It concentrated instead on raising money for special events such as a Second Amendment symposium and hearings into the confrontation between federal officers and members of a cult in Waco, Texas, in 1993. It also raised money in 1995 for right-to-carry legislation in state legislatures.[40] From the standpoint of the organization's leadership, these may be worthy causes, but their capacity to rally the membership to make contributions or motivate nonmembers to join do not generate the same sense of urgency as the actual threat of gun control legislation or a vocal anti-gun president.

Finally, the electoral victories in 1994 also seemed to have spawned competing activities within the organization for which funds needed to be raised. Members can give to fund programs, the PAC, or both. There do seem to be some financial problems, and the NRA has made efforts to curb its losses. In August it announced that it was eliminating about forty positions from staff at its national headquarters. The positions affected mainly "hunter service programs and other general operating programs."[41] The financial problems of the NRA have put pressure on the organization to evaluate its goals and activities, and it seems torn between those who want to spend more money on campaign activities and those who want it to serve the hunting and sporting interests of its members.[42]

The tension between various goals has resulted in the creation of competing organizations designed specifically to fulfill simply one goal related to gun ownership. For example, the Second Amendment Foundation, founded in 1974, provides a legal defense for gun owners. The organization was formed to provide members with a tax-deductible way to support Second Amendment freedoms. The Second Amendment Foundation has endured membership fluctuations similar to those of the NRA. In 1975, the year after its formation, the foundation could boast only 10,000 members. However, in the following year the group heavily emphasized membership recruitment, and its rolls swelled to more than 150,000. Most of the members were recruited through direct mail, a strategy that resulted in a huge budget deficit. With 550,000 current members, membership has grown steadily since 1975. The organization gained 75,000 members during the Brady Bill years and during President Clinton's push for gun control legislation.[43] Although it is not in direct competition with the NRA, the Second Amendment Foundation attracts many lower income gun-ownership advocates because of its lower membership fee. Membership in the Second Amendment Foundation costs $15 a year compared to $35 for the NRA. Furthermore, the operation budget of the Foundation is not nearly as large as the NRA's: $3,400,000 compared to $86,9000,000.[44] Approximately 40 percent of the foundation's members also belong to the NRA, and the two organizations jointly sponsor an annual Gun Rights Policy Conference.[45]

The same political threats, such as the Brady Bill and President Clinton's gun control campaign, that stimulate growth in the NRA's membership also mobilize organizations, such as Handgun Control, Inc., which represents the opposing view. Founded in 1974, Handgun Control, Inc.

(HCI) has become the nation's largest gun control lobbying organization. HCI works to enact stronger gun control legislation at the federal, state, and local level, mobilizes activists and allied organizations around gun control issues, and educates voters about candidates' positions on gun control. HCI experienced growth similar to the NRA and the Second Amendment Foundation during the Brady Bill years. Sarah Brady, wife of former White House press secretary James Brady, who was shot during an assassination attempt on President Ronald Reagan in 1981, joined HCI in 1985 and now serves as chair of the organization. Increasing from 240,000 members in 1988 to 400,000 members in 1993, Handgun Control, Inc., has been very conscious of the cost of membership increases. During the late 1980s up until 1991, HCI recruited heavily and felt the costs of doing so. With a budget of $8,306,000 in 1991, the organization decided to put less emphasis on recruiting in order to cut costs and reduced its operating budget to $5,120,000 in 1992.[46]

Organization: Problems and Possibilities

The organizational structure of interest groups can be categorized from the simple and centralized to the complex and federated.[47] The type of structure determines everything from the length of time it takes the organization to make a decision to the kind of input enjoyed by rank-and-file membership. Organizations that allow for input from rank-and-file members are more susceptible to challenges from members and key constituencies within the group. Finally, groups with a more complex decision-making structure generally receive more communications from rank-and-file members and actually solicit the expression of opinions.[48] Although the NRA is often criticized for responding to the more radical elements of its members, it is the decision-making structure that makes such challenges to the leadership possible, a point underscored when executive vice president Wayne LaPierre survived a challenge from Neal Knox at the 1997 annual convention.

The origins of this conflict can be traced to the 1977 NRA annual convention in Cincinnati, Ohio, where Knox first raised his voice in support of a stronger and more politically active NRA. Soon after Knox was appointed by then-NRA president Harold Carter to be the executive director of the NRA's Institute for Legislative Action. From 1978 to 1982 Knox built around himself a coalition of politically active hardliners who saw the future of the organization in promotion of Second Amendment rights through the NRA's influence in Washington, D.C. Fired in 1982 for lobbying efforts that conflicted with NRA policies, Knox remained actively involved with the organization. During the early 1990s Knox often published advertisements in the *American Rifleman* encouraging members to vote for certain board members and waged a war against the leadership of the NRA in *Guns & Ammo* and *Rifle* magazines. Knox returned to the

NRA in 1995 as the second vice president, after being elected by the same board members whom he had previously supported. Continuing to stress political activism, he was soon nominated to the position of first vice president in 1996.

Prior to the 1997 NRA annual convention, Knox was faced with a choice. Obviously dissatisfied with the ideological focus of the organization, Knox had to decide between voicing his dissatisfaction or exiting the organization completely. Knox became convinced that voicing his dissatisfaction would be a more effective strategy because he thought he would be elected executive vice president, thereby postponing the need to quit the NRA. And once he left, he realized, he would lose his forum. Leaving, therefore, was used as a last resort.[49]

Knox's sudden rise to power was possible through his control of the board of directors. Because the number of members who actually participate in the nomination of the directors is normally fewer than 5 percent, he was able to orchestrate the nominations of new directors and control the vote of board members whom he had helped to elect. He headed into the 1997 NRA annual convention stressing the defeat of President Clinton and the protection of the anti–gun control Congress.[50] Appealing to the hardliners in the organization, Knox attempted to overthrow executive vice president LaPierre. Knox was not only unable to overthrow LaPierre, but he also lost his own post as first vice president. Members who supported a more "family oriented" NRA joined together to reelect LaPierre and elect the actor, Charlton Heston, who had been a vocal and visible spokesperson for the NRA for years, as first vice president. Heston was elected to be the seventy-sixth member of the board of directors at the meeting and was soon after elected to his new position. Supporters of LaPierre and Heston hoped that the elections would finally put to rest the fanatical Knox, silence the rumors of an organization disabled with divisions, and wipe away the unhealthy image mainstream Americans seemed to have of the NRA.[51]

The NRA is governed by a board of directors that consists of seventy-five NRA members who are elected by mail ballot by the membership of the association, each of whom is entitled to vote, and one member elected at the annual meeting of the members. The right to hold the office of director is limited to NRA lifetime members who have attained an age of eighteen years and are citizens of the United States. Directors are elected for a term of three years, with the exception of the director elected at the annual meeting of members, who serves for a one-year term. The terms of office of one-third of the board expire each year.[52]

Members of the board are nominated from the general membership either by recommendations to the nominating committee, which selects members for the mail ballot, or by petition of at least 250 members. The director chosen at the annual meeting of members will come from the pool of members nominated but not elected.

Members of the executive committee are first elected as directors and are then elected by the seventy-six-member board of directors to serve on the executive committee. Over the years, the structure of the executive committee has changed slightly. In 1979, the office of second vice president was added. Other lower management positions on the executive committee have been added or changed over the years. These individuals oversee a complex system of thirty-six standing and special committees that work on matters of interest to the NRA membership.

Part of the success of the NRA can be attributed to the stability in major leadership positions. The NRA is a multimillion dollar enterprise with operations throughout the United States. It is not easy to find talented individuals who are capable of managing such far-flung enterprises. The executive vice president is the most powerful office in the organization because it oversees the day-to-day operations of the NRA. There have only been five individuals to serve in this position during the past twenty years, and two of those served for only one year.[53] This post is currently held by LaPierre, who has held the office since 1992. Before that time he served for six years as executive director of the Institute for Legislative Action (ILA), the political action committee and lobbying wing of the NRA. This pattern of upward movement within the leadership is certainly not uncommon. Gary L. Anderson served as executive director of operations before moving into the office of executive vice president. J. Warren Cassidy, like LaPierre, served as executive director of the ILA before becoming executive vice president.

The NRA is a national organization with affiliates and club members. Members have influence on the organization and the candidates it supports through a variety of means. Leaders encourage members to write, e-mail, and fax their opinions to the national office.

The leadership of the NRA feels a particular need to listen to the members because so much of the money that goes to the candidates and sustains the organization comes from the dues the members pay. Therefore, the national office solicits advice about which candidates to support, takes public opinion polls of the membership, and tries to keep members informed about campaign activities. The willingness of an organization to listen to its members contributes to the organization's well being; members will be less likely to continue to contribute to organizations that are not responsive.[54]

The interaction between the leaders and the members also enhances the NRA's effectiveness. When candidates for office know that the national organization listens to the rank-and-file members, the candidates become more responsive to members in their state or district. For this reason, the Institute for Legislative Action, its lobbying organization, oversees the Political Victory Fund (PVF), its political action committee.[55] When the NRA talks to an elected official about a particular policy, it wants this individual to understand that the members in the district or state can influence his or her electoral fortunes.[56] The NRA uses this strategy of combining lobbying and campaign activities at both the state and federal levels.

Representation and Political Influence

NRA electoral support goes only to those candidates who support the NRA objective: to staunchly defend the Second Amendment. Who is deemed faithful to this objective depends in part on the assessment of the local members. The NRA recruits election volunteer coordinators who assess the candidates in each congressional district and pass along their findings to the national office. Members are also free to lobby the national office on behalf of particular candidates. Disagreements between the national office and the rank-and-file members sometimes arise over who should receive electoral support. However, because most of the money that the NRA gives to candidates comes from solicitation of its members through the mail, the organization tolerates these disagreements.

Giving money to candidates is only one way in which the NRA gets involved in campaigns. The NRA has developed five distinct levels of involvement.[57] First, it grades candidates and publishes those grades in *The American Rifleman*, a magazine that all NRA members receive. Candidates for Congress can receive grades ranging from an "A" to an "F." Those candidates who most actively help the NRA to achieve its goals receive an "A." Individuals who actively oppose the NRA receive an "F." The important dimension of the grade is activity. Candidates who lead the charge for NRA principles receive the higher grades. Those individuals openly opposed get failing grades. Some candidates vote for the positions of the NRA but do not lead on the issues. These are the candidates who receive the "average" grades. An example of an average grade is the C+ grade received by California state senate candidate Joe Dolphin. Despite his membership in the NRA, Dolphin stated that a C+ accurately reflected his views: "I'm not an extremist in either direction."[58]

Endorsement of a candidate is the second level of involvement. Endorsements appear in the *American Rifleman*'s election guide. Only faithful allies of the NRA receive its endorsement. An endorsement is better than a good grade because of the signal that it sends to local members. Long-time friends of the NRA receive the endorsements from the national organization, even when local members may vehemently oppose it. The national organization believes that loyalty should be rewarded, even if the incumbent or candidate may not be popular in the local areas.

The next three levels of involvement pertain to material support. At the third level, the NRA gives a campaign contribution to the candidate. Some PACs give only to incumbents hoping to gain access after the election. Other PACs carefully target their donations seeking to turn the tide in a close race.[59] The NRA's wealth means it can do both. It contributes to loyal incumbents who have long fought the organization's battles, and it targets its contributions to those close races in which a contribution can make a difference. However, the NRA does not just throw money at candidates. It rarely gives the full legal amount to any candidate and it only gives to those candidates who ask.[60] At the fourth level, the NRA uses in-kind contributions, such as fund-raising and meet-and-greet events, to help the candidate. The national office involves local members in many of these functions to drive home the point that the candidate should be aware of the NRA rank-and-file members. Finally, the NRA uses independent expenditures to help its candidates. These kinds of expenditures run the gamut from radio and television ads to telephone banks and can be quite substantial. In 1994, the NRA spent more than any other single-interest PAC; its independent expenditures bankrolled more than a quarter of all such expenditures.[61] Once again, many of these independent expenditures rely on the work of the local members. In the *American Rifleman*, Tanya Metaksa urged local members to help local candidates in the 1996 election by "making the phone calls, stuffing the envelopes, canvassing the neighborhoods."[62] Using the local members at these various levels of involvement maximizes the effectiveness of the NRA. It harnesses the members' ideological zeal and translates it into a language candidates for any office can understand: campaign resources.

From 1977 to 1994, the NRA spent more than $14.6 million in elections to support or oppose presidential and congressional candidates. Over this time, the NRA preferred to give to Republican candidates, a preference that has deepened over the years (Figure 6-2). Expenditures and contributions on behalf of Republican candidates totaled more than $9 million, whereas Democrats received slightly more than $3.1 million. The total amount spent by the NRA gradually expanded from $383,690 in 1978 to more than $3,100,000 in 1994 (Tables 6-3 and 6-4). The NRA claims some impressive results for its efforts; 84 percent of its candidates won in 1996.

The 1996 presidential campaign stands out as a glaring failure among all the success. The NRA had two candidates for whom it had little or no enthusiasm. In an *American Rifleman* article titled "Bill Clinton Must Be Voted Out," Metaksa stated that if Clinton won another term in office, his "anti-gun cronies" would "add up to a gun owner's worst nightmare."[63] An NRA board of directors resolution urged "in the strongest terms that the members of the Association [NRA] use their collective power of the vote to remove Mr. Clinton from office."[64] Oddly enough, urging members to use the power of the vote did not translate into an endorsement of Senator Dole. The NRA believed that Dole had not been as faithful of a supporter as he could have been. Some cited Dole's decision to delay efforts to repeal the ban on assault weapons. Metaksa affirmed that an endorsement is "based on principle."[65] The failure of

Figure 6-2 NRA Political Contributions, 1978–1996

Dollar contributions

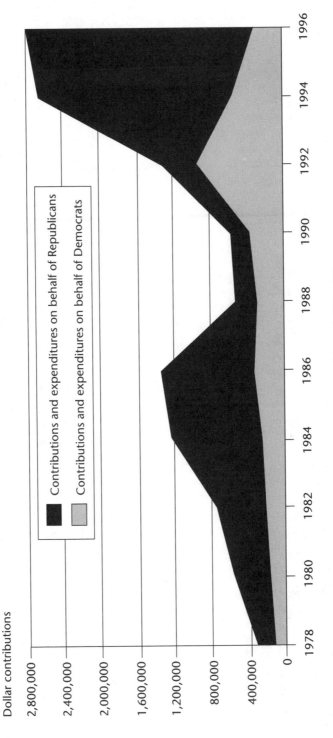

Source: Federal Elections Commission, *Committee Index of Candidates Supported/Opposed, 1978–1996.*

Table 6-3 NRA Contributions and Expenditures on Behalf of Republicans

	1978	1980	1982	1984	1986	1988	1990	1992	1994	1996
Contributions	$272,035	$336,035	$540,207	$ 500,215	$ 643,740	$488,487	$456,285	$1,098,354	$1,442,519	$1,288,371
Expenditures	15,745	201,190	193,761	721,287	693,030	4,370	81,222	202,969	1,205,189	1,537,580
Total	287,780	537,225	733,968	1,221,502	1,336,770	492,857	537,507	1,301,323	2,647,708	2,825,951

Source: Federal Election Commission, *Committee Index of Candidates Supported/Opposed 1978–1996.*

Table 6-4 NRA Contributions and Expenditures on Behalf of Democrats

	1978	1980	1982	1984	1986	1988	1990	1992	1994	1996
Contributions	$93,626	$ 98,268	$170,695	$200,109	$254,824	$284,269	$293,208	$632,642	$410,519	$262,600
Expenditures	2,284	63,796	38,589	49,442	60,790	0	61,898	329,861	152,626	44,572
Total	95,910	162,064	209,284	249,551	315,614	284,269	355,106	962,503	563,145	307,172

Source: Federal Election Commission, *Committee Index of Candidates Supported/Opposed 1978–1996.*

Senator Dole to support actively the agenda of the group placed him, however slightly, at odds with its principles. Therefore, it widely and publicly declared its intentions not to endorse him.

The actions of the NRA in this election serve as an example of how far some single-interest groups will go to preserve their ideological purity. The NRA clearly detested President Clinton and did everything it could to defeat him. At the same time, it was less than enthusiastic about Senator Dole. Rather than compromise on its principles, the NRA worked to defeat President Clinton but did not fully rally the faithful for Senator Dole. This compromise preserved the principles of the organization—not supporting any candidate that did not enthusiastically protect the Second Amendment—but produced what members perceived as a less than optimal electoral outcome.

Conclusion

The National Rifle Association is clearly one of the most powerful single-interest groups in the United States. Its influence is the result of a sustained and deliberate attempt to attract and retain a large and enthusiastic membership base. The NRA offers a variety of incentives to individuals and expends large sums of money to recruit new members and satisfy current members. These incentives range from social benefits consumed mainly by sportspersons to ideological satisfaction enjoyed largely by hard-core proponents of Second Amendment liberties.

However, the large membership and perceived power of the group do not mean that all is well within the NRA. Most complex organizations face tradeoffs as they seek to allocate resources among the various goals. In the case of the NRA, it must satisfy two distinct types of members: those who resist any attempt to regulate firearms or ammunition and those who join for the sporting and shooting activities. The latter are much less politicized and do not see some restrictions on the "right to bear arms" as unreasonable.

These two groups often contend for the heart and soul of the organization. The insurgency led by Neal Knox reflects the strength of the ideological elements of the membership, and the election of Charlton Heston to the board of directors indicates that the moderate elements have not completely disappeared—and even have some significant staying power. Such a tension will continue to exist so long as the NRA instantiates these two goals within its charter and so long as the federated structure of the organization allows all members access to the decision-making processes in the national office.

Finally, single-interest groups can fall prey to their own success. Membership and fund-raising declined in the wake of the Republican revolution in 1994. The NRA will have to maintain its commitment to a goal that generates enthusiasm (and contributions) from among its members while not alienating the moderate elements that enlarge its membership base in order to remain a vibrant and influential organization.

Notes

1. Hershey refers to these kinds of groups as *condensational.* She contrasts their tactics to groups she labels *referential.* Condensational groups symbolize the issue differently than referential groups. In the former case, the groups personalize the issues to enhance their emotional impact. In the latter case, groups speak of the objective elements of the issue, appealing more to reason than to emotions. Marjorie Randon Hershey, "Direct Action and the Abortion Issue: The Political Participation of Single-Issue Groups," in *Interest Group Politics,* 2d ed., ed. Allan J. Cigler and Burdett A. Loomis (Washington, D.C.: CQ Press, 1986).
2. For a discussion of the reasons for the growth in the number of interest groups, see Jeffrey M. Berry, 1993, "Citizen Groups and the Changing Nature of Interest Group Politics." *The Annals of American Academy* 528 (July 1993): 30–41.
3. David Truman, *The Governmental Process,* 2d ed. (New York: Alfred A. Knopf, 1971).
4. *Original Charter of the National Rifle Association,* 1871.
5. This also seems to be an example of what Graham K. Wilson refers to as encouragement of the growth of interest groups by their proximity to institutions such as political parties and the state. Wilson has argued that the NRA is an example of a group that exists because of early policies by the government that gave it a boost. Graham K. Wilson, *Interest Groups* (Oxford: Basil Blackwell, 1990). A similar argument is made by Burdett A. Loomis and Allan J. Cigler, "The Changing Nature of Interest Group Politics," in *Interest Group Politics,* ed. Allan J. Cigler and Burdett A. Loomis (Washington, D.C.: CQ Press, 1986).
6. For an excellent discussion of the history of the NRA, see Robert Spitzer's book, *The Politics of Gun Control* (Chatham, N.J.: Chatham House, 1995), 99–115.
7. Robert H. Salisbury, "An Exchange Theory of Interest Groups, *Midwest Journal of Political Science* 13 (February 1969): 1–32.
8. Alan C. Webber, "Where the NRA Stands on Gun Legislation," *American Rifleman* (March): 22–23.
9. David Brock, "Wayne's World; In May the NRA Will Decide Whether It Wants to Be a Modern Political Organization or an "Extremist" Group Sprung from a Liberal's Worst Nightmare," *American Spectator* (May 1997): 38.
10. Quoted in Charles Madigan and David Jackson, "NRA in the Cross Hairs: Lobby Battles Foes, Itself," *Chicago Tribune,* August 3, 1995, N1.
11. Peter B. Clark and James Q. Wilson, "Incentive Systems: A Theory of Organizations," *Administrative Science Quarterly* 6 (September): 129–166.
12. Brock, "Wayne's World," 38.
13. Scott Shepard, "National Convention; NRA's Message: 'The Gun Lobby Is People,' " *Atlanta Constitution,* May 19, 1995, 12A.
14. Ibid.
15. Peter Stone, "The NRA's Been Shaken, Too," *National Journal* 27 (1995): 1133.
16. John T. Young, David Hemenway, Robert J. Blendon, and John M. Benson, "Trends: Guns," *Public Opinion Quarterly* 60 (Winter): 634–649.
17. Ibid., 643.
18. Ibid., 642.
19. Ibid., 648.
20. Salisbury, "An Exchange Theory of Interest Groups."
21. Truman, *The Governmental Process.*

22. John Mark Hansen, "Political Economy of Group Membership," *American Political Science Review* 79 (March 1985): 79–96.
23. The Shooter's Liability insurance started at $300,000 and was set to increase $100,000 for each year of membership. The insurance was capped at $1,000,000.
24. Steven Holmes, "Rifle Lobby Torn by Dissidents and Capitol Defectors," *New York Times*, March 27, 1991, A20.
25. Truman, *The Governmental Process*.
26. Peter Stone, "Showing Holes: The Once-Mighty NRA Is Wounded, but Still Dangerous, *Mother Jones* 19 (1994): 39.
27. Charles Mahtesian, "Firepower," *Governing Magazine* 8 (1995): 16.
28. The membership figures were provided by Bernie Hoerr, director of Membership Programs in the Membership Division of the NRA.
29. I determined the number of bills relating to gun control by using the *Thomas Bill Summaries and Status, Previous Congresses, Index*. The *Index* includes a brief discussion of the subject of the bill, the bill number, and its sponsor. Any bill listed that mentioned any issue relating to the regulation or deregulation of firearms was included in this analysis.
30. Hansen, "Political Ecology of Group Membership," 81.
31. Ibid.
32. Micheal McBurnett, Christopher Kenny, and David J. Bordua, "The Impact of Political Interests in the 1994 Elections: The Role of the National Rifle Association" (Paper delivered at the 1996 annual meeting of the Midwest Political Science Association, Chicago, Illinois).
33. J. Warren Cassidy, "Here We Stand," *American Rifleman* (January 1991): 7.
34. Foundation for Public Affairs, *Public Interest Profiles, 1996–1997* (Washington, D.C.: CQ Press, 1996).
35. Peter Stone, "From the K Street Corridor," *National Journal* 27 (1995): 1774.
36. William F. Parkerson III, ed., "Leupold Advertisement," *American Rifleman* (January 1993): 14–15.
37. Stone, "Showing Holes," 39.
38. Wayne R. LaPierre, "NRA Members Overwhelmingly Support 'Fighting Back,' " *American Rifleman* (May 1994): 50–51.
39. Tanya Metaksa, executive director of the NRA's Institute for Legislative Action, interview by the author, July 18, 1996.
40. Ibid.
41. Stone, "From the K Street Corridor."
42. Katharine Q. Seelye, "An Ailing Gun Lobby Faces a Bitter Struggle for Power," *New York Times*, January 30, 1997, A1.
43. Allan Gottlieb, chair of the Citizen's Committee for the Right to Bear Arms and founder of the Second Amendment Foundation, interview by Carter Swift, November 24, 1997.
44. Christine Maurer and Tara E. Sheets, eds., *Encyclopedia of Associations*, vol. 1, pt. 3 (Detroit, Mich.: Gale Research, 1998).
45. Gottlieb, personal interview.
46. Budget and membership information was obtained from employees within the organization. Information was only available for the years 1988–1993.
47. Philip A. Mundo, *Interest Groups: Cases and Characteristics* (Chicago: Nelson-Hall, 1992).
48. Ibid.
49. Albert O. Hirschman, *Exit, Voice, and Loyalty* (Cambridge, Mass.: Harvard University Press, 1970).
50. Robert Dreyfuss, "Good Morning, Gun Lobby," *Mother Jones* (July/August 1996): 38–47.
51. Seelye, "An Ailing Gun Lobby Faces a Bitter Struggle for Power."

52. E. G. Bell, Jr., ed., "Exercise Your Rights: Assist in the Nomination of Directors," *American Rifleman* (July 1995): 56–57.

53. Harlon B. Carter served from 1977 to 1984, G. Ray Arnett in 1985, J. Warren Cassidy from 1986 to 1990, Gary L. Anderson in 1991, and Wayne LaPierre has served from 1992.

54. Anthony Nownes and Allan J. Cigler, "Public Interest Groups and the Road to Survival," *Polity* 27: 379–404.

55. Kelly Patterson, "Political Firepower: The National Rifle Association," in *After the Revolution: PACs and Lobbies in the Republican Congress*, ed. Robert Biersack, Paul Herrnson, and Clyde Wilcox (Boston: Allyn and Bacon, 1998).

56. Metaksa interview.

57. For a full discussion of how the NRA makes its decisions to allocate these resources see Patterson, "Political Firepower."

58. Gerry Braun, "Alpert Taking Tougher Stance," *San Diego Union-Tribune*, October 30, 1996, B1.

59. Paul S. Herrnson, *Congressional Elections: Campaigning at Home and in Washington* (Washington, D.C.: CQ Press, 1995), 109–110.

60. Metaksa interview.

61. National Public Radio, "Morning Edition," October 8, 1996.

62. Tanya Metaksa, "Memorandum: Election of Pro-Gun Candidates," *American Rifleman* 144 (September 1996): 33.

63. Tanya Metaksa, "Bill Clinton Must be Voted Out," *American Rifleman* 144 (November/December 1996): 36.

64. NRA Board of Directors, "Resolution Enumerating Reasons Why Bill Clinton Should Be Voted out of Office," *American Rifleman* 144 (November/December 1996): 37.

65. Metaksa interview.

II. ORGANIZED GROUPS
AND ELECTIONS

7

Parties and Interest Groups in Postreform Congressional Elections

Paul S. Herrnson

From the late nineteenth century until the 1940s, local political parties dominated the politics of the electoral process and organized interests played a secondary role. In the following decades the declining role of local parties and the increasing importance of technological innovations in campaigning led to an electoral system focused on candidates and their immediate organizations. In the new candidate-centered system, the needs of those seeking office, especially for money, created an opportunity for organized interests to increase their involvement in federal elections.

In this provocative chapter, Paul Herrnson argues that the "near collapse" of the regulatory regime governing federal campaign finance, which became obvious during the 1996 elections, has led to a new postreform era for parties and interest groups in electoral politics. Fund-raising by both parties and interest groups is at record levels, and the overlap of activities between both sets of organizations has increased. The creative use of soft money in elections is one defining characteristic of this new era, as is the impact of party and independent interest group efforts on the candidate-centered system. In 1996 party and group spending actually outpaced candidate spending in a number of close races.

In Herrnson's view, the postreform era has the potential "to drastically alter the dynamics of congressional election politics." He is not optimistic that any major reforms in campaign finance and the conduct of campaigns will take place in the near future.

Parties and interest groups carried out a number of new activities during the 1996 congressional elections. These include the redistribution of funds from parties to groups and groups to groups, and unprecedented unregulated "soft" money expenditures, many of which took the form of party and group agenda-setting efforts and issue advocacy. *Soft money* refers to money that is raised and spent outside of the federal campaign finance system, but is used to influence the outcome of federal elections.

The author would like to acknowledge research assistant Peter Burns for his help with this chapter.

This money, in contrast to so-called hard money, comes from sources and in amounts that are not prohibited under the federal system.[1]

For the first time, parties also spent huge sums on independent expenditures in Senate elections, which were formerly made only by interest group political action committees (PACs). The 1996 elections showed the continuation of four important trends in the conduct of congressional elections: the nationalization of campaign finance, the increased role of interest groups, the convergence of party and group campaign activities, and the increased cooperation between parties and groups. Perhaps more important, the 1996 elections were the first to seriously challenge the candidate-centered election system and the federal system of campaign finance regulation.

This chapter anaylzes these trends by tracing the evolution of the roles of parties and groups in congressional elections through four distinct periods. The first is the party-dominated era, which began in the nineteenth century and lasted through the 1940s. The second is the candidate-centered era, which began in the 1950s and lasted through the late 1970s. The third period, called the reform era because it was largely shaped by party and federal campaign finance, lasted through the early 1990s. The postreform era, which is characterized by the near-collapse of the campaign finance reform system put in place in the 1970s, is the final era in the twentieth century.

The Party-Dominated Era

During the party-dominated era, sometimes referred to as the golden age of political parties, local party organizations, often referred to as old-fashioned political machines, possessed a virtual monopoly over elections.[2] They controlled the nomination process, possessed the resources needed to organize the electorate, and provided the symbolic cues that informed the electoral decisions of most voters. Interest groups usually ran a distant second in their ability to influence the electoral process.

Local party leaders dominated candidate recruitment and selection during this era. Most politicians learned about the political process from party bosses who distributed food, jobs, or invitations to social events, while asking only for their loyalty on election day. A small number of these individuals became heavily involved in party politics. Party bosses selected some of these individuals to run for office. In cases in which nominees were chosen in closed caucuses the support of the party leaders was sufficient to win the nomination. Where direct primaries were held, the machine's endorsement was usually sufficient to ensure that the candidate won the primary, which in many cases was tantamount to winning the election.[3]

Parties also dominated the conduct of most campaigns during this period.[4] The parties' national committees carried out issue research and helped set the national campaign agenda during presidential election years. Local party committees organized rallies and parades, distributed buttons and other election paraphernalia, and played a central role in campaign communications. Local party committees also played a central role in gauging public opinion and mobilizing voters. Local party leaders kept tabs on the political opinions and voting intentions of their neighbors. They reported this information up the organizational ranks to their county party leader, who summarized the information for the state party chair who, in turn, prepared a condensed report for the national party committee. At the same time, local pols gathered information about public opinion and helped their neighbors register to vote. Later they knocked on doors, transported people to the polls, and performed other activities aimed at turning out supporters.[5] This two-way flow of communication helped party committees focus most of their efforts in competitive elections, including those of challengers and open seat contestants.

Party organizations at all levels raised money by soliciting contributions from civil servants, businesses, labor unions, and other individuals and groups that relied on the government for their livelihood. Candidates were also often expected to contribute to party organizations. Money was not as important in elections during the party-dominated era as it was during the latter half of the twentieth century; however, party committees made most of the financial transactions that occurred in connection with campaigns.[6]

Interest groups played secondary roles in candidate recruitment and campaigning during this era. Unions and other large membership groups that had high concentrations of members who had strong group identifications could have a measure of influence on candidate recruitment and campaigns in some areas. Unions, businesses, and other groups that gave contributions to parties also could affect the outcomes of elections.[7] However, most interest group activity was coordinated with party campaign efforts.

The Candidate-Centered Era

By the 1950s the party-dominated system had given way to a system in which candidates, not political parties, were the major focus of congressional campaigns, and candidates, not parties, bore the ultimate responsibility for election outcomes.[8] The transition to the candidate-centered system was brought about by legal, demographic, and technological changes in American society and reforms instituted by the parties themselves. The direct primary and civil service reforms passed during the Progressive Era deprived party bosses of their ability to handpick nominees and reward party workers with government jobs and contracts. This weakened the bosses' hold over candidates and political activists and encouraged candidates to build their own campaign organizations.[9]

Increased education and social mobility, declining immigration, and a growing national identity contributed to the erosion of the traditional ethnic neighborhoods that formed the core of the old-fashioned political machine's constituency. The rise of the mass media provided voters with more reliable sources of political information than local party activists.[10] Growing preferences for television, radio, and movies reduced the popularity of rallies, barbecues, and other types of interpersonal communication at which local party committees excelled. These changes deprived the parties of their political bases and rendered many of their communications and mobilization techniques obsolete.

Technological innovation also reduced candidates' dependence on local party organizations. Modern polling, data processing, and direct mail and electronic advertising gave candidates tools they could use to gather information about voters and communicate campaign messages. The emergence of a new corps of campaigners—the political consultants—enabled candidates to hire nonparty professionals to run their campaigns. Direct-mail fund-raising techniques also helped candidates raise the money needed to pay campaign staffs and outside consultants. These developments helped to transform election campaigns from party-focused grass-roots affairs into money-driven events that revolved around individual candidates and their campaign organizations.[11]

Party reforms passed by the Democrats following their tumultuous 1968 national convention weakened Democratic Party committees. Republican committees who adopted similar reforms or had them imposed on them by Democratic controlled state legislatures were also adversely affected. The reforms created powerful tensions within the parties because they opened the candidate selection process to all registered party voters who wished to participate in it. This resulted in the replacement of closed caucuses with participatory primaries, it denied local party leaders the authority to select delegates to their national conventions, and it encouraged candidate and issue activists to become more involved in party politics. Conflicts emerged over such basic issues as whether the party should focus on winning elections or advancing particular policies. As a result of these conflicts, many party organizations were neglected and weakened to the point where they were unable to furnish significant campaign support to candidates.[12] The reforms helped to further institutionalize the candidate-centered election system.

The declining roles of local parties and the changing needs of candidates created opportunities for interest groups to increase their involvement in federal elections. Increased federal spending and regulation gave groups the incentive to step up their lobbying efforts in Washington.[13] As lobbyists sought to educate members of Congress about their group's needs, members communicated the fact that they had needs of their own, many of which revolved around raising campaign money.

Economic interest groups increased their election activities during this period. The automobile industry, insurance companies, banks, and other business interests became well represented among major campaign contributors. Organized labor, led by the American Federation of Labor-Congress of Industrial Organizations' (AFL-CIO's) Committee on Political Education (COPE) also stepped up its election efforts.[14] A few ideological groups, such as the National Committee for an Effective Congress (NCEC), were created to provide candidates with endorsements and financial support. As revelations from the Watergate scandal showed, some groups contributed enormous sums of campaign money, both legally and illegally.[15]

The Reform Era

The public uproar in response to Watergate led Congress to pass the Federal Election Campaign Act of 1974 (FECA), the most comprehensive set of statutes governing federal campaign finance ever enacted. The Federal Election Commission (FEC) was created to enforce these statutes. As amended in 1976, the FECA allows national party organizations to accept individual contributions of up to $20,000 per year and PAC contributions of up to $15,000. State parties can accept contributions of up to $5,000 from individuals and PACs. National, congressional, and state party campaign committees can each give $5,000 to a House candidate at each stage of the election (primary, general election, and runoff, if one is required).[16] The parties' national and senatorial campaign committees can give a combined total of $17,500 in an election cycle to a Senate candidate. State committees can contribute an additional $5,000 to Senate candidates.

Parties can also make "coordinated expenditures" on behalf of candidates, which are typically for campaign services that a congressional or senatorial committee or some other party organization gives to an individual candidate or purchases from a political consultant on the candidate's behalf. Originally set in 1974 at $10,000 for all national party organizations, the limits for coordinated expenditures on behalf of House candidates are adjusted for inflation and reached $27,620 in 1992.[17] The limits for national party-coordinated expenditures in Senate elections vary by state population and are also indexed to inflation. They ranged from $55,240 per committee in the smallest states to $1,227,322 in California. State party committees are authorized to spend the same amounts in coordinated expenditures in House and Senate races as the parties' national organizations. In the event that a state party lacks resources to make its share of coordinated expenditures, and a national party organization—usually the parties' congressional or senatorial campaign committee—deems it important for the party to spend as much money as possible, the state and national party organizations form "agency agreements" that transfer the state party's quota for coordinated expenditures to the national party.

The FECA prohibits corporations, unions, trade associations, and other groups from making campaign contributions to federal candidates from their treasuries, but it allows these organizations to establish PACs to collect donations from individuals and distribute these funds as campaign contributions to federal candidates. PACs can also make independent expenditures for or against candidates as long as they are made without the candidate's knowledge or consent.

By legally sanctioning PACs, the FECA drastically changed the financing of congressional elections. Between 1974 and the 1992 elections, the PAC community grew from a little more than 600 to 4,729 committees. Most of the growth occurred in the business sector, with corporate PACs growing in number from 89 to 1,930. Labor unions, many of which already had PACs in 1974, created the fewest new PACs, increasing in number from 201 to 372. The centralization of the labor movement into a relatively small number of unions greatly limited the growth of labor PACs.[18] In addition, three new kinds of PACs emerged in 1977: PACs sponsored by corporations without stock, PACs sponsored by cooperatives, and "nonconnected" or ideological PACs. The nonconnected PACs increased to 1,377 by 1992, whereas the other two kinds of PACs numbered only 153 and 61 that year.

PACs collectively contributed just under $178.3 million in contributions to congressional candidates in the 1992 elections, over fourteen times more than they had given in 1974. By 1992, PAC funds accounted for approximately one-third of all House candidates' and one-fifth of all Senate candidates' campaign receipts. Corporate and other business-related committees accounted for almost 36 percent of these contributions, trade PACs accounted for 28 percent, labor union PACs 22 percent, and nonconnected PACs gave 11 percent. PACs sponsored by cooperatives and corporations without stock accounted for the final 4 percent. PACs also made $8.8 million in independent expenditures that year.

During the 1970s and early 1980s many PACs followed election-outcome oriented or ideological strategies, making contributions to candidates, including challengers, who shared their policy views. However, by the mid-1980s, high reelection rates, pressures from incumbents, and a desire to influence the legislative process encouraged most PACs to give the vast majority of their contributions to incumbents. The exceptions are nonconnected PACs, which tend to pursue ideological goals, some trade association PACs that pursue mixed strategies, and labor PACs, which use mixed strategies and give virtually all of their funds to Democrats.[19]

PAC activity increased in areas of campaigning that traditionally had been carried out by political parties. PACs such as the NCEC, the Committee for the Survival of a Free Congress (now called the Free Congress

PAC), AMPAC (the American Medical Association's PAC), and the Business Industry–Political Action Committee (BI–PAC) began to provide candidates with campaign services ranging from precinct targeting data, candidate training sessions, and public opinion polls to fund-raising assistance. COPE carries out grassroots organizing and voter mobilization efforts.[20]

The rise of PACs encouraged some observers of politics and political practitioners to speculate that PACs might overtake parties as the leading organizers of electoral politics. According to Larry Sabato, a leading scholar of PACs,

> Many political action committees are slowly but surely developing into rival institutions that raise money, develop memberships, recruit candidates, organize campaigns, and influence officeholders just as parties do (or are supposed to do). PACs already outfinance the parties, partly because they drain away potential gifts from them, permitting supporters to tell the Democratic or Republican committee they gave at the office.[21]

Lee Ann Elliot, former director of AMPAC and a Federal Election Commissioner, observed that PACs "are the political manifestation of social and behavioral changes taking place in America" and proclaimed them to be the election "precincts of the '80's."[22]

PACs may have taken on some of the roles traditionally carried out by precinct-based party committees. However, PACs were not the only political organizations to have adapted to the new political environment. First party organizations at the national level and then party committees in some states and localities began to adapt to the conditions of the reform era. Both parties and PACs contributed to the nationalization of campaign finance.

By the mid-1980s, party committees in Washington, D.C., and some states had made significant adaptations to the candidate-centered, high-tech, cash-based style of contemporary congressional elections. These organizations became wealthier, more professional, and capable of playing important roles in congressional elections. National party efforts to encourage candidates to run for Congress and their ability to provide candidates with important levels of campaign services suggested that PACs were not likely to replace parties in the electoral arena. Rather, it was more likely that the foundations of the candidate-centered system would remain in place and that national party organizations and PACs would play a bigger role in that system.[23]

By 1992, the Democratic national, congressional, and senatorial campaign committees raised nearly $104.1 million for their federal campaign accounts and more than $36.9 million in soft money, which technically lies outside of the federal campaign finance system and cannot be used to directly campaign for federal candidates. Their Republican rivals raised even more, collecting in excess of $192.1 million in federal dollars and

$51.7 million in soft money.[24] Although the parties' national committees collected most of these funds, the Democratic Congressional Campaign Committee (DCCC), Democratic Senatorial Campaign Committee (DSCC), National Republican Congressional Committee (NRCC), and the National Republican Senatorial Committee (NRSC) raised enough money to play important roles in congressional elections and attract the attention of reformers.

The GOP, which traditionally has been the wealthier and more effective of the two parties, contributed $9.0 million in cash and campaign services to candidates for the House, about $2.0 million more than did the Democrats in 1992. The Republicans also outpaced their opponents in Senate races, giving almost $20.9 million in assistance as opposed to the Democrats' $12.6 million.[25]

Some of the services the parties' congressional and senatorial campaign committees provided to their candidates included assistance with campaign management, polling, issue and opposition research, communications, and fund-raising. With few exceptions, the House and Senate campaigns that were the recipients of these services rated them more highly than comparable services provided by interest groups and PACs.[26]

The congressional and senatorial campaign committees have played, and continue to play, important roles in helping their most competitive and financially needy candidates raise money from wealthy individuals and PACs. The committees' PAC directors help candidates develop their fund-raising strategies and organize "meet and greets" where candidates can make pitches directly to PACs. The committees also manipulate the informational environment in which PACs and wealthy individual donors make their contribution decisions, helping to steer most campaign money to elections where they have the potential to have the biggest impact.[27]

These party campaign committees' fund-raising efforts on behalf of individual candidates point to the symbiotic relationships that have developed between parties and PACs.[28] Many PACs were, and continue to be, rich in cash but short on the kinds of information needed to execute contribution strategies. Most PACs, especially those representing business or labor interests, were also looking for new avenues of access to powerful legislators. National party organizations, though wealthier than they had been during the candidate-centered era, were continually preoccupied with fund-raising. The complementary needs and resources of these organizations led to the creation of several PAC clubs, such as the DSCC's Leadership Circle and the NRSC's Senatorial Trust Club.[29] For membership fees of several thousand dollars per year, PAC managers and lobbyists who join the clubs receive updates on congressional elections and opportunities to be briefed by congressional leaders, cabinet members, or other high-ranking party officials. Some relationships are less formal, consisting mainly of campaign updates that party officials disseminate to PACs about the latest developments in the campaigns waged by candidates involved in close races. Party–PAC relationships that revolve around the flow of money and information have contributed to the development of a national economy of campaign finance.

In 1979 Congress took measures intended to partially counter the trend toward the nationalization of campaign finance and to boost the role of state and local parties in federal elections. The 1979 amendments to the FECA allowed state and local party committees to carry out voter registration and get-out-the-vote drives in connection with federal elections; distribute yard signs, bumper stickers, and other campaign materials associated with volunteer campaign efforts; and permitted state and local party materials to make passing references to federal candidates without having those materials count against the FECA's contribution and spending limits. Although the amendments were intended to reinvigorate local parties, they created a soft money loophole that eventually led to an even greater nationalization of campaign finance.

The Postreform Era

The 1979 amendments to the FECA laid the groundwork for the postreform era, but it was not until the mid-1990s that the campaign finance system was on the verge of collapse. The FECA's regulatory regime imploded for several reasons. Rising campaign costs and static contribution limits made it inevitable that candidates, parties, and interest groups would search for new ways for campaign supporters to help them win elections. Heightened electoral competition, especially after the election of a Democratic president in 1992—the first in sixteen years—and the Republican takeover of Congress in 1994, intensified this search.

The Federal Election Commission's failure to adequately enforce the law, especially its seeming inability to investigate complaints and adjudicate cases in a timely manner, emboldened those involved in federal elections to hunt for cracks in the campaign finance law and test its boundaries. Their efforts, along with congressional amendments, court decisions, and regulatory rulings by the FEC, added to the weaknesses that existed in the 1974 FECA. Court rulings in *Buckley v. Valeo*, which equated money with speech, and *FEC v. Massachusetts Citizens for Life* and *Colorado Republican Federal Campaign Committee v. FEC*, which favored free speech above the other values that are central to American democracy, had an especially powerful role in ushering in the postreform era.[30]

Several features distinguish the postreform era from its predecessor: the growth in soft money that parties and interest groups raise and spend to influence federal elections; the growth of creative monetary transfers among party committees, interest groups, and candidates; the increase in party and group independent political communications and grassroots expenditures; and greater overlap in the roles of parties and groups in congressional elections. Many of these activities appear to have been carried out with the intent of maximizing party and interest-group influence and circumventing the original intent of the law. These developments have challenged the viability of the candidate-centered system.

Fund-Raising

The heightened competition that surrounded the 1996 elections led to record party fund-raising. The Republicans, led by the Republican National Committee (RNC), collected $416.5 million in hard money that could be spent directly on federal elections, 36 percent more than they had raised in 1992, the previous presidential election year. Their Democratic counterparts raised $221.6 million, 26 percent more than they had raised four years earlier. Both parties also raised and spent record sums of soft money. GOP national organizations raised approximately $138.2 million, a 178-percent increase over 1992, whereas the Democrats raised about $123.9 million, a 242-percent increase.

Party spending on congressional campaigns also reached record proportions. Republican contributions to House candidates and coordinated expenditures on their behalf reached $10.9 million. Similar GOP expenditures on candidates for the Senate amounted to $12.0 million. As is typically the case, Democratic contributions and coordinated expenditures lagged behind, reaching $8.3 million for House and $9.7 million for Senate candidates.

Interest groups also set records in political fund-raising. However, it is difficult to ascertain the full measure of their success because only PACs are required to disclose their finances. The political money raised by other interest group organizations is soft money that does not have to be reported to the FEC. PACs collected $437.4 million during the 1996 elections, a 12-percent increase over 1994. Business-related PACs were the biggest fund-raisers, with corporate PACs collecting almost $133.8 million, trade association PACs just under $106.0 million, and PACs sponsored by corporations without stock and cooperatives collecting an additional $12.4 million. Labor PACs collected $104.1 million, and nonconnected PACs raised almost $481.2 million.[31] Although there is no way to tell exactly how much these groups spent in soft money, anecdotal evidence suggests that they spent at least $50 million.[32]

Creative Money Transfers

Record fund-raising left national party organizations and some interest groups with an abundance of soft money that could be spent directly in state and local, but not federal, elections, and shortages of hard money that could be spent in federal and most state and local campaigns.[33] As a result, national parties and groups possessed more money than they needed to carry out organization building, issue advocacy, and grassroots activities, but had a shortfall of funds that could be distributed as candidate contributions or coordinated or independent expenditures. Party committees worked their way around this dilemma by using a variety of strategies. One approach used "money swaps"—informal agreements in which national party organizations make campaign contributions to state or local candidates or soft money transfers to state party organizations, and state party committees spend equal or slightly lesser amounts of hard money in competitive congressional races.[34]

Under another approach national party organizations carry out activities similar to foundations. That is, they collect money from benefactors and redistribute it to beneficiaries who spend it in ways that meet with their approval. In this case, the benefactors are individual donors, congressional incumbents, and interest groups, and the beneficiaries are other groups that spent the funds in ways that are designed to help their candidates. During the 1996 elections, both the DNC and RNC collected $500,000 or more in soft money from each of more than a dozen groups (see Table 7-1). The Democrats relied heavily on labor unions and the Republicans on the tobacco industry. Joseph E. Seagrams & Sons, a major liquor company, and its executives ranked among the top seven soft money contributors of both parties. Other groups also gave considerable sums to both parties even though they did not rank among the top twenty givers to both.[35]

Some of the money the parties collected from these groups was later redistributed to other groups. The RNC, which is the wealthier of the two national committees, distributed approximately $6 million to others. It gave an unprecedented $4.6 million in soft money to Americans for Tax Reform (ATR), an antitax group with ties to RNC chair Haley Barbour, and some other tax-exempt organizations that mobilize Republican-leaning voters. It also gave approximately $1.4 million to a small number of right-to-life groups. The Democrats redistributed only a few hundred thousand dollars. This money was given to the Rainbow Coalition and a few other groups that are committed to turning out minority voters, who usually support Democratic candidates.[36]

The parties derive a number of benefits from funneling money through these groups. In many cases, the groups have greater credibility than the parties among targeted populations, such as antitax activists and minority voters. The groups also have mailing lists, educational activities, communications networks, and outreach programs that they can use for political purposes. Party contributions also keep weakly allied groups from abandoning a party's coalition and backing other candidates, including popular independents. Perhaps most important, these contributions enable parties to spend additional sums to help their candidates without violating federal election laws that regulate the amount of soft money a national party can spend in an individual state.

Table 7-1 Top Soft Money Donors, 1995–1996

Democratic Party		Republican Party	
Name (Interest)	Amount	Name (Interest)	Amount
Joseph E. Seagram & Sons Inc./MCA Inc.[a] (beer, wine, liquor)	$1,180,700	Phillip Morris Co. Inc.[a] (tobacco)	$2,517,518
Communications Workers of America[a] (labor union)	1,128,425	RJR Nabisco Inc.[a] (tobacco)	1,188,175
AFSCME[a] (labor union)	1,091,050	American Financial Groups[a] (insurance)	794,000
Walt Disney Co.[a] (entertainment)	997,050	Atlantic Richfield ARCO[a] (oil and gas)	766,506
United Food & Commercial Workers[a] (labor union)	714,050	News Corp.[a] (communications)	744,700
Revlon/MacAndrews & Forbes Holding Inc.[a] (securities and investments)	673,250	Union Pacific Corp./ Southern Pacific Corp.[a] (transportation)	707,393
Lazard Freres & Co.[a] (securities and investments)	617,000	Joseph E. Seagram & Sons Inc./MCA Inc.[a] (beer, wine, liquor)	685,145
Laborers' International Union Of North America[a] (labor union)	610,400	Brown & Williamson Tobacco Corp. (tobacco)	635,000
Loral Corp.[a] (aerospace and defense)	606,500	U.S. Tobacco Co. UST[a] (tobacco)	559,253
MCI Telecommunications (communications)	593,603	AT&T[a] (communications)	546,440
Association of Trial Lawyers of America[a] (lawyers and lobbyists)	581,300	Enron Corp.[a] (oil and gas)	530,690
Integrated Health Services Inc.[a] (health care)	578,342	Eli Lilly & Co. (pharmaceuticals and medical supplies)	506,825

Table 7-1   *continued*

Democratic Party		Republican Party	
Name (Interest)	Amount	Name (Interest)	Amount
Federal Express Corp.[a] (transportation)	577,625	Mariam Cannon Hayes, Concord, N.C. (other)	500,000
Dream Works SKG[a] (entertainment)	530,000	Larry Fisher/ Fisher Brothers Management Co.[a] (real estate)	475,000
Milberg, Weiss, Bershad, Hynes, & Lerach[a] (lawyers and lobbyists)	530,000	Glaxo Wellcome Inc.[a] (pharmaceutical and medical supplies)	467,245
Arnold Hiatt, chair and CEO, Stride-Rite Footwear (textile)	500,000	Tele-Communications Inc.[a] (communications)	433,950
Atlantic Richfield Co., ARCO[a] (oil and gas)	486,372	General Motors[a] (automotive)	426,600
Phillip Morris Co. Inc.[a] (tobacco)	481,518	Blue Cross & Blue Shield Association[a] (insurance)	426,348
America Federation of Teachers[a] (labor union)	454,400	Chevron Corp.[a] (oil and gas)	426,006
AFL-CIO[a] (labor union)	454,135	Tobacco Institute (tobacco)	424,850

Source: Common Cause, http://www.commoncause.org/soft_money/topdem.htm and topgop.htm.

[a] Includes contributions from executives or subsidiaries.

Parties are not the only organizations that function like foundations. Some interest groups shift money back and forth among themselves and umbrella organizations they create in order to engage in partisan activity while enjoying the benefits of tax-exempt status and avoiding the FEC's reporting requirements. Included among these are GOPAC, the Abraham Lincoln Opportunity Foundation, and the Progress and Freedom Foundation, which were used by Speaker Newt Gingrich to recruit Republican candidates and disseminate a pro-GOP message.[37]

Party leaders, committee chairs, and some other congressional incumbents also function as de facto foundations, collecting money from individuals and PACs and redistributing it to needy House and Senate candidates. During the 1996 elections current and former members of Congress contributed more than $8.6 million from their campaign accounts or leadership PACs to 576 primary and general election candidates for the House and $2.2 million to 57 candidates for the Senate.[38]

Independent Political Communications

In addition to engineering new approaches to redistributing money, party committees and interest groups spent record amounts on independent political communications to influence candidates' election campaigns. The Supreme Court's ruling in the *Colorado Republican Federal Campaign Committee v. FEC* case made it legal for parties to make independent expenditures in the 1996 elections. Federal court rulings in *FEC v. Massachusetts Citizens for Life* and related court cases also made it legal for parties and groups to carry out issue advocacy campaigns. Some issue advocacy and independent expenditure ads were aired early in the campaign season to influence the national political agenda and the agendas in individual House and Senate contests. Later ads were used to supplement candidates' campaign advertisements and catch their opponents off guard. In some cases, the subject of a negative attack lacked the funds to respond, and in others there was little or no media time available for the victim of the attack to throw a counterpunch.

The vast majority of party independent expenditures made in 1996 were intended to influence Senate elections. Most were made by the two senatorial campaign committees. The Republicans made nearly $10 million of these: $4.7 million was spent to advocate the election of fifteen Republican Senate candidates and another $5.2 million was spent to advocate the defeat of fourteen Democratic Senate candidates.[39] The Democrats spent nearly $1.4 million against six Republican Senate candidates and another $50,000 advocating the election of three Democrats. Virtually all of the independent expenditures were made in races decided by twenty points or less, and the vast majority were made by the NRSC and the DSCC.[40]

Democratic and Republican state parties made less than $68,000 in independent expenditures in House elections, with GOP committees accounting for 88 percent of these. The DCCC and the NRCC opted not to make independent expenditures in 1996 because they were too involved in their competitive candidates' campaigns for any of their expenditures to be considered independent. The committees were also unprepared to hire new personnel who could claim to have no knowledge of these campaigns or committee strategy in them—a requirement for independent expenditures. Moreover, committee officials felt that issue advocacy campaigns provided a better alternative for helping their candidates in 1996. This is a judgment that several committee officials expect to revisit.

Both parties' national, senatorial, congressional, and state party committees spent large sums of soft money on issue advocacy in 1996.[41] Issue advocacy campaigns consist of ads that parties and some interest groups use to encourage citizens to support or oppose public policies or praise or criticize specific candidates. These ads cannot *expressly* advocate the election or defeat of a federal candidate, but just like regular candidate ads they can discuss candidates by name, feature their likenesses, and have a significant impact on election outcomes. Most are television or radio advertisements, but some take the form of direct mail. Whether issue advocacy ads can be coordinated with a candidate's campaign is a matter that is under challenge in the courts, but some coordination did occur in 1996. This coordination made issue advocacy ads an attractive form of communication for the party committees and groups that made them.[42]

The Democrats were the first to air issue advocacy ads for the purpose of influencing electoral politics. In mid-October 1995 they broadcast several ads to counteract President Clinton's low standing in the polls and to characterize the Republican-controlled Congress as radical extremists who wanted to help large corporations and wealthy individuals at the expense of working people. The ads focused on GOP proposals to downsize the growth of Medicare and Medicaid, cut spending on education, allow corporations to pollute the environment, and cut taxes for the wealthy. They were primarily intended to improve Clinton's reelection prospects, but the $42.4 million that the DNC spent on issue advocacy ads over the course of the election helped set the tone for many House and Senate campaigns.[43]

The DCCC, DSCC, and some Democratic state party committees ran issue advocacy campaigns that complemented those spearheaded by the DNC. The DCCC transferred $8.5 million to Democratic state committees to help finance television ads that were aired in sixty marginal House seats, most of which were occupied by first-term Republicans. The committee's Senate counterpart transferred $10 million for issue advocacy ads to fourteen states that hosted the nation's closest Senate races.[44]

The Republicans waited until late March to begin their issue advocacy campaign. The RNC spent $20 million between March and its August national convention to boost Bob Dole's campaign for the presidency. However, like the DNC's issue advocacy ads, the impact of these advertisements reverberated in campaigns at all levels.[45]

The NRCC televised six issue advocacy ads to help Republican House candidates running in thirty competitive districts.[46] The first three ads, which cost $7 million and were aired from the third week in July through Labor Day, were designed to clarify for the public the GOP's positions on welfare reform, congressional reform, and Medicare. The second three ads, which were aired during the last month of the election, cost roughly $20 million and were cosponsored by the RNC.[47] They were intended to remind voters in fifty-eight districts of some of the policy failures of the Clinton administration and to discourage them from electing a Democratic Congress.[48]

The NRSC spent about $2 million to televise issue advocacy ads in five states, having chosen to spend most of its money on independent expenditures. Many of the ads focused on welfare reform, the Republican plan to balance the budget, and Republican spending priorities. However, some addressed the vulnerabilities of specific Democratic candidates. For example, the committee ran a series of television and radio ads in Minnesota that labeled Sen. Paul Wellstone (D-Minn.) "embarrassingly liberal" and accusing him of being "stuck in the sixties, decades out of touch."[49]

Labor, business, and other interest groups also spent near-record sums on independent campaigning in the 1996 congressional elections. PACs spent $8.8 million in independent expenditures.[50] Approximately 90 percent of these were made by nonconnected PACs. Most of the independent expenditures that PACs made in connection with House elections focused on Republican candidates, primarily first-term representatives in competitive districts. Independent expenditures in Senate elections also focused mainly on GOP contestants for competitive seats. The majority of independent expenditures made in connection with elections in both chambers were designed to help GOP candidates.

The AFL-CIO and affiliated unions made the largest and most visible issue advocacy expenditures in 1996. Labor spent $35 million to help the Democrats try to retake Congress.[51] The unions targeted 105 House Republicans for defeat. Television commercials were broadcast in forty of their districts, voter video guides distributed in twenty-four, and radio ads aired in several others.[52] The ads focused on Republican-proposed cuts in Medicare and Medicaid, education, health insurance portability, and environmental protections. The unions also distributed 11.5 million voter guides that compared the Democratic and Republican candidates' on these issues in 114 House, 15 Senate, and 2 gubernatorial contests. The unions' election efforts met with considerable success. Forty-five of 105 AFL-CIO targets were defeated, including eleven first-term representatives and fifteen candidates who were the targets of AFL-CIO television ads or voter guides. Labor efforts also helped increase turnout among union voters by 2.32 million over 1992 levels in an election in which eight million fewer voters nationwide turned up at the polls.

Many business groups responded to labor's campaign, but none more so than the National Federation of Independent Business (NFIB). The NFIB mailed nearly 240,000 campaign voter guides designed to help probusiness candidates. Together with the U.S. Chamber of Commerce, the National Association of Manufacturers, the National Restaurant Association, and the National Association of Wholesaler–Distributors, the NFIB created The Coalition—Americans Working for Real Change. The Coalition spent $5 million in thirty-seven House elections to purchase 6,000 television commercials and 7,000 radio ads and mail two million letters to small business owners, mostly in support of Republican candidates. The NFIB claimed a success rate of 54 percent in 133 House and Senate races in which they had major involvement. The Coalition also enjoyed some success, receiving praise from RNC Chair Haley Barbour. The National Business Roundtable and some other business groups, however, were not as unified in their support for Republican candidates, and in fact their support may have hurt some of the candidates.[53]

Several noneconomic groups also carried out issue advocacy campaigns. Both the Sierra Club and the National Rifle Association aired television and radio ads and distributed voter guides.[54] Groups associated with the Christian Right, which played a critical role in helping the Republicans capture control of Congress in 1994, continued to play an important role in the congressional elections held two years later, especially in the South and parts of the Midwest.[55] The Christian Coalition, for example, used its church-based network to distribute more than fifty-four million voter guides to help conservative Republican candidates in 1996.[56]

Several tax-exempt organizations, which are not supposed to become involved in elections, also engaged in issue advocacy.[57] Among them are Americans for Tax Reform, a prolabor group called Project '96, and the Coalition for Our Children's Future, a tax-exempt organization with a declared mission to promote a balanced budget amendment to the Constitution. This last group spent an estimated $700,000 in Louisiana and California on highly partisan television ads, radio commercials, direct-mail, and telephone banks designed to help Republican candidates.[58]

Grassroots Activities

Parties and interest groups also spent record sums to organize registration and get-out-the-vote drives, set up telephone banks, distribute lawn signs, hang posters, and engage in other grassroots activities in 1996. Most of this was supported by soft money that was raised in Washington and distributed to local party and interest group committees. The federated structure of many political organizations enabled them to benefit from the advantages of centralized fund-raising and targeting and decentralized administration.

The Democratic national, congressional, and senatorial campaign committees spent about $40 million in soft and hard money to help finance state and local party-building programs, purchase voter lists and direct mail, and set up telephone banks. The DNC alone spent approximately $20 million to directly contact roughly 14.3 million people through direct mail and 11 million through telemarketing calls. The Republicans spent a record $48.3 million on their grassroots campaigning. These resources enabled the party to deliver 84.8 million pieces of targeted political mail and make 14.5 million voter identification or get-out-the-vote calls.[59]

Interest groups also spent huge sums on grassroots activities. The AFL-CIO and its affiliates trained nearly 175 union members to organize fifty-four targeted congressional districts. Another 3,200 union activists were trained in issue education and get out the vote activities. Later, the trainees focused registered and mobilized union members and their families. The unions also distributed $2 million to nonpartisan voter registration groups in labor-targeted districts. In 1996 organized labor succeeded in increasing turnout among union voters by 2.32 million over 1992 levels in an election in which 8 million fewer voters nationwide turned up at the polls.[60]

The NFIB also carried out a number of grassroots efforts. It sponsored a seminar in Washington to instruct small business owners and executives on running for office, campaign management, grassroots organizing, and coalition building. The NFIB also held a satellite conference to train 500 of its members across the country in political action, mailed 197,051 letters, and carried out a telemarketing campaign to recruit volunteers to help organize 103 congressional districts. Of course, a variety of noneconomic and non–Washington-based groups also mounted grassroots campaigns. Included among these are the Sierra Club, the Christian Coalition, and various abortion rights, prolife, racial, and ethnic groups.

Conclusion

Parties and interest groups have evolved in response to systemic, legal, and political change over the course of American history. Their roles in congressional elections have also evolved. During the period that stretched from the late nineteenth century through the 1940s local parties dominated elections and interest groups played a secondary role, often assisting party committees in their efforts. The candidate-centered era that followed was a period in which interest group influence grew largely as a result of the decline of local party committees and the changing needs of candidates. The reform era, which began with the passage of the 1974 FECA, witnessed the birth of the modern political action committee, the strengthening of national and some state party organizations, and the nationalization of a large portion of the campaign finance system. During this era, both parties and PACs adapted to the candidate-centered system and became influential players in congressional elections.

The near-collapse of the regulatory regime governing federal campaign finance paved the way for the postreform era, which began in earnest during the 1996 elections. This era is marked by record fundraising and spending by parties and interest groups and an increase in the overlap in the activities of both sets of organizations. One of the defining aspects of the postreform era involves soft money transactions that at one time would have been considered in violation of the spirit, if not the letter, of the law.

Party soft money is raised from wealthy interest groups and their representatives and has been traditionally spent on party building, voter mobilization efforts, and generic party-focused advertising. Interest group soft money, which has been raised mainly from corporate funds, union treasuries, and the operating funds of other organizations, was spent on similar activities. Some party and interest group soft money gets transferred back and forth from national to state committee accounts so that these groups can legally deliver money to the elections in which it will have the biggest impact. Some parties, groups, and candidates distribute soft money to each other or to the tax-exempt organizations they create for similar purposes.

Party and interest group soft money is also spent in new ways in the postreform era. One of the most important outlets for these funds are issue advocacy advertisements that closely resemble ads that candidates, parties, and PACs had previously financed exclusively with hard money. Many of these ads bear the names and likenesses of individual candidates and differ from hard money ads only in that they do not explicitly call for a candidate's election or defeat. Voter guides make up another popular outlet for soft money.

The second factor that may come to define the postreform era concerns the impact of party and interest group independent campaign efforts on the candidate-centered system. It is premature to claim that the issue advocacy campaigns, independent expenditure ads, and voter guides have undermined the viability of the candidate-centered system, but they have challenged it. These communications framed the terms of the debate and shaped the closing arguments in some 1996 House and Senate elections. Party and group spending outpaced candidate spending in a number of close races. The postreform era may drastically alter the dynamics of congressional election politics.

The third and perhaps most obvious factor that defines the postreform era is the inability or unwillingness of members of Congress to change the law that governs the federal election campaign finance system. Parts of the current campaign finance regime will have been in place for more than twenty-five years at the arrival of the new millennium. Congressional elections have changed substantially since that regime was established. Parties, interest groups, political consultants, and even some candidates have become accustomed to circumventing the law, and a much smaller portion of the spending that takes place in congressional elections is regulated by the federal government.

The 105th Congress, like most of its predecessors, has resisted amending the FECA. Members of the House and the Senate introduced more than 125 separate campaign finance reform bills, but none survived the legislative process. There are a number of reasons for this. Politicians often try to portray themselves as reformers while advocating changes that reflect their own self-interest. Most incumbents are preoccupied with protecting elements of the system that work to their advantage. Challengers are often as vocal about doing away with those advantages, at least until they become incumbents. Most Republicans want to increase existing limits on party spending so they can take advantage of their party's superior fund-raising ability, whereas most Democrats favor public subsidies coupled with spending limits, which would reduce the Republicans' financial advantages. Many members of the Senate advocate the elimination of PAC contributions, and most House members defend PACs, reflecting the greater dependence of members of the lower chamber on PAC funds. Philosophical differences over the role of money in politics also divide politicians and parties.

Reports of corruption, the efforts of reform groups, and public disapproval have not been sufficient to motivate members of Congress to overcome their differences in order to pass campaign finance reform. Elected officials appear to have a high tolerance for corruption and public displeasure with the way in which congressional elections are financed. However, there is a possibility that issue advocacy campaigns may motivate legislators to reform the campaign finance system. This form of independent spending deprives candidates, especially incumbents, of their ability to dominate the political agenda in their districts. Issue advocacy spending also heightens uncertainty in congressional elections because candidates can no longer estimate the funds that are going to be spent against them by merely checking FEC records of their opponent's cash on hand. The possibility that a candidate will face an influx of issue ads financed with soft money has heightened the uncertainty of congressional elections and resulted in candidates' feeling pressure to raise more funds. It may be that soft money and independent spending, which help define postreform congressional elections, will do what public pressure could not—motivate members of Congress to reform the campaign finance system. If not, the postreform era is likely to endure for a long time to come.

Notes

1. The term *soft money* was coined by Elizabeth Drew in *Politics and Money: The New Road to Corruption* (New York: Macmillan, 1983), 15. See also Herbert E. Alexander and Anthony J. Corrado, *Financing the 1994 Election* (Armonk, N.Y.: M.E. Sharpe, 1995), chap. 6; Robert Biersack, "The Nationalization of Party Finance," in *The State of the Parties*, ed. John C. Green and Daniel M. Shea (Landover, Md.: Rowman and Littlefield, 1996), 108–124.
2. See, for example, Frank J. Sorauf, "Political Parties and Political Action Committees: Two Life Cycles," *Arizona Law Review* 22 (1980): 446–450.
3. M. Ostrogorski, *Democracy and the Organization of Political Parties, Vol. 2: The United States*, ed. Semour Martin Lipset (Garden City, N.Y.: Anchor Books, 1964), 186–189.

4. Ibid.

5. Charles E. Merriam, *The American Party System* (New York: Macmillan, 1923), 308; Harold R. Bruce, *American Parties and Politics* (New York: Henry Holt, 1927), 164–165.

6. See, for example, Bruce, *American Parties and Politics*, 282–288.

7. Ibid.

8. Committee on Political Parties, American Political Science Association, "Toward a More Responsible Two-Party System," *American Political Science Review* 44 (1950).

9. See, for example, V. O. Key, *Politics, Parties, and Pressure Groups* (New York: Thomas Y. Crowell Company, 1958), 559; Eugene H. Roseboom, *A History of Presidential Elections* (New York: Macmillan, 1970), 263.

10. See Austin Ranney, *Curing the Mischiefs of Faction* (Berkeley: University of California Press, 1975), 110; Xandra Kayden and Eddie Mahe, Jr., *The Party Goes On*, 95; and especially Wilson Carey McWilliams, "Parties as Civic Associations," in Gerald, *Party Renewal in America*, ed. Gerald M. Pomper (New York: Praeger, 1981), 51–68.

11. Robert Agranoff, "Introduction/The New Style of Campaigning: The Decline of Party and the Rise of Candidate Centered Technology," in Agranoff, *The New Style in Election Campaigns*, ed. Robert Agranoff (Boston: Holbrook Press, 1972), 3–50; Sorauf, "Political Parties and Political Action Committees."

12. Nelson W. Polsby, *Consequences of Party Reform* (New York: Oxford University Press, 1983), chap. 2.

13. David B. Truman, *The Governmental Process*, 2d ed. (New York: Alfred A. Knopf, 1971), chap. 4.

14. Clyde Wilcox, "Coping with Increasing Business Influence: The AFL-CIO's Committee on Political Education," in *Risky Business? PAC Decisionmaking in Congressional Elections*, ed. Robert Biersack, Paul S. Herrnson, and Clyde Wilcox (Armonk, N.Y.: M.E. Sharpe, 1994), 20.

15. Herbert E. Alexander, *Financing Politics*, 4th ed. (Washington, D.C.: CQ Press, 1992), 15–22.

16. These are considered separate elections under the FECA. Party committees usually only give contributions to general election candidates.

17. Coordinated expenditure limits for states with only one House member are $55,240.

18. Frank J. Sorauf, *Inside Campaign Finance: Myths and Realities* (New Haven, Conn.: Yale University Press, 1992), 102–103.

19. Craig Humphries, "Corporations, PACs, and the Strategic Link Between Contributions and Lobbying Activities," *Western Political Quarterly* 44 (1991): 353–372; Sorauf, *Inside Campaign Finance*, 64–65, 74–75; Richard Hall and Frank Wayman, "Buying Time: Moneyed Interests and the Mobilization of Bias in Congressional Committees," *American Political Science Review* 84 (1990): 797–820.

20. On the increase in PAC activity see the chapters in Biersack et al., *Risky Business*.

21. Larry J. Sabato, *The Rise of the Political Consultants* (New York: Basic Books, 1981), 274.

22. Lee Ann Elliott, "Political Action Committees—Precincts of the '80's," *Arizona Law Review*, 22 (1980): 539, 544.

23. Paul S. Herrnson, *Party Campaigning in the 1980s* (Cambridge, Mass.: Harvard University Press, 1988), esp. chaps. 2–5.

24. Federal Election Commission, "Democrats Narrow Financial Gap in 1991–92," press release, March 11, 1993.

25. Ibid.

26. Herrnson, *Party Campaigning*, chap. 4, and *Congressional Elections: Campaigning at Home and in Washington*, 2d ed. (Washington, D.C.: CQ Press, 1998), chaps. 4 and 5.

27. Herrnson, *Congressional Elections*, 192–196.
28. Larry J. Sabato, *PAC Power: Inside the World of Political Action Committees* (New York: W. W. Norton, 1984), 144–149.
29. Ibid.
30. *Buckley v. Valeo*, 424 U.S. 1 (1976); *Massachusetts Citizens for Life, Inc.*, 479 U.S. 248 (1986); *Colorado Republican Federal Campaign Committee et al. v. Federal Election Commission*, 116 S. Ct. 2309 (1996).
31. Federal Election Commission, "PAC Activity Increases in 1995–96 Election Cycle," press release, April 22, 1997.
32. As will be discussed later, labor unions affiliated with the AFL-CIO spent approximately $35 million and business groups affiliated with a group that refers to itself as the "Coalition" spent $5 million.
33. The laws in most states are not as strict as those governing federal elections.
34. Anthony Corrado, "The Politics of Cohesion: The Role of the National Party Committees in the 1992 Elections," in *The State of the Parties*, ed. John C. Green and Daniel M. Shea (Landover, Md.: Rowman and Littlefield, 1996), 79–80; Diana Dwyre, "Spinning Straw into Gold: Soft Money and U.S. House Elections, *Legislative Studies Quarterly* 21 (1996): 411; and James A. Barnes, "New Rules for the Money Game," *National Journal*, July 6, 1996, 1501.
35. Common Cause, "The Soft Money Laundromat: Democratic Party Top Soft Money Donors, 1995–1996," http://www.commoncause.org/soft_money/topdem. htm, and "The Soft Money Laundromat: Republican Party Top Soft Money Donors, 1995–1996," http://www.commoncause.org/soft_money/topgop.htm.
36. Herrnson, *Congressional Elections*, 95.
37. Ibid., 126.
38. Ibid., 83–85.
39. Includes only expenditures made in connection with general election candidates. A small amount was made in connection with primary candidates who did not make it to the general election.
40. The GOP spent $424,000 in the Rhode Island Senate race in which Democratic Rep. Jack Reed defeated state treasurer Nancy Mayer by 27 percent of the vote. Only state and local parties in Louisiana, Maine, and Texas made independent expenditures in connection with Senate races in their states.
41. The ratio of soft to hard money that a national party can spend in a state, including funds spent on issue advocacy, is determined by the number of state and federal elections held in the state in a given election year. See Dwyre, "Spinning Straw into Gold."
42. Herrnson, *Congressional Elections*, 95–99, 120–126.
43. Brooks Jackson, "Financing the 1996 Campaign: The Law of the Jungle," in *Toward the Millennium: The Elections of 1996* (Boston: Allyn and Bacon, 1997), 238.
44. Herrnson, *Congressional Elections*, 97.
45. Ibid., chap. 4 and 97–98.
46. For reasons of cost, the ads were broadcast on radio rather than television in the Los Angeles and Philadelphia media markets. They were also broadcast on radio rather than television in Portland, where the television airwaves were already saturated with campaign ads.
47. The RNC contributed $8 million toward this ad campaign.
48. Herrnson, *Congressional Elections*, 88.
49. Ibid.
50. The record for independent expenditures is $9.5 million and was set in 1986.
51. Much of the information on the labor's issue advocacy campaign is drawn from Robin Gerber, "Building to Win, Building to Last: The AFL-CIO COPE Takes on the Republican Congress," in *After the Revolution: PACs and Lobbies in the*

Republican Congress, ed. Robert Biersack, Paul S. Herrnson, and Clyde Wilcox (Boston: Allyn and Bacon, 1998).

52. "Labor Targets," *Congressional Quarterly Weekly Report*, October 26, 1996, 3084; Jeanne I. Dugan, "Washington Ain't Seen Nothin' Yet," *Business Week Report*, May 13, 1996, 3.

53. Ronald G. Shaiko and Marc A. Wallace, "From Wall Street to Main Street: The National Federation of Independent Business and the Republican Majority," in Biersack et al., *After the Revolution*.

54. On the Sierra Club, see David M. Cantor, "The Sierra Club Political Committee: Spreading Some Green in Congressional Elections," and on the National Rifle Association, see Kelly D. Patterson, "Political Firepower: The National Rifle Association," both in Biersack et al., *After the Revolution*.

55. See the case studies in Mark J. Rozell and Clyde Wilcox, *God at the Grassroots: The Christian Right in the 1994 Elections* (Lanham, Md.: Rowman and Littlefield, 1995).

56. Ruth Marcus, "FEC Files Suit over Christian Coalition Role; Work with Republicans in Campaigns Alleged," *Washington Post*, July 31, 1996, A6.

57. Anthony Corrado, *Creative Campaigning: PACs and the Presidential Selection Process* (Boulder, Colo.: Westview Press, 1992), 80–84.

58. Charles R. Babcock and Ruth Marcus, "For their Targets, Mystery Groups' Ads Hit Like Attacks from Nowhere," *Washington Post*, March 9, 1997, A6.

59. Herrnson, *Congressional Elections*, 94–95.

60. Gerber, "Building to Win."

8

Thunder on the Right? Religious Interest Group Mobilization in the 1996 Election

James L. Guth, Lyman A. Kellstedt, Corwin E. Smidt, and John C. Green

The past two decades have witnessed a resurgence of political activity among the nation's religious interests. Especially noteworthy have been religious activists on the political Right, who have become convinced that government action must be taken to reverse the perceived moral decline of the nation. Christian Right mobilization has been widely credited with the resurgence of the Republican Party in national politics, including helping Republicans oust Democratic majorities in the House and Senate in 1994.

In this selection, James Guth and his colleagues examine the tactics and targets of Christian Right mobilization efforts in the 1996 elections. Using the results of a national survey of nearly 2,400 Americans, they find that religious contacting was extensive during the election, despite the lack of enthusiasm that many prominent conservative religious leaders felt for the Republican ticket headed by Bob Dole. Besides reaching their orthodox Evangelical targets, Christian Right communications found other sympathetic listeners as well, including more moderate Evangelicals, Mainline Protestants, and conservative Catholics.

The impact of Christian Right communications on voters in 1996 was substantial, with those contacted more likely to turn out and vote Republican. Direct contact with voters and indirect persuasion by activist laity were the most important influence tactics. The researchers suggest that in an era in which party mobilization of voters has diminished, organized religious interests represent "a crucial new set of intermediaries linking the public to the electoral process."

Organized interest groups influence American elections in many ways. They encourage citizens to run for office, provide financial aid to candidates, seek to shape party platforms, recruit activists to staff campaigns, and urge sympathizers to go to the polls to vote for favored candidates. Business organizations, labor unions, farmer associations, and a myriad other occupational and economic groups are veterans of such activities, and more recently have been joined by a host of ideological and "cause" organizations.[1]

Christian Right interest groups are an especially vocal entrant to the world of American campaign politics, engaging in virtually every aspect of electioneering. In this chapter, however, we focus on Christian Right activities in electoral mobilization: the effort to get friendly citizens to the polls and to persuade them to vote for the correct candidates. As we shall see, Christian Right groups have often argued among themselves about the most promising target audiences and the best strategies for activating those audiences. Nevertheless, their electoral campaigns have reached many religious people and have influenced recent national elections.

Christian Right Electoral Politics: Targets and Techniques

Over the past two decades, Christian Right organizations have debated the best way to mobilize voters, with two major issues in contention: First, who are the natural targets of mobilization? Should campaign efforts concentrate on Evangelical Protestants alone, or on potential supporters in other religious traditions as well? Second, what are the best techniques for activating religious conservatives? Are church-based efforts more effective, or are conventional political tactics superior?

From the very beginning, Christian Right groups argued over their "natural constituency." Although the first organizations appearing in the early 1980s focused on specific Evangelical Protestant constituencies, such as fundamentalists or Pentecostals, more recently the Christian Coalition and other groups have not only broadened their targets to include the entire Evangelical community, but they have also sought assistance from religious conservatives among Mainline Protestants, Roman Catholics, and African Americans. For example, prior to the 1996 elections the Christian Coalition sponsored the Catholic Alliance as a vehicle for reaching that community, and even courted conservative African American churches.[2] Despite these changes, the weight of scholarly opinion is that the Christian Right has not advanced very much beyond the walls of its original Evangelical strongholds. The entire argument has taken place, however, in the absence of much hard evidence.[3]

Whatever the target audience, the Christian Right has continually experimented with mobilization techniques. The pioneer organizations, such as Jerry Falwell's Moral Majority, the Christian Voice, and the Religious Roundtable, were all dominated by clergy and, as a result, stressed church-based techniques, especially pastoral mobilization. In this scenario, clergy were the key to electoral action: They encouraged parishioners to register, told them where candidates stood on vital issues, and provided clear guidance on how to vote. As Falwell told fundamentalist clergy in 1980, "What can you do from the pulpit? You can register people to vote. You can explain the issues to them. And you can endorse candidates, right there in church on Sunday morning."[4]

By the late 1980s, however, Christian Right leaders and political analysts alike had concluded that this approach did not work: Most clergy shunned overt electioneering and, in any event, many parishioners were unwilling to follow their lead, often times resenting the politicizing of the church.[5] As a result, second-generation Christian Right groups, such as the Christian Coalition and the Family Research Council, preferred to contact religious voters without implicating clergy in professionally distasteful or "risky" activity. The new electoral strategies emphasized the role of committed laity, who take the lead in both church-based and more conventional tactics. Recognizing that churches are still a "happy hunting ground" for religious conservatives, Christian Right activists would place "voter guides" inside churches (or on cars in church parking lots) on the Sunday before the election, or they would engage fellow parishioners in informal political conversations. Other activists would replicate the standard political tactics used by many interest groups: contacting voters directly through phone calls, fax messages, personal visits, or e-mail—taking advantage of the natural networks of communication among church people. Such efforts exemplify the classic two-step flow of influence by which group leaders mobilize the rank and file through trusted intermediaries.[6] Despite the clear shift in emphasis from church-based to conventional tactics, and from clergy to laity as key actors, in 1996 one could still find Christian Right organizations using each approach, singly or in combination.[7]

To assess this religious interest group mobilization in the 1996 national elections, we use data from a survey of 2,392 Americans conducted by the Survey Research Center at the University of Akron, funded by the Pew Charitable Trusts. These respondents were part of a two-wave study of potential voters, interviewed first during the summer of 1996 and then immediately after the election.[8] We address four key questions: (1) Which religious communities were most heavily targeted by interest group mobilization efforts in 1996? (2) Which mobilization techniques reached the largest audience? (3) What factors influenced the likelihood of citizens receiving such religious interest group contacts? (4) Did Christian Right groups achieve their objectives, increasing the vote for conservative (and Republican) candidates and enhancing turnout among religious conservatives?

Religious Tradition and Theological Location

To simplify the inquiry, we have limited our analysis to the four major Christian traditions in the United States: namely, Evangelical Protestants, Mainline Protestants, black Protestants, and white Roman Catholics (excluding black and Hispanic Catholics). Together these religious communities encompass the great majority of voters and almost all the targeted populations for both the massive Christian Right mobilization and the smaller countermobilization by liberal groups.[9] Historically these four traditions have also constituted the critical religious building blocs for party coalitions. From at least the turn of the twentieth century, Evangelical Protestants were a major component of the Democratic electorate, joined by most Roman Catholics and, by the 1950s, most black Protestants. Mainline Protestants, on the other hand, represented the religious core of the GOP, or as the old adage had it, the "Republican Party at prayer."[10]

In contemporary politics, however, these historic alignments are being reconfigured in complex ways, shaping and in turn being shaped by the activities of religious interest groups. First, there has been some realignment of the traditions themselves: Evangelicals—growing in numbers, upwardly mobile, and ideologically conservative—have become the biggest religious constituency of the GOP in recent national elections, joined by more Catholics than ever before. On the other hand, the Mainline Protestant community has not only shrunk in size, but some remaining members have also drifted away from their ancestral Republican home, shaking an old religious foundation of party politics.[11] At the same time that religious traditions are en route from one partisan loyalty to another, vital cross-cutting changes are occurring *within* these same traditions. According to James D. Hunter's vivid depiction, religious communities are being reshaped politically by "culture wars," heated divisions over abortion, gay rights, and other social issues. According to Hunter, the "orthodox" and "progressives" now line up on opposite sides of such issues, a split that runs right through the major traditions. Mainline Protestants, Roman Catholics, and even Evangelicals are dividing into competing factions, with the orthodox aligning with the Republicans and progressives with the Democrats.[12]

We can use the insights from both perspectives on religion's changing partisan role to pinpoint the targets of interest group mobilization. To classify voters for analysis, we first placed them in a *religious tradition* (Evangelical, Mainline, black Protestant, and Roman Catholic), based on denominational affiliation, and second, assigned them a *theological location* (we will use the terms *orthodox, centrist,* and *modernist*) within each tradition by using survey items on what might be called the "three Bs of religion": beliefs, belonging, and behavior.[13] Although the details of the procedure need not concern us here, we can summarize the traits of the three theological groups in each tradition: the *orthodox* are most committed to classic doctrinal formulations, tend to affiliate with traditionalist religious movements within the church, and are quite active in religious life. *Centrists* are less orthodox on the historic theological tenets of their tradition, tend not to adopt movement affiliations, and are somewhat less active in personal and corporate religious activities. Finally, *modernists* reject orthodox theological formulations or even adopt heterodox beliefs, often identify with liberal religious movements, and typically (though not always) exhibit lower levels of religious involvement. Remember, however, that the theological location of respondents was determined by issues central to their own tradition; comparisons of theological groups should be made primarily *within traditions*, and those across traditions should be made with great caution. For example, by any comparable measure Evangelical "modernists" are probably a good bit more orthodox theologically and organizationally active than their Mainline Protestant or Catholic counterparts. Because the number of black Protestants in the postelection survey is relatively small ($N = 180$), and because this tradition shows little evidence of theological polarization, we do not divide these respondents into theological groups.[14]

Although a good bit of variation remains within each religious tradition and theological location, the classification is quite helpful in identifying the targets and effects of religious mobilization. According to press accounts and scholarly assessments, interest group contacting—at least insofar as it was dominated by Christian Right organizations—was most often directed at Evangelicals, then at the orthodox among Mainline Protestants and Catholics, and finally at a small number of black Protestants. If Christian Right organizations really dominated political communications to voters from religious groups, we should find that the frequency of contact follows this pattern.

Of course, the Christian Right was not the only religious force active during the 1996 election. A diverse melange of liberal groups campaigned with different motivations. Some, such as Americans United (AU) and People for the American Way (PAW), attacked the Christian Right's "politicizing of religion," or its perceived violations of the separation of church and state. Others, such as The Interfaith Alliance (TIA) and the Call for Renewal, argued that more liberal public policies were required by religious faith, and they also criticized some Christian Right tactics. The TIA, led by prominent Mainline clergy, took a page from the Christian Coalition playbook by building grassroots organizations and distributing at least five million voter guides—although usually not in church. Many local liberal groups also joined this loosely coordinated effort. Thus, if we find that Mainline Protestants and modernists in other traditions were contacted frequently, we will credit liberal religious groups with a more effective campaign than most observers perceived.

Finally, other prominent religious institutions were involved in 1996, at least tangentially, but are more difficult to categorize. Some Catholic clergy spoke out against abortion during the campaign, but the nonpartisan information on candidates available in many Catholic parishes also stressed the liberal social welfare stances of the Catholic church. In a similar vein, some African American churches were targets of Christian Right activity, as noted previously, but many also received more liberal communications from other religious sources. Thus, we might expect a mixed impact in these traditions.

To determine the extent of religious interest group mobilization in 1996, we asked potential voters five questions: (1) "Did you discuss the election with friends at your place of worship?" (2) "Was information on parties and candidates made available in your place of worship before the election?" (3) Were you "contacted by a religious group, like the Christian Coalition or The Interfaith Alliance?" (4) Did "the clergy at your place of worship" speak out this year on "candidates and elections"? and (5) "Did the clergy or other leaders at your place of worship urge you to vote a particular way?" Although these questions do not cover all possible kinds of communications, they do include most of the major techniques used. In analyzing the results, we have counted respondents who did not know, could not remember, or refused to say whether they had been contacted as "no contact." Despite this conservative approach, we find that many Americans were the targets of political communication by religious interest groups and activists.

The Contours of Religious Contacting

What, then, was the shape of religious mobilization during the 1996 elections? Which people were most often the recipients of such contacts? And what techniques were most widely used—at least as perceived by potential voters? In Table 8-1 we list the proportion of citizens in the mass public, in each major religious tradition, and in their constituent theological locations who reported the five types of contact. First note that in the mass public only a minority received any single form of contact: Almost one in five discussed the election with a friend in church, 15 percent said that a voter guide was available in their place of worship, about one in eight was contacted directly by a religious interest group, and a similar number heard a discussion of the election by clergy, but only 7 percent reported that their pastors actually endorsed a candidate.

The proportion contacted grows, of course, among people with some minimal level of religious commitment. Nevertheless, contacts varied substantially by religious tradition (and by theological location in each). Although political discussion with friends in church was the most common contact in the mass public, Evangelicals engaged most often in such conversations, followed closely by black and Mainline Protestants. Catholics, on the other hand, seldom talked about the election with friends in church. Why this is so is not clear. Perhaps Catholic worship services and religious activities lack the "free time" and "free space" that riddle the schedules of most Evangelical, Mainline, or black Protestant churches; adult Sunday school hours, coffees between Sunday school and church, postservice meals, mid-week prayer meetings, choir practice (and so on) may offer Protestants more opportunities for political talk. Or, as some scholars suggest, the historic lack of emphasis on the role of laity in Catholic churches may have residual effects, discouraging lay participation of all sorts, or the larger size of the typical Catholic congregation may limit such activity.[15]

Political discussion varied by theological location as well, especially among Evangelical and Mainline Protestants, with the orthodox talking

Table 8-1   Religious Contact Sources by Major Religious
Traditions and Theological Groups, 1996 Election
(in percentages)

	Talk in church	Voter guides	Interest group	Clergy talk	Clergy endorse	At least one contact
Mass public	19	15	12	14	7	38
Evangelical Protestant	28	21	18	16	8	49
Orthodox	41	31	26	21	10	64
Centrist	23	12	15	15	9	43
Modernist	11	14	9	10	4	33
Mainline Protestant	24	13	13	12	6	41
Orthodox	39	17	17	15	8	53
Centrist	25	13	15	13	6	44
Modernist	6	10	7	6	4	25
Black Protestant	26	23	4	42	14	56
Roman Catholic	15	18	13	14	14	39
Orthodox	17	24	21	16	19	49
Centrist	15	17	10	16	10	37
Modernist	12	13	7	8	9	28

the most. About two-fifths of orthodox Evangelicals and Mainliners reported such exchanges, compared to less than one-fifth of the orthodox
Catholics. In both white Protestant traditions, political discussion declined sharply among centrists and modernists. These differences reflect,
in part, the denser social networks of religious traditionalists, who typically have many close friends in the congregation. Note also that the level
of discussion by modernists in all three white religious traditions is very
low, perhaps because modernists are least likely to attend church services
regularly or to have as many friends in the congregation.

Because it is hard to observe, political discussion in church takes a
low profile in most accounts of Christian Right techniques. Nevertheless,
Christian Right groups directly encourage such electoral proselytizing; it
is also a byproduct of their other campaign activities. And the growing
focus of religious interest groups on mobilizing laity in target congregations no doubt reflects their recognition of the critical nature of such
"two-step" political communications. We also know that such informal
exchanges can play a crucial role in shaping the political attitudes and
activities of specific religious communities.[16] On the whole, then, the
findings comport well with Verba, Schlozman, and Brady's emphasis on
church as a place where all sorts of political orientations are fostered.[17]

If press accounts and scholars have neglected the strategic role of informal personal discussions within congregations, they have often spotlighted the Christian Right's controversial provision of political guidance through "voter guides" at houses of worship, typically on the Sunday before the election. Such guides have become almost canonical in some churches, having been used by antiabortion groups as early as the 1970s.[18] In 1996 the Christian Coalition, Focus on the Family, and many other national, state, and local religious interest groups distributed at least forty-five million such guides, primarily in Evangelical and orthodox Mainline congregations, but also in some black Protestant and Catholic churches as well.[19] These documents were often criticized for their transparent Republican bias, and liberal groups such as The Interfaith Alliance counter-attacked with their own more "objective" guides, but certainly failed to match the Christian Right performance in distributing such materials.[20]

How extensive was this voter guide campaign? As Table 8-1 shows, fewer Americans had candidate information available in their place of worship than talked with friends there about the election, but the differences are not massive. As expected, the voter guide strategy fared best among orthodox Evangelicals, a third of whom found such materials in church. This number drops off substantially among centrist and modernist Evangelicals, whose experience was quite similar to that of all the Mainline groups. One-quarter of African American Protestants also said that election guides were available in church, a figure equaled by orthodox Catholics. If liberal groups hoped to match the Christian Right's showing, at least among their own natural centrist and modernist constituencies, it appears that they fell short. In all three white Christian traditions, modernists seldom found voting guides available (or perhaps were not in church to notice and to pick one up).[21]

Christian Right groups did not rely entirely on supplying information in bulk to parishioners at services. Movement organizations also used more conventional electoral techniques, contacting voters individually through telephone banks, door-to-door canvassing, mail, fax messages, and even e-mail. As Table 8-1 reveals, such efforts contributed almost as many contacts as voter guides, at least among Evangelical and Mainline Protestants. Black Protestants very seldom experienced such contacts, whereas Catholics were also somewhat less likely to be approached directly than to have voter guides in church. Once again, the orthodox in all three predominantly white traditions were most likely to receive contacts, whereas modernists were seldom the target.

Finally, there were still some attempts in 1996 to elicit pastoral guidance for parishioners' political choices. Although the Christian Right's early enthusiasm for clerical leadership had waned by the 1990s, the Christian Voters League and other groups still urged ministers to inform their parishioners about candidates and even let them know how a "good Christian" should vote. In 1996, however, very few church people reported that their clergy actually urged a vote for a specific candidate, but many more heard discussion of candidates from the pulpit. Only orthodox Catholics reported that "clergy endorsement" exceeded "clergy discussion" (19 and 16 percent, respectively). Other data show that Catholic priests outspoken on abortion were most prone to endorse candidates, at least according to parishioners. In the remaining religious traditions, clerical endorsement of candidates is lower yet: Even among black Protestants the figure is only 14 percent, despite frequent press accounts of such activities in African American churches, and very few white Protestants report endorsements.[22] It is obvious that the theological, organizational, legal, and constituency factors constraining direct pastoral endorsements were fairly effective in 1996. Many clergy in all traditions still adhere to old adages against mixing religion and electoral politics; others may fear the wrath of the Internal Revenue Service or the Federal Election Commission.[23] Most clergy are also reluctant to endanger fellowship within the congregation by introducing unwanted political controversies.

Although explicit candidate endorsements were rare in 1996, as in previous years, some clergy no doubt did employ more subtle ways of indicating their preferences.[24] As Table 8-1 reveals, significant minorities of church people listened to their minister or priest discussing candidates for office. Black Protestants led the way, with more than two-fifths recalling such pastoral discourse, confirming the historic political role of the African American clergy.[25] One-fifth of orthodox Evangelicals also heard pastoral commentary, followed closely by orthodox and centrist Catholics. Once again, the orthodox in each tradition are most likely to be contacted, but differences among theological groups are not as wide on clerical activity as on other forms of contacting.

What can we conclude about electoral action by religious interest groups in 1996? On the whole, evidence suggests that Christian Right interest groups hit their targets. Certainly, no one technique reached a majority in any religious community, but many individuals were contacted, both through church-based and more conventional campaign tactics. As a rough overall gauge of the extent of contacts, we calculated the proportion in each religious group who received at least one. As the final column in Table 8-1 shows, almost two-fifths of all Americans were contacted in some way, but this number rises to two-thirds of the orthodox Evangelicals, half of the orthodox Mainliners and Catholics, and more than two-fifths of the Evangelical and Mainline centrists. Many fewer modernists in all three white traditions had religious communications—only one-third of the Evangelical modernists and one-quarter of their Mainline and Catholic counterparts. Not only were more of the orthodox in all three traditions reached, but they were also contacted more frequently (data not shown). Although more black Protestants reported some contact than members of any other tradition (56 percent), much of this is accounted for by pastoral action. On the whole, orthodox Evangelicals have a considerable edge over their Catholic and Mainline brethren, and to a lesser extent, over black Protestants. Although not all the communications received by religious people were laden with clear ideological and partisan messages, the majority no doubt had a conservative and Republican coloration.

The importance of religious contacts should be put in broader perspective. In an era when party organizations have either atrophied or find it difficult to locate and activate sympathetic voters, religious interest groups are an important new force, an exemplar of the "new politics" of ideological organizations. Such groups have become significant electoral competitors (and often adjuncts) to party committees, candidate organizations, and other traditional interest groups. Although we cannot elaborate here, the religious contacting shown in Table 8-1 compares quite favorably with voters' contacts by party organizations (32 percent of the public), political candidates (30 percent), and business or labor groups (19 percent). And among orthodox Christians, especially Evangelicals, religious contacts often equaled or outnumbered "secular" ones. Religious interest groups, it is clear, constitute a crucial new set of intermediaries linking the public to the electoral process.

Determinants of Religious Contacting

As we have seen, there is significant variation in the frequency with which members of different faith communities are contacted by religious interest groups and activists. At this point, we need to explore the factors that influence the likelihood of receiving electoral communications. As our dependent variable, we calculated an additive index of religious contacting, using the five items in Table 8-1. We looked at several factors that previous research suggests may help determine the targets of political communications. First, we consider the religious location of the respondent, using combined measures of religious tradition and theological location, which we shall call *Evangelical orthodoxy, Mainline orthodoxy*, and *Catholic orthodoxy*, as well as several detailed measures of religious commitment and involvement.[26] Then we turn to what we call the *social theology* of respondents, beliefs that relate faith to the political process, and to *organizational accessibility*, the extent to which individuals are already organizationally and cognitively mobilized. Finally, we look at demographic traits that are often associated with political involvement. In the first column of Table 8-2 we report the bivariate correlations between the independent variables and the contacting index, and in the second column, the standardized regression coefficients from a multiple regression. The analysis includes not only citizens from the four major religious traditions, but all other respondents, who provide the suppressed reference or comparison group in the regression.

The correlations show that several variables are associated with the frequency of religious contact. It is not surprising that the combined mea-

Table 8-2   Influences on Religious Contacting: Correlations and Regression Coefficients

	Religious contacts	
	r	b
Religious location		
Evangelical Orthodoxy	.18**	.03
Mainline Orthodoxy	.03	.01
Black Protestant	.11**	.07*
Catholic Orthodoxy	.06*	.03
Religious commitment		
Church attendance	.34**	.15**
Financial contributions	.33**	.12**
Small group activity	.30**	.09**
Friends in congregation	.06*	.02
Social theology		
Faith vital for political decisions	.22**	.00
Religion in United States threatened	.13**	.03
Churches should not avoid politics	.16**	.01
Organizational accessibility		
Christian Right membership	.29**	.20**
Proximity to Christian Right	.17**	.02
Conservative identification	.15**	.04
Republican identification	.11**	.03
Social and demographic variables		
Southern residence	.08**	.04*
Midwestern residence	.04	.05*
Education	.08**	.06*
Income	.06*	.04
Age	−.03	−.04
Male	.01	.02
$R^2 =$		.23

r = Pearson product moment correlations; b = standardized OLS coefficients
* coefficient significant at $p < .05$
** $p < .001$

sures of religious tradition and theological location make a difference: Evangelical orthodoxy is related to contacting more strongly than being a black Protestant, and Catholic orthodoxy has a slight positive correlation. Mainline Protestant orthodoxy, however, does not differentiate these believers from the rest of the population.

As one might predict, religious contacting is also closely associated with measures of religious commitment. People who attend religious services frequently, make substantial financial commitments to their church, and participate in small group religious activities were all much more likely to report contacts, as evidenced by the solid positive coefficients. Having a large proportion of one's friends in the same church is also modestly associated with contacting, at least in the bivariate analysis. None of these results are surprising. Church attendance not only taps religious commitment, but also facilitates contacting: Regular worshipers are more prone to informal political discussions with friends, likely to be present to pick up a voter guide, or to find themselves on the mailing list of a moral concerns organization. In a similar way, financial contributions enhance the likelihood of appearing on the telephone-tree lists shared by religious interest groups. And regular participation in one of the small groups now so pervasive in American religious communities provides added opportunities for political talk and contacts.[27]

We also considered the possible influence of what we have elsewhere called "the civic gospel," a social theology that connects religious beliefs to public life. Christian Right organizations have promoted the civic gospel to justify a new religious insurgency in American politics, reversing the historic antipolitical effects of fundamentalist theology. Although it is a complex set of ideas, the civic gospel urges conservative Christians to link their faith explicitly to political choices, fight against the attacks on the rights of religious people, and mobilize churches to advance these objectives.[28] To tap adherence to the key notions of this new social theology, we asked respondents three questions: (1) How important are your religious beliefs to your political decisions? (2) Do you think religious faith is under siege in contemporary America? (3) Should churches enter the political fray or not? Those who share the tenets of the civic gospel should be the natural targets for the Christian Right. And in fact, each sentiment has a positive correlation with religious contacting.

Organizational and cognitive accessibility should also play a role in determining the reception of contacts. Naturally, people belonging to profamily and Christian Right groups, and those who do not belong but feel close to these groups, should report more contacts. Similarly, we expect that those with strong ideological or partisan attachments might also be more frequent recipients. As Table 8-2 reveals, membership activity in Christian Right groups has a fairly strong correlation with frequency of contacts, whereas proximity to these organizations has a slightly weaker one. Conservative ideological identification is also associated with being contacted, as is Republican partisanship. The latter correlation is not very strong, however, perhaps reflecting the Christian Right's frequent targeting of conservative Democrats and independents, rather than confirmed Republicans.

We also expected that several social characteristics would be related to contacting. For example, residents of more "religious" regions, such as the South and Midwest, should experience more contacts, along with older people, who are more involved in both religious and political networks. We also thought that several other traits often linked to political participation, such as being male, well educated, and wealthy might have some impact. But, in fact, only a few of these factors are related to contacting, and not very strongly at that. Those living in purported regional Christian Right strongholds—southerners and midwesterners—were indeed contacted slightly more often, although the latter coefficient just misses statistical significance. The better-educated also had more contacts, as did the wealthy, but age and gender did not have even a modest relationship with religious communications. Indeed, the weakness of all the coefficients for social characteristics is striking.

Which variables are the best predictors of religious communications? Many of the independent variables are interrelated, of course: Evangelical Protestants, for example, attend church more frequently, think that religion should influence their political choices, sometimes join Christian Right groups, and often reside in the South or Midwest. To sort out the independent effects of each variable, we employed multiple regression. The results in Table 8-2 reveal the impact of each variable, holding constant the influence of all the rest. As the results make clear, religious commitment and Christian Right affiliation dominate the equation. Members of Christian Right organizations, faithful church attendees, financial contributors, and those active in religious small groups are all more likely to experience contacts. Once these factors are taken into account, Evangelical, Mainline Protestant, and Catholic theological location have no independent effect; that is, people with similar Christian Right organizational ties, church attendance, contributions, and small group activity in each tradition are equally subject to contacting. The bivariate tendency of Evangelicals to receive more contacts is accounted for by their higher scores on these variables. Only affiliation as a black Protestant increases contacts above what these variables would predict. And when everything is accounted for, only residence in the South or Midwest and higher education add modestly to the frequency of religious communications. None of the social theology measures has any significant relationship to frequency of contacts, the proportion of one's friends in the congregation disappears, and partisanship and ideology also fall away.

These results reinforce the conclusions drawn earlier: Christian Right groups have strategically targeted the most committed believers in all the major traditions. Nevertheless, as the model explains only a quarter of the variance in religious contacting, we suspect that not all the target populations are effectively reached and that some contacts are probably wasted on voters with unpromising religious and political profiles.

The Impact of Religious Contacting

Our final question is the most crucial: How did all this religious interest group activity affect the election? Assessing the influence of interest groups has always been a notoriously risky task, intriguing and frustrating generations of political scientists. Such judgments are especially problematic in the electoral arena, where so many forces are at play. At the very least, success for Christian Right mobilization in the 1996 election required two results: (1) an increase in the proportion of the Republican vote for Congress and for the presidency, and (2) higher turnout among orthodox—and presumably Republican—religious constituencies. Table 8-3 reports the percentage of respondents voting for a Republican candidate for the U.S. House and for Republican Bob Dole in the presidential race, as well as the proportion who actually went to the polls on election day.[29] (To simplify a complex table we have omitted data for black Protestants—we shall comment on that tradition in the text—and have combined the clergy items into a single measure.)

Table 8-3   Bivariate Data: Electoral Impact of Religious Contacts[a]

	Evangelical			Mainline			Catholic		
	House	Dole	Voted	House	Dole	Voted	House	Dole	Voted
All (percentage)	75	65	54	60	56	60	53	46	55
Religious group									
Orthodox	85*	80*	67*	66*	70*	68	60*	54*	63
Centrist	67	59	45	61	52	54	54	41	55
Modernist	57	41	50	42	38	69	37	37	44
Religious contacts									
Church talk									
Yes	84*	72*	73*	62*	57	72*	71*	62*	69*
No	69	61	47	55	51	57	49	43	53
Voter guides									
Yes	83*	69	61*	56	58	67	75*	69*	60
No	72	64	52	57	52	59	47	41	54
Interest group									
Yes	87*	84*	72*	71*	74*	55	61	48	67*
No	70	60	50	55	50	61	51	46	53
Clergy action									
Yes	80	61	62*	54	47	72*	60	53	57
No	73	67	52	58	54	58	50	44	55
Summary									
Contacted	83*	72*	63*	63	57	61	59	50	62*
No contact	64	57	45	53	50	59	48	44	51
N =	(265)	(315)	(590)	(200)	(234)	(391)	(192)	(228)	(416)

[a] The numbers represent the mean Republican vote for House of Representatives and president and the percentage of those turning out to the polls.

* $p < .10$

At first glance, the evidence suggests that religious contacting was rather successful. As in other recent national elections, Evangelicals were clearly the Republican Party's strongest religious constituency, with 75 percent choosing a Republican House candidate and 65 percent voting for Bob Dole. They were followed by Mainline Republicans (60 and 56 percent, respectively), and Roman Catholics (53 and 46 percent). Evangelicals were still slightly less likely to vote than Mainline Protestants, although they almost matched white Catholics. The choice of candidates varied by theological location in all three traditions, however, with the orthodox much more Republican than modernists. The Evangelical orthodox were also more likely to vote than other Evangelicals, but there were no significant turnout differences among the Mainline or Catholic theological groups.

Perhaps the Republican propensity of Evangelicals and the orthodox in other traditions resulted from more frequent contact from conservative religious interest groups or activists. The rest of Table 8-3 lends weight to this notion: Those who discussed the election with friends in church, had voter guides available, were contacted by religious interest groups, and whose clergy discussed candidates or the election were generally more likely to favor a GOP candidate for the House, prefer Bob Dole for president, and actually go to the polls. It is not surprising that such tendencies were strongest among Evangelicals. For example, Evangelicals contacted by a religious group voted 87 percent Republican in House races, compared to only 70 percent of those not contacted. The comparable figures for a Dole presidential vote were 84 and 60 percent, respectively. Similarly, 73 percent of Evangelicals contacted actually voted, compared to 50 percent of those who were not contacted. The differences were smaller (and sometimes statistically insignificant) among Mainline Protestants and Catholics, who were less Republican than Evangelicals. Talking with friends about the election also increases the Republican vote and turnout in all three religious traditions, but most strongly among Evangelicals and Catholics.

The provision of voter guides also appears to produce more Republican choices and higher turnout among Evangelicals and Catholics—but not among Mainline Protestants. (Perhaps enough of the liberal voter guides got through to offset the Christian Right campaign.) Clergy activity seems to have more modest, and sometimes inconsistent, effects. Among Evangelicals, whose clergy are generally conservative politically, there was a slight pro-Republican effect in the House vote, which is reversed in the presidential race. In the Mainline tradition, where clergy tend to be much more liberal than their congregations, those hearing their pastors speak about the election and candidates were slightly less Republican, although the coefficients are not significant. Clergy action does, however, have a strong bivariate relationship with turnout in both Protestant traditions.

The last section of Table 8-3 summarizes the differences in electoral choice and turnout based on a simple division between those who received at least one contact and those who were not contacted at all. Among Evangelicals and Catholics, those contacted were both substantially more Republican and turned out at a higher rate than those who had no contacts. Among Mainline Protestants, however, those contacted were somewhat more Republican (the differences narrowly miss statistical significance), but were not more likely to vote.

A note on black Protestants: Although the number of respondents in this religious tradition in the survey was relatively small, we can still detect some clear patterns. Although there is some tendency for most contacts to be related to a higher Republican vote for the U.S. House, the impact of discussion with friends in church had a pro-Democratic effect. The Republican bias of voter guides, clergy action, and interest group contacts was totally absent in the presidential vote, however, which went almost unanimously for the Democratic candidate, Bill Clinton. Most striking was the strong tendency for African Americans contacted by any technique to *vote* more frequently. The gap in turnout associated with religious interest group contact was quite wide (75 to 42 percent), with similar results for voter guides (69 to 36 percent), church discussion (59 to 38 percent), and clergy action (52 to 39 percent). Thus, although the usual pro-Republican impact of religious contacting was only weakly present in the black church, religious contacts had a powerful effect on simple voter mobilization, producing a larger Democratic vote.

Before we jump to the conclusion that religious mobilization worked in the 1996 campaign, we need to take into account other factors related both to the frequency of contacting and to electoral choice and turnout. As we have seen, theological location matters, because the orthodox in all three major traditions are more likely to be contacted *and* more likely to vote and vote Republican. This may result less from contacting, however, than from the strong connection between orthodox theology, conservative ideology, and Republican partisanship. Thus, religious interest groups may be "preaching to the choir," seeking to influence or mobilize those who would inevitably vote and pull the correct lever anyway—simply in response to their strong and theologically based political preferences. Or perhaps the contacted vote Republican because they are disproportionately male, middle-class, and well-educated. Any full assessment of the impact of religious group activity requires that we control for the effects of these theological, political, and demographic variables.

To present a strong—and easily interpretable—test, we ran a multiple classification analysis (MCA) on the effects of theological location and types of contacts on electoral choice and turnout in the three major traditions. We included party identification, ideology, gender, age, family income, and education level as covariates (control variables), as each has a strong influence over vote choice or turnout. First, as any political scientist would remind us, party identification has long been the most potent way of explaining vote choice: Republicans vote Republican and Democrats favor Democrats. And that is the case in this instance as well. Political ideology also assists scholars in explaining the vote, even when partisanship is accounted for, and indeed, it has a modest independent effect in our study, with liberals liking Democratic candidates and conservatives choosing Republicans. In recent years, much has been made of the "gender gap"—the demonstrated tendency of women to vote for the Democratic ticket—and, again, our data show that women in each religious tradition were more Democratic than men. On the other hand, age, income, and education had very modest and often statistically insignificant effects on electoral choice, but all three substantially encouraged turnout, as the scholarly literature would suggest (data not shown).[30]

Our primary concern, of course, is not with replicating the findings of earlier voting research but with isolating the impact of theological orientation and religious interest group activities. Table 8-4 reports the same results presented in Table 8-3, but with the data for each theological and contact variable statistically adjusted for the effects of party identification, ideology, age, gender, education, and income, as well as for the other variables shown in the table. If under these very stringent conditions we still discover differences among those contacted, we can say that religious interest groups had some impact on the results.

What do we find? First, even with the controls religious communities still vary in partisan preferences; thus, their distinct voting choices are not simply the result of party identification, ideology, socioeconomic status—or even differential mobilization by religious interest groups. Evangelicals vote Republican more often than Mainline Protestants, who in turn favor the GOP more often than Catholics. In all three religious traditions, GOP voting tends to decline from orthodox to modernist, although that effect is most striking in the 1996 presidential race. Among Evangelicals and Catholics turnout is significantly different among theological groups, with the orthodox more likely to vote than other subgroups, but among Mainliners, the orthodox and modernists are closely matched. Thus, even with the imposition of extensive political and demographic controls, religious tradition and theological location retain a significant influence over electoral choice.

Second, religious mobilization effects also persist, but vary in predictable ways by religious tradition and type of contact. Talking with friends in church has a fairly strong net effect, producing a significantly higher GOP House vote among Evangelicals, a larger turnout in all three traditions, and more Republican votes for both House and president among Catholics. On the other hand, the availability of voter guides seems much less effective. Although voter guides have a slight pro-Republican effect on the presidential vote among Catholics, in most instances those reporting the availability of voter guides are actually *less*

Table 8-4   Multivariate Data: Electoral Impact of Religious Contacts[a]

	Evangelical			Mainline			Catholic		
	House	Dole	Voted	House	Dole	Voted	House	Dole	Voted
All (percentage)	75	65	54	60	56	60	53	46	55
Religious group									
Orthodox	76*	72*	61*	60*	63*	66*	55*	50*	61*
Centrist	73	66	48	62	56	56	54	43	54
Modernist	71	52	51	53	50	68	45	43	46
Religious contacts									
Church talk									
Yes	78*	65	66*	60	56	68*	59*	52*	64*
No	73	66	49	59	56	58	51	45	54
Voter guides									
Yes	75	61*	51	53	60	61	54	53*	54
No	75	67	55	61	55	60	52	45	55
Interest group									
Yes	80*	79*	66*	61	64*	52	53	39	62*
No	73	61	51	59	55	62	52	48	55
Clergy action									
Yes	71	53*	52	60	45	68*	56	47	51
No	76	69	54	59	58	59	52	46	56
Summary									
Contacted	78*	65	58*	62*	56	61	54*	46	60*
No contact	70	65	50	58	56	60	51	47	52
N =	(265)	(315)	(590)	(200)	(234)	(391)	(192)	(228)	(416)

[a] The numbers represent the mean Republican vote for House of Representatives and President, and the percentage of those voting, adjusted for the effects of party identification, ideological identification, gender, age, income and education.

* $p < .10$

likely to report a choice of the GOP House or presidential candidate, although only on the Evangelical presidential vote are the differences statistically significant. Thus, the bivariate association of voter guides with higher Republican voting often washes out with controls.

Although direct religious interest group contact is not the most frequent type of communication, it has the strongest effects among Evangelicals, certainly the key target of such efforts, adding 7 percent to the House GOP vote, 18 percent to the Dole tally, and 15 percent to turnout among those contacted. The impact of contacts among Mainline and Catholic parishioners is mixed, however, producing a stronger Dole vote (9 percent higher) among the former, and higher turnout among the latter (7 percent). Note, however, that the controls actually reverse the bi-variate impact of contacting on Mainline turnout and Catholic vote for Dole, although neither result is statistically significant. On the whole, though, direct contact has considerable impact—but only in certain religious contexts.

Clergy activity, however, might seem a waste of time. When everything is taken into account most of the differences are statistically insignificant and sometimes run in the opposite direction from those expected. Among Evangelicals, for example, clergy action is associated with a substantially lower vote for Bob Dole than obtained when clergy were silent. This may result not so much from any "backlash" effect but from the fact that Evangelical clergy who engage in endorsements tend to be much more conservative than their congregations. Thus, endorsements may occur more frequently in settings in which clergy who are very conservative (and vocal) are matched with relatively moderate congregations, which tend to be less Republican.

Another way to summarize the impact of religious contacting is to look once again at differences between those who received at least one such communication and those who did not. The final section of Table 8-4 provides this information, once again with all controls in effect. Being contacted increases the Republican House vote in all three traditions and increases turnout among Evangelicals and Catholics. Only on the presidential vote do we find no significant net effects. Overall, however, these findings are quite impressive, supporting arguments for the political efficacy of interest group activity. Clearly, religious interest group contacting is often effective among the Christian Right's primary target constituency, Evangelical Protestants, and in some other religious locations as well. And the techniques vary in effectiveness. Conventional interest group tactics, such as direct contact with voters, seem more effective than some of the church-based techniques, such as the much-debated provision of voter guides and pastoral action. Both seem ineffective in the short run and may even be counterproductive in some circumstances. One church-based tactic clearly works, however: Informal influences from church discussion partners have considerable impact, especially among Evangelicals, who engage in much political discussion in church, and among Catholics, who are less likely to do so.

Among black Protestants, all the patterns are much simpler: The controls for party identification, ideology, income, and the other variables eliminate most of the tendency of those contacted to vote more Republican in House races. This suggests that contacts by Christian Right groups in the African American community are aimed at the minority already leaning toward the GOP; such contacts have little effect on partisan choices among other black Protestants. One clear effect does survive: Black Protestants receiving *any* form of contact are more likely to vote (53 percent versus 31 percent after all controls). This confirms the irony noted previously that some Christian Right contacting may have had the undesired result of bringing more Democrats to the polls!

We must issue one final caveat: Our analysis may understate the long-run impact of religious interest group activity, especially with respect to the church-based activities. We suspect, for example, that the growing strength of Republican identification among Evangelicals results in part from a decade or more of insistent Christian Right blandishments to vote for Republican candidates, conveyed through a variety of mechanisms. Similarly, the politically conservative ministrations of many Evangelical clergy probably have a comparable effect over time. Most of these long-term and "indirect" effects would be captured in 1996 by the controls for party or ideology in our statistical analysis, not by the contacting items. Yet, at least indirectly, such political socialization substantially bolsters the Christian Right's long-term achievements.

Conclusion

We have established that religious contacting was fairly extensive during the 1996 campaign, despite the lack of enthusiasm that many prominent conservative religious leaders felt for the Republican presidential ticket. Press accounts of the extent of Christian Right activities are largely confirmed by citizens' reports of actual contact. Second, these communications clearly reached their primary target, orthodox Evangelicals, but also found other sympathetic listeners, such as Evangelical centrists, and orthodox Mainline and Catholic believers. In several respects, our evidence also confirms the continuing importance of African American churches as central points for political communication and, especially, voter mobilization, although much of that role is still in the hands of clergy. Third, the religious location of those receiving contacts suggests that the countercampaign by liberal groups did not reach many voters, despite substantial and sympathetic press coverage. These interest groups often seemed more adept at holding national leadership meetings and press conferences than in contacting their own constituencies, or perhaps in getting them to pay attention, although it is conceivable that the apparent ineffectiveness of contacting among Mainline Protestants, considered generically, is a result of countervailing messages from Christian Right and Christian Left.

We have also observed the diversity of contact strategies noted anecdotally in much previous work, with different religious groups subject to varying mixes of techniques. Only Evangelicals—and especially the most orthodox among them—seem truly "encompassed about with so great a cloud of [political] witnesses" (apologies to Hebrews 12:1, KJV) as to be sure of at least one contact, but many other religious people were reached as well. Finally, we have discovered more than prima facie evidence that the interest group activity gets results. In general, in all major traditions (even among black Protestants), those contacted were more likely to vote Republican and turn out at the polls. Especially among Evangelicals and Catholics, these results often survived very powerful controls for other prime influences on electoral behavior. Of the techniques used by religious interest groups, direct contact with voters and indirect persuasion by activist laity seem, on balance, to have been most effective, whereas voter guides and clergy activity had much less impact—at least in the short run.

There are several important questions still unanswered; some can be addressed with data in the present study; others will be settled by history. First, we need to incorporate our results on religious interest group contacting into a broader framework of mobilizing influences, including traditional political actors such as candidate organizations, party committees, and economic interest groups. These political agencies also target religious constituencies, and their efforts might counteract or reinforce those of Christian Right or other groups. For example, Evangelicals are carefully wooed by Republican Party organizations in some areas, and GOP candidates themselves may also find it advantageous to look for votes in that community. In 1996, fully 33 percent of orthodox Evangelicals reported such Republican contacts, twice the rate reported by Evangelical modernists (or any Mainline group). And although Democratic Party committees and candidates neglected Evangelicals, they cultivated African American Protestants. Thus, we must consider religious interest group influence in the context of a host of other campaign effects.

Some other issues can be settled only by the next few elections. Have Christian Right groups hit the apex of their ability to reach sympathetic audiences? Can they expand further their substantial beachhead in the Evangelical community? Can they make inroads among Mainline Protestants and Catholics, especially the religious traditionalists among them? What changes in mobilization strategies will occur as the limits of existing church-based and conventional techniques become evident? And finally, will liberal religious forces, whether denominational or parachurch, compete more vigorously with the Christian Right in the grassroots culture wars of the future? The answers to these questions may come with the initial presidential election of the new millennium.

Notes

1. For overviews of the electoral activity of interest groups, see Paul S. Herrnson, Ronald G. Shaiko, and Clyde Wilcox, eds., *The Interest Group Connection: Electioneering, Lobbying, and Policy Making in Washington* (Chatham, N.J.: Chatham House, 1997), pt. II; and Mark J. Rozell and Clyde Wilcox, *Interest Groups in American National Elections* (Washington, D.C.: CQ Press, forthcoming).

190 Guth et al.

2. For an account of the formation of the Catholic Alliance by the executive director of the Christian Coalition, see Ralph Reed, *Active Faith: How Christians Are Changing the Soul of American Politics* (New York: Free Press, 1996), 217–220. The reaction to the Alliance among Catholic liberals is illustrated by Ed Griffen-Nolan, "Coalition Fishing for Pro-Family Catholics," *National Catholic Reporter* (October 27, 1995), 5.

3. For various efforts of Christian Right groups in selected states to broaden their target constituencies, see the essays in Mark J. Rozell and Clyde Wilcox, eds., *God at the Grass Roots: The Christian Right in the 1996 Elections* (Lanham, Md.; Rowman and Littlefield, 1997).

4. Quoted in James L. Guth, "The Politics of the Christian Right," in *Interest Group Politics*, ed. Allan J. Cigler and Burdett A. Loomis (Washington, D.C.: CQ Press, 1983), 73.

5. For some possible reasons for the failure of the "clergy-oriented" strategy among evangelical clergy, see Ted G. Jelen, *The Political World of the Clergy* (Westport, Conn.: Praeger, 1993); also James L. Guth, "The Bully Pulpit: Southern Baptist Clergy and Political Activism, 1980–92," in John C. Green, James L. Guth, Corwin E. Smidt, and Lyman A. Kellstedt, *Religion and the Culture Wars: Dispatches from the Front* (Lanham, Md.: Rowman and Littlefield, 1996), 146–147.

6. Reed, *Active Faith*, 121–124. The classic discussion of the "two-step" flow of communications is Elihu Katz and Paul F. Lazerfeld, *Personal Influence* (Glencoe, Ill.: Free Press, 1955).

7. For a good overview of the range of mobilization strategies used by Christian Right groups across the country in 1996, see Rozell and Wilcox, eds. *God at the Grass Roots*.

8. For details of the survey, see Lyman A. Kellstedt, Corwin E. Smidt, John C. Green, and James L. Guth, "Is There a Culture War?: Religion and the 1996 Election" (Paper delivered at the annual meeting of the American Political Science Association, August 28–31, 1997, Washington, D.C.).

9. For the concept of religious tradition and the size of various American traditions, see David C. Leege and Lyman A. Kellstedt, eds., *Rediscovering the Religious Factor in American Politics* (Armonk, N.Y.: M.E. Sharpe, 1993); and John C. Green et al., *Religion and the Culture Wars*, chaps. 10, 13–14.

10. For the historic role of religious groups in American party coalitions see the essays in Mark Noll, ed., *Religion and American Politics: From the Colonial Period to the 1980s* (Oxford: Oxford University Press, 1990).

11. See Geoffrey C. Layman, "Religion and Political Behavior in the United States," *Public Opinion Quarterly* 61 (Summer 1997): 288–316.

12. For the original statements of the "culture wars" thesis, see James D. Hunter's two works, *Culture Wars: The Struggle to Define America* (New York: Basic Books, 1991) and *Before the Shooting Starts: Searching for Democracy in America's Culture War* (New York: Free Press, 1994).

13. We have used somewhat arbitrary labels to describe these religious factions that tend to stress the belief element, but we remind the reader that behavior and associational facets of religiosity are also incorporated in the isolation of these groups. In this respect, it is important to note that we have removed those citizens who exhibit only nominal religious characteristics, classifying them as secular. Thus, all those in the analysis have at least some level of religious commitment.

14. Inasmuch as African American Protestants remain overwhelmingly orthodox in their theological perspectives, and racial concerns dominate the community's politics, the divisions Hunter perceives in other major religious communities seem to have made few inroads here. Thus, we do not divide this tradition into theological groups.

15. For some observations on the differing political impact of Protestant and Catholic congregations on the politics of parishioners, see Sidney Verba, Kay Schlozman, and Henry E. Brady, *Voice and Equality: Civic Voluntarism in American Politics* (Cambridge, Mass.: Harvard University Press, 1995), 320–330.

16. For an important analysis of the informal political effects of membership in congregations, see Kenneth D. Wald, Dennis E. Owen, and Samuel S. Hill, Jr., "Churches as Political Communities," *American Political Science Review* 82 (June 1988): 531–548; also Paul Djupe, "The Plural Church: Church Involvement and Political Behavior" (Ph.D. diss., Washington University in St. Louis, 1997).

17. Verba, Schlozman, and Brady, *Voice and Equality*, 518–521.

18. For some of the early experiments with voter guides in churches, see Marjorie Hershey and Darrell M. West, "Single-Issue Politics: Prolife Groups and the 1980 Senate Campaign," in *Interest Group Politics*, ed. Allan J. Cigler and Burdett A. Loomis (Washington, D.C.: CQ Press, 1983), 31–59. A critical assessment of the accuracy of the Christian Coalition's voter guides is found in Larry J. Sabato and Glenn R. Simpson, *Dirty Little Secrets: The Persistence of Corruption in American Politics* (New York: Random House, 1996).

19. R. Scott Appleby, "Catholics and the Christian Right," and Allison Calhoun-Brown, "Still Seeing in Black and White: Racial Challenges for the Christian Right," in *Sojourners in the Wilderness: The Christian Right in Comparative Perspective*, ed. Corwin E. Smidt and James M. Penning (Lanham, Md.: Rowman and Littlefield, 1997), 93–113, 115–137.

20. For The Interfaith Alliance, see Richard L. Berke, "Mainline Religions Form Lobby for 'Alternate' View," *New York Times*, July 14, 1994, A11. For The Interfaith Alliance's voter guide program, see "A Voter's Guide to Election '96," The Interfaith Alliance homepage, http://www.tialliance.org/tia/vguides.html.

21. Many of the liberal interest groups did not try to distribute their voter guides in churches, for either theological or political reasons. The homepage version of The Interfaith Alliance guides, for example, warned that they were "not for distribution in houses of worship."

22. For a case of seemingly widespread candidate endorsement by African American clergy, see Brett Pulley, "Whitman Gains Seen among Black Clergy," *New York Times*, October 23, 1997, A1.

23. For sympathetic accounts of federal agency scrutiny of political activities by clergy and churches, see Rob Boston, "Religious Groups and Political Activity: Some Do's and Don'ts," *Church and State* 49 (May 1996): 105; and Joseph L. Conn, "Judgment Day," *Church and State* 49 (September 1996): 172–174.

24. We have reviewed the evidence on the political involvement of clergy in James L. Guth, John C. Green, Lyman A. Kellstedt, Corwin E. Smidt, and Margaret M. Poloma, *The Bully Pulpit: The Politics of Protestant Clergy* (Lawrence: University Press of Kansas, 1997).

25. On the historic political role of black clergy, see C. Eric Lincoln and Lawrence Mamiya, *The Black Church in African-American Experience* (Durham, N.C.: Duke University Press, 1990), 196–235.

26. We incorporated religious tradition and theological tendency as follows: For each of the three white traditions, nonmembers were scored "0," modernists in that tradition, "1," centrists "2," and orthodox, "3." Black Protestant affiliation was scored as a simple dummy variable, "1," with all others, "0."

27. See Robert Wuthnow, *Sharing the Journey: Support Groups and America's New Quest for Community* (New York: Free Press, 1994), 333–338. Wuthnow suggests that religious small groups reinforce political messages received from religious interest group leaders. We suspect they also facilitate transmission of these messages.

28. For a more detailed discussion of the "civic gospel," see Guth et al., *Bully Pulpit*, 63–72.

29. Like other postelection surveys, ours is affected by the tendency of respondents to "overreport" voting. We have corrected for this tendency in the tables by use of a formula designed to predict the likelihood of an actual vote. For details, contact the authors.

30. For a comprehensive review of the factors influencing vote choice in recent national elections, see Warren E. Miller and J. Merrill Shanks, *The New American Voter* (Cambridge, Mass.: Harvard University Press, 1996). For the factors influencing turnout, consult Ruy A. Teixeira, *The Disappearing American Voter* (Washington, D.C.: Brookings Institution, 1992).

9

Political Action Committees and Campaign Finance

M. Margaret Conway and Joanne Connor Green

Observers of American political life would be hard pressed to name a feature of contemporary electoral politics that has attracted more attention and aroused more emotion over the past decade than campaign spending by political action committees (PACs). By mid-1997 nearly 3,900 PACs had registered with the Federal Election Commission, and in the 1995–1996 election cycle they provided 31 percent of the campaign funds received by House candidates and 17 percent of Senate candidates' receipts. The impact of such spending on electoral outcomes and public policy decisions is a matter of widespread debate. But without question, PACs represent a key weapon in the arsenals of influence of many (though not all) interest groups.

In this chapter political scientists M. Margaret Conway and Joanne Connor Green survey the rise of PACs as potent political forces and assess their effects on electoral and legislative politics. Particular attention is given to PAC contribution strategies and to the conditions and circumstances that may maximize PAC influence. The authors explore the criticisms leveled at PAC politics and evaluate the various reforms that have been suggested to limit PAC influence. Conway and Green conclude that one problem of the possible reforms is that none addresses the "imbalance in the representation of interests through PACs," an imbalance illustrated by the rapid growth in the number of business-related PACs compared to their labor-based counterparts. In their view, despite hostility among reformers and the press, PACs are not likely to be abolished and their role in the political process will continue, as will the many controversies surrounding their activities.

In the two decades since federal laws and Supreme Court decisions conveyed legitimacy on political action committees (PACs), their numbers have increased by 637 percent, growing from 608 in 1974 to 3,875 in 1997 (see Table 9-1). Although the absolute number of PACs declined from 1988 to 1997, their role in the funding of congressional elections remained significant. During the 1995–1996 election cycle, PACs provided 31 percent of the funds received by House candidates and 17 percent of Senate candidates' receipts.[1]

Table 9-1 PAC Count, Selected Dates and Years, 1974–1997

Year/date	Corporate	Labor	Trade, member- ship, health	Non- connected	Cooperative	Corporation without stock	Total
1974	89	201	318				608
11/24/75	139	226	357				722
5/10/76	294	246	452				992
12/31/76	433	224	489				1,146
1977	550	234	438	110	8	20	1,360
1978	785	217	453	162	12	24	1,653
1980	1,206	297	576	374	42	56	2,551
1982	1,469	380	649	723	47	103	3,371
1984	1,682	394	698	1,053	52	130	4,009
1986	1,744	384	745	1,077	56	151	4,157
1988	1,816	354	786	1,115	59	138	4,268
1990	1,795	346	774	1,062	59	136	4,172
1992	1,735	347	770	1,145	56	142	4,195
1993	1,789	337	761	1,121	56	146	4,210
1995	1,674	334	815	1,020	44	129	4,016
1996	1,642	332	838	1,103	41	123	4,079
1997	1,602	332	826	956	41	118	3,875

Source: Federal Election Commission.

Note: For 1974–1976, the figure for trade/membership/health PACs includes noncommercial, cooperative, and corporation without stock PACs. On November 24, 1975, the FEC issued its "SUNPAC" advisory opinion. On May 11, 1976, the Federal Election Campaign Acts of 1976 (Pub. L. No. 94-283) were enacted. Unless otherwise indicated, all data are as of the end of the year.

Many questions about the role of PACs in American politics are addressed in this chapter, including, "What laws govern the activities of PACs?" "Have these laws been effective in achieving their intended aims?" "What has been the role of PACs in financing congressional campaigns?" "What types of candidates are favored and what types are disadvantaged by the existing laws?" "How do PACs make decisions about which candidates should receive contributions and how much to give?" "What strategies govern contribution decisions by PACs?" "Do the internal needs of the organization giving the money influence patterns of PAC contributions to congressional candidates?"

Two types of political action committees operate at the federal level: independent and affiliated. Independent PACs are officially independent of any existing organization and usually focus on a particular issue or advocate a particular ideology. Affiliated PACs are created by existing organizations such as labor unions, corporations, cooperatives, or trade and professional associations. They serve as a separate, segregated fund to collect money from people affiliated with the organization for contribution to candidates' political campaigns or for use as independent expenditures for or against a particular candidate.

Affiliated PACs obtain funds for use for political purposes through donations made by individuals associated with the group. Corporations and labor unions are not allowed to make direct campaign contributions from their treasuries, but treasury funds may be used to establish and administer a PAC and to communicate with people associated with the organization—such as corporate employees or shareholders and their families or labor union members and their families—for voter registration and get-out-the-vote drives.

Federal Law and the Growth of PACs

Political action committees are governed primarily by the Federal Election Campaign Act of 1971 (FECA) and amendments enacted in 1974, 1976, and 1979, as well as the Revenue Act of 1971. Also important are regulations and advisory opinions issued by the Federal Election Commission (FEC), which administers and enforces federal campaign finance laws, as well as several Court decisions interpreting federal laws.

To limit the influence of any one group or individual in the funding of campaigns for federal office, individuals and most organizations are restricted in the amount of money that they can give directly to a candidate in any one year. The current limits are $1,000 per election to a candidate for federal office, $20,000 per year to the national political party committees, and $5,000 per election to a campaign committee. No individual may contribute more than $25,000 to PACs regulated by the Federal Election Commission, national-level party organizations, and candidates for federal office in any one year. Federal campaign finance laws give a distinct advantage to multicandidate committees—those contributing to five or more candidates for federal office—whether they are independent or affiliated. A multicandidate committee may contribute as much money as it is able to raise, yet it is restricted to giving no more than $5,000 per candidate in each election. That permits a PAC to give a candidate up to $5,000 for a primary election, $5,000 for a run-off primary election if one is required, and $5,000 for a general election contest. There is no limit on how much a PAC may spend in independent expenditures on behalf of a candidate as long as it does not coordinate its campaign efforts in any way with the candidate, representatives of the candidate, or the candidate's campaign committee. Because PACs are able to raise and funnel large amounts to campaigns for federal office, their numbers have grown; public concern about their influence on members of Congress has grown as well.

The 1974 amendments to FECA permitted government contractors to establish PACs, thus greatly expanding the universe of businesses and labor unions eligible to use this form of political expression. The FEC's April 1975 decision to permit corporations and labor unions to use their treasury funds to create PACs and to administer their activities, including solicitation of funds from employees and stockholders, facilitated the establishment and operation of PACs.[2] Authorization of the use of payroll deductions to channel funds to PACs also stimulated the creation and continuing operations of PACs.

Supreme Court decisions as well played a major role in stimulating the creation of additional PACs. In *Buckley v. Valeo*, the Supreme Court in January 1976 indicated that the 1974 FECA amendments did not limit the number of local or regional PACs that unions or corporations and their subsidiaries could establish.[3] That decision also clarified the right of PACs to make independent expenditures (those not authorized by nor coordinated with a candidate's campaign) on behalf of a candidate. In 1976 further amendments to FECA restricted labor union and corporation PAC contributions to one $5,000 contribution per election, regardless of the number of PACs created by a corporation's divisions or subsidiaries or a labor union's locals. The process of clarifying what is permissible continues, with the FEC and other interested parties proposing amendments to existing laws and advisory opinions being issued by the FEC.

Although PACs had existed prior to 1974, their numbers were limited, and most were affiliated with labor unions. Between 1974 and 1997 the number of labor union PACs increased by just 65 percent, whereas the number of corporate PACs increased by 1,700 percent.[4] Thus, the first notable effect of changed laws and the FEC's interpretation of the laws was the explosive growth in the number of corporate PACs. Although the number of labor union and corporate PACs has increased significantly, most do not raise and contribute large amounts of money. During the 1995–1996 campaign cycle, only thirty-nine corporate PACs raised more than $500,000, with thirty-six each contributing that much to candidates from funds raised. Thirty-nine labor union PACs raised $500,000 or more, and twenty-nine contributed at least $500,000 to candidates.[5]

After clarification of the campaign finance laws in 1976, other types of PACs were created. The most prominent was the independent or non-connected PAC. Its numbers increased from 110 in 1977 to 956 in 1997; this represents an increase of 769 percent (see Table 9-1). One category of nonconnected PACs that has grown dramatically in the past decade is women's PACs. EMILY's List ("Early Money Is Like Yeast"—it makes dough rise) stands out because of its significant growth. Founded in 1985 by Ellen Malcolm to fund prochoice Democratic women candidates, the PAC has had remarkable growth. In 1986, EMILY's List raised more than $350,000 for two Senate candidates. By 1990, the PAC's members, using a technique called *bundling* (collecting donations to candidates and presenting them directly to the candidate by the PAC), donated $1.5 million to fourteen candidates. The members of EMILY's List contributed $6.7 million to women candidates in 1996 (an 1,814 percent growth in ten years). According to the FEC, EMILY's List spent the most amount of money of all types of PACs in 1996, with a total disbursement of $12,494,230.[6] Between 1977 and 1997, another category of PAC, those affiliated with trade associations, membership organizations, or health-related organizations, increased by 160 percent. During the 1995–1996 election cycle, twenty-eight nonconnected PACs raised $500,000 or more, and twenty-seven contributed that much to candidates. Forty-seven association- or health-related PACs raised at least $500,000, but fewer than thirty contributed at least that much.[7]

Despite the growth in the number of PACs, a significant proportion of them are relatively inactive. For example, among the nearly 3,900 PACs existing during the 1995–1996 election cycle, 817 (18 percent) did not make any contributions to candidates.[8]

Scholars, journalists, and many political leaders have expressed increasing concern about the role of PACs in federal campaign funding. PACs may have enormous influence, affecting who is viewed as a viable candidate, the outcomes of elections, access to the policy-making process, and the content of policy. Because PACs have become a major source of campaign funds for congressional candidates, an inability to obtain PAC support may mean a candidate cannot afford to run an effective campaign. If elected, the successful candidate must be ever mindful of campaign funding sources, both past and future. The escalating costs of congressional and senatorial campaigns force incumbent members of Congress to be watchful of how policy positions taken and votes cast on legislation may affect future fund-raising.

Not all aid from PACs, however, is always welcome. The entry of independent PACs into a contest may be unwelcome, even by the candidate the PACs favor. Moreover, a backlash may develop against independent PACs, particularly those that engage in negative campaigning, and that backlash can extend to the candidate supported by the independent PACs. Some candidates believe that identification with a particular PAC's issue positions, the negative campaign tactics often used by independent PACs, or the fact that a PAC is based outside the constituency hurts rather than helps the candidate's chances for electoral success.

PAC Decision Making

A number of variables influence PAC decision making on campaign contributions. These include the goals of the organization, the expectations of contributors to the PAC, the official positions within the organization of those making the decisions, their physical location (in Washington versus elsewhere), the strategic premises employed by the PAC, and the PAC's competitive position versus those of other organizations.[9]

An organization may follow a "maintaining strategy" and seek simply to continue to ensure access to those members of Congress to whom the sponsoring organization already has access. Or it may follow an "expanding strategy" and attempt to gain access to additional representatives or senators who would not normally be attuned to the PAC's interests because of the limited presence of the represented interest within the member's electoral constituency. The results of the limited amount of research done on this topic suggest that PACs generally emphasize a maintaining strategy, with only a third of contributions representing an expanding strategy.[10] PACs also tend to be more responsive to the needs of vulnerable representatives and senators who have befriended the PAC's interests.[11]

PAC decision-making patterns vary with the structure of the PAC. If the PAC has staff based in Washington, that staff tends to play a greater role in deciding to whom to contribute and how much to contribute. Contributions are also more likely to occur through the mechanism of a Washington-based fund-raising event.[12] PACs in which substantial funds are raised by local affiliates tend to follow the locals' more parochial concerns. That may not be the most rational allocation strategy to pursue, however. Rationality would require that the PAC allocate funds either to strengthen or broaden access or to replace opponents, but parochialism may require that an already supportive member of Congress receive substantial amounts of locally raised funds.[13] The degree of parochialism appears to vary by type of PAC interest—for example, defense-interest PACs are more locally oriented than labor-interest PACs.[14]

Partisanship and ideology also may influence PAC decision making—for example, defense PACs tend to be less ideological in their contribution decisions than labor, oil, and auto PACs.[15] Business PACs vary in the extent to which they pursue a partisan support strategy; usually this is associated with the vulnerability of a political party's incumbents. When political tides appear to be favoring Republicans, they may contribute more to Republican challengers than when the political climate is less favorable to that party.

Incumbents' voting records on key votes may be a major factor as well in influencing contribution decisions. An incumbent, for example, who voted against legislation the PAC considered of vital importance generally would be unlikely to receive a campaign contribution, but exceptions exist.[16] One study of PACs affiliated with Fortune 500 companies found voting records on key legislation to be the second most frequently cited criterion used in making contribution decisions (the most frequently cited was the candidate's attitudes toward business).[17] Some research suggests that corporate PACs' decisions about whether and to whom to contribute are also influenced by the size of federal contracts held by the company, the corporation's size, and whether or not the company's business is regulated by the federal government.[18] Contribution decisions by both corporate and labor PACs are also influenced by the jurisdictions of the committees on which incumbent members serve,[19] but some research indicates committee jurisdiction is more relevant in decisions regarding contributions to House incumbents than to Senate incumbents.[20]

Some PACs also must be concerned about competition for supporters, and that concern influences contribution patterns. Contributions that would leave the PAC open to criticism sufficiently severe to cost it future support from donors must be avoided. This is a particular problem for nonconnected PACs that raise funds through mass mail solicitations.[21]

Another factor that influences patterns of PAC contributions is concern about relative influence with key holders of power. If other PACs give to a member of Congress and PAC X does not, will that have an impact on relative access? Although some PACs act as though it would, others could pursue a different strategy, gaining the member's attention by giving to his or her challenger. The member of Congress might therefore become more attentive to gain support from the PAC. The effectiveness of that strategy, however, would be limited by the extent to which the PAC's preferred policy outcomes conflict with the strength of a contrary ideology held by the member of Congress or the intensity of support for a different policy position present in that member's constituency.

Role of PACs in Campaign Finance

PAC receipts, expenditures, and contributions to congressional candidates have increased significantly since the early 1970s. PAC receipts grew from $19.2 million in 1972 to $437.4 million in 1995–1997, and PAC expenditures increased from $19 million to $429.9 million.[22] PAC contributions to congressional candidates increased from $8.5 million for the 1972 elections to $201.4 million for the 1996 elections. Congressional candidates' dependence on PAC contributions increased significantly between 1976 and 1996.[23]

The changing technology of campaigns stimulates candidates' perceived needs for PAC funds. Extensive use of professional campaign management firms, surveys, television advertising, and the other requirements of modern campaigns have greatly increased campaign costs. Total spending in general election contests for the Senate increased by 1,007 percent between 1974 and 1996, with Senate candidates spending a total of $222.6 million in 1992 compared with $20.1 million in the 1975–1976 election cycle. Candidates for the general election races for the House of Representatives spent $446 million in 1995–1996, compared with $38 million in 1975–1976. The average campaign cost for a House incumbent seeking reelection in 1996 was $725,000. The average general election campaign cost for Senate incumbents was $4.1 million.[24] In 1974 no candidate for the House spent more than $500,000 in a campaign, but in 1992, 224 House candidates spent more than that in general election campaigns, with fifty spending more than $1 million.[25] In fact, the median expenditures of Republican incumbents in the House was $610,166 (up from a median of $416,080 in 1994). The median amount spent by Democratic House incumbents was $471,56 in 1996 (down from $501,155 in

1994). Spending by all Congressional candidates in 1996 increased by 5 percent from the record-breaking 1993–1994 election cycle, and 12 percent over the previous presidential cycle.[26]

The dependence on PAC funds to meet the large and ever-increasing costs of campaigns for Congress varies greatly by legislative chamber, incumbency status, and party. In 1996 Democratic House incumbents received 46 percent of their total campaign receipts from PACs, whereas Republican incumbents in the House obtained 37 percent of their funds from that source. Challengers and candidates for open seats received less, with, for example, Republican challengers receiving 10 percent of their funds from PACs and Democratic challengers receiving 23 percent. Senate candidates are less dependent on PAC money; in 1996 Democratic incumbents obtained 14 percent of their funds from PACs, and Republican incumbents received 31 percent from that source. Challengers and open-seat candidates in both parties in the Senate received even less from PACs; neither averaged more than 17 percent.[27]

If candidates obtained a greater share of their funds from other sources, public concern about the role of PACs in American politics would probably lessen. The federal campaign finance laws, however, limit how much political parties may contribute to congressional candidates and spend on their behalf. Although those limits are not met in all contests, they may be met in open-seat contests or in Senate contests, especially by the Republican campaign finance committees. Permitting parties to give more to their candidates and changing the campaign finance laws to permit citizens to give more to political parties would encourage reduced dependence on PAC funding.

To overcome the limits on party funding of congressional campaigns contained within the federal laws, several practices have developed whose effects can only be estimated. In the first practice the political party organizations guide individual or PAC contributions to particular candidates, and especially to those whom the parties believe have a good chance of winning if adequate funding can be made available. A PAC may collect contributions from members in the form of checks made out to a particular candidate and then present the collected checks to the candidate, a practice known as bundling. Thus the candidate knows that he or she received a substantial total contribution from the members of the interest group represented by the PAC. The second practice is to guide money—particularly money that may not be given under federal law but is permissible in some states, such as campaign contributions from corporate treasury monies (commonly called *soft money*)—to state political party organizations to be used for various campaign purposes such as generic advertising, voter registration drives, and voter mobilization drives on election day. These contributions can be used, of course, for a variety of campaign activities that promote the presidential ticket as well as congressional candidates.

During the 1995–1996 election cycle 77 percent of PAC contributions went to candidates for the House of Representatives.[28] Senate campaigns are much more expensive than House contests, and the $5,000-per-election restriction limits the impact of PAC contributions on Senate contests. In general, only a finite number of PACs are interested in any one contest, and most PACs do not give to any one candidate the maximum amount of money allowed under the law. Among the factors considered by PACs when determining whether and how much to give are the nature of the state or district and the interests of the PAC within that constituency and, for incumbents, committee assignments, past voting patterns, and help previously provided by the candidate to the PAC in support of its interests. Affiliated PACs tend to be associated with a particular business, industry, or other economic or social entity and may focus on contests in states in which the sponsoring interest group is particularly strong. Independent PACs have tended to focus more on Senate than on House contests, particularly in making independent expenditures.

Some members of Congress establish their own PACs. Leadership PACs have been created by party leaders within each chamber, and those who have presidential ambitions have formed PACs as well. These member PACs are used not only to fund research on public issues, speaking trips, and other support-building activity among the general public, but also to make campaign contributions to other candidates for Congress. Contributing to other congressional candidates builds support for the attainment and maintenance of formal positions of power within Congress and may accumulate support for a future presidential campaign. Candidate PACs have been used by Jack Kemp (R-N.Y.), Richard Cheney (R-Wyo.), Robert Dole (R-Kan.), Edward Kennedy (D-Mass.), and Bill Bradley (D-N.J.). Candidate PACs were also used by presidential candidates Ronald Reagan, Walter Mondale, George Bush, and Robert Dole.

Most prominent among the leadership PACs are those sponsored by members of Congress and used to raise and contribute money to other members or to nonincumbent candidates for Congress. In 1988, fifty-five members of Congress (twenty-five Republicans and thirty Democrats) had formed their own PACs; collectively they contributed more than $4.3 million to congressional candidates, with 56 percent going to nonincumbent candidates.[29] In 1992, Senator Dole's Campaign America PAC contributed $377,000 to congressional candidates, and House Speaker Tom Foley's House Leadership Fund contributed $244,000 to other candidates.[30] In 1995–1996, Dole's Campaign America disbursed $4,492,000. Senate Majority Leader Trent Lott's PAC, the New Republican Majority Fund, disbursed $1,386,000 in the 1995–1996 election cycle. In the first ten months of 1997, the PAC had raised $2 million.[31]

Leadership PACs serve as a vehicle for incumbents not facing a significant challenge to raise and contribute campaign funds to others. They also serve as mechanisms to foster support and loyalty to the member making the contribution. Some proposals for campaign reform target this type of PAC for elimination.

Strategies: Access and Replacement

Two types of strategy are used by PACs to obtain results from their contributions. One emphasizes contributing to obtain access to members of Congress who are positioned to be most helpful in advancing the policy interests of the PAC. The other focuses on electing people to Congress who will be more helpful to the PAC—that is, the goal is to replace members who are not supportive of the PAC's interests or ideology and to elect people to open seats who are viewed as supportive of the PAC's policy objectives.

The access strategy uses contributions to obtain access to members who can be of particular help to the PAC in obtaining its legislative goals. The consequence of this strategy is a disproportionate allocation of funds to incumbents. Those members serving on legislative committees whose jurisdiction includes areas of interest to the PAC are favored in PAC allocations. Also of importance are members who influence budgets for policies relevant to the PAC or who serve on major procedural committees such as the House Rules Committee. PACs also contribute to leaders of the House and Senate whose influence extends over the entire range of legislative policy. PACs are quite aware of a congressional member's voting record on legislation of interest to them, and many PACs make an effort to reward friends in Congress with campaign contributions. Many kinds of PACs appear to pursue an access strategy; indeed, incumbent support is the strategy generally pursued by most types of PACs.[32] In the 1995–1996 election cycle, 76 percent of corporate contributions went to incumbents. The percentage given to incumbents in the past, however, has varied with the situation, with corporate PACs giving to challengers when the electoral tides indicate that incumbents who have been less supportive of corporate interests may be vulnerable. Thus in 1980, 57 percent of corporate contributions went to incumbents, and 28 percent were given to Republicans challenging incumbent Democrats and to open-seat candidates.[33] With the Republican takeover of Congress, corporate PACs are now much more likely to give money to Republicans than Democrats (76 percent of contributions went to Republican candidates in 1995–1996), demonstrating the link between incumbency and policy preferences in the allocation decision.[34] Other types of business PACs are also highly likely to support incumbents. In contrast, labor union PACs tend to be supportive both of incumbent Democrats and of Democratic open-seat and challenger candidates. When Democratic incumbents are more vulnerable, a greater share of labor PAC funds goes to incumbents.

The second strategy of trying to replace members of Congress whose ideology and voting records do not coincide with those preferred by the

PAC is more likely to be pursued by nonconnected PACs. The proportion of their contributions going to challengers and open-seat candidates varies, with 72 percent in 1978, 33 percent in 1988, 41 percent in 1992, and 44 percent in 1996 being contributed to challengers and open-seat candidates.[35] Incumbents who are perceived as unlikely to be defeated usually have only limited amounts directed against them.

Sometimes, however, other criteria are involved in targeting. In 1982 Sen. Paul Sarbanes (D-Md.) was selected by the National Conservative Political Action Committee (NCPAC) to serve as an object lesson to other members of Congress. NCPAC assumed that other senators and representatives would see the ads run against Sarbanes on the Washington, D.C.-area television stations. The implied threat was that those whose voting records were not sufficiently in accord with NCPAC's preferences also would be the target of negative advertising campaigns. The negative advertising campaign against Sarbanes was not successful, however, and the ads were withdrawn before the general election campaign.[36] Although not effective in the Sarbanes campaign, other independent expenditure efforts have been perceived as successful. In 1984, for example, more than $1.1 million was spent to influence Illinois voters to cast their votes against Sen. Charles Percy (R-Ill.), who lost his reelection bid by 1 percent of the vote.[37] Independent expenditures also can be important in electing candidates; for example, Sen. Phil Gramm (R-Texas) benefited from more than $500,000 spent on his behalf in the 1984 Senate contest.[38]

Although nonconnected PACs raised $81.2 million in 1995–1996, they contributed only 30 percent of that amount to candidates. In contrast, corporate PACs contributed 60 percent of the $133.8 million they collected, and labor PACs contributed 46 percent of the $104.1 million they raised.[39] Nonconnected PACs find it necessary to spend far more to raise money than do affiliated PACs, who have the support of their sponsoring organizations. Nonconnected PACs also allocate more money for direct expenditures in support of or opposition to particular candidates. In 1991–1992, for example, they spent 9 percent of funds raised on expenditures for or against candidates. However in 1995–1996 only 4 percent was spent on independent expenditures.[40]

Partisan Allocation of PAC Contributions

The partisan distribution of PAC disbursements is highly influenced by majority-party control of Congress (reinforced by PACs' preference to donate money to incumbents as part of their access strategy). For example, in 1992 Democratic candidates as a group received 64 percent of campaign contributions made by PACs. However, in 1996, 54 percent of PAC contributions went to Republican candidates. With the Republican takeover of Congress in 1994, the GOP has had an advantage in the allocation of PAC contributions; however, the disparity is not as great as it had been when the Democrats controlled Congress.[41] The division of PAC money between the two parties' candidates, however, differed greatly by PAC, with 27 percent of corporate PAC contributions and 92 percent of labor union PAC contributions going to Democrats. Corporate PACs largely pursued an access strategy, allocating 76 percent of their contributions to incumbents; trade, membership, and health PACs pursued a similar course of action, granting 72 percent of their contributions to incumbents. Labor split its contributions differently, giving 51 percent to incumbents, 28 percent to challengers, and 20 percent to open-seat candidates. Non-connected PACs also divided their contributions, giving 56 percent to incumbents, 22 percent to challengers, and 22 percent to open-seat candidates. In terms of actual amounts, in 1995–1996 Democratic Senate candidates received less from PACs than Republicans did ($19.4 million versus $36.1 million). Democratic House candidates received nearly equal amounts from PACs as did Republicans ($79.4 million versus $79.7 million).[42]

PACs and the Policy Process

One way in which PACs affect policy is by influencing who wins House and Senate elections. PAC contributions can affect electoral outcomes in several ways. The first is to help incumbents by inciting reluctance among highly qualified potential candidates to enter the contest. Large sums of money in the incumbent's campaign coffers will intimidate many potential candidates and, in effect, act as a preemptive strike against them. The potential challenger, knowing the incumbent starts with a significant advantage in name recognition and typically with a favorable image with the voters, often concludes that the chance of defeating the incumbent is quite small and thus does not enter the contest.[43]

Large accumulations of campaign funds also permit early campaigning by the incumbent. The objective is to discourage potential opposition, or, if opposition does develop, to control the issue agenda of the campaign. Other goals of early spending include further increasing the incumbent's fund-raising and enhancing the popularity of potentially weak incumbents.[44]

After the campaign has begun, do challengers and incumbents benefit equally from campaign expenditures? One point of view is that the challenger benefits more, as higher levels of funding enable the challenger to establish name recognition and create awareness of his or her candidacy. Thus, substantial benefit accrues from initial expenditures. As more potential voters become aware of the challenger, however, the effectiveness of expenditures decreases.[45] Whether incumbents, who already have greater name recognition, benefit as much as challengers from their expenditures is the subject of considerable debate among scholars.[46] Through their expenditures incumbents may increase turnout, or they may prevent loss of support among those previously committed to them. Those incumbents who spend the most may be the most vulnerable, or they may be aiming for "overkill" to discourage future opposition or to gain public acclaim that will help them seek another office such as the governor's office, a U.S. Senate seat, or even the presidency.

The effectiveness of the challenger's expenditures may depend on whether political trends are favorable or unfavorable to the challenger's party.[47] If the challenger is a Democrat and factors not related to the candidate that influence congressional election outcomes—such as economic conditions and the level of approval of presidential job performance—favor the Republicans, the challenger's expenditures will buy less support than if these noncandidate factors were less favorable to the opposition.

In addition to influencing electoral outcomes, PAC contributions can influence public policy in other ways. For most PACs a primary objective of campaign contributions is to gain access to the member of Congress in order to present policy views and have them heard in the legislative setting. When an issue is not one of primary concern to a senator's or representative's constituency and not in conflict with a strongly held party position or the member's ideology, the recipient of campaign contributions from a particular source may be willing to vote in support of that interest group's issue position. It may be that the effects of campaign contributions are indirect, influencing who is lobbied when legislation of importance to a group is being considered and the receptivity of that legislator to the group's approach and arguments.[48]

Do campaign contributions generally influence legislative outcomes? Unfortunately, insufficient research exists to permit a definitive answer to the question. Studies that examine the relationship between campaign contributions and legislative roll-call votes have reached conflicting conclusions. Some suggest that PAC money affects recipients' support in roll-call votes for legislation. Studies supporting this conclusion analyzed votes on minimum wage legislation,[49] the B-1 bomber,[50] the debt limit, the windfall profits tax, and wage and price controls,[51] trucking deregulation,[52] and legislation of interest to doctors and to auto dealers.[53] A study examining the effects of labor's contributions on both general issues and urban issues concluded that their contributions had a significant impact on five of nine issues relating to urban problems and five of eight general issues, but business contributions were significant in only one issue conflict of each type.[54] One study reports that labor union contributions have an impact on support for labor's preferences on labor legislation only in some congressional sessions and not in others.[55] Other research concluded that contributions influence support for labor's preferred legislation.[56] Still other research, however, suggested that campaign contributions were not important on roll-call votes on such issues as the Chrysler Corporation's loan guarantee and the windfall profits tax[57] and dairy price supports.[58] One study examined a number of PACs and congressional voting behavior over an eight-year period and concluded that contributions rarely are related to congressional voting patterns. When they are, contributions are a surrogate for other support for the member from the interest group.[59] In summary, the evidence on the importance of PAC contributions in influencing congressional voting on roll calls is conflicting, and obviously further research on this topic is needed.

Campaign contributions may be given to reward past support rather than to gain future roll-call support. Furthermore, the most important effects of campaign contributions may not be on roll-call votes but on the various earlier stages of the legislative process such as the introduction and sponsorship of bills, the behind-the-scenes negotiations on legislative provisions, the drafting and proposing of amendments, and the mark-up of bills in subcommittees and committees.

Finally, factors such as constituency interests and ideology and party ties may determine whether campaign contributions influence legislative outcomes. If the issue is important to a significant part of the constituency, for example, constituency interests will likely prevail over PAC policy preferences. Thus, PAC money and the interest group concerns it represents may prevail only on less visible issues in which the influences of party, ideology, or constituency are not as important.[60]

Criticisms of Interest Group Activity in Campaign Finance

The increased role of PACs since the early 1970s in funding campaigns for Congress has generated substantial criticism. Certainly PAC funding plays a role in who is elected to Congress, even if the evidence about the impact of PAC contributions on roll-call voting is mixed and the research is too limited to draw firm conclusions about its influence on other stages of the congressional decision-making process.

Organization simplifies the representation of interests in a large and complex society, and PACs are one manifestation of the organized representation of interests. Criticism of the campaign finance system, however, has resulted in a number of suggestions for changes in federal law. One issue underlying the suggested changes is whether the total amount of PAC money a candidate may receive should be limited. Proponents argue that such a limitation will limit PAC influence; opponents point out that limiting PAC contributions will make it more difficult for nonincumbents to seek office.

Two ways to overcome this problem are (1) to permit individuals to make larger contributions to candidates and to political parties and (2) to permit political parties both to give more to candidates of the party and to spend more on behalf of party candidates. In general, the Democrats have opposed these suggestions as being more likely to favor Republicans, who could both raise more money from larger contributions and have more money to give to the party's candidates.

A means that political parties have used in attempts to skirt the limitations on contributions is to donate money raised by the national party organizations to state party organizations. Such money has been termed "soft" because it falls outside federal regulations on donation limits, but the use of it still affects federal elections. In 1995–1996, the Democratic national party organizations raised $123.9 million in soft money and contributed $121.8 million (an increase of 271 percent from 1992) for use by state and local party organizations to fund voter registration efforts, get-out-the-vote drives, and other party-building activities. During this same period the Republicans raised $138.2 million and contributed $138.2 million (an increase of 178 percent from 1992) in soft money.[61] In an attempt to address this issue, President Bill Clinton proposed to prohibit state and national parties from spending unregulated money (soft money) to influence federal elections.[62] To replace soft money, an increase in the maximum permitted size of individual contributions was proposed, as well as the creation of a new grassroots fund to be used by state parties to finance generic media and coordinated campaigns. In addition, Clinton's proposal included a provision to increase the level of public funding of presidential elections by $11 million for each candidate, thereby decreasing the necessity for the use of soft money.

Another criticism of PACs is that they weaken the role of the individual citizen in politics, a criticism based on the disparity between the amount an individual may contribute ($1,000) and the amount a PAC may contribute ($5,000). To increase the role of individuals, the maximum individual contribution could be increased or the maximum limit on PAC contributions reduced. Increasing the maximum an individual may give, however, increases the influence of those more affluent. PAC contributions would also be limited under the Clinton proposal. Presidential candidates could receive only $1,000 from any one PAC. Senate and House candidates could receive PAC contributions of $2,500 and $5,000, respectively, for both primary and general elections. Some reformers support eliminating PAC donations altogether; however, the constitutionality of such proposals is questionable.

An additional proposal put forth to reduce the dependence on PAC money is to encourage more individuals to give small contributions by permitting them to write off part of the contribution as a deduction from gross income in figuring income taxes or as a deduction from taxes owed. Some proposals would permit the deduction only for contributions to candidates or parties within the state where the contributor resides.

Yet another idea is to establish limits on the amount of money a candidate may spend on congressional elections. Because the Supreme Court ruled in *Buckley v. Valeo* that limiting the amount spent in congressional elections must be voluntary (the court equated campaign spending with freedom of expression), campaign-limit proposals are typically accompanied by the inducement of public financing. President Clinton proposed a system in which candidates who comply with spending limits would receive partial campaign funding from a government campaign fund.[63] If a candidate accepted the limits but the opponent did not, the candidate would receive more from the fund. But finding the money for such a fund in a very tight federal budget and convincing candidates to limit voluntarily how much they spend are highly unlikely in the present political climate. Another proposal to induce voluntary spending limits is to provide candidates who comply with spending limits free media time (or at least provide significantly reduced-cost media time). If spending limits are imposed, one must ensure that the limits are high enough to stimulate competition. If the limits are too low, the better-known incumbents will benefit and the lesser-known challengers will be further disadvantaged.

Discussion of Proposed Reforms

Campaign finance reform efforts focus on several issues. The first stems from concern over the spiraling costs of elections in the United States. More than $765 million was spent in congressional elections in 1995–1996, up from a little more than $391 million a decade previously.[64] Many see this outpouring of money as inappropriate and call for limits on the amount a candidate can spend in an election bid. A second major reform issue relates to the substantial role of PACs in funding congressional elections. PACs donated more than $201 million to candidates for Congress in the 1995–1996 election cycle.[65] Many have proposed to limit PAC influence in congressional elections by eliminating or limiting PAC contributions to candidates.

The essential problem relates to the perception of money's role in congressional elections. The evidence is mixed and the research too limited to draw firm conclusions about money's influence in other stages of the congressional decision-making process, but the perception that money buys elections is prevalent in popular culture, some sectors of the academic world, and among the press. Even if money does not buy elections or legislators' loyalty, it *appears* to have those effects. The seemingly improper nature of money in elections is itself of significant consequence. Elections legitimate governmental authority; if elections are biased toward moneyed interests, or appear to be so biased, their legitimacy is questioned. Campaign finance reform is partly motivated by a desire to squash these suspicions of impropriety. Reform is further motivated by a desire to make the electoral races more competitive to address widespread concern over the seemingly noncompetitive nature of congressional elections (especially those for the House of Representatives).

A potential problem that current proposals do not address is the imbalance in the representation of interests through PACs. For example, the rapid increase in the number of business-related PACs and the considerable potential for their future growth, compared to the much more limited potential for the growth of labor-related PACs, suggests that an imbalance in this kind of access–influence mechanism between these two types of interests exists and could become much greater. Although it could be argued that business PACs simply represent a repackaging of activities that occurred previously—free services, for example—the amounts being contributed to candidates are larger than in earlier elections. Of course, it also can be pointed out that labor PACs do much more than contribute money; they are very active in the mobilization of other types of resources as well. Other types of interests—those less affluent—are not represented through money-based mechanisms of representation such as PACs.

Fueled by growing public cynicism, Congress is again debating campaign finance reform. High profile congressional hearings into alleged abuses have spurred public concern. Revelations of money laundering and wealthy individuals buying access to top Republican and Democratic officials have been given a good deal of press attention. Also fueling momentum for reform is the Justice Department's investigation into the fund-raising practices of Vice President Al Gore and President Bill Clinton. The inquiry focuses around whether the president and vice president made telephone calls soliciting donations for the Democratic National Committee from the White House (the calls may be—or may not be—a violation of federal law). Former Republican National Chair Haley Barbour also stimulated scrutiny by the Justice Department, focusing on allegations that he received a $2.1 million loan from a Hong Kong businessperson. Of that money, $1.6 million was funneled into the RNC immediately preceding the GOP takeover in 1994, potentially violating a federal prohibition on foreign contributions. Also fueling demands for reforms were the revelations that political parties raised record amounts of soft money despite the investigations into potential corrupt practices. In the first six months of 1997, the Republicans raised $21.7 million and the Democrats $13.7 million in soft contributions.[66] To many analysts and to many in the public, it seems like Congress wants to expose corruption but is slow to alter the system that fuels it. All sides appear to be hesitant to change the current system for fear that the reforms will adversely affect their party and their personal electoral system. The public is cynical regarding the likelihood of significant reform.[67] A brief look at recent reforms and their failures will explain in part the high levels of pessimism currently present in the American electorate.

President Clinton proposed a campaign reform bill early in 1993. The bill had many of the essential characteristics of a bill vetoed by former President Bush in 1992. Clinton vowed to sign virtually any bill that dealt with electoral reform to demonstrate his commitment to campaign finance reform. The promise to sign any bill passed by Congress greatly changed the characteristics of the debate. During the previous administration, President Bush had indicated that he would veto campaign finance reform, so the Congress produced a less pragmatic bill. With Clinton's promise to sign any bill passed by the Congress, the task of enacting a reform bill became more difficult.

Also in 1993 the House passed a bill similar to President Clinton's proposals. The Senate passed quite different legislation, which did not establish public funding of congressional campaigns and which essentially banned PACs. Those campaigns that did not comply with spending limits would be taxed at the highest corporate rate. In contrast, the House bill offered public funding and other benefits to induce compliance with spending limits. In several other ways the two bills differed substantially. The current bipartisan proposal put forward by Senators McCain and Feingold is a scaled-back version of a more ambitious bill that failed in 1996. The bill, which is widely opposed by the Republican leadership, rank-and-file, and interest groups would significantly alter campaign finance practices. The McCain-Feingold bill contained three components. It would ban soft money and also provide incentives for candidates to voluntarily limit campaign spending. Issue ads would also be restricted by the bill by making a clear distinction between issue ads that take issue positions and those that are designed to defeat candidates.

Fundamental differences exist between Democrats and Republicans concerning desired campaign finance reform. Democrats historically have advocated limiting expenditures, whereas Republicans want to limit the sources of contributions. However, Democrats are divided over public financing of congressional elections, and Republicans are generally opposed to public funding of congressional campaigns. With the Republican takeover of Congress, distinctions regarding the means for reform is less clear. These differences between the House and Senate and between Democrats and Republicans in their views on campaign finance reform will continue to make it quite difficult to change laws governing financing of campaigns at the federal level.

In 1996 new tactics or extended use of previously employed tactics changed substantially the nature of campaign fund-raising by the political parties, PACs, and interest groups and directed vastly increased resources to House and Senate campaigns in attempts to influence outcomes. These tactics included the political parties raising substantially larger amounts of soft money (not federally regulated), the increased use of soft money to fund issue advocacy ads in targeted campaigns, the parties' use of independent expenditures to influence campaigns for the Senate and House, the swapping of soft money for hard money (federally regulated) among a party's committees at the state and national level or among states, and use of videotaped voter guides produced by interest groups that were broadcast on television to reach a maximum audience and that, because their sponsors could claim they were being used to inform and to stimulate turnout, were not federally regulated expenditures.[68]

Conclusion

These developments subvert the principles of disclosure, limitation, and regulation on which campaign finance reform efforts were based in the FECA and its amendments. Parties and interest groups are playing an increasing role in financing campaigns for Congress, but these new tactics enable the parties and interest groups to evade the requirements of federal law and FEC guidelines. Furthermore, the increased role of parties and interest groups weakens candidates' control over their campaigns and the messages delivered to potential voters. One consequence of this appears to be an increase in negative campaigning, with its detrimental effects on citizens' perceptions of politicians and politics.

The increased imbalance between the political parties' campaign expenditures on behalf of congressional candidates and the larger amounts of funds available to PACs and interest groups is detrimental in two ways. One is that the parties spend to promote electoral competition, whereas PAC–interest group spending tends to concentrate very heavily on the reelection of incumbents, thus weakening electoral competition. Second, although each party focuses on the broad interests of its supporting coalition, the interests served by PACs and interest groups are much more narrow.

The politics of PACs and PAC reform in the funding of campaigns for Congress present many problems. PACs are here and are not likely to be abolished, and their role in the political process will continue, as will the controversies about their role.[69]

Notes

1. FEC press release, April 14, 1997.
2. See Edwin Epstein, "The Emergence of Political Action Committees," in *Political Finance*, ed. Herbert Alexander (Beverly Hills, Calif.: Sage, 1979), 159–179.
3. *Buckley v. Valeo*, 424 U.S. 1 (1976).
4. FEC press release, July 25, 1997.
5. FEC press release, April 22, 1997.
6. http://www.emilyslist.org; FEC press release, April 22, 1997.
7. Ibid.
8. Ibid.
9. Theodore J. Eismeier and Philip H. Pollock, III, "An Organizational Analysis of Political Action Committees," *Political Behavior* 7 (1985): 192–216.
10. John R. Wright, "PAC Contributions, Lobbying, and Representation," *Journal of Politics* 51 (August 1989): 713–729.
11. J. David Gopoian, "What Makes PACs Tick? An Analysis of the Allocation Patterns of Economic Interest Groups," *American Journal of Political Science* 28 (May 1984): 259–281.
12. Larry J. Sabato, *PAC Power: Inside the World of Political Action Committees* (New York: Norton, 1985), 42–43.
13. John R. Wright, "PACs, Contributions, and Roll Calls: An Organizational Perspective," *American Political Science Review* 79 (June 1985): 400–414.
14. Gopoian, "What Makes PACs Tick?" 279.
15. Ibid., 271.

16. Some PACs will contribute to candidates who oppose them in the hope of minimizing the intensity or frequency of the opposition to their interests. Davies found this factor to be statistically significant; Hall and Wayman also suggest some PACs pursue a strategy of attempting to minimize the opposition. See F. L. Davis, "Sophistication in Corporate PAC Contributions: Demobilizing the Opposition," *American Politics Quarterly* 20 (October 1992): 381–410; R. L. Hall and F. W. Wayman, "Buying Time: Moneyed Interests and the Mobilization of Bias in Congressional Committees," *American Political Science Review* 84 (1990): 797–820.

17. Ann B. Matasar, *Corporate PACs and Federal Campaign Financing Laws* (New York: Quorum Books, 1986), Table 13, 58. When incumbents are involved in close contests, voting records may induce contributions for a candidate whose record is favorably assessed by a corporate PAC and against an incumbent whose record is viewed negatively. See K. T. Poole, Thomas Romer, and H. Rosenthal, "The Revealed Preferences of Political Action Committees," *American Economic Review* 77 (May 1987): 298–302.

18. R. B. Grier and M. C. Munger, "Committee Assignments, Constituent Preferences, and Campaign Contributions," *Economic Inquiry* 29 (January 1991): 24–43.

19. J. W. Endersby and M. C. Munger, "The Impact of Legislator Attributes on Union PAC Campaign Contributions," *Journal of Labor Research* 13 (Winter 1992), 79–97; M. C. Munger, "A Simple Test of the Thesis that Committee Jurisdictions Shape Corporate PAC Contributions," *Public Choice* 62 (1989): 181–186.

20. K. B. Grier, M. C. Munger, and G. M. Torrent, "Allocation Patterns of PAC Monies: The U.S. Senate," *Public Choice* 67 (1990): 111–128.

21. Eismeier and Pollock, "Organizational Analysis," 207–208.

22. FEC press release, April 14, 1997.

23. Ibid.

24. Calculated from FEC press release, April 22, 1997.

25. Ibid.

26. FEC press release, April 14, 1997.

27. Computed from data contained in the FEC press release, April 14, 1997.

28. Ibid., 2–3.

29. Larry Makinson, *Open Secrets: The Dollar Power of PACs in Congress, Center for Responsive Politics* (Washington, D.C.: CQ Press, 1990), 77.

30. FEC, "PAC Activity Rebounds in the 1991–1992 Election Cycle," *News from the FEC*, March 29, 1993, 25.

31. *New York Times*, October 13, 1997, A1.

32. Frank J. Sorauf, *Money in American Politics* (Glenview, Ill.: Scott, Foresman, 1988), 103.

33. FEC press release, March 2, 1982, and April 29, 1993.

34. FEC press release, April 27, 1997.

35. FEC press release, May 10, 1979, April 29, 1993, 3, and April 22, 1997.

36. Polls conducted by the *Baltimore Sun* indicated that the proportion of the public approving of Senator Sarbanes's job performance remained stationary, whereas the proportion disapproving increased from 20 percent to 29 percent between October 1981 and February 1982. During that period several NCPAC ads critical of Sarbanes's performance were shown on television stations broadcast to Maryland residents. See Karen Hosler, "Voter Shifts Favor Hughes, Hurt Sarbanes," *Baltimore Sun*, February 22, 1982, A1.

37. FEC press release, October 4, 1985.

38. Ibid.

39. Computed from data in FEC press release, April 22, 1997.

40. FEC press release, April 22, 1997.

41. Ibid.

42. Ibid.

43. In 1992, eleven members of the House were defeated in primary elections and nineteen lost in the general election.

44. Paul West, "'Early Media' Push '86 Campaign on the Air," *Baltimore Sun*, December 12, 1985, 1A.

45. See Gary C. Jacobson, "Money and Votes Reconsidered: Congressional Elections, 1972–1982," *Public Choice* 47 (1985): 43–46; and Jacobson, "The Effects of Campaign Spending in House Elections: New Evidence for Old Arguments," *American Journal of Political Science* 34 (May 1990): 334–362.

46. See Donald P. Green and Jonathan S. Krasno, "Salvation for the Spendthrift Incumbent: Re-estimating the Effects of Campaign Spending in House Elections," *American Journal of Political Science* 32 (November 1988): 884–907; Jacobson's response in "Effects of Campaign Spending"; and Green and Krasno's response in "Rebuttal to Jacobson's 'New Evidence for Old Arguments,'" *American Journal of Political Science* 34 (May 1990): 363–374. See also J. R. Lott, Jr., "Does Additional Campaign Spending Really Hurt Incumbents? The Theoretical Importance of Past Investments in Political Brand Name," *Public Choice* 72 (1991): 87–92.

47. Gary C. Jacobson, "Strategic Politicians and the Dynamics of U.S. House Elections, 1946–1986," *American Journal of Political Science* 83 (September 1989): 773–794; C. Wilcox, "Organizational Variables and Contribution Behavior of Large PACs: A Longitudinal Analysis," *Political Behavior* 11 (June 1989): 157–174; D. Epstein and P. Zemsky, "Money Talks; Detering Quality Challengers in Congressional Elections," *American Political Science Review* 89 (1995): 295–308.

48. J. Wright, "Contributions, Lobbying, and Committee Voting in the U.S. House of Representatives," *American Political Science Review* 84 (June 1990): 417–438.

49. Jonathan I. Silberman and Garey C. Durden, "Determining Legislative Preferences on Minimum Wage: An Economic Approach," *Journal of Political Economy* 94 (April 1986): 317–329.

50. Henry W. Chappel, Jr., "Campaign Contributions and Congressional Voting: A Simultaneous Probit-Tobit Model," *Review of Economics and Statistics* (February 1982): 77–83.

51. James B. Kau and Paul H. Rubin, *Congressmen, Constituents, and Contributors: Determinants of Roll Call Votes* (Boston: Martinus Nijhoff, 1982), Table 7.5, 96–97.

52. John P. Frendreis and Richard W. Waterman, "PAC Contributions and Legislative Behavior: Senate Voting on Trucking Deregulation," *Social Science Quarterly* 66 (June 1985): 401–412.

53. K. F. Brown, "Campaign Contributions and Congressional Voting" (Paper delivered at the annual meeting of the American Political Science Association, Chicago, September 1–4, 1983).

54. Kau and Rubin, *Congressmen, Constituents, and Contributors.*

55. A. Wilhite, "Union PAC Contributions and Legislative Voting," *Journal of Labor Research* 9 (Winter 1988): 79–90.

56. Gregory M. Saltzman, "Congressional Voting on Labor Issues: The Role of PACs," *Industrial and Labor Relations Review* 40 (January 1987): 163–179.

57. Diana M. Evans, "PAC Contributions and Roll-Call Voting: Conditional Power," in *Interest Group Politics*, 2d ed., ed. Allan J. Cigler and Burdett A. Loomis (Washington, D.C.: CQ Press, 1986), 114–132.

58. W. P. Welch, "Campaign Contributions and House Voting: Milk Money and Dairy Price Supports," *Western Political Quarterly* 35 (December 1982): 478–495.

59. Janet M. Grenzke, "PACs and the Congressional Supermarket: The Currency Is Complex," *American Journal of Political Science* 33 (February 1989): 1–24.

60. F. L. Davis, "Balancing the Perspective on PAC Contributions: In Search of an Impact on Roll Calls," *American Politics Quarterly* 21 (April 1993): 205–222.

61. FEC press release, March 19, 1997.

62. *CQ Weekly Report*, May 8, 1993, 1121–1122.

63. Ibid.
64. FEC press release, April 4, 1997.
65. FEC press release, March 19, 1997.
66. *CQ Weekly Report,* September 27, 1997, 2279–2284.
67. Ibid.
68. Paul Herrnson, Chapter 7, this book; Diana Dwyre, "Pushing the Campaign Finance Envelope: Parties and Interest Groups in the 1996 House and Senate Elections" (Paper delivered at the 1997 American Political Science Association annual meeting, Washington, D.C., August 28–31, 1997).
69. For more detailed discussions of the arguments for and against various reform proposals, see David B. Magleby and Candice J. Nelson, *The Money Chase* (Washington, D.C.: Brookings Institution, 1990), chaps. 8–11; Dan Clawson, Alan Neustadtl, and Denise Scott, *Money Talks* (New York: Basic Books, 1992), chap. 7; and Frank J. Sorauf, *Inside Campaign Finance* (New Haven, Conn.: Yale University Press, 1992), chap. 7.

III. INTERESTS AND THE POLICY PROCESS

10

Lobbying Friends and Foes in Washington

Beth L. Leech and Frank R. Baumgartner

Over the years, both scholarly and journalistic observers of lobbying have tended to emphasize one of two sets of tactics: (1) the marshalling of efforts to cajole and pressure those who oppose their positions or who remain undecided on an issue that affects an interest, and (2) the provision of numerous services to those legislators and other governmental officials who favor the group's position. In recent years, a generally arid and unproductive scholarly literature has grown up around whether interests lobby their "friends" or their "foes." Lobbyists find such a dichotomy as lacking a firm base in reality—especially to the extent that one set of activities is performed to the exclusion of others, at least on major issues.

In this article Beth Leech and Frank Baumgartner merge these literatures, noting, "There is no contradiction between the 'service bureau' tradition of scholarship and the 'pressure group' school." Rather, interests shape their tactics to their targets, and place them in context. The authors find that the most common tactic used by lobbyists is persuasion aimed at undecided legislators to support an interests' position. And the "persuasion" can come in the form of service (information) or pressure. Moreover, Leech and Baumgartner note that groups seek to find legislators to lobby on their behalf—again, with the possible alternative tactics of offering services or applying pressures. In short, lobbyists adapt as contexts change. Such a conclusion is simple, yet it moves us toward more productive analyses of lobbying behaviors and the choices made by organized interests.

Scholars have traditionally adopted one of two seemingly opposing views in discussing interest-group lobbying tactics. One view focuses on the efforts of groups to pressure undecided or opposing government of-

The research reported in this chapter was funded by National Science Foundation Doctoral Enhancement Grant #SBR–9631232, with additional financial support from the Program in American Politics at Texas A&M University. Leech was supported during the collection of these data by an NSF Graduate Research Fellowship and the Department of Political Science at Texas A&M. Any opinions, findings, or conclusions expressed here are those of the authors and do not necessarily reflect the views of the National Science Foundation.

ficials through such tactics as argumentation, letter-writing campaigns, demonstrations of constituency support, or the threat to oppose them in the next election. Another body of scholarship focuses on the services that groups render to government officials allied with them in mutually reinforcing systems of reciprocal support. In this chapter we show why groups should be expected to follow both strategies. There is no contradiction between the "service bureau" tradition of scholarship and the "pressure group" school of research. We review these scholarly traditions, discuss the goals that groups are trying to achieve with each approach, and note how these goals are complementary rather than mutually exclusive. We go on to present data on lobbying friends and foes from a large survey of interest groups active in Washington, using these data to show how groups typically use a combined strategy of working with their governmental allies and attempting to win converts on the other side as well. A complete understanding of lobbying tactics must recognize that lobbyists simultaneously have many targets. At the same time as they work with one group of allies within and outside of government, hoping to affect the content of a new policy, they cannot ignore the need to garner support for the policy among a broader range of potential supporters. Most groups are both pressure groups and service providers; their tactics depend on their targets.

The Choice

One common view of interest group lobbyists depicts them as arm-twisters who force government officials to go against their better judgment to do the group's bidding. In this view, letter-writing campaigns put pressure on officials, PAC contributions attempt to buy legislative votes, and personal visits with government officials take a threatening tone. Groups argue with legislators that if they do not work with them there may be consequences at the next election, either because the group will withhold cooperation and contributions or because the group will mount an active campaign against the legislator or in support of a rival. This depiction of interest group–government relations is accurate in some cases, but another view of lobbying is equally accurate. Interest groups and their lobbyists spend much of their time working with their friends within government, lobbying cooperatively rather than conflictually. In the cooperative view, letter-writing campaigns can provide support and political cover for governmental allies, PAC contributions help friendly legislators get reelected, and personal visits are a time to share information and plan political strategies.

The distinction between conflictual and cooperative lobbying strategies dates back at least as far as the description of interest groups as "service bureaus" rather than "pressure groups," which was put forth in *American Business and Public Policy*, a classic study of trade legislation in the late 1950s.[1] Although many previous depictions of lobbyists had assumed that their job was to badger officials who disagreed with them, *American Business and Public Policy* found that lobbyists spent most of their time consulting with their friends and allies in government, providing information, and rendering services to those officials. The portrayal of lobbying as a non-conflictual activity taking place among friends carried through in other writings of the communications school as exemplified by political scientist Lester Milbrath and others.[2] These authors emphasized how little impact lobbyists had on legislators' decisions and viewed the role of lobbyists as benign, because the information transmitted simply made legislators better informed rather than pressuring them to change their views.

The term *pressure group* is seldom used in recent studies, but the concept of a lobbying strategy based on conflict rather than cooperation has hardly been abandoned. The hypothesis being tested in many of the PAC studies conducted in the 1980s was that campaign contributions pressured legislators to vote with the contributing group. Other frequently used lobbying tactics also can be seen as pressure tactics: Letter-writing campaigns and other shows of district strength, for example, can serve as electoral threats against legislators should they vote the wrong way. Even lobbying that provides information only about the issue at hand, and not about constituency sentiment, can be seen as conflictual when it is directed at an official who remains to be convinced, because such an exchange takes on the qualities of a minidebate, which the lobbyist wins or loses. Rather than simply *providing information*, as groups would to allied officials, group lobbyists must *convince* officials who oppose their position. Arguments may be on the substance of the policy issue in question or on the electoral consequence of voting against the group, but in those cases in which the target is a legislator predisposed against or undecided, the aim of the lobbying communications is quite different from a situation in which the target is an official who already agrees with the group. What would be pressure to one is service to the other.

There is no reason to think that groups must limit themselves to one or another of these strategies. Groups are of course constrained by limited lobbying resources, but they should be expected in some cases to work with allies and in other cases to try to convince undecided or opposing legislators. The question is to define the circumstances under which they will choose to lobby friends rather than foes, and the circumstances under which they would do both.

Why Lobbying Allies Makes Sense

A number of possible explanations have been suggested for why interest groups choose to lobby governmental allies. One reason is simply because all of the government officials the interest groups must contact to achieve their political goals already share the same point of view as the interest group. In other words, interest groups do not *choose* to lobby allies, they simply have no other option. This is the argument made by Ken Kollman, a political scientist at the University of Michigan, using data from a survey of Washington interest groups collected by the late Jack Walker, also of the University of Michigan. Kollman finds that as a result of subsystems and bias within the congressional committee system, "Committees tend to share the same biases as the interest groups surrounding them."[3] In a study of witness testimony in congressional hearings on pesticides and smoking issues, political scientists Bryan Jones, Frank Baumgartner, and Jeffery Talbert found that different committees systematically invited different types of interest-group lobbyists to testify before them. Those committees with a bias in favor of the pesticides or the tobacco industries typically invited a surfeit of like-minded lobbyists to give them information; those committees whose members were intent on changing things invited a wholly different set of witnesses to testify.[4] Part of the reason for focusing on allies may be that many issue areas are home to cozy subsystems in which most of the important players already agree with each other. Absent some controversy, they typically work with those who already agree with them. This is the standard finding of a long list of studies focusing on policy subsystems.

One of the farm commodity groups included in the survey reported on in this chapter illustrated this type of lobbying in describing its dealings with the U.S. Department of Agriculture (USDA): "We're dealing with a friendly agency," the organization's government relations specialist said. "It's not a regulatory thing. We're not going to have to persuade them that our position is the right one." The organization's lobbying interactions with the USDA thus consist mainly of information sharing. An official from the USDA will call the organization with information about proposed actions by the USDA or by foreign governments that might affect the members of the organization. The organization in turn briefs the USDA on what the impact of that governmental action would be on its members and, in turn, on the economy. Occasionally there is conflict among organizations representing different commodities, and in that case a more conflictual style of lobbying, including letter-writing campaigns and congressional pressure, may emerge. But for the most part, the group and the governmental officials with whom they deal are on the same side. A long tradition of scholarship, traceable across the entire twentieth century, notes the importance of consensual subsystem relations among agency officials and friendly interest groups.[5]

Another reason for lobbying governmental allies is because those allied officials are the most likely to sponsor legislation, and a sponsor is the first thing needed by any interest group hoping to change a policy with new legislation. In their primer for lobbyists titled *How to Win in Washington*, Ernest and Elisabeth Wittenberg, themselves longtime Washington lobbyists, noted the importance of finding a congressional sponsor. "Get a Horse" is their advice: A "horse" is a member who will take on the cause of the interest group as her own, who will, in effect, carry the group's water in the legislature.[6] Similarly, when adverse legislation is initiated by a rival, allies within Congress are key to efforts to amend or to soften the impact of the proposed changes. Whether the interest group supported the original bill or not, it needs allies within committee if it hopes to change language within a bill or add amendments to it.

Political scientists Marie Hojnacki and David Kimball point out that groups spend more time lobbying their allies in committee, where legislation takes shape.[7] When the bill is considered on the floor, the same lobbyists may adopt a different approach, seeking to gain the votes of a broader range of allies. In committee, they need not only the votes, but especially the active participation of a small number of active friends. Political scientists Richard Hall and Frank Wayman illustrate the importance of this strategy in their study of participation within committee. They show that members vary dramatically in activity in the mark-up sessions. Some propose a great number of amendments, others are typically less involved.[8]

Clearly, at the early stages of the legislative process, an active set of close allies within government can be important in terms of affecting the content of legislation. According to Hojnacki and Kimball and to Hall and Wayman, groups would be expected to follow different strategies at different stages, working especially with a small group of allies first as they attempt to affect content, then broadening their targets later as they attempt to get the legislation passed or defeated on the floor. An organization lobbies its allies on a committee in the hopes that a staff member will share proposed legislative language with the organization and listen to input and advice from the organization on additional changes to the bill. The organization stays in contact with its allies so that if the committee calls for hearings on the issue, the organization is asked to testify. Even if the organization opposes the bill in question, close contact with allies at this stage is important. Weakening the language in a bill that your organization opposes can minimize the potential losses your organization might suffer should the bill eventually be enacted.

Allied governmental officials also may be persuaded to lobby other officials on the issue in question. No one else has greater access to other members of Congress than a fellow member. No one else has greater access to employees of an agency than another employee. If that member can intervene on behalf of your group with other members of Congress, or if that employee can feed your group information about the regulatory process, your group will have the advantage. But such contacts must be maintained, and thus interest-group lobbyists spend much of their time keeping in touch with their friends and allies within government, sharing information and exchanging favors.

In a recent article discussing lobbying from the perspective of the member of Congress, Scott Ainsworth, a political scientist at the University of Georgia, reminded us that members need the help of lobbyists to achieve their own legislative goals. Using the concept of a "lobbying enterprise," Ainsworth noted that like-minded individuals work together on a variety of legislative issues. These coalitions can be informal, small, and temporary, or they can grow into large and institutionalized organizations such as a caucus or a study group. Ainsworth wrote, "Unlike legislative coalitions, lobbying enterprises include members and nonmembers alike. In addition, lobbying enterprises are more stable and become semi-institutionalized. In the U.S. Congress, lobbying enterprises are centered around individual legislators, caucuses, and committees. Lobbying enterprises allow lobbyists to coordinate their efforts with legislative allies" just as they allow legislators to coordinate their efforts with lobbyists, Ainsworth argued.[9] Interest groups often work with their legislative allies, then, because their allies recruit them into a lobbying enterprise.

Members of course want to be known for good public policy and not only for doing favors, and so they are often willing to go to considerable lengths to promote popular interests from their districts or public policy issues on which they have a particular investment of time and energy.[10] In exchange, they may want information, further support, and help in pushing the issue along. The idea that groups are on the outside, pressuring recalcitrant government officials into doing their bidding and against their will, is wholly incomplete. Most major groups, and many small ones, benefit from long-standing relations with government officials who are predisposed toward helping them. Their lobbying strategies are thus a combination of coordinating with their friends at the same time as they work with enough of their sometimes foes to craft legislative majorities.

Who Lobbies?

The data presented in this chapter come from the National Survey of Government Relations, a survey of nearly 800 interest groups maintaining offices in the Washington, D.C., area.[11] The survey was conducted by mail between April 1996 and March 1997. The interest groups included in the study include a wide range of organizational types: clubs, citizen groups, professional associations, businesses, large institutions such as universities, and even the Washington offices of state and local governments. Table 10-1 divides the respondents to the survey into seven categories: businesses, trade associations, professional associations, unions, governmental associations, nonprofit-sector groups, and other institutions. The business category includes the government relations offices of individual businesses and corporations such as General Motors, Sears and Roebuck, and Microsoft. A few of the businesses are actually based in the Washington area, but more than 80 percent are based elsewhere, maintaining a separate Washington office for lobbying efforts. (If they did not maintain a separate Washington office, they would not have

Table 10-1   Types of Organizations

	Percentage	N
Businesses	19	149
Trade associations	28	222
Professional associations	17	137
Unions	3	21
Governmental organizations	3	25
Nonprofit-sector groups	28	225
Other institutions	2	18
Total	100	797

Note: Percentages may not sum to 100 because of rounding.

been included in our sampling frame.) Among the other types of groups, 80 percent or more have their headquarters in the Washington, D.C., area.

Trade associations, of course, represent groups of businesses—for instance, the American Hotel and Motel Association, the American Sugar Beet Growers, and the Chamber of Commerce. These are not-for-profit membership organizations that represent the profit sector. They tend to provide services and information to their members, and often one important service is lobbying activities on behalf of the industry. The third category is professional associations. In some ways, these associations are similar to trade associations, because they also provide occupation-related information and services to their members. Members of professional associations are far more likely to be individuals, whereas members of trade associations are usually businesses, and professional associations are far less active in lobbying activities, as we will see. Examples of professional associations include the American Medical Association (which is quite active in the lobbying arena), the National Association for Dental Assistants, the American Political Science Association, and the Society for Professional Journalists. Like the first three categories, unions are occupationally focused. Like professional associations, unions have members who join because of their occupations; unlike professional associations, unions have the legal right to represent those members in contract negotiations. They also are far more active politically than the professional associations tend to be.

The fifth category in Table 10-1, governmental organizations, includes the Washington offices of states, cities, and counties, as well as governmental associations such as the National League of Cities. The governors of most states and the mayors of many large cities maintain Washington offices in order to monitor legislation and lobby on issues affecting their local economies and budgets. Although they themselves represent governmental entities, they have no formal role in the federal decision-making process, and thus use many of the same lobbying tactics as the other interest groups in the study. Because lobbying is their sole reason for being in Washington, and because they tend to be quite well connected, these offices are among the most active in the survey.

The sixth category, nonprofits, includes citizen groups, social clubs, issue-advocacy organizations, charities, and religious groups. Examples of this type of group would be the Sierra Club, Handgun Control Inc., the American Lung Association, and Knights of Columbus. The final category includes other types of organizations that do not fit easily into the previous categories, but primarily consists of large institutions such as universities, stock exchanges, and nonprofit hospitals.

Lobbying Activities

The groups represented in our survey vary not only by whom they represent, but also by how large their lobbying staffs are and how often they lobby. Table 10-2 shows the number of staff members devoted to government relations in each of the group types. Table 10-3 shows how often these associations report being active in government relations. The tables make clear that some groups, particularly businesses, trade associations, government organizations, and unions tend to have larger staffs and to lobby more frequently than others. Still, most groups in the sample, no matter what the type, have significant staff resources and are quite active in government relations activities.

Table 10-2 shows that the groups tend to have quite substantial staff resources. Seventy-six percent of the groups have at least two full-time

Table 10-2   Number of Government Relations Staff Members

Question: "How many staff members do work that involves federal government relations as part of their duties? Federal government relations would include monitoring government activities, preparing reports or comments about proposed policies, or contacting government officials."

	None	One	Two to five	Six to twenty	More than twenty	N
Business corporations	1%	4%	48%	31%	17%	149
Trade associations	6	16	52	22	5	218
Professional associations	13	21	51	15	1	131
Unions	10	14	19	33	24	21
Governmental organizations	4	0	50	33	13	24
Nonprofit-sector groups	19	18	39	19	4	218
Other	6	6	61	22	6	18
Overall percentage	10	14	47	22	7	779

Note: Percentages may not sum to 100 because of rounding.

Table 10-3   Frequency of Government Relations

Question: "How often is this organization active in government relations, including monitoring government activities, preparing reports or comments about proposed policies, mobilizing citizens regarding proposed policies, or contacting government officials?"

	Never	Once a year or less	Several times a year	Monthly	Weekly	Daily	N
Business corporations	1%	2%	6%	2%	7%	81%	149
Trade associations	5	6	8	4	13	64	222
Professional associations	9	5	13	8	17	49	131
Unions	10	0	10	5	5	70	20
Governmental organizations	4	0	0	0	0	96	24
Nonprofit-sector groups	11	2	17	7	19	44	220
Other	13	0	6	13	6	63	16
Overall percentage	7	3	11	5	14	60	783

Note: Percentages may not sum to 100 because of rounding.

lobbyists, and 29 percent have more than five. When we turn, in Table 10-3, to government relations, we see that the groups are generally very active. Sixty percent responded that their organization engaged daily in government relations, whereas just 7 percent said they never did so. There was quite a bit of variation based on group type, with government organizations being most likely to report that they were involved daily with federal government relations, followed by businesses, unions, and trade associations. Professional associations and nonprofit-sector organizations were least likely to lobby daily. Part of the explanation for the patterns evident in this table have to do with resources: In general, organizations with larger budgets and larger staffs tended to engage in government relations more often.

Who Is Lobbied?

Rather than asking groups which lobbying tactics they usually used or selecting the issues beforehand, the survey asked respondents to identify the issue with which they had most recently been involved, and then to answer a series of questions based on that issue. The range of issues involved was quite broad, including many of the most publicized bills of 1996 and many issues that received no outside attention, meaning that our findings should relate to lobbying in general, not just lobbying on a particular type of issue.

Three questions asked respondents to describe whom they had lobbied on the issue in question. The first question asked whether their organization had "consulted with people in government who already agreed with our policy position." The second asked whether they "tried to persuade government officials who were undecided about the policy issue." The third asked whether they "tried to persuade government officials who were opposed to our policy position." Respondents could characterize each of these statements as poor or good descriptions of their lobbying activities by marking five-point scales next to the statements. The results of their responses are shown in Table 10-4.

The most common type of lobbying target was undecided officials, followed by allied officials. Groups were least likely to spend time trying to persuade officials who clearly disagreed with them, although it is worth noting that more than half of the groups did, in fact, lobby these opposing officials on the issue in question. This pattern held true nearly across the board, regardless of the type of group involved, as we can see in Figure 10-1. Although some types of groups (governmental associations, trade associations, businesses) have higher overall levels of lobbying, the general pattern remains. Most types of groups tended to lobby undecided officials, followed by allies, followed by opponents. An exception to this pattern was unions, which were slightly more likely to lobby allied officials than any other targets. The differences are quite small, however: The number of unions indicating that they had targeted allied officials was only one union greater than the number indicating that they had targeted undecided officials. The data presented in Table 10-4 and Figure 10-1 clearly show that the majority of organizations lobbied all three possible targets on the issue in question. Rather than limiting themselves only to friends or only to convincing opponents, organizations tend to try to do it all.

Table 10-4   Lobbying Targets

Question: "How good a description are each of the following sentences of this organization's efforts regarding this issue? We consulted with people in government who already agreed with our policy position. We tried to persuade government officials who were undecided about this policy issue. We tried to persuade government officials who were opposed to our policy position."

	Poor description of issue	Neutral	Good description of issue	N
Consulted with allied officials	21%	15%	63%	709
Persuaded undecided officials	11	13	76	715
Persuaded opposing officials	20	22	58	713

Note: Percentages may not sum to 100 because of rounding.

Figure 10-1 Choice of Lobbying Target by Group

Percentage of groups

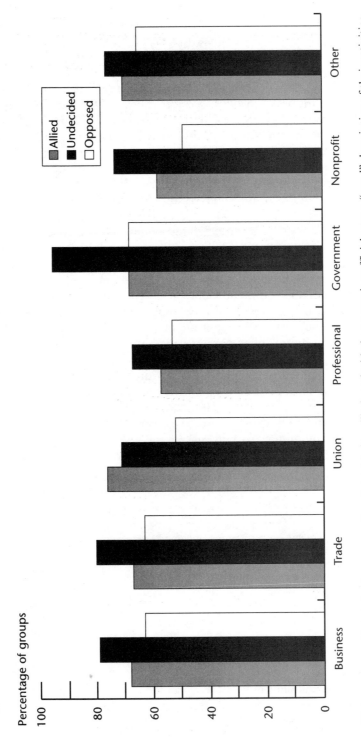

The percentage of organizations responding that lobbying allied, undecided, or opposing officials was a "good" description of their activities. (For question wording, see Table 10-4.)

Institutional Allies

What of Kollman's idea that interest groups lobby allies simply because they are there? The survey asked respondents whether they could identify a congressional committee, executive agency, or other governmental entity that was generally supportive of their organization's policy positions on the issue in question. Regardless of the type of group involved or how active they were in lobbying activities, most organizations could name such an institutional ally, and nearly half could name three or more. There were three series of questions, one regarding congressional allies, one regarding allies within agencies, and a third regarding allies within other governmental institutions.

The first series of questions asked respondents whether a congressional committee was involved in their policy issue; 578 of them said yes. Table 10-5 shows that of those 578 respondents, 83 percent were able to name a congressional committee or subcommittee that seemed supportive of their organization's policy position. Almost half (44 percent) could name three or more allied committees. The second series of questions asked whether a government agency was involved in the issue; in 592 of the cases the answer was yes. Fully 76 percent of the respondents could name an agency that was supportive of their position; 33 percent could name three or more. Other supportive institutions were noted by 79 percent of the groups.

The flip side to this supportive institutional structure is, of course, the presence of opposing or adversarial governmental agencies or congressional committees. Table 10-6 shows that this was also quite common. Approximately two-thirds of the respondents could name at least one hostile committee (64 percent), at least one hostile agency (60 percent), and at least one hostile institution (68 percent). Thus in most of the cases discussed by our respondents, the reasons for choosing to lobby al-

Table 10-5 Supportive Institutions of Government

Questions: "Were any subcommittees or committees [executive or regulatory agencies, other types of governmental actors] active in this issue? If yes: Did any subcommittees or committees [executive or regulatory agencies, other types of governmental actors] seem supportive of this organization's policy position? If yes, please indicate which ones."

	None	One	Two	Three or more	N
Supportive committees listed	17%	20%	19%	44%	578
Supportive agencies listed	24	30	13	33	592
Other supportive institutions listed	21	31	10	38	457

Note: Percentages may not sum to 100 because of rounding.

Table 10-6   Hostile Institutions of Government

Questions: "Were any subcommittees or committees [executive or regulatory agencies, other types of governmental actors] active in this issue? If yes: Did any subcommittees or committees [executive or regulatory agencies, other types of governmental actors] seem hostile to this organization's policy position? If yes, please indicate which ones."

	None	One	Two	Three or more	N
Hostile committees listed	36%	17%	6%	40%	578
Hostile agencies listed	40	23	6	31	592
Other hostile institutions listed	32	23	6	39	457

Note: Percentages may not sum to 100 because of rounding.

lies must be more complex than a simple lack of opponents. Combined, Tables 10-5 and 10-6 show that interest groups typically find themselves in a lobbying environment characterized by the presence of substantial numbers of supportive and hostile governmental institutions. The typical group finds that it has a number of allies within government. Typically, there are also hostile agencies or committees, though Table 10-6 shows that the level of governmental hostility to the interest groups in our sample appears to be lower than the level of support shown in Table 10-5.

Lobbying by Proxy

As we noted previously, it may be that interest groups often lobby their allies in government because those officials then may lobby other officials on behalf of the group. Although anecdotal evidence and political scientist John Kingdon's study of congressional voting behavior[12] have suggested that this type of indirect lobbying, or lobbying by proxy, goes on, there has been little evidence about its prevalence. Our survey asked three questions about this type of lobbying: whether the interest group asked a member of Congress to contact another member of Congress about the issue in question, whether the interest group asked a member of Congress to intervene with a government agency on its behalf, and whether the interest group asked a White House official to contact another government official about the issue in question.

The results of the survey show that this type of indirect lobbying is quite common indeed. Asking a member of Congress to contact another member was the most common type of indirect lobbying, with 67 percent of the organizations reporting that they had used this tactic on the particular policy issue they chose to discuss. Asking a member of Congress to contact an agency was somewhat less common (45 percent of the organizations), and asking a White House official to lobby on behalf of the

group was the least common of the three (30 percent of the organizations). Within those percentages, however, there was some striking variation by group type, as we can see in Table 10-7. Businesses and unions
were far more likely to ask a government official to lobby on their behalf:
89 percent had used at least one of the three indirect lobbying tactics
on the issue in question. By contrast, only 61 percent of the nonprofit-
sector organizations and 54 percent of the professional associations had
used such tactics. Is this difference in types of interest groups the result
of favoritism by government or a particular approach favored by one
group or another? Table 10-8 shows that the difference is most likely the
result of differences in group resources.

Interest groups are not alone in their lobbying battles in Washington.
Groups of all types and of all sizes find the Washington environment to
be crowded both with institutional allies and foes. Table 10-8 shows how
the largest groups, in particular, are able to make good use of their allies.
More than 90 percent of the largest groups indicated that they were able
to count on the efforts of at least one governmental ally to lobby on their
behalf. One respondent noted that this pattern makes perfect sense:

> The larger the [government relations] staff, the more likely you are
> to have people who have personal or close relationships with elected
> officials and can comfortably ask them to do such a favor. In a small
> office you may have one or two people covering 535 members [of Con-
> gress] plus agencies, so you don't have the time or ability to get to
> know elected officials or agency people on an intimate level.

Table 10-7   Indirect Lobbying by Type of Group

Questions: [Respondents were asked to indicate whether they used any of the
following lobbying tactics in relation to the issue they discussed.] "Asking a member
of Congress to contact an agency on behalf of this organization. Asking a member of
Congress to contact members of Congress. Asking someone from the White House
to contact another government official."

	Used one or more indirect lobbying tactic	N
Business corporations	89%	132
Trade associations	75	194
Professional associations	54	66
Unions	89	19
Governmental organizations	76	21
Nonprofit-sector groups	61	185
Other	69	16
Overall percentage	70	690

Note: Percentages may not sum to 100 because of rounding.

Table 10-8   Indirect Lobbying by Size of Lobbying Staff

Questions: [Respondents were asked to indicate whether they used any of the following lobbying tactics in relation to the issue they discussed.] "Asking a member of Congress to contact an agency on behalf of this organization. Asking a member of Congress to contact members of Congress. Asking someone from the White House to contact another government official."

Staff	Used one or more indirect lobbying tactic	N
No full-time lobbying staff	23%	53
One staff member	50	101
Two to five staff members	74	322
Six to twenty staff members	86	155
More than twenty staff members	92	48
Overall percentage	70	679

Note: Percentages may not sum to 100 because of rounding.

It is important to recall that our survey did not ask interest groups to generalize about their typical behavior or to discuss all the cases they had been involved with in the past six months. Rather, we asked about the most recent issue on which they lobbied. This means that the largest groups can almost always count on the active support of governmental allies in their lobbying efforts. They rarely fight alone.

Conclusion

The general parameters of our findings are clear: Organized interests in Washington rely heavily on allies within government as they work to make a difference in policy decisions. The decision to work with allies by no means comes at the expense of efforts to broaden a supporting coalition. Most groups simultaneously work with allies and try to persuade nonallied officials; cooperative and conflictual lobbying strategies are used in tandem on the majority of issues. There is, of course, variation in lobbying behavior by different types of groups and across different types of issues. Groups adapt their strategies to the issue at hand. In most cases, however, they choose a multifaceted lobbying strategy, working simultaneously with friend and foe.

Based on a new survey of almost 800 interest-group lobbyists in Washington, we have presented three primary findings: First, 70 percent of our respondents could identify an institutional ally—a congressional committee, agency, or other governmental body—that supported their group's position on the issue in question. Second, most respondents used a wide-ranging lobbying strategy, contacting allies, undecided officials, and opponents on their issue. Although most lobbied all three targets, the largest percentage of respondents said persuading undecided officials provided the best description of their activities. Third, 70 percent of the respondents said they had asked a government official (either a member of Congress or someone in the White House) to lobby on their behalf. This finding varied strongly by group type, with 89 percent of businesses and governmental associations reportedly using this tactic, but only 61 percent of nonprofits and 54 percent of professional associations doing so. Such lobbying by proxy also was extremely dependent on the size of the organization's government relations staff. Those groups with the largest staffs are also the ones most likely to enjoy the support of a lobbying ally within government.

All in all these findings suggest that lobbying in Washington is difficult to assess without reference to the work of groups in concert with allied agencies and officials within government. On any given issue, lobbyists typically find on their side a number of other groups and a number of interested governmental actors. Their lobbying behaviors are typically aimed simultaneously at mobilizing their allies and at convincing those not already on their side. This all-out strategy seems to hold across many types of issues: Our data set includes issues that were highly controversial and salient as well as many that were never the subject of media attention. Some groups lobby more than others, of course, but groups typically adopt a mixed lobbying strategy on any given issue: They provide information to their allies who may be in a position to make persuasive arguments, they attempt to mobilize their friends within government, and they naturally try to convince those that they can. Our data suggest that groups have incentives not merely to try to convince legislators or other decision makers of their views, but also to encourage government officials themselves to become active lobbyists for them. The social nature of lobbying means that lobbyists and organized interests are not always on the outside looking in. Considering the degree to which groups operate within issue networks combining governmental and nongovernmental actors into loose coalitions on most policy disputes, our models of lobbying should incorporate these relations.

Notes

1. Raymond A. Bauer, Ithiel de Sola Pool, and Lewis A. Dexter, *American Business and Public Policy: The Politics of Foreign Trade* (New York: Atherton Press, 1963).
2. Donald R. Matthews, *U.S. Senators and Their World* (New York: Random House, 1960); Lester W. Milbrath, *The Washington Lobbyists* (Chicago: Rand McNally); Andrew M. Scott and Margaret A. Hunt, *Congress and Lobbies: Image and Reality* (Chapel Hill: University of North Carolina Press, 1965); Lewis Anthony Dexter, *How Organizations Are Represented in Washington* (Indianapolis, Ind.: Bobbs-Merrill, 1969); L. Harmon Zeigler, *Interest Groups in American Society* (Englewood Cliffs, N.J.: Prentice-Hall, 1964).

3. Ken Kollman, "Inviting Friends to Lobby: Interest Groups, Ideological Bias, and Congressional Committees," *American Journal of Political Science* 41 (1997): 519–544 (quote from 519).
4. See Bryan D. Jones, Frank R. Baumgartner, and Jeffery C. Talbert, "The Destruction of Issue Monopolies in Congress," *American Political Science Review* 87 (1993): 673–687.
5. For a review, see Frank R. Baumgartner and Beth L. Leech, *Basic Interests: The Importance of Groups in Politics and in Political Science* (Princeton, N.J.: Princeton University Press, 1998).
6. See Ernest Wittenberg and Elisabeth Wittenberg, *How to Win in Washington*, 2d ed. (Cambridge: Basil Blackwell, 1989).
7. Marie Hojnacki and David Kimbal, "Organized Interests and the Decision of Whom to Lobby in Congress" (Paper delivered at the annual meeting of the American Political Science Association, San Francisco, California, 1996).
8. See Richard L. Hall and Frank W. Wayman, "Buying Time: Moneyed Interests and the Mobilization of Bias in Congressional Committees," *American Political Science Review* 84: 797–820; and Richard L. Hall, *Participation in Congress* (New Haven, Conn.: Yale University Press, 1996).
9. Scott H. Ainsworth, "The Role of Legislators in the Determination of Interest Group Influence," *Legislative Studies Quarterly* 22 (1997): 518.
10. See David R. Mayhew, *Congress: The Electoral Connection* (New Haven, Conn.: Yale University Press, 1974); William P. Browne, *Cultivating Congress* (Lawrence: University Press of Kansas, 1995).
11. Surveys were sent to 1,585 organizations chosen randomly from among all organizations listed in *Washington Representatives 1995* as maintaining offices in the Washington, D.C., area. Of the 1,585 organizations, 143 were later found to have been inappropriately sampled because they did not maintain offices in the Washington area, and as a consequence they were dropped from the study. Of the remaining 1,442 surveys, there were 797 completed surveys, 310 refusals, and 335 nonresponses. The overall response rate was 55 percent (that is, 797 responses from 1,442 sample items). The rate of response by businesses and corporations was 44 percent; the nonbusiness response rate was 58 percent.
12. John W. Kingdon, *Congressmen's Voting Decisions* (New York: Harper and Row, 1973).

11

Advocates and Analysts: Think Tanks and the Politicization of Expertise

Andrew Rich and R. Kent Weaver

Information has become the coin of the realm for Washington lobbyists, even more important than campaign contributions or expense-paid trips. And the institutions that produce, disseminate, and slice and dice that information are that late-twentieth-century phenomenon: think tanks. The Brookings Institution, whose precursor was founded in 1916, still represents the epitome of the first generation of tanks—a "university without students" that employs social science methods to arrive at well-considered empirical conclusions. Over the past twenty-five years, however, more ideological think tanks have emerged, with the Heritage Foundation as the model. These latter institutions made little pretense of performing original research; rather, their books, press releases, and studies reflected their dominant ideologies (mostly conservative).

In this chapter Andrew Rich and R. Kent Weaver carefully differentiate among the various kinds of think tanks and make some tentative conclusions about their capacities to influence the policy debate. In particular, they find—not surprisingly for those who follow op-ed pages and congressional testimony—"in today's . . . crowded think tank universe, they are increasingly perceived, and many have in fact become, contentious advocates in balkanized debates over the direction of public policy." Who, indeed, can you trust?

Information rivals money as a powerful currency in contemporary American politics and policy making. Even if politicians care only about their political careers and not about particular policies, they still need information about the likely political consequences of the choices they must make. Because most public officials care about policy as well as political outcomes, they have an almost insatiable demand for information about policy problems, how current policies work (or do not work), and potential alternatives. Demands for information have increased in recent decades, along with growth in the size and commitments of government and in the number of government personnel involved in setting policy. The ranks of information suppliers have grown as well.[1]

Information comes to policy makers in many forms and from many sources. Much of this information is what Allen Schick calls "ordinary knowledge": it is unsystematic information, not based on any special claim to expertise in particular policy areas.[2] Letters and telephone calls from citizens and exposé articles in the popular press constitute this kind of information—often signaling the direction of public support for policy proposals and serving as early warning signs of policy failures. Public opinion polls produce information about the attitudes of the public toward current policies and potential alternatives, and editorials and opinion pieces in newspapers and magazines provide insight into elite opinions.

Other information received by policy makers, what Schick calls "policy research," is based on the claims of its authors to special substantive expertise in particular policy areas. Policy research uses systematic social science methods in the collection and analysis of data to ensure that findings are "objective"—not tainted by the biases of those who have generated or paid for the research. Here, too, policy makers have many sources of information from which to choose. Policy evaluation divisions within individual agencies of the federal executive branch have been established to meet demands for reliable, unbiased policy research. Distrusting the executive branch, Congress has established the Congressional Budget Office, General Accounting Office, and Congressional Research Service to provide independent sources of expert information to the legislature. A number of sources of policy research have been established outside of government as well, both in universities and in other types of organizations. In addition, many interest groups supply specialized expertise, often using social science methods to increase the legitimacy of the information that they provide to policy makers.[3]

With so many sources of both ordinary knowledge and policy research available, policy makers—especially members of Congress—are inundated with more information than they can possibly absorb. They have to be selective in choosing messages to listen and respond to; their choices can have a critical impact on policy outcomes. In this chapter, we focus on the supply of, demand for, and effects of information provided by one particular and important type of political institution: independent, nonprofit, public policy research organizations, commonly known as *think tanks*.

Think tanks have long served as an "expert but neutral" alternative source of information to the interested, and therefore suspect, information provided by traditional interest groups in American politics. This role differentiation has eroded over the past two decades, however, with changes in the way that both think tanks and interest groups operate. Like interest groups, think tanks have proliferated in number, especially in Washington, D.C., and in state capitals. Single issue think tanks have become more common, as have coalition arrangements among think tanks on specific issues. Think tanks have also paralleled interest groups in rapidly adopting new technologies and media for use in disseminating their research and opinions.

Perhaps the most important development in the think tank industry in recent years is the especially rapid growth in the number of think tanks with avowed ideologies—particularly politically conservative organizations. Think tanks, especially the more ideologically focused ones, have been active and visible participants in contentious and divisive debates associated with virtually every contemporary policy issue, from national struggles over welfare reform to regional squabbles over school finances and performance. In these policy battles, expertise has frequently been used, and viewed by many participants, more as ammunition for partisan and ideological causes than as balanced or objective information that can and should be widely acceptable among policy makers. These developments have blurred the traditional distinction between think tanks and interest groups and jeopardized the reputation of think tanks as sources of neutral expertise.

The Early National Think Tanks

Think tanks have been a feature of the U.S. policy-making process for most of this century. Business and political elites came to support and rely on the first national think tanks in responding to problems exacerbated by the Industrial Revolution in the early decades of the twentieth century. The social science disciplines of economics, sociology, and political science became established fields of inquiry in the same period, and confidence grew in the uses of expertise as means for correcting social problems.[4] Think tanks were formed to create the knowledge that might help solve growing problems of poverty and inequality.

The Russell Sage Foundation, created in 1907 with a gift from Margaret Olivia Sage in honor of her late husband, was one of the first national philanthropic efforts to support the use of social science expertise to address quite visible industrial age problems. It "played a central role in a national movement to alleviate poverty through the professionalization of social work, the study of social problems, the shaping of legislation, and the creation of private agencies designed to meet specific needs."[5]

The Institute for Government Research (IGR), founded in 1916 and loosely modeled after Russell Sage, was established with the support and backing of John D. Rockefeller, Jr., and other prominent businesspeople of the day.[6] It was initially intended to develop and promote administrative efficiency in the federal budget-making process and played an integral role in the establishment of the executive-branch Bureau of the Budget in 1921.[7] In 1927, the IGR combined with two other organizations—the Institute of Economics and the Brookings Graduate School of Economics and Government—to form the Brookings Institution. Through its first decades, the newly consolidated organization remained principally oriented toward developing efficient ways for government to administer its growing commitments.

Demand for social science "experts" who could provide ways for government to solve social and economic problems intensified after the stock market crash of 1929 and the onset of the Great Depression. President Franklin Roosevelt formed his "brains trust" of social scientists to advise him on New Deal programs, inviting academically trained professionals to join his staff. With the national government increasingly active in domestic affairs and, with the advent of World War II, in international affairs, demands for usable policy research and technical analysis from think tanks intensified. The economic theories of John Maynard Keynes were gaining prominence and were reflected in new government programs—and increased demand for informed expertise to design them. As the ranks of experts grew and their ties to public officials strengthened, disagreements erupted among them over the appropriate roles of a growing government. The Brookings Institution, for example, became an outspoken critic of New Deal programs and of government fiscal management in general.[8]

During the course of these debates, several dozen more think tanks formed. The Committee for Economic Development (CED) was one of the most prominent among them, started by a group of businesspeople in 1942 to develop a postwar employment policy. In contrast to Brookings, the CED generally supported government fiscal management, as long as it was accompanied by policies to encourage private-sector jobs. The CED played a highly visible role in the development of the postwar, job-promoting Employment Act of 1946. The American Enterprise Association, another business-backed think tank, was founded in 1943 (and renamed the American Enterprise Institute in 1960). It took a more critical view of government intervention, but initially had a much lower profile than the CED.[9]

Additional new think tanks of this period included organizations such as the RAND (an acronym for Research and Development) Corporation, which was founded in 1946. Initially a government-contracted subsidiary of Douglas Aircraft that provided research to the Air Force during World War II, RAND became an autonomous organization after the war, producing broad strategic analyses for the Department of Defense.[10]

Although think tanks at times produced politically contentious and conflicting research, think tank expertise was sought and generally respected by policy makers throughout the early and middle part of the century. Although think tanks were not the only source of this expertise, they were one of its most prominent, consistent, and visible providers. In particular, academically trained economists became sought-after advisors by virtually anyone seeking to affect policy outcomes.[11] As Herbert Stein, an economist with the CED in the 1940s, 1950s, and 1960s, observed of the immediate postwar period, "It was a time when sophisticated economics became used in the policy discussion process—mainly Keynesianism and anti-Keynesianism. You began to have economists in the government, so the language of the policy discussion became much more sophisticated, and everybody needed an economist if they were going to participate in the debate."[12]

Through the 1950s and 1960s, the ideas and expertise produced by think tanks generally reflected the near consensus that developed among elites around the appropriateness of government management of social and economic problems. Even when new think tanks were established by policy entrepreneurs of a conservative bent, they usually followed prevailing norms about think tank organization, hiring academically trained staff and avoiding any appearance of having links to a single political party.[13]

The Ascendance of Conservative Ideology

By the end of the 1960s, as government grew larger, the desirability and possibility of achieving social change through government programs began to be challenged. Some of the problems themselves—notably the movement for civil rights for African Americans and the Vietnam War—were highly divisive. Increasingly vocal critics described the government as ineffective and overextended at home and abroad. Combined inflation and unemployment in the 1970s—*stagflation*—contributed further to the decline of confidence in "expertly devised" government programs, as well as to growing doubts about Keynesian principles in general.

Growth in government fueled organization among those who disapproved of it. Although there was much on which they did not agree, political conservatives were by the 1970s united by strong opposition toward Communism and a shared belief that government resources were better channeled toward the nation's defense and the fight to overcome Communism than to what were viewed as bloated and ineffective domestic welfare programs. A group of relatively small, politically conservative foundations and wealthy individuals were among those that took interest in providing support for these principles in public affairs. Joseph Coors, chair of the Colorado brewing company, provided seed money for the Heritage Foundation, an avowedly conservative think tank founded in 1973. Richard Scaife, heir to the Mellon family fortune, also made substantial contributions to Heritage and other conservative political efforts through his family foundations. More than a dozen additional conservative foundations and individuals formed a nucleus of support for all varieties of conservative organizations that emerged through the 1970s and 1980s—think tanks prominent among them.[14] At the same time, a number of liberal foundations shifted their funding priorities away from policy research toward grassroots organizations and demonstration projects of social programs, increasing the ideological gap in funding availability.[15]

The explicit intent of conservative efforts was to destabilize the statist, "progovernment" convictions that had dominated American politics to this point. Voices for a limited and restrained government created new think tanks with decidedly different attributes from those that had existed before. Heritage's founding in 1973 was a turning point, the first of a new vintage of think tanks that combined "a strong policy, partisan, or ideological bent with aggressive salesmanship and an effort to influence current policy debates."[16] The group of political entrepreneurs who started the Heritage Foundation initially sought to create a highly responsive policy apparatus that could react quickly to liberal proposals in Congress. By the late 1970s,

> an increasingly confident Heritage Foundation set an ambitious goal: to establish itself as a significant force in the policy-making process and to help build a new conservative coalition that would replace the New Deal coalition which had dominated American politics and policy for half a century.[17]

Through the 1970s and 1980s, ideological, overtly political and advocacy-oriented think tanks modeled after the Heritage Foundation proliferated. Most were politically conservative organizations, but liberal and centrist ones emerged as well. The staffs of these organizations tended to be ideologically homogeneous, and the leadership of these new think tanks used each of their research products as vehicles to advance their underlying ideologies.

Categorizing Think Tanks

Generalizing about the increasingly complex range of think tanks is fraught with risks. It is nevertheless helpful to think of the contemporary think tank "industry" as incorporating three distinct types of institutions (Table 11-1), differentiated in terms of their broad missions, products, sources of support, and staff backgrounds. A number of institutions straddle the boundaries between categories. *University without student* think tanks, including organizations such as the Brookings Institution and the Russell Sage Foundation, are staffed primarily by individuals with doctoral degrees drawn largely from university faculties. Given their academic training, high emphasis is generally placed on social science norms of objectivity and completeness in research among their scholars, with publication often taking the form of books and scholarly articles. Most of these organizations receive the bulk of their support from private foundations and institutional endowments.

Contract research think tanks, such as the RAND Corporation and the Urban Institute, draw the bulk of their revenues from government contracts—as their label implies. Their research agendas usually focus on issues specified by their contracting agency, and research products often take the form of monographs and detailed research reports rather than

Table 11-1   Categories of Think Tanks in the 1980s

	Universities without students	Contract researchers	Advocacy tanks
Mission	Produce objective policy analyses with forward-looking policy prescriptions	Produce objective, often quite narrow and targeted, policy analyses to satisfy government contracts	Produce timely and accessible policy analyses targeted at specific policy-making audiences to have immediate impact on the policy-making process
Support	Principal support from private foundations and institutional endowments, with supplemental support from contracts and corporations	Principal support from government contracts, with some supplemental support from private foundations	Principal support from individuals, corporations, and foundations
Products	Books and scholarly articles	Research reports and monographs	Policy briefs and press releases
Staff	Primarily academically trained scholars (PhDs)	Mix of researchers, some with PhDs and other with master's degrees in public policy or administration	Primarily politically experienced professionals, often with graduate degrees
Examples	Brookings Institution, Russell Sage Foundation	RAND Corporation, Urban Institute	Heritage Foundation, Cato Institute

Source: Based on discussion in R. Kent Weaver, "The Changing World of Think Tanks," *P.S.: Political Science and Politics* (September 1989): 563–579.

long books. Because their projects frequently involve large evaluation studies of government programs, these think tanks often use large teams of researchers headed by social science Ph.D.s that also include researchers with master's degrees in public policy and related fields.

Advocacy tanks are the newest variety of think tanks. By the mid-1980s, this category included organizations ranging from the Heritage Foundation, the libertarian Cato Institute, and the socially conservative Rockford Institute on the right to the labor-oriented Economic Policy Institute on the left. Advocacy tanks generally aim to be more responsive to and have a more immediate effect on policy makers—particularly those involved in the legislative process—than either university without student or contract research think tanks. They often rely at least as much on individuals and corporations for support as on private foundations, although a new politically active corps of conservative foundations makes gifts to ideologically conservative advocacy tanks. The products of these organizations most often take the form of short, easily read policy briefs that synthesize and put a particular "spin" on existing research rather than report on original findings. Although many on their staffs have graduate degrees, these think tanks are more likely to employ people with established political and policy credentials—experience on Capitol Hill, in the executive branch, or with a campaign—than those with a long list of scholarly publications.

Advocacy tanks pose a two-fold challenge to traditional university without student and contract research think tanks. First, they compete with older organizations for limited funds, media attention, and access to policy makers. Far more important, however, is their challenge to the legitimacy of the older organizations' claim to provide impartial and highly credible expertise. Leaders of many advocacy tanks, especially those on the political right, argue that the difference between themselves and traditional think tanks is not that their publications are value-based whereas those of the traditional think tanks are based on objective research. Instead, they claim, *all* research is value-based, but they are at least open about their values, whereas traditional think tanks hide their (liberal) values beneath a veneer of social science methods and jargon. To the extent that these claims are accepted by policy makers and the public, all think tanks risk having their expertise discounted or even dismissed as emanating from a hostile ideological camp. Moreover, whatever the actual quality or objectivity of advocacy tank research, the self-conscious association of their products with particular guiding ideological principles generates further doubt among policy makers and the public about the very possibility of value-free, objective research.

In addition to the growth of ideologically oriented think tanks, boundaries between the advocacy and analysis communities have become blurred along a number of other lines as well. Some public interest groups, such as the Center for Science in the Public Interest, have made the production and promotion of research their principal method for affecting policy, often committing more resources to research than to the mobilization efforts for which they have traditionally been known. A few interest groups, notably the American Association of Retired Persons (AARP), have established their own subsidiary research institutes. And some think tanks, notably the Progressive Policy Institute and the short-lived Project for the Republican Future, have been established explicitly to redirect debate within the Democratic or Republican parties rather than to provide advice equally to both political parties.[18]

Think Tanks in the 1990s

A look at American think tanks in the 1990s reveals a broad and diverse array of organizations. They range in size from the relatively staid and defense policy-oriented RAND Corporation, with a 1996 operating budget of almost $118 million obtained primarily from government contracts, to tiny, more ideologically aggressive organizations such as the conservative, Connecticut-based Yankee Institute for Public Policy Studies, which focuses on policy issues in its home state and has an annual budget of less than $50,000. Amid this great diversity, a number of patterns are evident related to the proliferation, ideological proclivities, locations, research scopes, and products of contemporary think tanks.

Proliferation

Providing an accurate count of the number of think tanks operating in the United States at any given time is nearly impossible. There are no accrediting agencies for think tanks as there are for colleges and universities, so there is no definitive listing. There are serious definitional issues, too: As the boundary between think tanks and advocacy groups grows fuzzier, it is less clear which groups should be included in the think tank category.

Acknowledging these constraints on achieving a definitive count, it is possible to get a plausible count of think tanks that existed in 1996, based on cross-references from a number of data sources.[19] Figure 11-1 provides data on the emergence of think tanks principally oriented to affect national policy making, and Figure 11-2 provides comparable data on think tanks with a state and regional focus. Our data include only organizations that were still in existence as of 1995. Therefore, the steep climb in new organizations during the 1970s through 1990s might be slightly exaggerated because older organizations that had ceased to exist by 1995 are not included.[20] Nevertheless, the data suggest that the number of independent public policy-oriented think tanks more than doubled between 1970 and 1985, approaching 200 organizations by the end of that period. The number of think tanks has continued to grow in recent years, with the number of ideologically motivated organizations increasing at the quickest pace. By the end of 1996, our data indicate that roughly 305 think tanks were in existence, of which about two-thirds concentrated primarily on national-level policy making.

Conservative Ascendance

Definitive judgments about the presence or nature of an ideology associated with each think tank are tricky to make. For tax and other reasons, most think tanks are less than forthright about the guiding political ideologies in their research and publications. As tax-exempt 501(c)3 nonprofit

Figure 11-1   Nationally Focused Think Tanks, 1996

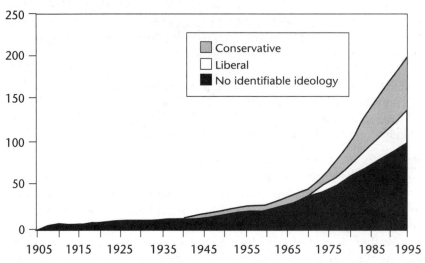

Figure 11-2   State and Regionally Focused Think Tanks, 1996

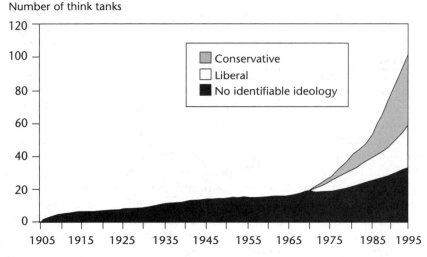

organizations, they are prohibited from devoting "more than an insubstantial part of [their] activities to attempting to influence legislation" or from "directly or indirectly participat[ing] in, or interven[ing] in (including the publishing or distributing of statements), any political campaign on behalf of or in opposition to any candidate for public office."[21] Our coding is based on a content analysis of the 1995 and 1996 mission statements and annual reports of each of the organizations in the database.[22]

The data suggest that a substantial portion of contemporary think tanks—nearly half—do not have an identifiable ideology on a left–right scale.[23] Our analysis nevertheless reveals tremendous growth in the number of avowedly ideological think tanks. Of the 195 nationally or state-focused think tanks founded since 1976, 55 percent are identifiably ideological in orientation. Among nationally focused think tanks, nearly twice as many conservative think tanks as liberal ones began between 1976 and 1995. Among state and regionally focused think tanks, nearly three times the number of conservative as liberal think tanks emerged.

The pattern of conservative dominance over liberal think tanks continues to hold when the relative size of think tanks is taken into account. Think tanks of no identifiable ideology receive the greatest proportion of resources—more than half. In part, this reflects the very large government-contract research organizations that fall into this category (for example, the RAND Corporation and the Urban Institute). When "no identifiable ideology" think tanks are excluded, conservative think tanks account for more than three-quarters of the remaining budget resources.[24]

A Washington-Centered World

Amid the expanded ranks of ideological think tanks and a densely populated organizational environment generally, proximity to decision makers is a distinct advantage for think tanks seeking to contribute to national-level policy debates. Of think tanks focused on national-level policy making, 54 percent of organizations founded before 1971 are head-quartered in Washington, D.C. An even higher share—63 percent—of nationally focused think tanks founded in 1971 or later years is based in the nation's capital. Moreover, many think tanks based outside Washington, such as the RAND Corporation, Hudson Institute, and the National Center for Policy Analysis, maintain Washington outposts in an effort to increase their visibility and access to policy makers.[25]

Issue Specialization

Specialization and "niche marketing" have been an additional reaction of newer think tanks seeking visibility among policy makers. Although many of the older think tanks attempt to cover a broad range of policy issues, a number of the newer institutions specialize in one or a few issues—or, in the case of foreign policy think tanks, a single region of the globe. Examples of relatively new Washington-based think tanks with a narrow focus include the Institute for Research on the Economics of Taxation, the Economic Strategy Institute (trade policy), the Institute for International Economics, the Center for Immigration Studies, and the Washington Institute for Near East Policy.

Specialization can be especially helpful in attracting targeted funding, media attention, and the ear of particular policy makers to new institutions that do not have established reputations on which to draw. Such "niche marketing" also carries risks, however: If funders and policy makers lose interest in a think tank's narrow research focus, an organization may have trouble surviving.

Working in Coalitions

Think tanks have also increasingly sought to work in coalitions on specific issues.[26] Collaboration with other institutions helps think tanks to raise their visibility and helps them reach out to funders and policy makers with whom they might otherwise have trouble developing relationships. Coalitions can have the added benefit of demonstrating broad support for policy proposals, particularly when the coalition transcends real or perceived ideological lines. A recent series of joint projects on congressional reform and campaign finance reform by the conservative American Enterprise Institute and the Brookings Institution, an organization often perceived as liberal-leaning (although seeking to be centrist), is a case in point.

Working together may also prevent duplication of effort among organizations with similar points of view. In the debate over welfare reform in 1995 and 1996, for example, the Center on Budget and Policy Priorities and Center on Law and Social Policy, both opposed to the conservative direction of reform proposals being debated by Congress, engaged in an informal division of labor in the analysis of the myriad issues under consideration.

Changing Products

Finally, amid all of these developments, the design of think tank products and their strategies for research dissemination have changed. Since its early days in the 1970s, the Heritage Foundation has prided itself on an ability to produce timely, short, faxable briefs on any pending issue that may reach Congress. In recent years, many of the older think tanks have begun to emulate features of Heritage's aggressive style. For example, the Brookings Institution launched a new series of five- to ten-page policy briefs in July 1996 to allow Brookings' scholars to hold forth on current policy debates in a timely, brief, and readable format.[27] The American Enterprise Institute (AEI) responded to the changed political environment by reformatting its magazine, *American Enterprise*, in the late 1980s. AEI is producing fewer and shorter books and is placing a greater emphasis on monographs and other shorter and more quickly produced publications. Carlyn Bowman, resident fellow and former editor of *American Enterprise*, observed, "We're pretty convinced that people just don't read books in the way that they once did. You can produce things more quickly that are shorter. You can get out a monograph or an occasional paper or something of that sort, and I think you can perhaps be more influential."[28]

Access to the Internet has also prompted changes in how think tanks disseminate research products and organizational information. Almost all but the smallest think tanks have established a presence on the World Wide Web, and the Web has become a particularly useful venue for the rapid and timely dissemination of brief opinion pieces by think tanks. There are even special Web sites that provide links to think tanks and advocacy organizations of particular ideological persuasions. Townhall (http:\\www.townhall.com), based at the Heritage Foundation, focuses on conservative organizations, and the Electronic Policy Network (http:\\epn.org), operated by *American Prospect* magazine, provides links primarily to liberal-oriented think tanks.

Increased Focus on State Capitals

These myriad developments among think tanks at the national level have been mirrored among the rapidly proliferating ranks of state and regionally focused think tanks. Most state-focused think tanks are relatively small—only a few have annual budgets of more than $1 million, and almost none of more than $5 million. Nevertheless, they have considerable opportunities to influence state-level policy making, because they are usually competing against far fewer think tanks and advocacy groups for the attention of policy makers in state capitals on issues such as school choice and affirmative action.[29]

The conservative ascendance among think tanks is even more striking at the state level than at the national level. Almost half (45 percent) of state and regionally focused think tanks—forty-seven organizations dispersed among most states—are avowedly conservative, compared to only 20 percent that are identifiably liberal. In many states, conservative think tanks have the field virtually to themselves—a situation that a coalition of liberal foundations has tried to address in the 1990s by financing rival research and advocacy groups in several states. Conservative think tanks at the state level have also benefited from organizations such as the State Policy Network that helps policy entrepreneurs start new institutions and provides advice as they grow.[30]

Assessing Access and Influence

Amid the growth and diversity among contemporary think tanks, the question remains: Which among them are actually influential? Under what conditions? Are the patterns associated with their development—particularly the growth in avowedly conservative institutions—reflected in their visibility and perceived influence? These questions resist definitive answers, but evidence points toward some preliminary indications.

Think tanks have always had a variety of channels of access to the policy process. They pursue "formal access" to policy makers, as in testimony at hearings of congressional committees and government commissions. Some think tanks, notably contract researchers, issue formal reports distributed directly to policy makers. Think tank personnel often have opportunities to perform government service (in appointed positions, on government commissions, etc.). Think tank staff also have informal access to public decision makers, given their shared participation over time in networks of experts working on specific issues. For Washington-based think tank staff, informal access may come in a form as simple as shared car pools with congressional staff. Finally, think tanks impart their research and ideas through the news media, often by writing on op-ed pages of major newspapers and through interviews granted by their scholars and spokespersons.

Some of these channels of access and potential influence are more susceptible to measurement than others. For media visibility, we have tracked references to forty-three of the most prominent think tanks operating in American politics between 1991 and 1996 in six national circulation newspapers: *New York Times, Washington Post, Wall Street Journal, Christian Science Monitor, Washington Times,* and *USA Today.* We calculated the proportion of references received by each think tank for the six years in the six newspapers, weighting for the relative circulation size of each newspaper. Several patterns are evident in this data. Think tanks with no identifiable ideologies consistently receive roughly half of all coverage, in rough proportion to their number of organizations in the think tank population. Conservatively oriented think tanks, on average, receive more of the remaining newspaper visibility than liberal organizations by a margin of four to one—a far greater difference in coverage than what is accounted for merely by the difference in number of conservative to liberal organizations. This coverage gap occurs not because of a bias in the media toward conservative think tanks, but because conservative think tanks collectively have far more resources than their liberal counterparts. Larger budgets allow these institutions to employ more staff, cover a broader range of issues, and have greater visibility.

Geography also affects media visibility. Think tanks located in the Washington area are likely to have far greater visibility in national newspapers than those based elsewhere, even controlling for budget size, ideology, and other factors.[31] A similar bias toward Washington-based think tanks emerges in major city newspapers elsewhere in the country: Nationally focused think tanks based outside the nation's capital tend to be much less visible, controlling for budget size, except in their home-state newspapers. State-focused think tanks, as might be expected, are almost invisible outside their home states.[32]

Available data on "formal" access as measured by testimony before Congress suggest similar patterns. Congressional testimony tends to be dominated by D.C.-based think tanks, with much lower levels of testimony, controlling for institutional budget size, by nationally focused institutions based elsewhere. Congressional testimony by representatives of state-focused think tanks is virtually nonexistent.

Data on congressional testimony demonstrate powerful effects of gatekeeping by the majority parties in Congress. Prior to the Republican takeover of Congress in 1994, staff members from the Brookings Institution were the most frequent think tank testifiers at congressional hearings in most years, often followed by witnesses from the more conservative American Enterprise Institute. In 1995, with Republican legislators and staff controlling the bulk of witness slots, the Heritage Foundation became the most frequently represented think tank, followed by AEI, the libertarian Cato Institute, and Brookings, in that order. Testimony by liberal think tanks lagged far behind.[33]

The advantages in number, size, and visibility of conservative think tanks is also reflected in their *perceived* influence in the political process. In a 1997 survey of 110 congressional staff and Washington-based journalists, 68 percent of respondents identified conservative think tanks as having a greater impact on policy making than liberal think tanks; only 5 percent named liberal think tanks as being most influential.[34]

Forty-two percent of survey respondents identified the Heritage Foundation—the largest conservative think tank with a 1996 budget of nearly $30 million—as the institution with the single greatest impact in the political process. The Brookings Institution came in a relatively distant second, being named by 28 percent of the respondents. When asked to rank thirty prominent think tanks on a scale of one to five in terms of their impact, the same respondents again gave Heritage the highest overall mean score. The combined scores of the conservative think tanks averaged significantly higher than either the liberal think tanks or the organizations with no identifiable ideology.

Although ideologically conservative think tanks scored high in our survey of journalists and congressional staff with regard to their *impact* in the political process, they—and ideological think tanks in general—were evaluated quite differently with regard to their *credibility*. In scaled assessments of the credibility of the thirty think tanks named in the survey—similar in format to the scaling with regard to impact—the average score for think tanks with no identifiable ideology was significantly greater than for either conservative or liberal think tanks.[35]

Conclusion

The ascendance of avowed ideologies among contemporary think tanks and the politicization of their expertise have reduced the faith and credibility accorded their products. Herbert Stein, an economist who has worked with think tanks since 1945, concluded,

> My sense of the whole thing is that we've had a great proliferation of think tanks and that there has been a great dilution of their impact. We have a whole range of things that are called think tanks but that are different because many of them are single purpose think tanks [and] they are also more policy-promoting. They tend to have pre-set agendas that they are pushing, and you can predict what they are going to say. They are not, I think, so much interested in studying problems as in promoting previously determined answers. And that's known.[36]

Along these same lines, AEI's Carlyn Bowman lamented, "I wonder what is happening sometimes to the think tank currency, whether it's becoming a little bit like paper money in Weimar [Germany]—currency without a lot of value because of the proliferation and because of the open advocacy of some of the think tanks."[37]

If the politicization of expertise has altered and diluted the impact of think tank expertise, unresolved are the consequences of the disproportionate numbers, visibility, and impact of conservative think tanks for the political process. To the extent that these differences appear traceable to the greater sources of support available to conservative think tanks, the potential for liberals to level the organizational playing field seems limited.

What is clear is that substantial shifts have occurred among the attributes and efforts of think tanks in recent decades, and their evolution is reflected in a politicization of expertise in American politics. Think tanks were widely perceived as objective and highly credible producers of policy expertise for policy makers in the early and middle decades of the twentieth century. In today's far more crowded think tank universe, they are increasingly perceived, and many have in fact become, contentious advocates in balkanized debates over the direction of public policy.

Notes

1. For a discussion of the connections among these developments, see David Ricci, *The Transformation of American Politics: The New Washington and the Rise of Think Tanks* (New Haven, Conn.: Yale University Press, 1993).
2. See Allen Schick, "Informed Legislation, Policy Research Versus Ordinary Knowledge," in *Knowledge, Power and Congress*, ed. William Robinson and Clay Wellborn (Washington, D.C.: Congressional Quarterly, 1991).
3. See Jeffrey M. Berry, *The Interest Group Society*, 3d ed. (New York: Longman, 1997), 128.
4. For a discussion of the development and institutionalization of the social sciences, in the United States, Europe, and Japan see Dietrich Rueschemeyer and Theda Skocpol, *States, Social Knowledge, and the Origins of Modern Social Policies* (Princeton, N.J.: Princeton University Press, 1996).
5. David C. Hammack and Stanton Wheeler, *Social Science in the Making* (New York: Russell Sage Foundation, 1994), 12.

6. The IGR also took regional bureaus of municipal research as models for its organization, most notably the New York Bureau of Municipal Research. These regional bureaus sought to provide the types of expertise about administrative efficiency to urban centers that IGR sought to bring to the national level. See Charles Thomson, *The Institute for Government Research* (Washington, D.C.: Brookings Institution, 1956).

7. On the IGR and the Brookings Institution's early days, see Donald T. Critchlow, *The Brookings Institution, 1916–1952: Expertise and the Public Interest in a Democratic Society* (DeKalb: Northern Illinois University Press, 1985). The IGR actually emerged from a group of Progressive businesspeople and scholars who had been associated with President Taft's Commission on Economy and Efficiency in 1910. The commission had been charged with devising an executive-controlled budgetary process. Its recommendations were not implemented before Taft left office in 1913. See James A. Smith, *Brookings at Seventy-Five* (Washington, D.C.: Brookings Institution, 1991).

8. Smith, *Brookings at Seventy-Five*, 27.

9. The CED received more than sixty citations in the *New York Times* in its first seven years of existence. This compared with zero citations received by the American Enterprise Association during its first seven years. Citation numbers are based on a search of *The New York Times Index*. On the relative visibility of the CED and the AEA in their early days, see also James A. Smith, *The Idea Brokers: Think Tanks and the Rise of the New Policy Elite* (New York: Free Press, 1991), 175.

10. For background on the RAND Corporation, see Bruce L. R. Smith, *The RAND Corporation: Case Study of a Nonprofit Advisory Corporation* (Cambridge, Mass.: Harvard University Press, 1966). On recent developments, see Roy J. Harris, Jr., "After the Cold War, Rand Remakes Itself as a Civilian Expert," *Wall Street Journal*, June 18, 1993, A1.

11. See Peter A. Hall, *The Political Power of Economic Ideas: Keynesianism Across Nations* (Princeton, N.J.: Princeton University Press, 1989), for a discussion of the expression and diffusion of Keynesianism in the United States and Europe during the twentieth century.

12. Interview with Herbert Stein, Senior Fellow at the American Enterprise Institute, Washington, D.C., September 24, 1997.

13. See James Allen Smith, *Strategic Calling: The Center for Strategic and International Studies, 1962–1992* (Washington, D.C.: CSIS, 1993).

14. For an analysis of the efforts by conservative foundations to affect public policy in recent years, see Sally Covington, *Moving a Public Policy Agenda: The Strategic Philanthropy of Conservative Foundations* (Washington, D.C.: National Committee for Responsive Philanthropy, 1997). For a discussion of the specific ties between conservative philanthropy and think tanks, see W. John Moore, "Wichita Pipeline," *National Journal*, May 16, 1992, 1168–1174, or Nurith C. Aizenman, "The Man Behind the Curtain," *The Washington Monthly* (July/August 1997): 28–34. For a contrasting view by the head of a conservative think tank, see Leslie Lenkowsky, "The Paranoid Perspective in Philanthropy," *Chronicle of Philanthropy* (June 12, 1997): 61–62.

15. For a discussion of these developments, see David Callahan, "Liberal Policy's Weak Foundations," *The Nation*, November 13, 1995, 568–572.

16. R. Kent Weaver, "The Changing World of Think Tanks," *PS: Political Science and Politics* 22 (1989): 563–578, at 567. See also Niels Bjerre-Poulsen, "The Heritage Foundation: A Second-Generation Think Tank," *Journal of Policy History* 3 (1991): 152–172.

17. Lee Edwards, *The Power of Ideas: 25 Years at the Heritage Foundation* (Ottawa, Ill.: Jameson Books, 1997), 32.

18. On the Progressive Policy Institute, which is organizationally a unit of the Democratic Leadership Council, see Jon F. Hale, "The Making of the New Democrats," *Political Science Quarterly* 110 (1995): 207–232, and Dan Balz, "Moderate, Conservative Democrats Buck 'Constraints,' Form Think Tank," *Washington Post*, June 30, 1989, A21.

19. Our figures were arrived at after combining references from three think tank directories, four books, several scholarly articles, and scores of newspaper and magazine stories. The directories are Lynn Hellebust, ed., *Think Tank Directory: A Guide to Nonprofit Public Policy Research Organizations* (Topeka, Kans.: Government Research Service, 1996); Robert L. Hollings, *Nonprofit Public Policy Research Organizations: A Sourcebook on Think Tanks in Government* (New York: Garland, 1993); and Eleanor Evans Kitfield, *The Capitol Source* (Washington, D.C.: National Journal, 1995). The books are James G. McGann, *The Competition for Dollars, Scholars and Influence in the Public Policy Research Industry* (New York: University Press of America, 1995); Joseph G. Peschek, *Policy-Planning Organizations: Elite Agendas and America's Rightward Turn* (Philadelphia: Temple University Press, 1987); Smith, *The Idea Brokers*, 1991; and Diane Stone, *Capturing the Political Imagination: Think Tanks and the Policy Process* (Portland, Ore.: Frank Cass, 1996). The articles are Donald E. Abelson, "From Policy Research to Political Advocacy: The Changing Role of Think Tanks in American Politics," *Canadian Review of American Studies* 25 (1996): 93–126; and Laura Brown Chisolm, "Sinking the Think Tanks Upstream: The Use and Misuse of Tax Exemption Law to Address the Use and Misuse of Tax-Exempt Organizations by Politicians," *University of Pittsburgh Law Review* 51 (1990): 577–640.

Our data actually establish a record of 555 independent think tank-like organizations operating in 1996. Of this number we eliminated 250 from our final group of organizations either because they lack a focus on the political and policy-making process—at any level of government—or because they maintain an affiliation with a corporation, interest group, or larger think tank (usually either as a subsidiary or by sharing office space).

Two examples of such excluded organizations are (1) the Academy for State and Local Government, which functions as a "policy and research center for its Trustee organizations"—organizations such as the Council of State Governments and the National Governors' Association, and (2) the American Family Foundation, which is a "secular nonprofit tax-exempt research center and educational organization" whose purpose is "to study psychological manipulation and high-control and cultic groups" (Hellebust, *Think Tank Directory*, 5, 11). The former organization is closely tied to and run by government officials. The latter organization, although performing independent research, is oriented toward public education and counseling rather than toward effecting public policy change.

20. As confirmation of the relatively small number of public policy think tanks in 1970, see Paul Dickson, *Think Tanks* (New York: Atehneum, 1971), 30, where he discusses "a handful of truly independent, nonprofit, self-determining think tanks."

21. Reg. Section 1.501(c)(3)–1(b)(1)(v).

22. Without explicit acknowledgment of a guiding political ideology, we chose key words and phrases associated with the concerns of conservative and liberal ideologies in order to make our determinations—phrases such as "in defense of a free-market economy and limited government" and "oriented toward a progressive and democratic expansion of participation in policy making," respectively. Those organizations whose published statements do not readily place them in either broad ideological category make up the third category of think tanks—those with "no identifiable ideology." In categorizing think tanks into only these three groups, we do not mean to ignore the real and substantial ideological differences

that exist among think tanks in each group—varying brands of conservatism, for example. However, as the dominant brands of ideology competing in contemporary American politics, the categories do illustrate the lopsided distribution among the contemporary population of ideological think tanks, with new conservative think tanks outnumbering liberal ones by a ratio of almost two to one.

23. This high proportion of think tanks of no identifiable ideology may in part be a function of the relatively conservative coding scheme for ideology that we used. Think tanks choose words carefully in mission statements and annual reports and can relatively easily use language that evades our coding scheme, leaving them in the "no identifiable ideology" category. In addition, most contract research think tanks—some of which are very large—do not fit easily into an ideological category.

24. Analysis of the budget size of think tanks relies on data from Hellebust, *Directory of Think Tanks*, 1996.

25. See, for example, Christopher Madison, "Rebounding Hudson," *National Journal*, December 12, 1992, 2838–2841.

26. Kevin Hula, "Rounding Up the Usual Suspects: Forging Interest Group Coalitions in Washington," in *Interest Group Politics*, 4th ed., ed. Allan J. Cigler and Burdett A. Loomis (Washington, D.C.: CQ Press, 1995), 239–258.

27. On recent changes at Brookings, see Paul Starobin, "Rethinking Brookings," *National Journal*, July 22, 1995, 1875–1879, and Burt Solomon, "Ferment at Brookings," *National Journal*, October 18, 1997, 2080–2083.

28. Interview with Carlyn Bowman, resident fellow at the American Enterprise Institute, Washington, D.C., September 24, 1997.

29. See W. John Moore, "Local Right Thinkers," *National Journal*, October 1, 1988, 2455.

30. See Joyce Price, "Conservative Think Tanks Gain in Number, Respect Nationwide," *Washington Times*, February 2, 1995.

31. See R. Kent Weaver and Andrew Rich, "Think Tanks in the National Media" (Paper delivered at the annual meeting of the American Political Science Association, Washington, D.C., August 28–31, 1997).

32. R. Kent Weaver, "Think Tanks, the Media, and the American Policy Process" (Paper delivered at the annual research conference of the Association for Public Policy Analysis and Management, Washington, D.C., October 30, 1993).

33. R. Kent Weaver, "Private Think Tanks in the United States," in *Think Tanks in Germany and the U.S.A.*, ed. Werner von der Ohe, forthcoming.

34. The question to which respondents replied was, "And finally, regardless of your own political views, when you consider ideological think tanks, which do you think have a greater impact in politics: conservative-oriented or liberal-oriented think tanks?" Fourteen percent of respondents thought that conservative and liberal think tanks have an equal impact; 7 percent thought which group had the greatest impact depended on the issues under consideration, and 6 percent declined to answer the question. This question was part of a survey conducted between July 15 and September 26, 1997, in collaboration with Burson Marsteller Worldwide. Samples were stratified for congressional staff to match the partisan makeup of Congress by chamber. Journalist responses split between reporters for D.C.-focused or national publications (for example, the *New York Times*, *Roll Call*, and the Associated Press) and journalists who are D.C.-based representatives for local and regional newspapers.

35. For more details on the survey and statistical results, see Andrew Rich, "Perceptions of Think Tanks among Congressional Staff and Washington-based Journalists," a report to Burson Marsteller Worldwide, December 1997.

36. Stein, interview.

37. Bowman, interview.

12

Reverse Lobbying: Interest Group Mobilization from the White House and the Hill

Ronald G. Shaiko

> For 200 years—probably longer—Americans have in general
> believed that lobbying is done by citizens, businesses, member-
> ship groups, and other interests taking their grievances to the gov-
> ernment in hopes of changing (or retaining) the laws of the land.
> David Truman's *Governmental Process* defined American politics
> at mid-century as a struggle among groups to influence policies
> through their influence on governmental actions. Pluralism as a
> theory depends in part on the capacity of groups to organize and
> gain representation. But one secret of American politics from the
> founding to the millennium is that much lobbying and even some
> organization of groups has derived from the actions of legislators,
> executives, and bureaucrats. The American Farm Bureau Federa-
> tion and the Chamber of Commerce, as examples, were both be-
> gun in response to governmental initiatives.
>
> This chapter by Ronald Shaiko illuminates how both Presi-
> dent Clinton and the Republican Congress have worked systemat-
> ically to rally interests to support their policy initiatives. Drawing
> on interviews and observation, Shaiko demonstrates how "reverse
> lobbying" is pervasive on many important issues. Of particular
> value is his inclusion of both the legislative and executive branches
> in his analysis. The president is every bit the instigator of lobbying
> as is the Speaker. Shaiko's article fits with many others in this vol-
> ume in that his analysis shows how pervasive lobbying has be-
> come—to the extent that almost all exchanges of information are
> politically charged. And the article makes the point that we need
> to recognize from where policy initiatives are really coming.

The relationships between organized interest groups and policy makers in Washington are often defined in a pluralist fashion as multiple
competing interests seeking to advocate policy positions and to persuade
federal officials to support their positions.[1] Although this approach cap-

The author wishes to thank Ron Klain, Bruce Gates, Pat Griffin, Barry Jackson, Monica Vegas,
Erik Reid, and the more than two dozen lobbyists representing the national police organizations
active in 100,000 Cops and the corporations, associations, and interest groups affiliated with
Project Relief for their time and effort. Their insights and comments strengthened this chapter
significantly.

tures the general essence of interest group lobbying, it also simplifies the complex nature of the relationships between policy makers and interest groups in Washington. Today, these relationships are much more interactive. In fact, they are, at times, reversed. Perhaps the most common form of reverse lobbying—"the legal tradition by which officials lobby lobbyists" wherein "the roles of predator and prey are flipped"—occurs in the context of campaign fund-raising.[2] Organized interest groups and their lobbyists are prime targets for campaign solicitation by members of Congress seeking reelection. In the same way, presidential campaign committees direct these interest groups and their representatives through the maze of legal pathways that individual, political action committee, and soft money contributions may flow. In these instances the direct linkages between political contributions and policy outcomes are less clear, yet widely chronicled by the media as well as a variety of public interest watchdog groups.

In this chapter, reverse lobbying will be analyzed in the context of the direct political engagement of organized interest groups by members of Congress and officials in the White House in the midst of ongoing policy debates, but will also link these activities to the conduct of electoral politics in Washington.

The Rules of Political Engagement

Members of Congress and their staffs are virtually unrestrained in their abilities to engage constituents and organized interests in policy debate, though the craft of reverse lobbying in Congress tends not to involve major letter-writing campaigns. Rather, members and congressional staff seek to mobilize coalitions of interest group lobbyists so that the interest group leaders may then organize and mobilize their memberships to support or to oppose proposed policies.

Reverse lobbying or "public engagement" strategies employed by the White House and executive departments and agencies are regulated by a variety of federal statutes.[3] The most relevant regulatory statute is the Anti-Lobbying Act of 1919 (18 U.S.C. § 1913). In an April 1995 internal memo to Justice Department officials, then assistant attorney general Walter Dellinger provided guidelines regarding the limitations on orchestrated grassroots campaigns conducted by the Clinton administration that targeted members of Congress—reverse lobbying.[4] Dellinger stated, "The Department of Justice consistently has construed the Anti-Lobbying Act as not limiting the lobbying activities personally undertaken by the President, his aides and assistants within the Executive Office of the President, the Vice President, cabinet members within their areas of responsibility, and other Senate-confirmed officials appointed by the President within their areas of responsibility."[5]

Under the Anti-Lobbying Act, government employees *may not:*

engage in substantial "grassroots" lobbying campaigns of telegrams, letters, and other private forms of communication expressly asking recipients to contact Members of Congress, in support of or opposition to legislation. Grassroots lobbying does not include communication with the public through public speeches, appearances, or writings.

Although the 1989 Barr Opinion does not define the meaning of "substantial" grassroots campaigns, the opinion notes that the 1919 legislative history cites an expenditure of $7500—roughly equivalent to $50,000 in 1989—for a campaign of letter-writing urging recipients to contact Congress.[6]

Dellinger also acknowledged the findings of the comptroller general relating to interactions with organized interest groups in grassroots lobbying activities. In this context, government employees *may not:*

1) provide administrative support for the lobbying activities of private organizations, 2) prepare editorials or other communications that will be disseminated without accurate disclosure of the government's role in the origin, and 3) appeal to members of the public to contact their elected representatives in support of or opposition to proposals before Congress.[7]

Beyond the Anti-Lobbying Act limitations, White House and executive branch officials may not coordinate efforts to mobilize support for administration policies with allied interest groups that are recipients of federal funds through contracts and grants. Close relationships often emerge between executive agencies and the contractors delivering public goods and services. To the extent that the federal agency and the contractor interests coincide, the possibility exists for coordinated support for the continued funding of existing agency programs. The General Accounting Office has, on numerous occasions, conducted investigations of such agency activities, as prompted by Congress.[8]

In the current phase of divided government, congressional attentiveness to Clinton administration activities relating to possible violations of these statutes and provisions has increased, as would be expected. Beyond the consequences of divided government, however, the methods of operation employed by the Clinton administration and the Republican Congress, particularly in the House of Representatives, are quite similar in their efforts at engaging organized interest groups.

Interest Group Engagement in the Clinton Administration

During the first term of the Clinton administration, the operation of the White House maintained much of the character of the Clinton–Gore campaign organization. In fact, many of the key players in the campaign became important policy actors in the Clinton White House. As a result, many of the policy initiatives undertaken during the first term were organized on the campaign's highly successful "war room" model. Just as the campaign reached out to its allies in the interest group sector for their resources (for example, financial support, membership mobilization, and political intelligence gathering), the Clinton White House sought assistance from a wide variety of interest groups as it constructed its war rooms on major policy issues.

For better or worse, the archetypal example of the Clinton outreach effort was its health care reform campaign waged in 1993 and 1994. Apart from the widely publicized health care summits organized by the war room leadership in the White House, which brought together more than 1,000 policy actors representing a wide, yet not totally inclusive, array of political interests, much smaller groups of the more powerful interests were called to the White House. In early 1993, the White House organized a series of meetings that included sets of lobbyists representing major corporate, association, and medical interests. In each meeting, the group of lobbyists were told that they were the only outsiders who were called into the White House to discuss the health care strategy. Unfortunately for the White House health care war room, lobbyists who attended separate meetings began to compare notes. After several weeks, it became clear that the White House had held a fairly large number of meetings in which differing strategies were discussed. Although this method of operation did not lead to the failure of the Clinton health care plan, it did not serve the cause well either.[9]

A second and related problem with the Clinton war room engagement strategy was that there were, in fact, multiple war rooms at work simultaneously, each competing for media attention and the attention of organized interest groups. For example, while Hillary Rodham Clinton and Ira Magaziner were managing the health care war room, the crime bill war room, operating through a team that linked the White House and the Justice Department, was busy engaging organized interests, particularly police organizations, and the media in a debate over providing communities with 100,000 new police officers. In a number of instances the Clinton White House competed against itself for media attention, as well as for spots on the issue agendas of the major interest groups aligned with the president. Suffice it to say that the Clinton administration, particularly during its first term, employed reverse lobbying at levels unmatched by recent presidents. Likewise, the new Republican majority in the 104th Congress did much the same thing.

Interest Group Engagement in the Republican Congress

One cannot understand the success of the Contract with America in the House of Representatives during the first 100 days of the 104th Congress (January–April 1995) without understanding the role of reverse lobbying. The House Republican leadership engaged in a ten-point policy campaign for passage of the Contract with America by soliciting the support of roughly a dozen major, friendly interest groups. Access to the internal decision-making apparatus of the House Republican leadership was granted to these organizations on two conditions: (1) each group had to support every item in the Contract with America, and (2) each had to contribute to the funding of the media and grassroots campaigns essential to pass all the items. These key interest group leaders were then charged with mobilizing scores of other interest groups to support each item of the Contract with America.

Various accounts of the success of the Contract in the House identify the significant role played by these coalitions of interest groups,[10] the expensive media and grassroots campaigns orchestrated by these groups,[11] and the important role of the interest group engagement strategy employed by House leaders, particularly House Conference Chair John Boehner (R-Ohio).[12]

Beyond the first 100 days of the 104th Congress, the House Republican leadership maintained its outreach program with key interest groups as Boehner—and more recently Sen. Paul Coverdell (R-Ga.), having organized a similar program in the Senate—have met regularly with the lobbyists representing the lead interest groups aligned with the Republican Party in Congress. Journalist Michael Weisskopf argued that such "reverse lobbying may come more naturally to many Republicans who have long-standing ties to big business."[13] This, indeed, may be the case. Nevertheless, big business is represented within the Republican outreach program only through the U.S. Chamber of Commerce. All of the other seats at the table are held by representatives of small business (for example, National Federation of Independent Business, National Retail Federation, National Restaurant Association) or by representatives of membership organizations (for example, Christian Coalition, Americans for Tax Reform). Moreover, these continuing linkages, although common in the U.S. House of Representatives, have not taken hold in the contemporary U.S. Senate.

White House Reverse Lobbying: 100,000 Cops

The relationship between the Clinton administration and the major national law enforcement organizations can be traced back to the 1992 presidential campaign when candidate Bill Clinton openly courted the law-and-order vote by presenting his crime plan, which included placing 100,000 new law enforcement officers on the nation's streets by the year 2000. Wresting the issue of crime away from the Republican Party was a key element in reshaping the Democratic constituency at the national level for the Clinton–Gore campaign. By encapsulating the crime initiative within the call for 100,000 Cops, the Clinton campaign had accomplished the dual goals of shifting the debate on crime and providing the media and the public a clear message that cut through the complexities of federal crime policy.

Converting campaign promises into public policy is a more difficult undertaking, yet not entirely different from electioneering. Although the Clinton–Gore campaign received no formal endorsements from the major police organizations in 1992, the electoral outreach effort orchestrated by candidate Clinton was followed by institutionalized outreach by the Clinton administration. In the months following the initial introduction of the Clinton legislative proposal on crime in July 1993, the crime bill war room began to take shape in the White House. Ron Klain, chief adviser to candidate Clinton on criminal justice issues and original architect of the 100,000 Cops initiative, moved from his position in the White House counsel's office to become chief of staff for Attorney General Janet Reno in early 1994. This shift was important for two reasons. First, the relationships between the Justice Department and the White House during the first year of the Clinton presidency were strained, with Reno not particularly convinced of the efficacy of community policing, the cornerstone of the 100,000 Cops plan. Klain was the person to convert Reno to the ways of the White House. Second, Klain would provide the direct link to the White House necessary to facilitate the war room strategy on crime.[14] From the White House, Rahm Emanuel, then deputy communications director, would serve as the leader of the war room. Together, Klain and Emanuel orchestrated the public engagement strategy for passage of the Clinton crime bill in 1994.

The Crime Bill and Public Engagement

The omnibus crime bill proposed by the Clinton administration took the legislative form of the Violent Crime Control and Law Enforcement Act. First proposed in the summer of 1993, the sweeping provisions of the bill (H.R. 3355) provided $30.2 billion in law enforcement funding over a six-year period. The centerpiece of the legislation was the COPS Program—Community-Oriented Policing Service Program—an $8.8 billion program through which the attorney general would award grants to individual law enforcement agencies to aid in the hiring or rehiring of police officers, thus fulfilling the Clinton campaign pledge to "add 100,000 new cops" to the law enforcement ranks in the United States by the year 2000.

The reverse lobbying strategy employed by the crime bill war room was ingenious in that the plan included not only tactics focused on the passage of the crime bill in the Congress, particularly in the more difficult House of Representatives, but also efforts to ensure the successful implementation of the COPS Program once passed by Congress and signed by the president. The Klain–Emanuel team organized a three-pronged strategy to pass the legislation and to begin the implementation process for 100,000 Cops: (1) direct lobbying, (2) national outreach, and (3) constituency group mobilization. Direct lobbying would involve the president, the vice president, the attorney general, the senior Justice Department staff, and several senior White House officials. At the height of the legislative battle in the House of Representatives, one could find ten to fifteen Justice Department officials on the Hill on a daily basis, each working on undecided members of both parties. By the end of the battle in the House in August of 1994, the president was on the telephone with wavering Democrats in the House. However intensive, in many ways these tactics reflected conventional administration lobbying on a major piece of legislation.

Beyond the halls of Congress, the White House took the issue to the streets. As such, the crime bill war room was particularly attentive to the special limitations on the administration in mobilizing public support for the crime bill. In the earliest planning meetings of the war room team, there was explicit discussion of the Anti-Lobbying Act as it would relate to any activities undertaken by the Justice Department or the White House in mobilizing both the public at large and particular constituency groups concerned with the crime bill. These two methods, national outreach and constituency group mobilization, were linked in that the interest groups most attentive to crime issues, such as law enforcement organizations, would serve as the conduits through which the Clinton administration could reach the wider public.

The law enforcement constituency in the United States includes roughly 600,000 police officers, sheriffs, federal agents, and related personnel. The crime bill war room solicited the support of the major law enforcement organizations and managed to attract the vast majority of the national groups, associations, and unions (see Table 12-1). The single holdout in the law enforcement community was the Police Benevolent Association (PBA), with more than 100,000 members in state and local associations across the country. Given a total constituency of 600,000 members nationwide, multiple membership in the police organizations is evident as combined memberships in the dozen organizations listed in Table 12-1, along with the PBA membership, total close to 800,000 members. In fact, there are several local PBAs included in the National Association of Police Officers (NAPO) and Fraternal Order of Police (FOP) memberships. Although a few police organizations are not listed, these represent the largest and most politically significant groups in the law enforcement community. The absence of the PBA in the crime bill war room reflects the unhappiness of the PBA with the Brady Bill and the Assault Weapons Ban. The PBA later joined forces with the National Rifle Association (NRA) and other progun organizations as the Law Enforcement Alliance of America, in opposition to the crime bill.

The dozen police organizations mobilized by the war room were brought into the White House and the Justice Department for strategy sessions with the president, the attorney general, and the war room team.

Table 12-1   National Law Enforcement Organizations Mobilized
by the Clinton White House

Associations	Membership
Fraternal Order of Police (FOP)	270,000
National Association of Police Organizations (NAPO)	200,000 members/ 4,000 organizations
International Union of Police Associations (IUPA)	80,000
National Troopers Coalition (NTC)	45,000
International Brotherhood of Policy Officers (IBPO)	40,000
International Association of Chiefs of Police (IACP)	14,000
Federal Law Enforcement Officers Association (FLEOA)	13,000 federal agents
National Organization of Black Law Enforcement Executives (NOBLE)	3,500 members
National Sheriffs Association (NSA)	3,000 county sheriffs
Major City Police Chiefs Association	< 100 members
Police Executive Research Form (PERF)`	a
Police Foundation	a

[a] These organizations are think tanks associated with the law enforcement community. PERF is directed by the top administrators of major law enforcement agencies and provides consulting services to federal, state, and local entities as well as job search services. The Police Foundation is a privately funded, independent research organization created in 1970 through Ford Foundation funding.

Not only were the police organizations lobbied on the importance of the COPS Program, they were asked to provide guidance in the design and implementation of the program. According to one Justice Department official, "If we could get them to buy into the program, make them feel as if they had a stake in its success, we would be more than halfway home."[15] In order to accomplish this, the program would have to serve all law enforcement constituencies. In many ways, the congressional language added to the Clinton proposal that called for COPS Program funds to be divided equally between large jurisdictions (cities with populations greater than 150,000) and small and rural communities (under 150,000) aided in appeasing the interests of both big city police unions and the local police chiefs with staffs of five or fewer officers.

In order to conduct a national public engagement campaign through earned media—that is, free media coverage of political events orchestrated by the White House or Justice Department—the war room called on the police organizations to provide the venues for the attorney general to sing the praises of the crime bill and 100,000 Cops in particular. If the war room team had its way, Reno would have never spent a day in Washington during the summer of 1994. As it was, Reno was made available for media events organized by police organizations and law enforcement agencies anywhere in the United States for one week a month during a six-month stretch of 1994.

One June 1994 exchange between Klain and his war room compatriots provides a flavor of the mission to keep Reno on the road. Klain, just notified of Gov. Mario Cuomo's cancellation of a media event in Albany, New York, with Reno, scrambled to fill the slot. "What are we doing with [Drug Enforcement Administration Director] Tom Constantine?" "Dragging his butt all the way up to Albany," someone says. "Boom, we've got it. A press conference. State police. Constantine and her [Reno]. Effect of the Crime Bill on New York state." Moving on, he saw further uses for this team: "We should get some rural targets for her. She can do media stuff with rural guys. This is Sheriff Bob and Attorney General Reno on the crime bill—that kind of thing."[16]

Throughout the legislative battle, the war room provided talking points and other materials to the police organizations that made the strongest case for the crime bill and for 100,000 Cops. As the battle drew to a close in August of 1994, police organizations with close ties to undecided members of the House were pressed into service by the war room team. In a late skirmish in the House, many Republicans, supported by a concerted NRA effort on eliminating the Assault Weapons Ban, as well as more than fifty Democrats with this and other concerns relating to death penalty provisions, voted down the rule on the crime bill conference committee report on August 11. Legislators often vote against a procedural measure, such as the rule establishing conditions for debate on a bill, when they find it difficult to oppose the measure itself (for example, 100,000 Cops).

President Clinton wasted little time taking his case to the American public via the second largest police organization in the nation.

> On the evening of August 12, at a rally at the National Association of Police Organizations meeting in Minneapolis, Clinton stood surrounded by uniformed officers and American flags as he blamed special interests for the House vote defeating the rule for floor consideration of HR 3355, as he attacked Republicans for playing politics with America's safety, and as he tapped widespread public support for a ban on assault weapons. The evening news pictures were vintage Reagan. Within a week, a *USA Today* poll showed that confidence in Clinton's handling of crime had bounced up to 42 percent from 29 percent just a month earlier.[17]

After minor modifications, a second conference report passed the House on August 24, and the Senate followed suit four days later. In a September Rose Garden ceremony, flanked by representatives from the police organizations mobilized by the White House, President Clinton signed the crime bill into law. By winning over all but one of the national police organizations, the White House developed effective legislative allies who proved to be persuasive spokespersons with the public at large.

Rapid Implementation of COPS Program

With the direct lobbying phase of the three-pronged strategy completed by the passage of the crime bill, the Clinton administration sought to institutionalize the COPS Program as quickly as possible by remobilizing the police organizations and reengaging the general public on the importance of the COPS Program. To these ends, the attorney general held a two-hour meeting with representatives of the twelve police organizations the day after the Rose Garden signing ceremony. This outreach effort by Reno registered positively with the police groups. As one police representative stated, "We were used to being courted during congressional fights. It was nice to be asked what we thought after it was all over."[18] During the next two months Reno held three additional meetings with the police groups. Associate Attorney General John Schmidt also held three large meetings with all of the police representatives and ten one-on-one meetings with individual organization leaders.

In addition to the substantive advice from the police organizations, the police representatives were consulted on naming a director for the COPS Program in the Justice Department. Officials there thought it important to have an active duty police chief or sheriff as the director of this new program. Each police organization was asked to submit a list of candidates to Reno; the list of seventy-five names was winnowed to four finalists within the Justice Department. At that point all twelve police organizations were given the list of finalists to ensure that there were no objections prior to the final selection by Reno. In the end, Hayward, California, Police Chief Joseph Brann was chosen, a member of three of the twelve organizations.

Public engagement by the Clinton war room team following passage of the crime bill easily matched their efforts leading to the legislative success. From the day after the presidential signing until election day in November, Justice Department officials appeared at fifty-five meetings and conferences across the nation, pitching the 100,000 Cops message. Reno made four personal appearances at major law enforcement conferences and President Clinton spoke at the annual meeting of the International Association of Chiefs of Police.

Whether the Clinton White House had already acknowledged the possibility of losing control of Congress in the upcoming congressional elections, thereby threatening the existence of the COPS Program, or was simply seeking to expedite the implementation of its most recent successful legislative initiative, the efforts to mobilize support for and, more important, participation in the 100,000 Cops initiative were extensive. The new COPS office in the Justice Department created an outreach system that surpassed the legislative effort earlier in the year. Talking points were disseminated to law enforcement agencies and police organizations across the country as often as three times a week during the fall of 1994 (see box, p. 265). These fact sheets served to inform the supporters of

Box 12-1   Example of Talking Points Produced by Department of Justice for Police Organizations

---

MAKING AMERICA SAFE
Implementing the Violent Crime Control Act
October 11, 1994

How the Violent Crime Control Act
Will Put 100,000 Cops on the Beat

- President Clinton has pledged to the American public that his Administration will add 100,000 police officers to law enforcement agencies across the country. This is one reason President Clinton fought so hard to ensure the Violent Crime Control Act passed by Congress contained $8.8 billion in funding for the COPS Grant Program.
- Some people, however, say the Violent Crime Control Act won't fund 100,000 police officers. They're just plain wrong and the facts prove it. Here's why:
    — Under the Act, **$8.8 billion** is available for the administration's community policing initiative;
    — An initial 3 percent (or $264 million) may be used for technical assistance and training. **Funds remaining for hiring police = $8.54 billion.**
- Of the remaining $8.54 billion, *no more than* 15 percent may be used for purposes other than hiring police officers. The Department of Justice assumes that about 14 percent (or $1.195 billion) will be used for other criminal justice purposes. **Funds remaining for hiring police = $7.345 billion.**
- The Act will provide three-year grants of up to $75,000 to pay for as much as 75 percent of the cost of salary and benefits for each new officer.
- Taking the funds remaining for hiring police ($7.345 billion) and dividing by the maximum federal grant ($75,000), the total number of police projected to be funded by the Violent Crime Control Act is **97,920.**
- Now, **2,080** police have already been funded this year. Adding these police officers to the **97,920** police officers funded under the Violent Crime Control Act bring the total number of new police officers to **100,000.**

RESPONSE CENTER 1-800-421-6770
202-307-1480

100,000 Cops and to provide responses to Republican challenges to the program. A response center with an 800-number was established to field inquiries from prospective COPS awardees.

New grant initiatives in the COPS Program were also introduced through the talking points network. For example, in the week following the transmission presented in the box, two new programs—COPS FAST and COPS AHEAD—were announced. COPS FAST (Funding Accelerated for Smaller Towns) reduced the paperwork needed to apply for COPS grants by jurisdictions under 50,000 residents to a one-page, fill-in-the-blank application. COPS AHEAD (Accelerated, Hiring, Education, and Deployment) allowed jurisdictions with more than 50,000 residents to "begin recruiting and hiring new police officers now in anticipation of later COPS grant funding." The intended goal of these programs was to have as many police officers in positions created by the COPS Program as quickly as possible, in the face of the pending November elections.

The Republican Revolution and the Fight against Repeal

The results of the 1994 elections were disastrous for the Clinton White House and the Democrats. Losing both houses of Congress placed in jeopardy every major policy initiative of the Clinton administration, and the 100,000 Cops Program was no exception. A major item in the Contract with America was The Taking Back Our Streets Act (H.R. 3)— the Republican response to the Clinton crime bill. In reality, the Republican crime agenda included six legislative initiatives,[19] and one of the crime bills, the Local Law Enforcement Block Grant Act (H.R. 728), would have effectively eliminated the 100,000 Cops Program and replaced it with block grants to local governments.

As the first session of the 104th Congress began in January 1995, the crime bill war room redoubled its efforts to fight for the COPS Program in the face of new Republican majorities in both houses. The mobilization of police organizations in support of the program was matched with an upgraded national outreach effort. The third prong of the strategy, direct lobbying, was reinstituted. President Clinton decided that the 100,000 Cops initiative was too important to be killed by the new Republican Congress. On February 1, 1995, President Clinton, Attorney General Reno, and White House Chief of Staff Leon Panetta held a strategy session with the twelve police organization leaders. By that point, the Justice Department claimed that 17,000 new police officers were on the streets in just the first four months of the COPS Program. The talking points network was being bombarded with fact sheets, statistics on new police placements, updates on COPS FAST and COPS AHEAD, and even responses to Republican charges against the Program—"Debunking the Myths: The 100,000 Cops Program Works!!!"

As the crucial vote on H.R. 728 approached in the House, Clinton threw down the gauntlet in his weekly radio address on February 11, 1995:

> I made a commitment, a promise to put 100,000 more police on our streets, because there is simply no better crime fighting tool to be found. And I intend to keep that promise. Anyone on Capitol Hill who wants to play partisan politics with police officers for America should listen carefully: I will veto any effort to repeal or undermine the 100,000 police commitment, period.

Despite his effort, the House went on to pass H.R. 728 by a vote of 238 to 192, by far the closest margin of victory of any of the six crime provisions in the Contract.[20] Later that summer, the Senate agreed to fund the House provision on local block grants in their Commerce–State–Justice appropriations bill. The final bill passed by both houses included only block-grant funding. Honoring the commitment made in his February radio address, Clinton vetoed the bill. This action resulted in the shut down of the federal government in December of 1995.

In the end, the Republicans blinked, having suffered the negative consequences of the government shut down far more than the Clinton administration. As of the end of 1997, the Justice Department COPS Program Office reported that more than $3.7 billion has been appropriated for 100,000 Cops since its initial passage in 1994, with annual appropriations for fiscal years 1996 and 1997 of roughly $1.4 billion. Though disputed by a variety of sources, partisan and academic, the Justice Department stated that funding had been approved for more than 65,000 police officers, as of December 1997.[21] In addition to the survival of the 100,000 Cops program, President Clinton received one additional reward for his efforts with police organizations. For the first time in its history, the Fraternal Order of Police endorsed a Democrat for president in 1996—Bill Clinton.

Congressional Reverse Lobbying: Project Relief

At the heart of the so-called Republican revolution was the basic goal of reconfiguring the relationship between the federal government and the American people. Central to that goal was easing the burden of federal regulation on American business, and especially American small business owners. As Haley Barbour, then chair of the Republican National Committee, observed on election night in 1994: "The Republican Party is the party of small business, not big business; the party of Main Street, not Wall Street." The small business theme endures as the cornerstone in the new Republican philosophy of governance. Representative J. C. Watts (R-Okla.), responding to President Clinton's State of the Union Address in January of 1997, echoed the theme: "The strength of America is not on Wall Street but on Main Street, not in big business but in small business with local owners and workers."[22]

During the first 100 days, though, the new Republican leadership in the House of Representatives scrambled to give substance to the small business theme. One of the earliest examples of the lengths to which the new House leadership would go to demonstrate the distinction between their allegiances with big business and small business interests in Washington was the expression of displeasure with the leadership of the U.S. Chamber of Commerce by newly elected House Republican Conference Chair John Boehner (R-Ohio). His public chastisement of the Chamber's support of the Clinton economic stimulus package in the 103d Congress led to the firing of senior vice president Bill Archey and the elevation of two Republican allies within the Chamber, Bruce Josten and Lonnie Taylor, to the positions of senior vice president and vice president for congressional affairs, respectively. Only after this public mea culpa was the Chamber granted access to the Boehner coalition operation.[23]

Tom DeLay as Mr. Deregulation

Within the new Republican House leadership ranks, there was no better candidate to give voice to the campaign for federal deregulation as chair of the Contract Task Force on Deregulation than newly elected Majority Whip Tom DeLay. Prior to being elected to Congress in 1984, DeLay owned and operated the Albo Pest Control Company in suburban Houston. His constant dealings with federal and state regulatory agencies drove him into politics: "I was really angry. It got me thinking that the government was the cost of doing business, so I got involved."[24] In 1978, he won a seat in the Texas House of Representatives by beating the deregulatory drum. Six years later, he was elected to the U.S. House, where he continued on his deregulatory mission. His first successful effort contributed to the deregulation of the trucking industry. Into the 1990s, DeLay continued to challenge what he and his colleagues perceived as heavy-handedness of federal regulatory agencies such as the Environmental Protection Agency (EPA) and the Occupational Safety and Health Administration (OSHA).

As the 1994 elections approached, however, DeLay sensed that dramatic change was at hand. At an August 1994 meeting of the National American Wholesale Grocers' Association (NAWGA), now known as Food Distributors International, at the Greenbrier Resort in Berkeley Springs, West Virginia, Representative DeLay spoke of his vision to the assembled grocers. On the morning following the elections, he posited, the Republican Party would control the U.S. House of Representatives for the first time in forty years; the Senate would also return to Republican control. The resulting shift in political power in Congress would produce sweeping change in government regulatory policy. Thus, the germination of Project Relief had begun.[25]

NAWGA would become one of the founding members of Project Relief and its lobbyist, Bruce Gates, would go on to serve DeLay as executive director of the Project Relief effort. The first official meeting of Project Relief was held within a week of the November 8 elections. Twenty representatives of corporations, associations, citizens organizations, and policy organizations supportive of deregulation met with DeLay to discuss the substance of the new deregulatory regime as well as the strategies and tactics to be employed in order to achieve the policy goals of the coalition. Of the ten major task forces organized under conference chair John Boehner's leadership, the DeLay effort was the first organized and was the most elaborate constructed during the first 100 days of the 104th Congress.

Project Relief Coalition Building

In less than three months, between the November elections and the first day of the 104th Congress in January 1995, DeLay and the Project Relief team had managed to solicit the support of approximately 350 interest groups. The first public pronouncement on the new deregulatory agenda came on December 14, 1994, when DeLay held a press conference announcing Project Relief. DeLay urged all organizations interested in relieving the regulatory burdens of the federal government to join forces with Project Relief. He even offered the new Project Relief 800 number—1-800-9XS-REGS, for interested citizens to call for additional information.[26]

Tom DeLay did considerably more than "solicit" and "urge" participation by interest groups in Project Relief, as he used all available pressure to extract adequate resources from interest group leaders to support of his cause. Journalist Hanna Rosin concluded, "On special interests, DeLay's been positively brazen. On K Street he's known as 'the Hammer' for his skill at pounding lobbyists for cash. As head of Project Relief, DeLay was host, cashier, and bouncer, throwing parties in House chambers and collecting cash at the door."[27]

DeLay personally solicited the support of scores of interest groups and associations supportive of federal deregulation. In Washington circles, such direct solicitations are often played down to mask the raw political relationship between elected officials and interest group representatives. In the trade and industry association newsletters and magazines, the unvarnished story is often told, however. In publications such as *Food & Drink Daily*, *Pest Control*, and *Lawn & Landscape Maintenance*, association members learned DeLay's request to have their organization join Project Relief.[28] For example, *Lawn & Landscape Maintenance* reported,

> The American Association of Nurserymen will join forces with Project Relief, the leading national coalition dedicated to helping businesses seek relief from excessive government regulation. AAN's participation

comes at the request of new Republican House Majority Whip Tom
DeLay. Through Project Relief, AAN will help pursue a more aggres-
sive regulatory reform agenda with the new, Republican-led 104th
Congress, according to Ben Bolusky, government affairs expert with
AAN.

"We will be working with other business leaders and Republican
leaders to enact regulation and reform as part of the Contract with
America in the first 100 days, and beyond," said Bolusky.[29]

Such requests from a top-ranking Republican leader in the new
104th Congress raise two important questions: (1) What if your interest
group was not invited to participate? and (2) If your group was invited,
what if you say no to the invitation? In the first instance, environmental
groups were not welcome in the Project Relief coalition. They would
have no impact on the deregulatory agenda as long as the Republicans
were in charge. In the second instance, groups who did not respond to
DeLay's call to arms did so at their peril. DeLay and others in the Republican House leadership often used the train analogy to make their
points regarding support for the new Republican agenda. Interest groups
were told that the Republican leadership train was leaving the station. An
interest group could either get on board or be left behind.

Within a twelve-week period, virtually all of the major organized
business interests and many minor interests had signed on to Project Relief (see box, p. 271 for a partial membership list). The membership included a wide array of major corporations (AMOCO, Amway, Boeing,
Coors, Federal Express, General Electric, UPS, and Union Pacific), large
umbrella business groups (U.S. Chamber of Commerce, National Association of Manufacturers, Business Roundtable, and National Federation of
Independent Business), trade and industry associations, including more
than a dozen contractors groups, as well as taxpayer, property rights, and
religious citizens groups (Americans for Tax Reform, Citizens for a Sound
Economy, Defenders of Property Rights, Christian Coalition, and Family
Research Council).

Organizational Mission and Strategy

Because of the sheer magnitude of the coalition, a division of labor
was designed to organize the various aspects of the Project Relief en-
deavor. With more than 300 interest groups mobilized, it was clear that
without some degree of organizational discipline, the effort might become a multiheaded monster, spinning off in all directions. To that end,
Bruce Gates created several teams within the coalition, directed by a
steering committee, made up of some of the most powerful women and
men in the lobbying industry.[30] Lobbyist Kim McKernan of the National
Federation of Independent Business chaired the strategies team; Susan
Eckerly of Citizens for a Sound Economy was the legislative director.[31]

Box 12-2   Interest Group Membership in Project Relief

Advancement for Sound Science
  Coalition
Agricultural Retailers Association
Air Conditioning Contractors of
  America
Alliance of Independent Store
  Owners
American Association for Small
  Property Owners
American Association of
  Christian Schools
American Association of
  Nurserymen
American Association of
  Physicians and Surgeons
American Automotive Leasing
  Association
American Bakers Association
American Consulting Engineers
  Council
American Electronics
  Association
American Farm Bureau
  Federation
American Feed Industry
  Association
American Forest and Paper
  Association
American Frozen Food Institute
American Hardware
  Manufacturers
American Home Owners
  Association
American Hotel and Motel
  Association
American Independent Refiners
American Insurance Association,
  Incorporated
American Land Rights
  Association
American Loggers Solidarity

American Portland Cement
  Association
American Road and
  Transportation Builders
  Association
American Sod Producers
  Association
American Subcontractors
  Association
American Trucking Association
American Warehouse Association
American Wholesale Marketers
  Association
Americans for Tax Reform
AMOCO
Amway Corporation
ASARCO
Ashland Incorporated
Associated Builders and
  Contractors
Associated General Contractors
  of America
Associated Landscape
  Contractors
Associated Specialty Contractors
Association of Concerned
  Taxpayers
Association of Home Appliance
  Manufacturers
Association of Telemessaging
  Services
Automotive Recyclers
  Association
Beer Institute
Bell Atlantic
Bell South
Biotechnology Industry
  Organization
Blue Ribbon Coalition
Bronze Craft Association
Business Roundtable

(continued)

Box 12-2   *(continued)*

California Forestry Association
California State Grange
CBI Industries Incorporated
Center for Regulatory Studies
Chemical Manufacturers
  Association
Chemical Specialty
  Manufacturers Association
Chevron
Christian Coalition
Citizens for a Sound Economy
Coalition for Auto Repair
  Equality
Coalition for Flexible
  Compliance
Coalition of Energy Taxes
Committee for a Constructive
  Tomorrow
Community Bank League of
  New England
Competitive Enterprise Institute
Concerned Women for America
  of Kansas
Conservative Victory Committee
Consumer Alert
Coors Brewing Company
Council of Fleet Specialists
Council of 100
Curry County Oregon Project
Defenders of Property Rights
Distilled Spirits Council of the
  United States
Electronic Data Systems
  Corporation
Entergy
Environmental Conservation
  Organization
Environmental Policy Task Force
EST, Incorporated
Ethan Allen Institute
Family Research Council

FC Industries, Incorporated
Federal Express
FerroAlloys Association
Financial Executives Institute
Flexible Packaging Association
Fluor Corporation
Food Marketing Institute
Foundation for Environment
  and Economic Progress
Gas Appliance Manufacturers
  Association
Gelman Sciences
General Electric
Glaxo, Incorporated
Gold Prospectors Association of
  America
GPEC
Grocery Manufacturers of
  America
Halogenated Solvents Industry
  Alliance
Helicopter Association
  International
Independent Electrical
  Contractors
Independent Insurance Agents
  of America
Institute for Regulatory Policy
International Bankers
  Association of America
International Council of
  Shopping Centers
International Fabricare Institute
International Foodservice
  Distributors Association
International Mass Retail
  Association
International Window Film
  Association
Koch Industries
Lafarge Corporation

Box 12-2 *(continued)*

Machinery Dealers National
Association
Maine Alliance
Maine Oil Dealers
Manufactured Housing Institute
Maytag Corporation
Mechanical Contractors
Association
Minnesota Licensed Beverage
Association
Mutual Savings Bank
National Aggregate Association
National American Wholesale
Grocers Association
National Asphalt Pavement
Association
National Association for the
Self-Employed
National Association of
Biomedical Research
National Association of
Convenience Stores
National Association of
Manufacturers
National Association of Plumbing
and Heating Contractors
National Association of Private
Enterprise
National Association of Realtors
National Association of RV Parks
and Camps
National Association of Small
Business Investment
Companies
National Association of the
Remodeling Industry
National Association of Truck
Stop Operators
National Association of
Wholesaler-Distributors

National Cotton Council of
America
National Electrical Contractors
of America
National Electrical
Manufacturers Association
National Federation of
Independent Business
National Food Processors
Association
National Glass Association
National Grocers Association
National Landowners
Association
National Lumber and Building
Material Dealers
National Ocean Industries
Association
National Paint and Coatings
Association
National Pest Control
Association
National Rail Construction
Association
National Restaurant Association
National Retail Federation
National Roofing Contractors
Association
National Shoe Retailers
Association
National Soft Drink Association
National Tire Dealers and
Retreaders Association
National Tooling and Machining
Association
National Utility Contractors
Association
National Welding Supply
Association
National Wilderness Institute

(continued)

Box 12-2 *(continued)*

New Jersey Federation of
  Republican Women
Non-Ferrous Founders
Non-Prescription Drug
  Manufacturers Association
North Carolina Fisheries
  Association
Painting and Decorating
  Contractors
Pet Industries Joint Advisory
  Councils
Petrochemical Energy Group
Petroleum Markets Association
  of America
Plumbing Manufacturers
  Institute
Private Landowners of
  Wisconsin
Professional Lawn Care
  Association
Project 21
Promotional Products
  Association
Real Estate Services Providers
Reliance Resources
Resilient Floor Covering Institute
Retail Bakers of America
Seniors Coalition
Servicemaster
Sheet Metal and Air
  Conditioning Contractors

Sierra C.A.R.E.
Small Business Exporters
Small Business Survival
  Committee
Snack Food Association
Society of American Florists
Society of Glass and Ceramic
  Decorators
Society of the Plastics Industry
Spring Manufacturers Institute
Stop Taking Our Property of
  Indiana
SYSCO Corporation
Texas Association of
  Nurserymen
Traditional Values Coalition
Trans Coalition for Clean Air
U.S. Chamber of Commerce
U.S. Business and Industrial
  Council
Union Carbide
Union Pacific Corporation
United Parcel Service
United Veterans of America
Urban Mobility Corporation
W. R. Grace and Company
Washington Contract Loggers
Wild Rivers Conservancy
  Federation
Wood Machinery Manu-
  facturers

Aiding in organizing the congressional deregulatory forces, Rep. David McIntosh (R-Ind.) served as DeLay's deputy and would organize the vote-counting war room during the latter stages of the effort.[32]

With DeLay's previous record of heavy-handed dealings with lobbyists in fund-raising activities, the media and watchdog organizations paid particular attention to Project Relief, and numerous press accounts linked its participants to Republican fund-raising during the 1993–1994 election cycle. The Environmental Working Group analyzed 115 PACs tied to the 350 interest groups affiliated with Project Relief and found that $10.3 million in PAC contributions went to Republican candidates, party campaign organizations, and GOP leadership PACs.[33] Other reports and commentaries argued that the financial force of Project Relief was even greater: "Project Relief alone has spent an astounding $30 million in its efforts to undermine the nation's health, safety, and environmental laws."[34] Project Relief was also identified as a "$51 million coalition opposed to regulation."[35] It is not clear how these reporters arrived at such "astounding" figures; nonetheless, such media coverage constrained the efforts of DeLay and the coalition partners.[36] Given the heightened media exposure of Project Relief, Gates made it clear that the government deregulation aspect of the Contract with America would not involve a multimillion dollar media campaign effort funded by supportive interest groups, as was undertaken by the Contract Task Force on Tort Reform, for example. Although journalists Weisskopf and Maraniss set the communications budget for Project Relief at $500,000, Gates claims that this aspect of the campaign never totaled more than $100,000.[37] There were no national media commercials produced by Project Relief, which employed only limited newspaper advertising and direct mail efforts.

The strategy was largely confined to mobilizing support within the House of Representatives through member-to-member lobbying and targeted interest group lobbying of wavering members of both parties. The deregulatory agenda for the first 100 days took the form of The Job Creation and Wage Enhancement Act (H.R. 9). Within H.R. 9, there were six bills linked to the deregulatory plank in the Contract,[38] but DeLay and company were most concerned with the veto-proof passage of the Private Property Protection Act, which called for a moratorium on all new federal regulations.

As the legislative battle began to take shape, DeLay called on the Project Relief leadership to give substance to the moratorium legislation. On December 14, 1994, following the elections, DeLay had written a letter to President Clinton asking for a 100-day freeze on federal rule-making. Low-level administration officials rejected his request out of hand two days later. DeLay was more than willing to up the ante, as his lobbyist allies wrote a bill that proposed a thirteen-month moratorium on all federal rule-making activities.[39]

Proud of his capacities to organize and execute political strategies, Delay made little attempt to hide the relationship he had developed with his interest group allies. His political opponents, including the Democratic leadership in the House and various interest group adversaries, were aghast at what they viewed as improper access to the policy-making process by lobbyists who were writing legislation for the Republican leadership. In reality, what was taking place within the Republican leadership ranks was not at all uncommon, and a few Democratic lobbyists admitted that they had drafted legislation for some of the House Democrats who were screaming loudest against DeLay and the Republicans.[40]

As the 100-day march in the House continued, the moratorium legislation was queued for a floor vote on February 23, 1995. Under the direction of David McIntosh, a war room was assembled off the House floor, occupied by a handful of Project Relief lobbyists. In the days leading up to the floor vote, legislative director Eckerly and strategies director McKernan developed complex lists of supporters and opponents, including leaners—for and against—in both parties. The coalition leaders targeted a number of Blue Dogs, southern Democrats in the House who had often supported previous deregulation initiatives. Each House member who remained a possible "yea" vote received attention from a Project Relief advocate, who worked every conceivable angle to convince their legislative targets to support the moratorium bill. This largely inside-lobbying strategy employed by DeLay and Project Relief proved effective. DeLay attracted more than fifty Democrats and held 95 percent of the Republicans, losing only a dozen votes from the more moderate, environmentalist wing.

The moratorium bill passed by a vote of 277 to 148, clearly a legislative victory for DeLay and Project Relief. It did, however, fall short the two-thirds mark needed to override a potential Clinton veto, and it faced a much tougher challenge in the U.S. Senate. Absent the context of the Contract with America and the 100-day commitment to pass the GOP legislative agenda, the deregulatory effort floundered in the Senate. Project Relief was a creature of the Republican House leadership. Neither its method of operation nor its substance meshed well with the slower, more deliberative nature of the Senate, even under Republican leadership.

Deregulation and Project Relief after the Contract

Although the moratorium bill failed to pass in the Senate during the 104th Congress, the political context of the government deregulation debate was significantly altered by the efforts of Project Relief. Moreover, Tom DeLay could continue on his rampage against "the gestapo of government," the Environmental Protection Agency,[41] and other regulatory reform legislation circulated within both houses. Absent the heat and light of the first 100 days, in 1996 the Congress did pass and President Clinton did sign legislation with far-reaching consequences for federal government regulation for decades to come. Returning to the small business theme of the Republican Party, the law is titled The Small Business Regulatory Enforcement Fairness Act of 1996 (SBREFA), and it creates a host of mechanisms for advocates of government deregulation to stymie the federal rule-making process, especially for small business.

The Washington climate clearly has changed regarding government deregulation. With more than 350 interest groups mobilized through Project Relief watching closely, one might expect the winds of deregulation to continue blowing, even as the coalition has disbanded.

Table 12-2   Individual and PAC Contributions, DeLay Congressional Committee and DeLay Leadership PAC, 1993–1994 and 1995–1996

	Election Cycle	
Reporting Entity	1993–1994	1995–1996
Tom DeLay Congressional Committee		
PAC contributions	$393,376	$1,065,875
Individual contributions ($200+)	248,180	459,794
Total	$641,556	$1,525,669
Americans for a Republican Majority		
PAC Contributions	$ 26,500	$ 254,361
Individual Contributions ($200+)	246,500	333,392
Total	$273,000	$ 587,753

Source: Federal Election Commission, 1993–1994 and 1995–1996 final reports.

Politically, the linkage between Project Relief participants and DeLay has endured. During the 1995–1996 election cycle, DeLay and other Republican leaders were not hesitant to tap into the financial resources of the 350 interest groups and their PACs for electoral support. DeLay himself serves as a microcosm of the Republican fund-raising enterprise and the influence of majority status in the House. In both 1994 and 1996, DeLay ran for reelection and operated a leadership PAC— Americans for a Republican Majority. Analyzing the relationship between individual and PAC contributions to his campaign committee and his PAC during both cycles, a clear pattern emerges (see Table 12-2). PAC contributions to his campaign committees almost tripled, to more than $1 million; similar contributions to his leadership PAC multiplied almost ten-fold. In neither instance did individual contributions even double. Prominent among the PAC contributors to his 1996 campaign committee and PAC are many of the participants in Project Relief.[42]

Conclusion

In each of the preceding case studies, reverse lobbying was presented in a distinct institutional setting. The analysis of reverse lobbying by the White House, as practiced by the Clinton administration, offers insight into the relationships between organized interests and policy makers in the executive branch. Similarly, examining reverse lobbying in the Republican House of Representatives sheds light on the interactive nature of the relationships between lobbyists and members of Congress. In each instance, the act of reverse lobbying demonstrates the permeability of our institutions of governance in Washington. Whether in Congress or in the White House, those who govern control access to the inner sanctum of public policy making. By soliciting access to the policy process, actors in both institutions acknowledge the symbiotic relationship between themselves and organized interests.

White House operations benefit from public engagement that links interest groups and their constituencies with the positions articulated by the president. By organizing and mobilizing attentive publics, the president is better positioned to challenge the Congress, particularly in the era of divided government. Knowing when to employ reverse lobbying is made easier by continual public opinion polling by White House political operations. Reverse lobbying can also work when it limits the scope of mobilization to direct lobbying of members of Congress; the message is simply different, often less linked to constituency interests.

Congressional efforts at reverse lobbying in the 104th and 105th Congresses were qualitatively different from past Democratic efforts. The difference lies not in the access granted to the policy-making process, although the Republicans have raised interest group access to a new level. Rather, the difference lies in the institutionalization of reverse lobbying in the Republican House of Representatives. Discussions with lobbyists formerly on the "inside" during Democratic control of the House offer two distinct conclusions about how the Republicans "do business" with their interest group allies. First, there is an overriding sense of envy. These lobbyists are envious of the degree to which lobbyists allied with the Republican leadership actually have direct connection to the substance of the legislative agenda. As one labor lobbyist stated, "For years we bankrolled every initiative that the Democratic leadership wanted to sell to the American people, yet we were rarely asked what we thought."

The other conclusion is one of being overworked. Using Rep. John Dingell (D-Mich.) as an example, another labor lobbyist lamented the loss of majority status by the Democrats in the House as well as the subsequent cuts of committee staffs by one-third. In the 103d Congress, Dingell chaired the House Energy and Commerce Committee, which at that time held jurisdiction over more than half of legislation passed by Congress each year. As such, Dingell controlled a staff of roughly 125 employees working for the majority. In the 104th Congress, as ranking member of the renamed Commerce Committee, he had fewer than thirty staffers at his disposal. The lobbyist asked, "Who do you think is doing the work of the one hundred staffers that Dingell no longer commands?" For the answer, the lobbyist pointed to the several floors below him at the union headquarters.

Whether setting the agenda as one of the majority party or serving in the minority, members of Congress have the ability to employ reverse lobbying in a variety of circumstances. So, too, can the president, regardless of whether the Congress is controlled by his party or the opposition. The most significant negative consequence of reverse lobbying in both institutions is the linkage between policy advocacy and political money. The congressional example of Project Relief illustrates the inextricable linkage between money and interest group advocacy, particularly in DeLay's hot pursuit of political money. For interest groups participating in reverse lobbying, real danger lies in law makers' expectations of reciprocation for access granted and influence registered through legislative language written or removed.

Nor is the White House immune to such activities. Pat Griffin, assistant to the president for legislative affairs during the time of the passage of the crime bill and the fight over the repeal of 100,000 Cops, stated that the reverse lobbying effort on 100,000 Cops was one of only a very few instances where the White House did *not* seek contributions from the affected interest groups in 1996. Media accounts of the linkages between White House access and political contributions during the Clinton administration have filled volumes. The potential connections between granting access to the policy-making process through reverse lobbying by both institutions and the extraction of political contributions from interest group invitees remain numerous and varied. Interest groups and their lobbyists should enter these relationships only with the understanding that this political symbiosis is based on mutual self-interest, often with financial strings attached.

Notes

1. For a pluralist account of congressional lobbying, see Richard C. Sachs, "Lobbying," in *The Encyclopedia of the United States Congress*, ed. Donald C. Bacon, Roger H. Davidson, and Morton Keller (New York: Simon and Schuster, 1995), 1302–1312. For an assessment of institutionalized versus individualized pluralism relating to presidential policy making, see Samuel Kernell, *Going Public: New Strategies of Presidential Leadership*, 2d ed. (Washington, D.C.: CQ Press, 1993), 9–47.
2. Jodi Enda, "Lawmakers Lean on Lobbyists for Contributions," *Philadelphia Inquirer*, November 5, 1995, G1.
3. For an analysis of public engagement strategies in foreign policy making, see Ernest J. Wilson, III, "Interest Groups and Foreign Policymaking: A View from the White House," in *The Interest Group Connection: Electioneering, Lobbying, and Policymaking in Washington*, ed. Paul S. Herrnson, Ronald G. Shaiko, and Clyde Wilcox (Chatham, N.J.: Chatham House, 1998), 238–257.
4. Walter Dellinger, "Memorandum for Component Heads: Anti-Lobbying Act Guidelines," U.S. Department of Justice: Office of Legal Counsel, April 17, 1995, 1–3.
5. Ibid., 1.
6. Ibid., 2; the 1989 *Barr* opinion refers to an interpretation of the Anti-Lobbying Act by Assistant Attorney General William Barr in the Bush administration.
7. Dellinger, "Memorandum," 3.
8. General Accounting Office (GAO), "Alleged Lobbying Activities: Office of Substance Abuse Prevention," GAO/HRD-93-100, May 1993, 1–16.

9. The author's account of the meetings held at the White House is based on several interviews in 1994 and 1995 with lobbyists who participated in these meetings. On December 18, 1997, U.S. District Court Judge Royce C. Lamberth, in a nineteen-page opinion, found that Ira Magaziner had misled the court by claiming that the White House health care task force included only government employees. As a result, the task force was allowed to hold its meetings in secret and disclose very little of its activities. The lawsuit that generated the Lamberth opinion was filed by the Association of American Physicians and Surgeons, Inc., and two other interest groups. AAPS brought the lawsuit against the White House claiming that outside interest groups were participating in the Task Force. "Lamberth said he was 'convinced' that Ira Magaziner, Clinton's health care adviser, deliberately misled him in a sworn statement that said that the task force's working group comprised government employees only and not special interest groups." Lamberth "ordered the government to pay sanctions of $285,864 because of the White House and Justice Department's 'dishonest' and 'reprehensible' conduct in failing to reveal to the court key information about the health care task force." See Toni Locy, "Government Ordered to Pay Sanctions for Dishonesty about Health Care Task Force," *Washington Post*, December 19, 1997, A21.
10. See, for example, Colton C. Campbell and Roger H. Davidson, "Coalition Building in Congress: The Consequences of Partisan Change," in *The Interest Group Connection: Electioneering, Lobbying, and Policymaking in Washington*, ed. Paul S. Herrnson, Ronald G. Shaiko, and Clyde Wilcox (Chatham, N.J.: Chatham House, 1998), 116–136; James G. Gimpel, *Fulfilling the Contract: The First 100 Days* (Boston: Allyn and Bacon, 1996); and Darrell M. West and Richard Francis, "Selling the Contract with America: Interest Groups and Policymaking" (Paper delivered at the Annual Meeting of the American Political Science Association, Chicago, August 1995).
11. West and Francis, "Selling the Contract with America."
12. Michael Weisskopf, "Lobbyists Shift into Reverse: Politicians Pursue Interest Groups to Deliver Health Care Votes," *Washington Post*, May 13, 1994, A3.
13. Weisskopf, "Lobbyists Shift into Reverse."
14. Ruth Shalit, "The Kids Are Alright," *The New Republic*, July 18 and 25, 1994, 23–28, 30–31.
15. Interview with Justice Department official conducted by Erik Reid, U.S. Department of Justice, February 1995. This and several additional interviews conducted by Reid were shared with the author on the grounds that the identities of the officials and police organization representatives would not be attributed.
16. Shalit, "The Kids Are Alright," 23.
17. Bruce C. Wolpe and Bertram J. Levine, *Lobbying Congress: How the System Works*, 2d ed. (Washington, D.C.: CQ Press, 1996), 133.
18. Interview with police organization representative conducted by Erik Reid, U.S. Department of Justice, February 1995.
19. The six legislative provisions subsumed under The Taking Back Our Streets Act were Victim Restitution Act (H.R. 665), Exclusionary Rule Reform Act (H.R. 666), Effective Death Penalty Act (H.R. 729), Violent Criminal Incarceration Act (H.R. 667), Criminal Alien Deportation Act (H.R. 668), and Local Law Enforcement Block Grant Act (H.R. 728).
20. Gimpel, *Fulfilling the Contract: The First 100 Days*, 56–66.
21. Scores of Republicans in the House have voiced their dismay at the statistics produced by the Justice Department regarding the number of new police officers funded by the COPS Program. Writing in the fall of 1996, political scientist John J. Dilulio, coauthor of *Body Count: Moral Poverty and How to Win America's War against Crime and Drugs*, was also skeptical: "The 100,000 Cops provision of the 1994 Crime Bill remains notable mainly as one of the cleverest policy ploys in re-

cent political history. For instance, while administration officials have stated publicly that 40,000 cops have been hired under the bill, the actual number as of July 1996 was probably closer to 19,000, of whom only 12,000 were new hires (the rest were already on the force but 'redeployed'). When asked about this reckoning at a recent press briefing, Reno simply punted." See John J. Dilulio, "Questions for Crime-Buster Clinton," *The Weekly Standard*, September 2, 1996, 24.

22. Barbour and Watts quoted in Ronald G. Shaiko and Marc A. Wallace, "From Wall Street to Main Street: The National Federation of Independent Business and the New Republican Majority," in *After the Revolution: PACs and Lobbies in the New Republican Congress*, ed. Robert Biersack, Paul S. Herrnson, and Clyde Wilcox (Boston: Allyn and Bacon, forthcoming 1998).

23. Karen Riley, "Restructured Chamber Acknowledges Error, Woos GOP," *Washington Times*, January 18, 1995, B7.

24. Hanna Rosin, "Whiplash," *The New Republic*, February 19, 1996, 18.

25. For a journalistic account of the DeLay effort, see Michael Weisskopf and David Maraniss, "Forging an Alliance for Deregulation: Rep. DeLay Makes Companies Full Partners in the Movement," *Washington Post*, March 12, 1995, A1; reprinted in David Maraniss and Michael Weisskopf, *"Tell Newt to Shut Up"* (New York: Touchstone Books, 1996), 11–21. The account presented here differs from the Weisskopf–Maraniss description of events relating to Project Relief. Not being burdened by a newspaper deadline, the author was able to discuss the details with the major actors involved well after the effort had ended. Access to those not reached by Weisskopf and Maraniss allows for broader verification of the timing of events and the activities of Project Relief.

26. Mimi Hall, "DeLay Hopes to Whip Regulation into Shape," *USA Today*, December 15, 1994, 6A; and Bill Lambrecht, "Project Relief Opens Fire on Regulation," *St. Louis Dispatch*, December 15, 1994, 3A.

27. Rosin, "Whiplash," 20.

28. John Donnelly, "Food Industry Groups Spearhead Push for Regulatory Reform," *Food & Drink Daily*, December 19, 1994, 1–2; "How a PCO Stopped the Federal Steamroller," *Pest Control*, June 1995, 66; and "Environmental Forum: Trimming Bureaucracy," *Lawn & Landscape Maintenance*, February 1995, 10.

29. "Environmental Forum: Trimming Bureaucracy," 10.

30. Within the leadership ranks of Project Relief, there were as many women as men. The women who served in Project Relief were drawn not only from citizens organizations, but also from the top lobbying departments of the nation's leading corporations, trade associations, and think tanks. Prominent female lobbyists in the Project Relief leadership included Kim McKernan of National Federation of Independent Business, Susan Eckerly of Citizens for a Sound Economy, Dorothy Strunk representing UPS, Elaine Graham of the National Restaurant Association, Mildred Webber, a political consultant who aided DeLay in fund-raising activities, and Wendy Lee Gramm of the Center for Regulatory Studies, wife of Sen. Phil Gramm (R-Texas). In my own analysis of the more than 11,500 lobbyists who have registered with the House and Senate under the new lobbying disclosure law, I found that 29 percent of the registered lobbyists were women. Clearly, within the Project Relief leadership, women lobbyists were well represented. See Mary Lynn F. Jones, "The Lobbying Business: It's No Longer Just a Man's World," *The Hill*, October 15, 1997, 1.

31. Peter H. Stone, "Follow the Leaders," *National Journal*, June 24, 1995, 1640–1644.

32. McIntosh earned his deregulatory stripes as deputy director of Vice President Dan Quayle's Council on Competitiveness, prior to being elected to Congress in 1994; see Jeffrey M. Berry and Kent E. Portnoy, "Centralizing Regulatory Control and Interest Group Access: The Quayle Council on Competitiveness," in *Interest*

Group Politics, 4th ed., ed. Allan J. Cigler and Burdett A. Loomis (Washington, D.C.: CQ Press, 1995), 319–347.

33. See, for example, Gareth Cook, "Laws for Sale: Lobbyists in Congress Let Lobbyists Write the Laws," *Washington Monthly*, July 1995, 44.

34. Bob Herbert, Editorial, "A Lesson in Blood," *New York Times*, August 7, 1995, A13.

35. Douglas Turner, "New Laws Seen as Threats to Safeguards," *The Buffalo News*, April 9, 1995, 4.

36. Such wide disparity in the costs associated with this coalition effort reflects one of the shortcomings of the Lobbying Disclosure Act of 1995. These coalition efforts are rarely reported because the activities undertaken by coalitions are largely directed at issue advocacy in the form of grassroots lobbying. The Lobbying Disclosure Act does not include a provision for the disclosure of grassroots lobbying activities; therefore, there is no official record of the expenditures of such efforts. See Alice Love, "Lobby Disclosure Is Riddled with Loopholes," *Roll Call*, September 7, 1995, 1.

37. Weisskopf and Maraniss, "Forging an Alliance for Deregulation," A1.

38. The six provisions included Unfunded Mandate Reform Act (H.R. 665), Paperwork Reduction Act (H.R. 830), Risk Assessment and Cost-Benefit Act (H.R. 1022), Regulatory Reform and Relief Act (H.R. 926), Private Property Protection Act (H.R. 925), and Tax Incentives for Job Creation Act (H.R. 1215).

39. Weisskopf and Maraniss, "Forging an Alliance for Deregulation," A1.

40. See Alice Love, "Lobbyist-Written Bills Not Unique to GOP Congress," *Roll Call*, April 17, 1995, 1. Love quotes Wright Andrews, president of the American League of Lobbyists and a partner in Andrews & Butera, a multiclient lobbying firm: "I can assure you I have drafted provisions and amendments to bills over the years that have been introduced by Democrats."

41. On the House floor, on July 28, 1995, during final debate on a bill that would have barred the EPA from any further enforcement efforts, Tom DeLay referred to the EPA as "the gestapo of government." The bill was rejected, 212 to 200.

42. DeLay received more than $1.5 million in campaign contributions for his 1996 re-election campaign; his opponent raised less than $30,000. DeLay won the election with 68 percent of the vote.

13

Instrumental Versus Expressive Group Politics: The National Endowment for the Arts

Robert H. Salisbury and Lauretta Conklin

In 1965, with the publication of *The Logic of Collective Action*, economist Mancur Olson profoundly changed the nature of interest group scholarship. Olson demonstrated, both in theory and example, that interest groups did not organize spontaneously—indeed, that it was economically irrational for individuals to join large membership organizations. Olson reinvigorated the field of interest group politics, yet his elegant theory ran headlong into a contradictory fact—large membership groups, such as environmental organizations, were growing rapidly and were not offering the selective benefits (for example, a glossy magazine or a backpack) that Olson considered essential. Lots of folks joined groups for "expressive" reasons; they believed in a policy or a cause and wanted to demonstrate their preference, even if this action was not, strictly speaking, rational in economic terms.

In this chapter Robert Salisbury and Lauretta Conklin approach Olson and groups not from the traditional perspective of interests offering specific incentives for joining, but from a broader perspective of political participation. Salisbury and Conklin observe that, "At the core of expressive political action is the idea that political success is not a necessary condition." Rather, "making the effort is its own reward." They follow their theoretical observations with an analysis of support for the National Endowment for the Arts (NEA), especially as it confronted opposition from cultural conservatives, both in and out of the Congress. Expressive politics has offered substantial support for the NEA, but as the struggle over its very existence has continued for more than a decade, Salisbury and Conklin note that the NEA has found it difficult to rally backing for many specific projects that serve as magnets to "expressive attack." The NEA, even with President Clinton's proposed budget increases, remains vulnerable.

Conventional interest group theory, especially in its more popular and journalistic modes, assumes that most groups, engaged in lobbying activity in any of its multitudinous forms, seek policy objectives that will redound to the material self-interest of their members. The interest in question may be large or small, broad or narrow, widely inclusive or restricted to a few beneficiaries. Whatever its specific shape and substance, the assumption is that the observable behavior may appropriately be analyzed and explained in terms of economistic rationality.

A further and larger body of "theory" postulates that much public policy is the result of demands made on policy makers by interest groups. The stylized version of this theory holds that groups persuade politicians to do their bidding by offering incentives in the form of votes, campaign money, or something else of value such as problem-related information. Insofar as interest groups muster more substantial incentives than, say, political parties, policy makers will turn to them for guidance.[1] Within any given policy domain many different interests may secure some degree of substantive advantage, but in general it is expected that those groups commanding the most resources or offering the most incentives will receive the lion's share of the policy benefits.

Note that in this model politicians are generally reactive to initiatives from groups. Countering this version of things has been the recent cohort of state-centered scholars who have argued that in many situations it has been public officials themselves who have initiated policy proposals, sometimes with little or no prior demand from organized groups. It may well be that after a program is enacted groups come into being that thereafter mobilize support for the program in question, in which case the "second stage" of the process operates more or less as set forth in our initial formulation.

In either of the two versions sketched, the demands and interests of organized groups are treated as central to the policy continuities that have characterized U.S. politics for the past sixty-odd years. To be sure, if and when voter or financial mobilization on behalf of a program were to wither away, or if there were to be a more powerful countermobilization, the policy in question might be expected to shrink or even disappear, but exhortative campaign rhetoric notwithstanding, neither programmatic cancellations nor dramatic shifts in policy direction have been common in modern times.

It is obvious that through all the sound and fury of recent American politics the scope and impact of interest groups has not greatly diminished, and that self-interested groups pursuing their instrumental policy concerns continue to generate stabilizing, perhaps sclerotic[2] or even morbific[3] effects on the system. And yet we are left with some disquieting thoughts. One stems from the theoretical uncertainty into which standard interest group theory was cast by Mancur Olson's seminal 1965 publication, *The Logic of Collective Action.*[4] Olson offered the persuasive argument that whatever might motivate group lobbying activity, rational individuals generally could not be expected to join organizations in order to support the advocacy of self-serving policies unless they were offered selective benefits available only to members. The question then became one of explaining how it was that in fact so many groups did come into existence. Much subsequent research has gone into the question of who joins organized interest groups and why. A fair portion of this work sug-gests that Olson's hypothesis is only partly valid. In the real world of po-litical advocacy not only do quite a lot of people join groups and otherwise contribute to efforts at policy influence when they might free-ride, but they often do so even when they stand to receive no specific benefit from a favorable policy outcome.

Strict economistic rationality has not served very well in developing our understanding of other forms of political participation either; altruism, philanthropy, sociotropic voting, and other such motivations seem to be quite common. We would argue along with Verba, Schlozman, and Brady that interest group activity, at either the individual or organizational level, can best be understood as a specific variety of political participation, and that the investigations in one sphere of participation should be compati-ble, theoretically and empirically, with others.[5] Voting turnout, campaign contribution, and all the other forms of activism are close kin to interest group participation, and there is little warrant for segregating organized group lobbying from other forms of policy advocacy.

Thus the question recurs: If narrowly defined self-interest does not adequately explain interest group participation, what does? Some schol-ars, notably James Q. Wilson,[6] have suggested that the way to broaden the theoretical base for thinking about group membership is by adding "solidary" and "purposive" to "material" motives or benefits. That is, peo-ple may join in order to enjoy good fellowship *(solidary)* or in order to sup-port lobbying efforts for policies they believe in *(purposive)*. The latter is especially important because this was what Olson had said would *not* hap-pen without selective incentives, benefits of membership that were not dependent on lobbying, or policy success. But Moe[7] and others have found that in fact people often do join in order to support lobbying, and, in addition, they believe that their individual participation makes a dif-ference to the outcome. Although, as Rothenberg[8] has shown, group join-ers sometimes make mistakes or change their minds, it does not seem reasonable to attribute all "nonrational" behavior to error or flightiness. Some of it could perhaps be accounted for by philanthropic motives. The relationship between self-interest and generosity has not been very thor-oughly explored, despite the fact that the "economistic" argument would seem to assume the overwhelming empirical primacy of self-interest rather narrowly defined. In any event, however, much politically relevant participation seems in actuality to rest on the concerns and values people hold; self-interested perhaps, in the sense that they are felt to be con-nected to the individual believer's well-being, but in no direct sense bringing personal material advantage.

A further complication arises in the research and commentary on political participation, whether in interest groups or other institutional modes. In "standard" empirical theory "interested" political activity is assumed to be *instrumental*, motivated by a desire to affect the outcome of a policy-making process and conditioned, therefore, by at least a modicum of rational calculus of policy benefits against the costs to be incurred by the instrumental actions. Nearly three decades ago, however, an argument was advanced that cast serious doubt on this assumption.[9] A good deal of interest group activity, it was suggested, was primarily *expressive* in character, motivated by the desire to support a cause, to declare a policy position, to take a stand openly and forcefully, to assert something of value and importance, whether or not the assertion had any significant impact on the policy process.

A substantial share of the "interest group politics" throughout the American experience can be understood as some form of expressive politics; policy advocacy offered and supported by people—individuals and groups—who believed in (or opposed) the moral or ethical desirability of particular governmental actions and, without reference to their own material self-interest, contributed in some fashion to the effort to enact (or defeat) the proposal. Broad "movement" campaigns such as abolition, prohibition, and anti–child-labor efforts are obvious examples, but there are many others that can usefully be interpreted, at least in part, in terms of expressive motivations. People get involved because they *care* about an issue and think they *ought* to contribute.

Riker and Ordeshook suggested that a sense of duty was what explained the fact that so many people voted when, in terms of rational self-interest maximizing, they would not be expected to bother.[10] Indeed, a sense of duty appears to underlie expressive political behavior of many kinds, not just voting, and characteristically it is a sense of moral duty. Many of the policy issues evoking expressive involvement are framed in terms of ethical principles, sometimes in the secular form of good and evil, but often in the essentially religious terms of sin and righteousness.

Political movements in American politics have frequently displayed a large element of religious fervor—abolition, prohibition, and civil rights are obvious examples—and not uncommonly these movements have actually been based in large measure in churches and religious organizations.[11]

Some expressive issues are more mundane, less passionate, more matters of taste. Support for public spending on the arts and humanities is largely of this type perhaps. Such policy preferences may be more or less routine consumption goods, but even though they lack a deeply moralized commitment, they are expressive in that some people or organizations are willing to invest in the expression of support whether or not they believe that their action will affect the outcome or that they themselves will derive any direct benefit. One study reported that 89 percent of the public believed that the arts were important to the community even though no more than 71 percent had attended any specific arts event.[12]

At the core of expressive political action is the idea that political success is not a necessary condition. It is the moral declaration itself that is the essential justification of the effort, and making the effort creates its own reward. The modes of expressive political declaration are numerous and diverse. They may range from a letter to a newspaper or testimony before a legislative committee to a protest march or a sit-in demonstration. Some expressive causes receive rather quiet devotion, and others may generate enough noise to resemble a field of battle. Indeed, a sense of embattlement, of standing against powerful enemies requiring all-out commitment for survival, may generate greater enthusiasm, including a surge in group membership, than would electoral or legislative success. Expressive groups are easy to form, requiring little more than a declarative line and a return mailing address, but such groups are also easy to factionalize. An improved "line," an alternative construction of the moral obligation implied by one's "Holy Writ," may yield significant membership response, assuming, of course, that a mailing list of potential sympathizers is handy. Expressive interest groups often seem to have a short half-life, however. Many political movements manifest strong surges that seem likely to sweep opponents away but decay with equal speed. The civil rights movement of the 1960s and the surges of the Christian Right, first in the late 1970s and again a decade later, illustrate the apparent fragility of heavily moralized political movements.[13] Even those that achieve a degree of institutionalization—Ralph Nader's consumer movement, or environmentalism, for example—appear to thrive more in the face of political threat than with success.[14]

Our point is that important distinctions should be drawn, first, between policy interests that are material and self-serving and those that promise no particularized benefits to their advocates, and second, between those political exertions that are intended to be instrumental in bringing about some policy result and those that are primarily expressive, generating "benefits" to contributors simply by virtue of the public assertion of some value or point of view.

Expressive politics is defined by expression; by what is "said," by the arguments advanced, the rhetorical devices employed, and the symbols and values invoked. Moreover, as rhetoricians have long recognized, arguments are situated in particular contexts involving speaker and audience and are framed in language thought to be attractive to the intended audience. If an interest group desires to reach a broad audience and mobilize it for a letter-writing campaign, its tactics, including the language used, will be quite different from the group that hopes to retain an industry-specific tax break or a local highway improvement.

It seems clear from the research of Walker[15] and others that the near-explosion of interest groups that has come on the political scene since about 1960 has included a large proportion of non–self-interested, expressive groups. Walker found that the interest organizations established after 1960 included a disproportionate share of nonprofit "citizens" groups. Hadwiger reports that in the agricultural policy domain externality-alternative interests attained prominence in this same period.[16] Rising levels of income and education enabled a wide variety of consumption goods to be indulged, including foreign travel, casino gambling, and dining out, but also, we would suggest, participation in diverse expressive interest groups. To be sure, these same factors have helped the growth in the number and strength of more traditional self-interested instrumental groups, and the great expansion in recent decades of the K Street Corridor population was not solely, or even perhaps primarily, a result of the arrival of the externality–alternative interests. Nonetheless, we would surely expect that in recent years many more such groups could be seen contending over the institutional spaces of policy formation than in the days of the Rayburn–Johnson Congress[17] and the Bauer, Pool, and Dexter[18] lobbying system.

We would not suggest that, because expressive groups may "satisfice" their supporters with resonant rhetoric, they are indifferent to policy outcomes. Surely, they would rather prevail and hope, at least someday, to do so. But their typical arsenal of political weaponry is likely to emphasize mass mailings, protest marches and boycotts, and other techniques for using the mass media. Expressive groups are relatively easy to factionalize and vulnerable to shifting currents of moral conviction or consumer taste. As a consequence, on average and compared to groups based on economic self-interest, they are not likely to establish PACs. PACs are typically created by groups with on-going instrumental policy concerns for which sympathetic consideration from public officials is needed, and PAC contributions are designed to secure access to legislators on a continuing basis. Expressive groups may well spend substantial sums of money, if they have it, but primarily on presenting their positions in public forums and attempting to mobilize support from the larger society.

What these rather speculative excursions suggest is that, although they are all within the purview of interest group politics, expressive groups and self-interested instrumental groups are different; different in the motives and values that animate their activity, different in the political and organizational contexts from which they are likely to emerge and thrive, different in the modes of action they favor, and different in their dynamics across time. To explore some of these differences we focus on the interests involved in advocacy pro and con for the National Endowment for the Arts.

The Case of the NEA

The National Endowment for the Arts (NEA) is an example of a program that came into existence rather more in spite of interest group concern than as a result of group demand.[19] The National Endowment for the Humanities (NEH) side of the 1965 national endowment creation was strongly supported by the major groups of higher education interests, but the "arts community" was ambivalent at best.[20] Actors Equity and the American Federation of Musicians endorsed the program but did little else, and the American Symphony Orchestra League, perhaps the best organized of the potential NEA beneficiaries, was sharply divided, with many of the best established orchestras strongly opposed to a federal role in arts support.[21] And in 1965 there were not many American opera companies, ballet troupes, or even nonprofit theater organizations to provide articulate, self-interested constituency-backing for congressional action.

A few states had created agencies to assist the arts,[22] by far the most substantially funded being New York under the leadership of Gov. Nelson Rockefeller. Few local governments had formally designated arts programs, but of course many had museums that received at least indirect public assistance in the form of free land and tax exemption.[23] Essentially, however, the NEA cannot be said to have been called into existence by interest group pressure. Elite sponsorship both in and out of public office, much of it based in New York City, was far more determinative.[24] Once in operation, however, the NEA began to build a structure of organized group support through a reasonably explicit strategy of distributive policy.

At first, the Endowment followed the Ford Foundation pattern of grants designed to help beleaguered symphonies and art museums get onto a more secure fiscal base. After President Nixon appointed Nancy Hanks as NEA chair, however, there ensued a conscious cultivation of the civic elite that controlled the big arts institutions, and with the prospect of significant financial assistance these previously skeptical interests provided enthusiastic endorsements for the NEA. Reflecting this emergence of an arts constituency, Leonard Garment, then special assistant to Nixon, wrote a most instructive memorandum to his boss:

> Support for the arts is good politics. By providing substantially increased support for cultural activities, you will gain support from groups which have hitherto not been favorable to this administration.
>
> We are not referring to the hard-core radicals who offer little in the way of constructive dialogue when they plead for more support for cultural projects. We are talking about the vast majority of theater board members, symphony trustees, museum benefactors, and the like who, nevertheless, feel very strongly that federal support for the arts and humanities is of primary importance. It is well for us to remember that these boards are made up, very largely, of business, corporate and community interests.[25]

A second component in the construction of an interest group constituency for the NEA involved the formation of state and local arts agencies. Initial enthusiasm for the NEA had been especially centered in New York City, Chicago, and a few other metropolitan centers that had large arts organizations in place and whose representation in Congress and access to the White House were closely tied into the big city elites Garment referred to. Starting in 1967, however, NEA offered block grants to all the states to help create state agencies that would act as wholesale suppliers to arts organizations and performers within their respective boundaries.

Netzer concluded that "state art councils resulted not from the autonomous rise of interest in patronizing the arts on the part of state governments but from the availability of NEA funds for the purpose."[26] On the other hand, in several states arts enthusiasts among civic elites had begun to recognize their potential political strength and were gaining a degree of legislative acceptance. In any event, by 1972 every state had its agency in place, as did the District of Columbia and several U.S. territories.[27] In turn, state agencies facilitated the establishment of local government units, and along with other local organizations, both public and private, nearly four thousand such bureaucracies have come into existence since the mid-1960s.[28] NEA contributions to the budgets of these state and local units are generally quite small, and, as we shall see, their enthusiasm for battling politically on NEA's behalf appears to be fading. Nonetheless, over the past thirty years state and local arts agencies provided a substantial interest group constituency in support of NEA appropriations, one that is spread across the entire nation.

A third element in NEA's self-interested support coalition has been composed of the truly impressive array of performing arts organizations that have come into existence since 1965. Nonprofit professional theater groups increased from twenty-two in 1965 to more than 400 by 1990. Dance companies increased by a factor of eight. Opera companies quintupled. More than 150 symphony orchestras were created,[29] and existing groups greatly expanded their budgets and lengthened their seasons. By 1975 the Bureau of Labor Statistics counted more than one million writers, artists, and entertainers.[30] More significant politically, perhaps, was the geographic dispersion of arts interests. Dozens and scores of communities developed local performing arts organizations and folded them into the structure of their civic pride along with the local park system and the high school basketball team. Thus among all the performing arts and across the nation there was a widely heralded "cultural boom," manifested not only in the extraordinary expansion of groups, budgets, and audiences, but also in a major enlargement of public approval of the arts as important and valuable components of American life, deserving of governmental support as well as private philanthropy. Surely, this would seem to have signified a secure public policy niche for the Endowment, not very large as a share of the federal budget to be sure, but well insulated by broad group support against any forays from rogue politicians.

Throughout the 1970s, the NEA flourished, significantly assisted by what Netzer described as "a nationwide corps of lobbyists."[31] Appropriations grew rapidly, and numerous initiatives were taken in Congress to expand and strengthen the Endowment's programs. Much of this flowering of enthusiasm appears to have resulted from Hanks's talented leadership,[32] building not only a broad base of interest group support but attracting a considerable degree of bipartisan endorsement as well. During this decade some 40 percent of the House Republicans generally *opposed* the occasional efforts to slash NEA appropriations, whereas approximately one-third of the southern Democrats voted *for* these cuts.[33] Hanks's successor, Livingston Biddle, was somewhat less effective politically, but until 1981 the Endowment remained on a relatively high plateau of support from both organized groups and politicians.

During the Reagan administration, however, the NEA became enmeshed in a new phase of budgetary politics in company with many other domestic programs. The Reagan administration did not propose to eliminate the Endowment entirely; even the Heritage Foundation did not suggest so drastic a step. With impetus provided by OMB Director David Stockman, however, cuts of some 50 percent were recommended,[34] and it was clear that the NEA was on Stockman's hit list. As with a good many other programs with carefully constructed constituency support, champions arose on both sides of the aisles of Congress to beat back the worst of the attacks. NEA appropriations were modestly reduced in Reagan's first year but thereafter began again to rise in absolute terms, though never fully returning to a growth mode in constant dollars. Meanwhile, however, states and local governments increased their spending on the arts so that the overall level of public support, while fluctuating some as the economy flourished or faded, remained comparatively robust.

During the Reagan–Bush years two persistent themes, never entirely absent from debates over public support for the arts, were expressed in vivid terms. One theme was simply to question whether it was an appropriate role of the federal government to spend tax money on the arts.[35] This conventional fiscal–constitutional conservative concern was especially appealing to "traditional" Republicans and others committed to keeping taxes low and government small. Opponents of this view argued that the arts budget was too small to make much difference to taxpayers and that modest government support for arts programs could make a critical contribution to arts institutions and to the quality of cultural life across the country, in small towns as well as metropolitan centers.[36] A large majority of the congressional Democrats and "moderate" Republicans endorsed this position. And as long as this was the dominant theme of debate, as it generally was until 1989, NEA appropriations were reasonably secure.

In 1989, however, the Endowment ran into a firestorm of criticism along a somewhat different front. The famous grants to photographers Andres Serrano and Robert Mapplethorpe not only raised a host of questions regarding what constitutes art and who, if anyone, should have the authority to provide its financing; they occasioned the mobilization of public opposition to the very existence of the NEA itself. The debate's fault line shifted away from the affordability of arts subsidies and the relative priority to be accorded the arts as compared with rivers and harbors or tobacco supports. The NEA was now caught up a debate over obscenity (Mapplethorpe) and sacrilege (Serrano). The agenda had been transformed from disputes over what was expedient in the service of self-interest to what was morally defensible, framed primarily in terms of artistic freedom versus declarations of high moral dudgeon and religious outrage.[37] Accompanying this dispute was the perennial argument in American political rhetoric over who was better qualified to decide how to allocate public funds,[38] experts (artists and high-culture enthusiasts who knew what was worthy) or popular majorities (who knew what they liked)? In short, the National Endowment for the Arts had become embroiled in flamboyant expressive political conflict.

A major source of this conflict was the so-called Religious Right. The American Family Association, led by Reverend Donald Wildmon, galvanized its 500 chapters and 400,000 mailing list to protest. The Christian Coalition and the Heritage Foundation undertook national advertising campaigns not only against the controversial grants but against the NEA itself. "The arts—decentralized, unprepared, and politically innocent (sic)—provided a convenient, and juicy target. . . . it was a situation made in heaven. It had sex, religion, and politics, all wrapped up into one. The National Endowment became a clear, easy target."[39] The National Committee against Censorship in the Arts was formed to counter this attack, and People for the American Way, the ACLU, and a variety of other pro-NEA groups, including American Arts Alliance (AAA) and many beneficiary organizations rallied their supporters on the expressive political front.[40]

This brief recital of NEA's political biography leads us to develop some notions about the patterns of activity that interest groups concerned about NEA affairs might be expected to display. In the next section of this chapter we investigate a few of these patterns using some rather elementary but convenient empirical indicators. In the course of this examination we shall try to show that although some of our priorities were fulfilled, some were not and require us to reformulate in a nontrivial way the standard conception of how interest group politics works.

Niche Politics and Expressive Forays

Insofar as the NEA enjoyed a relatively low political profile commensurate with its modest budget and was insulated from attack by a robust array of articulate and well-organized beneficiaries of its largesse, we would expect to find media attention and explicit interest group activation to display similarly modest levels. In most years this would mean that the Endowment was rarely in the news and that group activity was manifested mainly in those years when the program was up for reauthorization. Alternatively, when the program was enjoying a growth mode, both media attention and interest group involvement should be at markedly higher levels. In either case, however, if our understanding is correct, the groups involved ought to have been composed of program beneficiaries: performing artists, arts enterprises of various sorts, public agencies involved in arts administration, and perhaps some representatives of arts audiences.

When the NEA became a battleground of expressive political dispute, however, this transformation should have been reflected in significantly increased media attention and in both the volume and composition of interest group activation. Not only should more groups get involved; they should include substantial numbers of organizations devoted to "principle," offering relatively abstract arguments pro and con and stressing the moral values at stake, not just the size and shares of the fiscal pie. Expressive politics is unlikely to be confined to the infrequent occasions when a program is reauthorized. Opportunities for outrage or enthusiasm may arise at almost any time. There is always something morally reprehensible to assail. Even during the Hanks era there were occasional outcries of expressive protest and counterprotest over specific NEA projects. In most cases, however, we expect an expressive cause not to be able to sustain its high pitch for very long. Other issues and different frames will soon displace the particularities of a given expressive controversy even as the instrumentally oriented interests continue soberly to pursue their self-interests. The organized groups that specialize in expressive causes often remain in the game, but the programmatic specifics and much of the particular rhetoric may change.

In order to test our intuitions we examine first the frequency of newspaper stories mentioning the National Endowment for the Arts from its establishment in 1965 to 1995. As Figure 13-1 demonstrates, newspaper attention to NEA affairs fluctuated modestly from year to year, with an uptick in 1981 during the Stockman attack, until the sudden burst of attention in 1989 and 1990, the years of the Serrano–Mapplethorpe controversy. A more refined breakdown of these frequencies (not included in this chapter because of length restrictions) reveals some further variations. For example, both appropriations and NEA programmatic goals received somewhat greater media attention in years of significant statutory revision or reauthorization. In the main, however, the media coverage data appear to support our expectation that the NEA enjoyed a relatively peaceful niche until the surge triggered by the controversial photographic awards. Moreover, we suggested that surges of expressive political concern are likely to be relatively short-lived, and this expectation also gains credibility from the data.

Data on interest group mobilization are not difficult to find, but they are not readily assembled in a fashion that permits unambiguous interpretation of their significance. A fairly straightforward manifestation of

Figure 13-1   Number of Articles on the NEA over Time

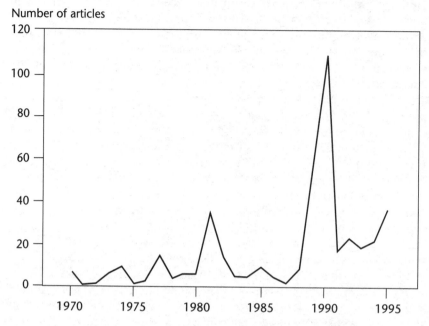

Source: *New York Times Index: A Book of Records.*

group activity can be found, however, in the form of testimony before congressional committees. For a program like NEA, hearings on appropriations are held every year, but many times these are relatively perfunctory and do not attract much interest group participation. Reauthorization hearings may bring forth broad-ranging group involvement, but these only occur every few years when a given authorization expires and bear no particular connection to other currents in the political stream. Situations that seem promising for expressive program attack or support may arise at almost any time, however, and when they do it is common for politically entrepreneurial members of Congress to introduce legislation and hold hearings at which interested groups are invited to express themselves. We would therefore expect to find, first, that in the period of NEA's maximum popularity Congress members sought to build on the "culture boom" and afford arts groups the opportunity to urge program expansion. Second, we would expect that reauthorizations would necessitate supportive group mobilization. If, however, reauthorization constitutes a more or less standard example of "interest group liberalism," we would not expect expressive groups to be much in evidence.

When the NEA runs into political trouble, however, as it did in 1989–1990, there should be a significant surge in legislation proposed—

most of it negative—in hearings held, and in the outpouring of interest groups expressing their concerns regarding the desirability of the program and, especially, offering pronouncements on the moral aspects of the dispute. As Figures 13-2 and 13-3 show, most of our expectations are apparently fulfilled. Legislative proposals to expand NEA were abundant in the heady days of the 1970s, especially during the Carter presidency, and the number of groups testifying in support of the Endowment fully reflected the growth in organized arts constituencies that was occurring during these years. Reauthorization in 1981 and the budget-driven attacks on NEA in the first Reagan years were likewise reflected in the data on group participation. And it is clear from a study of the lists of groups testifying at congressional hearings on NEA matters (see Tables 13-1 and 13-2 for sample rosters of witnesses) that all of them, without exception, were speaking on behalf of artists, arts organizations, and arts administrators—in short, self-interested groups.

In 1989 and 1990, as predicted, there was a huge surge in statutory proposals, in hearings, and in group mobilization. The Endowment had suddenly become a favorite target for fervent expressions of moral outrage, and congressional hearings afforded well-publicized institutional arenas in which these jeremiads could be given with ample media coverage,

Figure 13-2   Bills of Expansion and Restriction for the NEA, 1970–1995

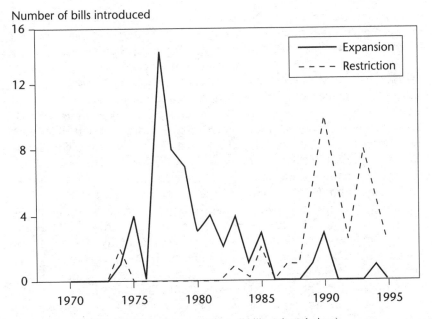

Source: Congressional Research Index (count includes all bills and resolutions).

Figure 13-3　Number of Witnesses Appearing on Behalf of the
NEA, 1965–1995

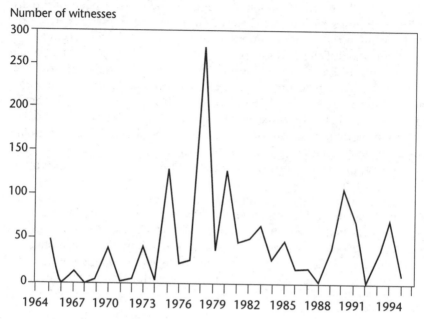

Source: Congressional Information Service.

resulting in great satisfaction to expressive group members and others of
similar convictions. The only difficulty with this interpretation is that, although there was indeed a surge in interest group participation in the
hearings, very little of it involved organizations we would call *expressive*.

People for the American Way, an organization started by television
producer Norman Lear in the 1980s to defend the principles of New Deal
Liberalism against the onslaught of conservatives, especially the Christian Right, was the most prominent expressive organization, testifying
several times in support of NEA funding, all after 1989. In 1990 Phyllis
Schlafly, organizer of the very conservative women's group, Eagle Forum,
and Jane Chastain of the Concerned Women for America, also a conservative organization, testified in opposition to the Endowment. Otherwise,
until 1995, the dozens of witnesses appearing before Congress on questions involving the NEA represented organizations of artists and arts administrators, self-interested groups acting instrumentally. A part of this
may have been because, at least in the House, Democrats controlled the
committees and therefore had a predominant say in selecting the witnesses invited to appear. In 1995, with Republicans in charge, William
Bennett (of Empower America) was an anti-NEA witness as was Gary
Bauer of the Family Research Council. Even in 1995, however, the bulk

Table 13-1   Hearings and Attending Witnesses, 1980

Hearings	Witnesses
Hearing on the older american	2 NEA representatives
Appropriation hearing	1 NEA representative
Appropriation hearing	8 council and association representatives 4 artists
Appropriation hearing	2 NEA and NEH representatives
Reauthorization of National Foundation for Arts and Humanities and Museum Services Act	30 institution and foundation representatives 36 council and association representatives 2 artists 1 politician 7 other
Reauthorization of National Foundation for Arts and Humanities and Museum Services Act	18 institution and foundation representatives 17 council and association representatives 1 artist 1 politician 3 other

of the group representatives were from NEA "constituents." Moreover, Republicans had controlled the Senate from 1981–1987, and expressive groups were not in evidence then either. We are forced to conclude that despite what appeared to have been a rich opportunity for interests with passionately held beliefs rooted in moral principles to enter the legislative fray against a program that was vulnerable to attack as both elitist and immoral, they did not do so. At least, they did not use the forum of congressional hearings for their expressive purposes.

Did that mean that despite the temptation these groups, especially those on the political right where the criticism of NEA was concentrated, were quiescent? Of course not! But to bring the full array of interests into the picture we must reconfigure the conventional formulation of interest group–politician relationships. We began this chapter by suggesting that traditional models assume that interest advocacy comes from "outside," and that politicians respond to group demands by enacting policies that confer benefits on group members (and free-riders also, perhaps). But politicians may also be interest advocates. Members of Congress hold principles dear; so do officials in the executive branch, and in the judiciary. Any officeholder—indeed, anyone aspiring to office—may decide to urge a particular course of public policy action, including appropriating or blocking funds for the NEA. In fact, a considerable number of members of Congress did testify in 1989 and 1990, both for and against the

Table 13-2   Hearings and Attending Witnesses, 1990

Hearings	Witnesses
Grantmaking policies and employment profile of the NFAH	3 NEA and NEH representatives 5 institution and foundation representatives 2 council and association representatives 1 other
Reauthorization hearing	1 NEA representative 1 institution and foundation representative 2 council and association representatives 6 artists
Reauthorization hearing	1 NEA representative 1 institution and foundation respresentative 3 council and association representatives
Appropriation hearing	1 NEA representative 8 institution and foundation representatives 16 council and association representatives 12 artists 2 other
Appropriation hearing	1 NEA representative
Reauthorization hearing	1 NEH representative 10 politicians
Reauthorization hearing	1 institution and foundation representative 5 council and association representatives 2 politicians
Reauthorization of NFAH and Institute of Museum Services	2 NEA and NEH representatives 5 institution and foundation representatives 13 council and association representatives 2 other

NEA. In subsequent years, too, members spoke up in considerable number, both on the floor and as committee witnesses. A modest rash of bills restricting the NEA was introduced following the excitements of 1989 after years of nearly complete quietude on this front.

It is especially attractive to elected politicians to engage in expressive politics—that is, to articulate the broad values and the policy implications thereof that they, the politicians, believe may appeal to voters; not necessarily to the well-organized or attentive voters, but to that portion of the electorate whose votes may be driven by broad and general commitments and beliefs but are little affected one way or another by the material specifics of a program. This is not to suggest, of course, that organized expressive interest groups are of no political importance, either as advocates themselves or as mobilizers of support for elective officials. But precisely because electoral processes involve vastly larger publics, the appeals that are most likely to resonate effectively will also be broad and framed when feasible in language that evokes widely shared beliefs.

The phenomena we refer to as political movements typically depend on this quality of broad-reaching affect because in most cases movement leaders must raise the consciousness of a commonality of interests among those they hope to mobilize, and to do so they have recourse to rhetorical themes and symbols that are "traditional"—in other words, deeply rooted in the culture and suffused with "moral sentiments." As we noted earlier, the special significance of churches, especially Protestant denominations, in underwriting political movements throughout the whole American experience can hardly be overstated.

Conclusion

When the National Endowment for the Arts came under attack in 1989, it was able to rally impressive group support, both instrumental and expressive. As it had done in 1981 and following, and despite the lurid denunciations from conservative religious groups, the NEA held on, though just barely, to its administrative life. By now, however, the Endowment was embroiled in a far more serious threat than moral outrage had posed. In 1995–1996 the NEA, along with dozens of other small and some quite large federal programs, had been caught up in the politics of the budget. The taxing and spending issues of budget politics in the 1990s involve a vast array of self-interested groups, of course, but they have more and more often been debated in terms of high moral principle. The expressive rhetoric of budget-balancing has pushed the Endowment to the political margin where debate concerning the moral character of the arts or the legitimacy of elite judgments regarding grants make relatively little difference. "Congressional pruners weren't talking obscenity . . . they were talking deficit."[41] In the latter 1990s spending priorities and program affordability seem largely to have taken over the expressive political terrain.

In this context it is not exactly startling to discover that some of the NEA's constituents have begun to accommodate themselves to the possibility that the Endowment may not survive, or if it does will no longer be of much instrumental use to them. When the grants controversy exploded in 1989 the National Association of State Arts Agencies (NASAA) suggested that the bulk of NEA funding be turned over to the states.[42] At their 1996 convention the National Assembly of Local Arts Agencies found that only a small proportion of their members regarded the survival of the NEA as their most pressing concern. On average, local agencies get only a little more than 2 percent of total government funds from the NEA,[43] and so, although they lamented the shrinkage of the NEA budget, they appear to have turned their principal energies to finding alternative (and larger!) sources of financial support. Some have suggested that this shows once again the inherent difficulty of assembling and maintaining an effective support coalition of arts organizations; that despite the successes of the 1970s, the arts involve too many distinct, too often competitive constituencies. At the same time, flexibility of individual institutions affirms the survival of arts activities in spite of debate about the NEA.

A part of the NEA's political weakness, however, lies in its expressive position, in the very substance of the debate over federal support for the arts. As we noted, the budget argument has tended to swallow up many programs quite apart from whatever else might be said about them. In addition, however, the NEA has some distinct rhetorical disadvantages in the context of American political discourse. We can do no more than touch on them here, but through all the debates over governmental support for the arts has been the theme of majoritarian preference. Government should do what "the public" wants; so runs the first tenet of democratic belief. And although poll majorities reveal a generalized approval of public funds for "high culture," it has seldom been difficult to mobilize broad disapproval of avant garde, atonal, or abstract aesthetic creations. NEA supporters may embrace with enthusiastic zeal the principle that the arts are truly essential to a civilized society and that providing public money for their support is therefore in the public interest "rightly understood." But grants do not go to "the arts" in general; they are given to particular organizations and individuals for specific creative purposes, and inevitably many of these will be disapproved of by popular majorities. NEA-supported tastes are minority tastes, virtually by definition, and the audiences for NEA-sponsored work, despite their impressive growth since 1965, are minority audiences—largely white, metropolitan, and middle-class.

Until the day arrives when the advocacy of "high culture" is a viable theme of electoral success in American politics, the NEA and public support for the arts will remain vulnerable to expressive attack. In general, the tensions between instrumental self-interest and broad-spectrum expressive politics, between narrow-gauge lobbying and moralizing exhortations directed at mass audiences, will surely continue to give definition to the American political process.

Notes

1. John Mark Hansen, *Gaining Access* (Chicago: University of Chicago Press, 1991).
2. Mancur J. Olson, *The Rise and Decline of Nations* (New Haven, Conn.: Yale University Press, 1982).
3. David B. Truman, *The Governmental Process* (New York: Knopf, 1951).
4. Mancur Olson, *The Logic of Collective Action* (Cambridge, Mass.: Harvard University Press, 1965).

5. Henry E. Brady, Sidney Verba, and Kay Lehman Schlozman, "Beyond SES: A Resource Model of Political Participation," *American Political Science Review* 89 (June 1995): 271.

6. James Q. Wilson, *Political Organizations* (New York: Basic Books, 1973).

7. Terry Moe, *The Organization of Interests* (Chicago: University of Chicago Press, 1980).

8. Lawrence S. Rothenberg, *Linking Citizens and Government Interest Group Politics of Common Cause* (New York: Cambridge University Press, 1992).

9. Robert Salisbury, "An Exchange Theory of Interest Groups," *Midwest Journal of Political Science* 8 (1969): 1.

10. William Riker and Peter Ordeshook, *An Introduction to Positive Political Theory* (Englewood Cliffs, N.J.: Prentice-Hall, 1973).

11. Robert H. Salisbury, "Political Movements in American Politics: An Essay on Concepts and Analysis," in *New Perspectives: American Politics*, ed. L. J. Barker (National Political Science Review, 1989), 213–231.

12. Fannie Taylor and Anthony Barresi, *The Arts at a New Frontier: The National Endowment for the Arts* (New York: Plenum Press, 1984), 144.

13. Doug McAdam, *Political Process and the Development of Black Insurgency, 1930–1970* (Chicago: University of Chicago Press, 1983).

14. John Mark Hansen, "The Political Economy of Group Membership," *American Political Science Review* 79 (March 1985): 79.

15. Jack Walker, *Mobilizing Interest Groups in America* (Ann Arbor: University of Michigan Press, 1989).

16. Don F. Hadwiger, *The Politics of Agricultural Research* (Lincoln: University of Nebraska Press, 1982).

17. Kenneth Shepsle, "The Changing Textbook Congress" in *Can the Government Govern?* ed. John E. Chubb and Paul E. Peterson (Washington, D.C.: Brookings Institution, 1989).

18. R. Bauer, I. De S. Pool, and L. A. Dexter, *American Business and Public Policy* (New York: Atherton, 1963).

19. Joseph W. Zeigler, *Arts in Crisis: The National Endowment for the Arts Versus America* (Chicago: A Capella Books, 1990), 16.

20. Gary Larson, *The Reluctant Patron: The United States Government and the Arts, 1943–1965* (Philadelphia: University of Pennsylvania Press, 1983), 47.

21. In 1953, 99 percent of orchestra board members opposed the institutionalization of national arts support. See J. W. Zeigler, *Arts in Crisis: The National Endowment for the Arts Versus America* (Chicago: A Capella Books, 1990), 16.

22. Kevin Mulcahy, "Government and the Arts in the United States" in *Public Policy and the Aesthetic Interest,* ed. Ralph A. Smith and Ronald Brown (Urbana: University of Illinois Press, 1992), 12.

23. For a thorough historical account of taxation, government, and the arts see Alan L. Feld, Michael O'Hare, and J. Mark Schuster, *Patrons Despite Themselves: Taxpayers and Arts Policy* (New York: New York University Press, 1983).

24. Taylor and Barresi, *The Arts at a New Frontier*, 30, 51.

25. Richard Swaim, "The National Endowment for the Arts 1965–1980," in *Public Policy and the Arts,* ed. Kevin V. Mulcahy and C. Richard Swaim (Boulder, Colo.: Westview Press, 1982), 185–186.

26. Dick Netzer, *The Subsidized Muse: Public Support for the Arts in the United States* (Cambridge: Cambridge University Press, 1978), 90.

27. Taylor and Barresi, *The Arts at a New Frontier*, 148.

28. *Jobs, The Arts and the Economy, 1994.* Publication highlighting findings from NALAA's "Arts in the Local Economy" (Study conducted by the National Assembly of Local Arts Agencies, January, 1994. Project funded by Charles Stewart

Mott Foundation, National Endowment for the Arts and the thirty-three Arts in the Local Economy Participants), 14.

29. David B. Pankratz, *Multiculturalism and Public Arts Policy* (Westport, Conn.: Begin and Garvey, 1993), 52.

30. Taylor and Barresi, *The Arts at a New Frontier*, 145.

31. Netzer, *The Subsidized Muse*, 90.

32. Margaret Jane Wyszomerski, "The Politics of Arts: Nancy Hanks and the National Endowment for the Arts," in *Leadership and Innovation: A Biographical Perspective on Entrepreneurs in Government*, ed. Jameson W. Doig and Erwin C. Hargrove (Baltimore: Johns Hopkins University Press, 1987).

33. Based on June 14, 1973, amendment to reduce the fiscal 1974 authorization for arts and the humanities by $64 million, from $145 million to $81 million.

34. Milton Cummings, Jr., "Government and the Arts: An Overview," in *Public Money and the Muse: Essays on Government Funding for the Arts*, ed. Stephen Benedict (New York: W. W. Norton, 1991), 57.

35. For further discussion of the debate, see Milton Cummings, Jr., "Government and the Arts: An Overview," and Kathleen Sullivan, "Artistic Freedom, Public Funding and the Constitution," in *Public Money and the Muse: Essays on Government Funding for the Arts*, ed. Stephen Benedict (New York: W. W. Norton, 1991).

36. Ronald Berman, "Art Versus the Arts," in *Public Policy and the Aesthetic Interest*, ed. Ralph A. Smith and Ronald Brown (Urbana: University of Illinois Press, 1992), 108.

37. According to Arthur Levitt, Jr., "The NEA's Battle—Unlike Anything the Arts World Had Ever Experienced, at Least on a National Level—Was Marked by Distortions, Heated and Emotional Debate, Divisive Actions and Inflammatory Rhetoric," in *Public Money and the Muse: Essays on Government Funding for the Arts*, ed. Stephen Benedict (New York: W. W. Norton, 1991), 20.

38. See Michael Macdonald Mooney, *The Ministry of Culture Connections among Arts, Money and Politics* (New York: Wyndham Books, 1980), 242. See also Joan Jeffri, "The Artist in an Integrated Society," in *Public Money and the Muse: Essays on Government Funding for the Arts*, ed. Stephen Benedict (New York: W. W. Norton, 1991), 102.

39. Levitt, "The NEA's Battle," 24.

40. Zeigler, *Arts in Crisis*, 116.

41. *Washington Post*, February 9, 1994.

42. On May 16, 1990, Reps. Tom Coleman (R-Ma.) and Steve Gunderson (R-Wis.) proposed an increase of 60 percent in funding to the states. Paul J. Dimaggio, "Decentralization of Arts Funding from the Federal Government to the States," in *Public Money and the Muse: Essays on Government Funding for the Arts*, ed. Stephen Benedict (New York: W. W. Norton, 1991), 217.

43. *National Assembly of Local Arts Agencies*, Monograph 7 (November 1994).

14

Culture Wars on the Frontier: Interests, Values, and Policy Narratives in Public Lands Politics

John Tierney and William Frasure

> The Frontier. The Wild West. Part of the culture of the
> American West has been a willingness to chafe under undue re-
> strictions, to resolve matters without putting them to a vote or
> dragging a criminal before a court. The contemporary West retains
> some of this resistance to deliberation, to compromise, when it
> comes to using the land. In the 1990s, the conflict is not between
> cattle barons and sodbusters but between those who would use
> federal lands in very different ways. Ranchers and recreational ve-
> hicle aficionados, with their respective nineteenth- and twentieth-
> century appreciations of a land to be used with no minimal re-
> strictions, face environmentalists who see federal lands as the last
> great place, whose virtues should be conserved in the face of the
> economic and sport demands of their opponents.
>
> In this chapter, John Tierney and William Frasure offer a
> detailed portrait of how the struggle over the use of federal lands
> has sparked passionate, sometimes intemperate, arguments from
> many, if not all, interests. Although the involved interests employ
> the ordinary tools of the group politics trade, the authors empha-
> size the narrative elements of this and other "culture wars" issues.
> The harsh, pointed, accusatorial rhetoric may well restrict the op-
> portunity to practice the ordinary politics of deliberation and com-
> promise. More than a century after the Census Bureau announced
> that the frontier was "closed," frontier politics flourishes in the
> contemporary West, albeit with writs and rhetoric, not six-guns
> and vigilantes.

The federal government owns almost 30 percent of the land surface of the United States. Most of that public land (93 percent of the government's 650 million acres) is in twelve western states—the eleven contiguous westernmost states of the lower forty-eight and Alaska. In these "public land states" the U.S. government owns more than half of the land. Controversies abound over how those lands are to be managed and

---

The authors thank Burdett Loomis, Francis Rourke, Ronald Shaiko, and Susan Tierney for their helpful comments an earlier drafts of this chapter.

to what uses they are to be put. Indeed, the federal government's management of western public lands arouses some of the most divisive political conflicts in contemporary American politics. Whether the specific quarrels concern grazing fees or timber cuts, mining laws, or reintroducing wolves to Yellowstone Park, the opponents wage their battles fiercely. Journalists who portray these fights as a "war for the West" echo a metaphor often invoked by the antagonists, who see their core values at stake in a struggle over incompatible ways of life.

Typically arrayed along one side of these issues are mainstream national environmental interest groups committed to nature preservation—organizations such as the Sierra Club, the Wilderness Society, and the National Wildlife Federation—and groups advocating on behalf of particular animals or regions, such as The Wolf Fund and the Greater Yellowstone Coalition. Standing on the other side are various business interests, including both individual corporations such as Weyerhauser (timber) and Anaconda (mining) and trade associations, such as the National Cattlemen's Association. The business organizations aligned on the "commodity" or "user" side of public lands issues have been joined in recent years by new groups that have cropped up to oppose the activities and interests of environmental groups. More implacable in their policy positions than many of their industrial and commercial allies, these groups, espousing the "wise use" of natural resources, mobilize around a shared fear of governmental intrusion and a joint commitment to private property rights.

This chapter explores the conflict between these loose coalitions of groups over issues of management and control of the nation's western public lands. Rather than focusing on how these organized interests lobby Congress or otherwise wage their battles in the nation's capital, our concerns lie with the broad ways these groups try to expand the scope of their conflicts and attract others to their cause. In particular, this chapter examines the positive and negative narratives each side tells in an effort to frame issues, define problems, and question the legitimacy of their opponents. An especially interesting subtext of these activities is formed by the opposing sides' virulent dislike for one another and by the intensity of their antipathy to their opponents' policy preferences. The concluding section draws out some of the consequences that obtain when group conflict is so passionate, fueled not just by different interests but by the clash of fundamental values.

Politics When Passions Abound

Most conflicts in American interest group politics do not take on a particularly passionate character. Typically, groups contend over some economic goal—a federal subsidy, a tax break, a bit of regulatory relief, an advantage over a competitor. Such economic interests, though pervasive and important, are not the sort that inspire deep and enduring animosities. Thus, when the hard-cider industry pushes for a reduction in the federal excise taxes imposed on hard cider makers, or the Archer-Daniels-Midland Corporation pushes for a federal subsidy of its ethanol products, those who spar over the appropriateness of such claims to federal help do so without serious animosity because the issues themselves do not involve fundamentally different sets of values and world views.

But many contemporary social issues do invite deep *cultural conflict*, defined as "political and social hostility rooted in different systems of moral understanding."[1] Hot-button issues such as abortion, homosexuality, guns, pornography on the Internet, or the provision of condoms in high schools inspire intransigent and belligerent interest group behavior. The people whose deeply held values place them on opposite sides of such cultural divides tend to be genuinely spiteful toward one another, portraying their adversaries as demons intent on making their own (bad) values and world view dominant. James Davison Hunter, a prominent observer of contemporary culture wars in America, noted that such disputes are "between groups who hold fundamentally different views of the world . . . fundamentally opposing visions of the meaning of America: what it has been, what it is, and what it should be." Indeed, as Hunter noted, the disputants over such issues come to adopt "the language of confrontation, battle, even war" as a way to "understand their own involvement." He quoted one activist whose metaphorical language is typical: "[T]his is a war of ideology, it's a war of ideas, it's a war about our way of life. And it has to be fought with the same intensity, I think, and dedication as you would fight a shooting war."[2]

Some conflict over the public lands is easily understandable, given the enormous economic stakes involved in these controversies. The federal domain is huge, and it contains many billions of dollars worth of resources—timber, pasture, coal, oil and gas, valuable minerals, recreational space, unsurpassed scenery, and fish and game. Thus, much of the intensity of public-lands conflict is based on self-seeking human nature, clashing economic interests, and the power of material motives. But many such controversies seem to roil at levels out of any obvious proportion to the material interests involved. America's public lands provide an arena in which a variety of interests organize around inseparable matters of economic consequences and cultural meaning.

Policy Battles in the "War for the West"

Residents of the western states are intimately familiar with the kinds of issues that give rise to these intense political antagonisms; they live with them every day. A list would be very long, but might include conflicts between those desiring increased fees for ranchers grazing cattle on public land and the ranchers who naturally object; those who want to preserve the habitats of various animals and those who worry about the consequences for the economic livelihood of their communities; advocates of maintaining current allocation patterns of timber allotments or mineral rights and those who want such resource extractions curtailed; oil and gas companies that want to drill on the periphery of Yellowstone National Park and those who worry that such drilling will disrupt the geothermal activity that makes the park such a distinctive place for tourists and nature lovers.

These controversies often seem boring, pedestrian, and arcane: How much should a family wishing to tour Yellowstone National Park have to pay to enter? What role should economics play in decision making over rangelands? What level of government should have authority for decisions about public lands?

But other controversies are intrinsically interesting to all but the most jaded, because they tap into mythic visions of the American West. Should wolves, long extinct from the Yellowstone region, be reintroduced to the area by government, despite the objections of cattle ranchers who fear for the safety of their livestock? Which side has the stronger claim in a continuing conflict between recreational rock climbers who love the challenge posed by Wyoming's Devil's Tower, rising above the Black Hills, and the Lakota Sioux Indians, who want rock climbing banned there at a sacred time of year when tribe members gather for ceremonies with profound cultural and spiritual significance for them?

What is remarkable about these issues is that, on the surface, many of them seem well-suited to the sort of straightforward allocational decision making—who gets what?—that the American political system handles fairly well. But the more profound conflicts are taking place at the level of people's core values and beliefs and are thus not subject to normal political bargaining.

Take the controversy over appropriate levels for federal grazing fees. From one perspective, this is a straightforward distributive policy that we might expect to produce the most familiar kind of congressional logrolling and bargaining. It should be simple to resolve with some difference splitting: The fee might be set higher than what the cattle ranchers want but lower than what environmentalists and opponents of "corporate welfare" desire. But in the West, economics does not always produce the bottom line.

Great issues of cultural meaning unavoidably get wrapped into this otherwise mundane controversy. Aside from its great economic importance to the western states, the cattle industry is associated with the frontier, the ranching life, cowboys, and all of the allied myths of individualism, free enterprise, and self-reliance. On the other side are opponents of the grazing industry who articulate an environmental ethic: cattle wreak environmental destruction and throw off the natural ecological balance (soil erosion and damage to riparian areas), pose threats to human health (red meat is "bad" for one's health), and represent capitalism's conquest of nature (including Native Americans).

In short, the grazing fee issue is not seen by those embroiled in it as simply an allocational who-gets-what kind of matter, easily subject to compromise. Instead, both sides understand it as an all-out moral war: The ranching industry interprets fee-hike proposals as attempts to eliminate grazing from public lands and end the West's ranching traditions, and many of the most vocal environmentalists would agree.

The grazing fee controversy illustrates how and why most of these conflicts over public lands policy acquire unusual ferocity from their association with conflict over cultural values, lifestyles, what it means to be a westerner, even what it means to be an American. At stake in the range of western public lands issues are competing views about the proper scope of federal governmental authority and whose values will underlie the policies that govern the management of a half-billion acres of western lands owned by the U.S. government.

The severity of the political conflict surrounding public lands issues stems from the inherent difficulty of reconciling these different sets of cultural values or negotiating trade-offs among them. Not only are settled outcomes hard to produce, but the political process of arriving at those solutions is itself inflammatory, exacerbating the conflicts rather than calming them. The contestants may want solutions, but they know that as the government makes policies, and thus favors some interests and harms others, it is doing more than merely distributing economic benefits and burdens. Decisions seem to authenticate the values of the winners and repudiate those of the losers. Such an outcome, especially as it is perceived as one of cultural validation (the implied adoption of a set of values, a view of what life in the region is all about and who "belongs" there), can turn policy choices that seem simple and even trivial—should the Park Service, say, release a dozen wolves into the Yellowstone back country?—into a serious, prolonged, and emotionally divisive political contest.

The Opposing Sides

The organizations attentive to federal lands policy vary greatly in the nature of their constituencies, the scope of their agendas, the appeal of their cause, their credibility, and the array of politically useful resources they bring to the fray. Despite this great diversity, and despite the fact that the range of issues in this policy arena gives rise to shifting lines of cleavage and varying coalitions of sometimes odd bedfellows, it helps to distinguish between those groups that represent "preservationist" interests (or typically are allied with them) and those groups that represent "user" interests (or typically are allied with them). The views of people on these opposite sides are associated politically with conventional ideological divisions of left and right, as they have developed in contemporary America,

and are deeply rooted in American traditions: The preservationists generally espouse communitarian values, active government, and the ideals of
"postmaterial" culture; the users tend to be advocates of private property
rights, personal autonomy, individualism, and limited government.

The disagreements between these sets of interests have been manifest in their conflicting philosophies of resource management as well as
in their different policy preferences. In recent decades, federal land management policy has shifted away from the allocation of land-based capital
to user interests and toward the preservation of lands for enjoyment by
more diverse constituencies. This controversial shift threatens traditional
users and has not reassured preservationists, who see it as not occurring
quickly or thoroughly enough.

The Users

The "user" side is made up of those who look to the public land as a
source of livelihood, economic benefit, and commercial use; they see the
claims of entitlement of local communities to a voice in the management
of nearby public lands as being more compelling than the claims of the nation as a whole. The users tend to find most of their political support in
local politics in the public land states—local and state governments, state
party organizations, business associations—and in the probusiness orientation of the national Republican Party. There is a great diversity of
organizational types on the user side. Given the depth of governmental
penetration into the economy—in particular, on issues affecting mining,
timber, oil and gas interests—it is not surprising that big corporations such
as Weyerhauser and Boise Cascade (paper) play a leading role in many
public lands disputes. Trade associations are also prominent—groups such
as the National Cattlemen's Association, the American Mining Congress,
the Rocky Mountain Oil and Gas Association, and the National Forest
Products Association.

Industry coalitions are also a common feature on the user group landscape, as groups of firms or trade associations find it politically expedient
to coordinate their activities in pursuit of shared goals. Most of these
coalitions aim to put the environmental community on the defensive, in
part through tactics that environmental groups themselves have long employed: adopting wholesome-sounding names, engaging in direct-mail
fund-raising, orchestrating grassroots lobbying campaigns, even organizing demonstrations. The National Endangered Species Act Reform Coalition, for example, was formed when a group of utility companies in the
Southwest wanted to work together to fight reauthorization of the 1973
Endangered Species Act. The coalition included the American Farm Bureau Federation, the Arizona–New Mexico Coalition of Counties, and the
Tristate Generation and Transmission Association, an electric utility cooperative based in Denver.[3]

In recent years, many other groups with memberships that mix individual citizens with commercial interests have cropped up in opposition to the activities and interests of environmental groups. More implacable in their opposition than many of the corporate interests they align with, these groups mobilize around a shared fear of governmental intrusion, a joint commitment to private property rights, and a dedication to the "wise use" of natural resources. Among the organizations that fall under the wise-use banner are the Center for the Defense of Free Enterprise, the Oregon Lands Coalition, and People for the West!

Most of these groups are strongly opposed to environmental measures that would change traditional policies allowing "multiple use" of the public lands. These groups also bristle at what they regard as the tiresomely paternalistic attitudes and meddlesome activism of folks from the big cities or from the East Coast who think of themselves as more committed and able than the locals at protecting the West's great natural resources.

Some of these user groups, such as the National Inholders Association, unite citizens who have property in or near national parks and who are incensed, as Christopher Bosso has noted, "about what they consider unfair, even confiscatory, federal and state policies that place severe restrictions on the use of their land, in the process reducing its development or resale value."[4] Similarly, many people have rallied under the wise-use banner because of their intense resentment of policies that, aimed at protecting or promoting endangered species such as spotted owls, wolves, or grizzly bears, either "lock up" federal lands or threaten the economic livelihoods of people in those locales. To these people, such issues boil down to what one observer termed "a moral question over a family's right to earn an honest living."[5] At the far-right fringe of the wise-use movement can be found groups that advocate opening virtually all federal lands to resource exploitation and equate federal land policy with Communism. Moreover, as Bosso has noted, those fringes include "a host of others in the traditional anticommunist right who, having lost their longtime nemesis, see environmentalism as the new scourge of private property, individual rights, and all else they hold to be truly American."[6]

Environmentalists condemn the wise users as ideological extremists who "are willing to distort the facts and use the 'big lie' to stir up public hysteria" and committed to "running the environmentalists out of business."[7] (The wise-use people, of course, regard the environmentalists in the same grim terms.)

The Preservationists

Aligned on the opposite side from the users on most public lands issues are the preservationists who see the public lands as areas of exemplary environmental qualities, or at least potentially so—especially the values represented by wilderness, wildlife, and natural ecosystems. This side sees the claims of entitlement of a national constituency to be much stronger than that of local communities. Like the users, they find some support in local politics—from urban and academic centers in the public-land states and in growing statewide environmental organizations. But more important, they enjoy national backing from powerful environmental groups with great influence in Washington, D.C., and gain support from the pro-environmentalist orientation of the national Democratic Party.

The vast constellation of politically active environmental organizations in the United States includes many groups concerned primarily with issues other than the disposition or management of federal public lands—toxic wastes, recycling, acid rain. Our concern, however, is primarily with those environmental organizations committed to nature preservation—that is, attentive to issues affecting national forests, parks, wilderness preserves, and species protection. Included among these organized interests are some of the nation's oldest and most esteemed political organizations.

The Sierra Club is the best known preservationist organization. Because it was the first such group in the United States, it has stood as a prototype of sorts for many nascent citizens' groups of all kinds over the years. Founded in 1892, in its early years the Sierra Club devoted itself to preserving national forests and primitive areas and creating national parks. That mission acquired new political support over the next few decades with the emergence of other organizations variously devoted to the protection of land resources or particular wildlife species. The formation of the National Audubon Society in 1905, the National Parks and Conservation Association in 1919, and the Izaak Walton League in 1922 rounded out the "first wave" of environmental group formation.

The second big wave of environmental interest group formation began in the 1960s, with an average of eighteen new groups emerging each year between 1961 and 1980.[8] But most of these organizations, such as the Environmental Defense Fund, the Natural Resources Defense Council, and Environmental Action, were principally concerned with pollution. The constellation of organized interests principally concerned with the conservation of land resources and wildlife was already well established by the 1960s, and this first set of environmental interests actually developed many of the effective political strategies often credited to the second set. Even though most of the land and wildlife conservation groups already were formed by the 1960s and 1970s, their memberships grew in response to the reawakened interest in the environment that was characteristic of the period.

The decade of the 1980s also proved a flush period for many of these organizations, as they diversified their resource bases and attracted memberships and other resources from citizens concerned that the conservative Reagan administration was determined to withdraw the governmental safeguards of environmental protection put in place in the preceding twenty years. The Sierra Club, for example, saw its budget double (to about $40 million) and its membership more than triple (to 630,000) from 1980 to 1990.[9]

Skeptical observers of the preservationist movement often portray supporters of these organizations as representative of a "privileged class." Critics ridicule a stereotype of gentrified elitists who wear Birkenstocks on their feet and Patagonia shirts on their backs, have Ansel Adams photographs on their walls, and feel somewhat guilty about the teakwood coffee table, even though it nicely accommodates both the tray of white wine and cheese and the Sierra Club picture book—all to accommodate a self-image of being one with the Earth. Unfair or distasteful though such stereotypes may seem to committed preservationists, the fact remains that the backbone of the environmental movement runs through higher income groups. Environmental organizations are not unusual in this regard; organized interests in general—and social movements especially—draw disproportionately from the higher socioeconomic strata. If there seems to be anything in particular that distinguishes environmental activists, it is their levels of higher education.[10] In both the Wilderness Society and the Sierra Club, more than three-quarters of the members are college graduates.

Just because their socioeconomic characteristics allow for ready generalization and parody does not mean that environmental activists are all alike or that their groups approach issues from the same perspective. For example, organizations such as Ducks Unlimited and the National Wildlife Federation cater to the interests of hunters, at least some of whom surely would rankle at being called environmentalists. The Nature Conservancy, with the largest budget of any organization in the environmental movement, is politically centrist, cozy with the corporate community, and comfortable with its mission of saving the world by buying land. And at the fringes of the environmental movement are groups that "occupy an unimaginably big tent":

> [They] are bound together by a belief that environmentalism is a profound choice about core values, not simply issues or interests. They include technophobes, for whom contemporary life has destroyed the primal linkage between humanity and nature, and technophiles with an unalloyed faith in the environmental solutions to be found in new scientific and technical breakthroughs. . . . The greens include feminists and misanthropes, socialists and libertarians. Many are populists, yet many are elitists with some disdain for the economic fears and cultural values of the mainstream electorate.[11]

Framing the Issues and Telling Policy Stories

Whenever organized interests are involved in intense struggles, the political conflict gets played out in many different ways, on many different levels. Some of the groups' political activity (such as efforts to influence the outcomes of elections) is aimed at trying to affect the mix of people who have the authority to make policy decisions. But most of their activities constitute an effort to "frame the issues"—to affect what aspect or "face of the issue" people see when they look at it.[12] This is what interest groups are doing as they present information and arguments to political elites and to mass audiences—testifying at congressional and administrative hearings, meeting officials directly for "insider" lobbying, inspiring letter-writing or telegram campaigns, going to court, publicizing research results and technical information, holding press conferences, talking to journalists, and so on.

Central to all these activities is the construction of arguments about the "social significance, meaning, implications, and urgency" of the situation under discussion.[13] Defining problems and framing issues typically involves the use of narratives, or stories—especially the telling of "causal stories" that imply very different policy choices for solving a problem. As Deborah Stone has argued,

> Problem definition is a process of image making, where the images have to do fundamentally with attributing cause, blame, and responsibility. Conditions, difficulties, or issues thus do not have inherent properties that make them more or less likely to be seen as problems or to be expanded. Rather, political actors deliberately portray them in ways calculated to gain support for their side ... [and] compose stories that describe harms and difficulties, attribute them to actions of other individuals or organizations, and thereby claim the right to invoke government power to stop the harm.[14]

As a consequence, often the best way to understand complicated policy issues, as Richard Neustadt and Ernest May have suggested, is not to ask "What's the problem?" but rather "What's the story?" behind the issue.[15] This is especially true, according to policy analyst Emery Roe, when a policy issue has "become so uncertain, complex, and polarized—their empirical, political, legal, and bureaucratic merits unknown, not agreed upon, or both—that the only things left to examine are the different stories ... [used] to articulate and make sense of that uncertainty, complexity, and polarization." And, Roe has suggested, the policy narratives of greatest interest are those that "dominate the issue in question," and are offered by one party or another in an effort to "underwrite and stabilize the assumptions for decision making."[16] Typical narratives, according to Stone, are stories of decline ("things are getting worse and here's what's to blame for it") or control ("if we're decisive and deliberate enough, we can fix this bad situation"). And common elements of these narratives are metaphors and myths.[17]

Advocacy groups on both sides of public-lands politics struggle to "institutionalize" their viewpoint through these processes of problem definition, framing, and storytelling. It is not surprising that advocates on both sides do what they can to frame their case in a constructive, appealing way, linking it to positive values. Discussing the ways in which advocacy groups craft their "positive appeals," James Davison Hunter noted, "By grounding the 'rightness' or legitimacy of their claims in logic, science, humanitarian concerns, or in an appeal to tradition or God, each side endeavors to persuade its opponents, as well as all others who might listen, of the superiority of its claims."[18] We can see such positive appeals at work in the ways the preservationists and the users frame the issues and in the stories that they tell.

The Preservationists' Positive Appeals

The platform on which preservationists base their positive appeals is supported by several sturdy pillars, each of them with its own strong claims to legitimacy in American public life—nature, science, and economics. Although not every issue evokes appeals to all three of these elements, each of them shows up over and over in the preservationists' discourse.

Nature. The preservationists have the advantage of having a powerful idea at the core of their ethos, or as their central motivating force—the idea of the Arcadian West as the repository of America's wilderness treasure, a living land where values associated with nature and ecology demand special priority. And they are able to call on a rich, idealistic tradition of respect for such values in American culture and public thought, reaching back through such figures as Henry David Thoreau, John Muir, and Aldo Leopold. This tradition promotes wilderness mostly for its contributions to human moral life. Wilderness, in this view, is spiritually uplifting; it cleanses and builds character. The experience of wilderness is as important as wilderness itself. Its idealization is as much a reaction against the vices of civilization as an affirmation of nature's intrinsic virtues. Throughout the twentieth century, this romantic, visionary sense of the complex web of dependency that binds all of nature has been rationalized, formalized, and fashioned into the science of ecology, which, in its many guises, is the intellectual fuel for contemporary preservationism.

Ecological Science. Ecological ideas link disparate elements of the environmental movement, confer scientific respectability to the thoughts of political activists and a sense of public importance to the activities of scientists, and serve as a powerful basis for explanations of why those who lack the spiritual sensibilities of Muir or Thoreau ought to adopt a version of their values merely out of self-interest.

With the imprimatur of ecological science, contemporary preservationists point to what they see as the harmful excesses of the user or extractive industries. The stories they tell are almost uniformly the familiar policy stories of decline. In their view, cattle grazing is causing soil erosion and damage to riparian areas; timber cutting is destroying wildlife habitats; mining is leaving unspeakable scars on treasured landscapes; excess tourism is causing environmental degradation in national parks. Those stories of decline are accompanied by stories of control, again backed up by ecological understandings. In recent years, many preservationist interest groups (along with a cadre of environmental scientists) have advocated approaching the entire catalog of resource management ills in a unified way, consistent with the holistic perspective of environmentalist ideologies and the conceptualizations of ecology. Such advocacy most commonly falls within the rubric of "ecosystem management"—a policy that prescribes that resources should be managed as entire ecosystems. Indeed, as Alston Chase noted, it was the Sierra Club that introduced the ecosystem model to popular culture when it published the book, *The Closing Circle*, by biologist Barry Commoner.[19]

In many ways the idea of ecosystem management has come to be infused in virtually all the policy controversies that make up the contemporary "war for the West." For example, the idea in recent years of reintroducing wolves to the northern Rocky Mountains in and around Yellowstone National Park was pursued by the Interior Department's Fish and Wildlife Service on the basis of that agency's statutory mandate to conserve endangered and threatened species and the habitat on which they depend. But some environmental preservation groups argued that the government had an affirmative obligation to restore wolves to the area, emphasizing the presence of wolves as an essential, not merely desirable, component of the greater Yellowstone ecosystem. Environmental activists we interviewed spoke of the wolf as "the only missing mammal species in this ecosystem," a "missing link," necessary for "putting the ecosystem back into natural balance." The story being told by advocates of wolf restoration is a story of control: The government can manage the ecosystem in the greater Yellowstone area by restoring its most important predator. This particular story assesses few costs (some sheep and cattle), but it inferentially leads to a broader story line—that a new western economy can thrive as the dominant extractive industries decline.

Economics. Preservationists make much of the observation that, in roughly a generation, the character of the population of the public land states has changed considerably—from one in which most incomes were earned from activity dependent on use of the public lands to one in which that is no longer the case.[20] Certainly, the traditional multiple-use industries constitute a smaller share of the western economy in the 1990s than they did a generation earlier. Grazing, timber, and mining have indisputably shrunk in importance. Oil and gas have fluctuated in keeping with their boom-and-bust character. Only recreation has clearly grown in economic significance.

The environmentalists argue that the West has changed so much that the traditional multiple-use industries are now superfluous. In this view, site-specific natural resources, extracted and processed by industry, are typically no longer the base of local economies in the West. Armed with visions of new kinds of "sustainable" economies, environmentalists hope to shift the economic base to low impact, environmentally sensitive industries. Meetings of environmental groups and the pages of environmentally oriented publications often feature discussions of utopian economic visions involving small, clean, information and service companies heavily reliant on sophisticated telephones and computers, or of arts and crafts and cottage industries turning out quality products, handmade by rustic artisans. One speaker at the 1993 annual meeting of the Greater Yellowstone Coalition extolled, as an example for other communities, a small business that makes canvas camp-stools in a small Wyoming town. The rather dubious moral of his story was that a proliferation of such businesses might release the region from its dependence on ranching, logging, and other extractive industries.

The Users' Positive Appeals

The users' groups also employ positive appeals in an effort to define the problem and persuade political elites and the mass audience of the legitimacy of their claims. Because successful efforts of this sort require a sensitivity to the realities of contemporary opinion and an understanding of the power of marketing, many of these groups start by choosing organizational names that associate them with politically appealing principles such as free enterprise and private property. Examples include the Center for the Defense of Free Enterprise, the American Land Rights Association, and the League of Private Property Voters. It is ironic that environmental preservation itself is a value that even groups on the "user" side like to appropriate for themselves. Recognizing that environmental values are widely popular, many such groups have adopted environmentally friendly names: Northwesterners for More Fish, the National Wetlands Coalition, Alliance for Environment and Resources, Citizens for the Environment, and Environmental Conservation Organization.[21] The bold use of such names by organizations opposed to the environmental agenda can be seen as either a cynical subversion of the meaning of language or as a sign of just how thoroughly the ascendance of environmentalism over the past thirty years has permeated American society—so thoroughly that even groups opposed to environmental advocates seem to feel it necessary to take on those names in order to have a chance at success.

Apart from finding attractive labels for themselves, advocacy groups on the user side argue, point for point, on the economic and commercial realities of public-lands use, weaving narratives dramatically different from those told by the preservationists. Just as the preservationists draw on the force of nature to bolster their own discourse, the users have their own storehouse of potent appeals—especially emotional narratives of the mythic American frontier and threats to the western "way of life," all complemented by stories of governmental officials and ecological scientists running amok.

Economic and Commercial Realities. Although the preservationists depict a glowing economic future for the American West with "sustainable communities," the users tell a quite different story of crisis or calamity. They see environmentally motivated federal policy as undermining extractive industries that depend on use of the public lands, putting the backbone of the western economy at risk. That narrative remains compelling, even though these industries constitute a smaller share of the western economy now than they did a generation ago. This "calamity" story's persuasive power hinges on the idea of spillover economic effects—showing that in addition to the industries and workers directly hit by government policy, a whole host of ancillary commercial activities and workers would be affected. They argue, for example, that in a ranching community there are many privately owned businesses such as auction barns, feed suppliers, veterinarians, and others that depend on the ranchers for their livelihoods. Indeed, restaurants, hardware and grocery stores, construction firms, lawyers, and accountants—in fact, the entire economy of many small towns—are often rooted in a local public-land-based industry. So, the story goes, when policies threaten the public-lands industries, the threat of economic calamity spreads across whole communities.

There is another tale of commercial reality, with a different spin, that is meant to counter environmentalists' accusations that the users are harming the land. This narrative is a portrait of the user, not as the land's pillager but as its protector. One version of it comes in the Weyerhauser corporation's image advertising—the commercials that present it as "the tree-growing company." Another, less contrived, version argues that, far from being insensitive to problems of overgrazing, soil erosion, damage to riparian areas, and the like, ranchers who lease federal land are, in fact, its best protectors. Thus, it makes no sense for ranchers to be disregarding of the very land on which their livelihood depends.

The Frontier Culture and the Western "Way of Life." Advocates on behalf of the user interests know that there is emotional power in narratives that emphasize the exceptionalism of the American West, suggesting that there is something unique about the region's attitudes, traditions, and politics. Much of this, of course, revolves around the legacy of the "frontier." The popular, conventional view has been that the conditions of settlement on the frontier produced a civilization of industrious, self-reliant, courageous, venturesome individualists. Cowboys and ranchers were the symbolic ideals of this culture.

Bolstered by evocative symbols, the users' depiction of westerners' individualist values is every bit as powerful as the preservationists' portrayal of a West based on wilderness values. They get a lot of political mileage out of this notion of the Frontier West, an unforgiving land where tenacious, hardscrabble pioneers hacked and fought and persevered to make hostile places productive. And indeed, for a lot of people in the West today, especially those in small towns and rural communities who depend on agriculture and traditional industries, the frontier ideals of independence and self-reliance remain powerful beacons of identity.

The users' groups thus have an easy time tapping into the political agitation that roils beneath the surface of daily life in the West. The most potent and incendiary tactic is to portray the traditional West as being stripped of its character and values by granola-crunching environmentalists from back East. Many people in the public land regions feel resentment over the intrusion into their lives and communities by people who are largely unaffected by the consequences. When environmentalists push for land to be set aside for a new wilderness area, or when they stop activity on federal lands in order to protect some endangered species, the people who live and work in those areas see such moves as threatening cultural extinction.

Skepticism about Science and Government. The fears and resentments of many land users in the West are fueled as well by hearty skepticism about science and government. More precisely, they are suspicious of what they regard as the scientific pretensions of the preservationists and the intrusiveness of government policy in their lives.

Whereas environmental preservationists believe fundamentally in the capacity of government policy, informed by science, to balance ecosystems and control biological outcomes, people on the user side are more likely to see intervention in natural processes as fraught with danger, certain to yield unexpected, possibly disastrous, results. They find affirmation for this view in the work of growing numbers of ecologists who say that efforts to keep ecosystems in harmonious balance are misplaced because "nature is actually in a continuing state of disturbance and fluctuation."[22] Moreover, these skeptics see ecosystem–management policies not as the logical consequence of reasoned science but as a subterfuge for the gradual closing of more and more federal land to grazing and other uses.[23] Science, in this view, is not the foundation stone of policy, but a pretextual veneer meant to make it acceptable.

Their wariness on this score is heightened by the perception that their adversaries have gradually captured the federal land management agencies that previously had served the users' interests. They feel threatened as they see the Forest Service, the Fish and Wildlife Service, and the National Park Service become increasingly populated by professionals with advanced degrees, often hailing from areas of the country other than the West, and often drawn to their vocations by ecological ideals. So, in the view of the users, a government that once worked to advance their interests has now been overrun by their adversaries and is now committed to a contrary set of interests and principles.

The skepticism about science and the wariness of government produce a potent combination, an amalgam that skillful advocates use to whip up opposition to the preservationist agenda. This is not a hard sell. In a climate of increasing popular hostility to government and growing frustration with government programs across the board, it is easy to dismiss the notion that large agencies headquartered in Washington, D.C., should be allowed to "play God" by trying to manage whole ecosystems.[24]

Framing the Negatives: Defining the Enemy as Extremists

Positive appeals, framings, and moral claims only carry organized interests so far in their efforts to persuade political elites and mass audiences of the virtues of their cause. In order to increase the chances of shifting popular opinion in their favor and against the opposition, interest advocates in the culture wars supplement their positive strategy with a "deliberate, systematic effort to discredit the opposition." James Davison Hunter explained this *negative* strategy:

> In the culture war, this negative aspect of the conflict has taken on a life and force of its own; indeed, neutralizing the opposition through a strategy of public ridicule, derision, and insult has become just as important as making credible moral claims for the world that each side champions. Arguably, this negative persuasion has become even more important, for in public discourse, "dialogue" has largely been replaced by name calling, denunciation, and even outright intolerance.[25]

In the culture wars, just as it is in military conflicts, both sides find it useful to portray the enemy as an "evil empire." Their object, of course, is to suggest that the opposition consists of people who, at worst, have evil intentions or, at best, are removed from the mainstream of American life. Although tactics of this sort are generally useful to both sides, whichever side is the underdog at a given point may have a special incentive to use incendiary scare tactics and appeals to fear and bigotry in an effort to rally people to their side (fear being a more powerful political motivator than positive appeals). In the 1990s the rhetorical excesses of a demonizing nature seem to be more prominent among the user interests, perhaps because they feel besieged by the successes of the modern environmental movement.

There are countless illustrations of the ways in which activists on the "user" side demonize their environmental opponents. Environmental preservationists end up being branded as "nature fascists" ready to "destroy industrial civilization"—extremists who attach more importance to insects and lesser species than to humans, who put nature preservation ahead of the economic livelihood of whole communities. Such notions are captured in such epithets and labels as "tree huggers," "toadstool worshipers," "bunny lovers," and "land embalmers."

Another theme in the portraits painted of preservationists is that they are themselves "unnatural" in some way, the implication usually being that they are homosexual. Sometimes the charge is quite direct, as when a female speaker at an environmentalists' rally in California in 1990 was shouted down by protimber activists in the crowd who chanted, "lesbian! lesbian!" as she began to talk about the biosphere.[26]

Sometimes environmental preservationists are depicted as somehow un-American, supportive of ideas such as one-world government and associated with Communism, socialism, or other ideologies deemed antithetical to American values. For example, Ron Arnold, one of the leaders of the wise-use movement, linked Communism and environmentalism when he told a pesticide trade group in 1984 that, "Environmentalism is an already existing vehicle by which the Soviet Union can encourage the Free World to voluntarily cripple its own economy."[27] This same theme is invoked more frequently by environmentalists' opponents through the "watermelon" metaphor: Environmental preservationists, they say, are "green on the outside but red on the inside."[28]

User-side activists aim this sort of inflammatory rhetoric not just at their preservationist opponents but at others, such as government officials, who are seen to be aiding and abetting the preservationist cause. One example of this occurred in January 1991 when Yellowstone National Park Superintendent Robert Barbee encountered an angry crowd of user group activists who showed up at a public hearing on the agency's "vision document" on the future of Yellowstone:

> There were seven hundred people there. You can't imagine the virulence of the outcry. I was Saddam Hussein, a Communist, a fascist, everything else you could think of. One lady got up there, jaw quivering, used her time to say the Pledge of Allegiance, then looked at me and called me a Nazi. They loaded the hall.[29]

These tactics of demonizing the opposition are by no means the exclusive tools of people on the user side of public-lands issues. The environmental preservationists do it, too. One of their more frequently cited assertions, for example, is that the wise-use movement is a political branch of the Reverend Sun Myung Moon and the Unification Church. Other assertions suggest a connection between the wise-use movement and the Religious Right—and even a link to right-wing regimes in Latin America.[30]

Another favorite tactic of environmental groups is to allege that their opponents, especially those in the wise-use movement, have a penchant for violence. Sierra Club Books in 1994 published *The War against the Greens* by David Helvarg, a book largely devoted to detailing stories of environmentalists whose personal safety or property have been threatened or harmed by antienvironmental extremists:

> In the last six years, the anti-enviro ranks have grown from resource users protecting their federal subsidies and property owners unhappy with land-use regulations to the fringes of America's expanding un-

derbelly of violence, where social causes become excuses for sociopaths motivated by fear, greed, and hatred, or private security agents working on behalf of outlaw industries.[31]

For their part, activists among the user groups insist that they are not alone in having among their ranks a few people willing to resort to harmful or violent protest to make a point. After all, they say, environmental groups such as Earth First! have attracted a lot of attention to their cause through harmful and dangerous acts of vandalism. They have pulled up surveyor stakes from Forest Service logging roads, burned or disabled expensive logging and mining equipment, and injured or endangered people through tree spiking—the driving of saw-shattering spikes into trees on public lands scheduled for clear-cutting.

The violent and destructive behavior by people on both sides is, however, far less common than a reading of the popular press might suggest. By and large, interest group activists on both sides eschew these sorts of tactics, which they quickly see as counterproductive in terms of public relations. Still, each side continues to foster the notion that their opponents have yet to forsake such actions, thus retaining a potent argument about their adversaries' demonic character.

Questions about their opponents' legitimacy also flow from assertions that although their own organizations are quite democratic, participatory, and infused with grassroots support, groups on the other side are closed, elitist, and not nearly as democratic as they like to suggest. In particular, each side points out that their adversaries, although portraying themselves as citizens' associations, are actually heavily funded by corporate America. Preservationists eager to expand or protect wilderness areas note Yamaha, Suzuki, and Kawasaki help fund organizations representing outdoor recreationists and off-road vehicle users. Environmental interests portray the wise use and property rights groups as being little more than fronts for greedy corporations and those who would profit from the public lands.[32]

It is ironic that the environmental groups find themselves vulnerable to countercharges in kind. The Audubon Society, for example, brings in hundreds of thousands of dollars each year from oil and gas interests. The National Wildlife Federation reaps similar amounts each year in annual membership fees from corporations such as Monsanto and Du Pont that are members of NWF's Corporate Conservation Council.[33] And the World Wildlife Fund–Conservation Foundation lists among its major donors various companies criticized for their poor record on environmental matters—Philip Morris, and oil giants Mobil, Chevron, and Exxon.[34] Indeed, environmental groups are embarrassed by the fact that so many of them receive large corporate donations, which often have been accepted after considerable internal dissension.

The argument over corporate funding is at its heart a dispute over political legitimacy, with organizations on each side suggesting that their opponents are not the simple, citizens' action groups they claim to be. Such efforts to question the legitimacy of rival groups extend beyond the issue of financial backing and reach to the very character of the organizations themselves. The environmentalists argue that the wise-use groups are little more than "letter-head" organizations, headed by a few entrepreneurial leaders but with a shallow or nonexistent membership base. Critics of the mainstream environmental preservation groups argue that these organizations long ago shed their character as democratic citizens' action groups; these critics claim that they are staff-run organizations concerned with protecting their stakes in Washington power games.

Conclusion

A commonplace observation about contemporary American politics is that recent years have brought a decline in civility and comity in our political culture, in public life—an increase in discord, rancor, polarization, and extremism. This decline in civility has permeated the interest group arena as well. Any reasonably alert observer can assemble a list of organized interests that seem intransigent, belligerent, intolerant, and driven by deep-seated animus toward their adversaries. They can be found on the political right and the left, and include such mutually hostile groups as the National Abortion Rights Action League and the National Right to Life Committee, ACT-UP, and the Christian Coalition.

Although plentiful today, these bitter interest group conflicts over nonmaterial interests and values are not new to public life; rather, they have been a consistent refrain in American politics since its inception, as the struggles over slavery, the franchise, temperance and prohibition, and ethnic assimilation readily attest. The deepest source of recurring dissension involves the defense of the moral and cultural values that underlie a way of life. Typically, the group antagonists have displayed the same behaviors examined here in the public lands case: Each side tries to depict itself as defenders of enduring values, of the "public interest," and of the institutions and traditions of American life, while depicting the opposition as the foes of those things.

Such continuing disputes have similar consequences, whether the matter in contention is abortion or gun control or the seemingly prosaic policies of public land management. First, these issues are exceedingly difficult to resolve because the American political system is poorly equipped to resolve conflicts in which passions run deep. Elected officials approach fundamental conflicts of this sort with great trepidation, preferring to deal with them through symbolic measures that have little substantive effect. When administrators try to make decisive policy, their decisions typically are challenged in the courts, putting the judiciary in the position of filling the policy-making void. But court-shaped policy is also suspect in the eyes of critics who doubt the ability of the judiciary to make timely, informed, and balanced decisions. Moreover, interests with the most resources can embark on a costly strategy of litigation and delay.

Mindful of these institutional and procedural impediments to resolution, an effort has been made in some domestic policy arenas to employ alternative approaches to resolving disputes (for example, mediation and negotiation). Only recently has the public lands arena begun to see such efforts. Perhaps most conspicuous are the working groups pulled together at the instigation of President Clinton's secretary of the interior, Bruce Babbitt, to develop less centralized, more collaborative structures for public range management. Other efforts to replace conflict with compromise and negotiation have emerged on issues such as how to improve the air quality over the Grand Canyon and how to balance timber interests with the protection of grizzly bear habitat in the Selway–Bitterroot Wilderness area of Idaho.[35] Despite these initial efforts at using mediation or related approaches, the techniques of alternative dispute resolution are unlikely to yield much success because of the considerable political impediments in their way.[36]

Second, because of the fragmentation of power in the American political system, even major changes in the configuration of power (partisan control of different institutions) make little difference in terms of settling these issues. For example, interests within the preservation community had high hopes for their agendas when Bill Clinton was first elected to the presidency. Similarly, the user groups' hopes soared in the wake of the Republicans' stunning congressional victory in 1994. But in neither case did the change in partisan control over these institutions yield expected dramatic policy shifts. So numerous and potent are the tools of obstruction and delay in the American policy-making system that the anticipated benefits of electoral victory are often rendered illusory in issue arenas infused with great passion. That institutional and procedural reality is magnified by the often-observed fact that such electoral victories have the countervailing impact of expanding the memberships of interest groups aligned on the opposing side and deflating the memberships of groups aligned with the victors. Thus, when Ronald Reagan was president, the environmental interest groups enjoyed a tremendous surge in membership and revenues; and when Bill Clinton won the presidency, those groups experienced a sizeable diminution of their ranks while their opponents were enjoying gains.

Third, conflicts in the culture wars also are hard to resolve because the antagonists never see the battles as "over." This pattern is often observed in other issue areas as well, but it seems considerably more pronounced in the culture wars. The losers in one round redouble their efforts for the next battle, often trying to shift it to a more favorable political venue. And the winners in these culture wars do not tend to see themselves as winners; at the least, they are loathe to portray themselves that way. For example, the environmental preservationists have emerged victorious in many recent battles in public lands politics, but one would never know it from their rhetoric or behavior. This is explained in part by the "war" mentality these groups acquire: They are always gearing up for the next battle, whatever it is, and wherever it might take place. But the phenomenon of denying that they are "ahead" is also surely attributable to groups' organizational maintenance needs: They can more readily rally contributions from the supporters on whom they depend by scaring them with the prospect of imminent defeat than by soothing them with reports of achievement or glorious victory.

Fourth, culture war conflicts such as those over public-land management are hard to resolve because they are conducted in a fashion that is antithetical to deliberation. The principal way in which such conflicts are waged—with each side conveying information and framing its case to the mass public through symbolically charged narratives—involves very little, if any, deliberation. As Burdett Loomis has observed, "The more public the performance, the less likely will there be any meaningful deliberation."[37]

This final conclusion carries some irony with it, because some public policy scholars have argued that in recent years the pluralist "politics of interests" has come to be supplanted by a new kind of politics. In this new order, the participants, both government officials and interest group representatives, advance ideas and values, not just interests. Moreover, they rely on deliberation ("purposive processes of moral discourse") as they "seek to achieve a policy product that is better, more dedicated to the public interest, than the mere pluralist, compromised sum of the preferences of interest groups."[38] The argument has real merit for explaining the otherwise anomalous passage of some of the most important policy reforms of the 1970s and 1980s.[39] But there is a whole category of policy issues (the public lands controversies and the social issues that make up the contemporary culture wars) that seem to stand outside this "new politics" framework. The irony is that in this alleged age of the "politics of ideas," no other issues come close to these in terms of the extent to which values and ideas dominate the discourse. Still, these are the very issues our leaders seem to have the most trouble handling and that seem, perhaps because of the passions they invoke, somehow impervious to processes of reasoned deliberation.

Notes

1. James Davison Hunter, *Culture Wars: The Struggle to Define America* (New York: Basic Books, 1991), 42.
2. All quotes in this paragraph are from Hunter, *Culture Wars*, 63–64.
3. See Eliza Newlin Carney, "Industry Plays the Grass-Roots Card," *National Journal*, February 1, 1992, 281, 282.
4. See Christopher J. Bosso, "Into the Third Wave: Environmental Activism in the 1990s" (Paper delivered at the 1992 Annual Meeting of the American Political Science Association, Chicago, September 3–6, 1992), 16.

5. Keith Schneider, "When the Bad Guy is Seen as the One in the Green Hat," *New York Times*, February 16, 1992, E3.
6. Bosso, "Into the Third Wave," 17.
7. Quote from a piece of direct mail from the Sierra Club, 1992.
8. Victor B. Scheffer, *The Shaping of Environmentalism in America* (Seattle: University of Washington Press, 1991), 113.
9. Financial Report, *Sierra* 76 (May/June 1991): 94–96. The club's own numbers are higher than those reported by some scholars. But the overall trend of growth in the 1980s in environmental groups' memberships and budgets is quite remarkable. See, for example, Robert C. Mitchell, Angela G. Mertig, and Riley Dunlap, "Twenty Years of Environmental Mobilization: Trends among National Environmental Organizations," in *American Environmentalism: The U.S. Environmental Movement, 1970–1990*, ed. Riley Dunlap and Angela Mertig (Washington, D.C.: Taylor & Francis, 1992), Table I, 11–26.
10. Denton E. Morrison and Riley E. Dunlap, "Environmentalism and Elitism: A Conceptual and Empirical Analysis," *Environmental Management* 10 (1986): 581–589.
11. Bosso, "Into the Third Wave," 20–21.
12. See Steven Kelman, *Making Public Policy* (New York: Basic Books, 1987), 26.
13. David A. Rochefort and Roger W. Cobb, "Problem Definition: An Emerging Perspective," in *The Politics of Problem Definition: Shaping the Policy Agenda* (Lawrence: University Press of Kansas, 1994), 3.
14. Deborah Stone, "Causal Stories and the Formation of Policy Agendas," *Political Science Quarterly* 104 (1989): 282.
15. Richard Neustadt and Ernest May, *Thinking in Time: The Uses of History for Decision-Makers* (New York: Free Press, 1986), 106.
16. Emery Roe, *Narrative Policy Analysis: Theory and Practice* (Durham: Duke University Press, 1994), 3, 34. As Roe also noted, these narratives may "retain some explanatory or descriptive power [in the view of the narrators], even after a number of the points or assumptions upon which they are based are understood to be in doubt and subject to serious qualification" (37).
17. Deborah Stone, *Policy Paradox: The Art of Political Decision Making* (New York: W. W. Norton, 1997), chap. 6.
18. Hunter, *Culture Wars*, 136.
19. See Alston Chase, *In a Dark Wood* (Boston: Houghton Mifflin, 1995), 103.
20. For example, in 1988, two preservationist groups—the National Wildlife Federation and the Wilderness Society—launched a campaign saying that preserving the old growth forests would not hurt loggers because the industry was dying anyway. See Chase, *In a Dark Wood*, 275.
21. Jane Fritsch, "Nature Groups Say Foes Bear Friendly Names," *New York Times*, March 25, 1996, A1, A12.
22. William K. Stevens, "New Eye on Nature: The Real Constant Is Eternal Turmoil," *New York Times*, July 31, 1990; quoted in Chase, *In a Dark Wood*, 361.
23. Typical of the sort of pattern that gives rise to such concerns was the way in which various environmental groups and land management agencies, using ecosystem arguments, gradually expanded their estimates throughout the 1980s of how large the "greater Yellowstone ecosystem" is. See Alston Chase, *In a Dark Wood*, 358.
24. The phrase "playing God" in this context comes from Alston Chase, whose *Playing God in Yellowstone: The Destruction of America's First National Park* (New York: Harcourt Brace Jovanovich, 1987) is a provocative and controversial skewering of the National Park Service's efforts to implement "natural regulation," a precursor of ecosystem management.
25. Hunter, *Culture Wars*, 136.

26. A description of the incident is found in David Helvarg, *The War against the Greens* (San Francisco: Sierra Club Books, 1994), 5.
27. Quoted in Jacqueline Vaughn Switzer, *Green Backlash: The History and Politics of Environmental Opposition in the U.S.* (Boulder, Colo.: Lynne Rienner, 1997), 209.
28. See Mark Dowie, *Losing Ground* (Cambridge: MIT Press, 1995), 94. Reference to the watermelon metaphor also appears in Switzer, *Green Backlash*, 209.
29. This anecdote appears in Helvarg, *The War against the Greens*, 79, and in Switzer, *Green Backlash*, 210.
30. See Switzer, *Green Backlash*, 211–212.
31. Helvarg, *The War against the Greens*, 14.
32. Helvarg, *The War against the Greens*, 120.
33. See Bill Gifford, "Inside the Environmental Groups," *Outside* (September 1990): 69–82.
34. Switzer, *Green Backlash*, 139.
35. These examples are from Switzer, *Green Backlash*, 296.
36. See Barry G. Rabe, "The Politics of Environmental Dispute Resolution," *Policy Studies Journal* 16 (Spring 1988): 585–602.
37. Burdett Loomis, "Interests, Narratives, and Deliberation: 'Saving Medicare' and Passing Kennedy–Kassebaum" (Paper delivered at the annual meeting of the American Political Science Association, San Francisco, August 29–September 1, 1996), 16.
38. This characterization is by Martin Shapiro, "Of Interests and Values: The New Politics and the New Political Science," in *The New Politics of Public Policy*, ed. Mark K. Landy and Martin A. Levin (Baltimore: Johns Hopkins University Press, 1995), 7. The authors whose essays appear in this volume are those who might be said to constitute the core of the "new politics" school.
39. Examples include the deregulation of the trucking, aviation, and telecommunications industries; the 1986 and 1990 immigration reform acts; the 1986 Tax Reform Act; Aid to Children with Special Needs; Superfund; the Clean Air Act, and various other important measures.

15

Abortion Interests: From the Usual Suspects to Expanded Coalitions

Laura R. Woliver

In the wake of the Supreme Court's historic 1973 *Roe v. Wade* decision that made abortions legal, interests became active on both sides of the issue. Indeed, the intensity of abortion politics has gone unrivaled in American politics over the past twenty-five years. The venues for this political activity have ranged from abortion clinics to state legislatures to the Supreme Court. Although abortion is surely one of our society's most difficult issues, for individual interests—and even lawmakers—it is often straightforward. That is, so-called "prochoice" and "prolife" groups have their own distinct agendas and bases of support; likewise, most legislators develop clear records on abortion, and they follow the patterns that they have established earlier in their careers. Abortion is a tough issue, but one in which the sides are seemingly well-defined.

In this chapter, Laura Woliver examines how abortion policy has been shaped by interest groups over the past quarter century. She then proceeds to consider how apparently peripheral interests have become increasingly important in abortion politics. For example, some doctors weigh in on medical research issues that require fetal tissue, whereas others worry about disruptions in the patient–physician relationship. Farther afield, historians have noted their findings that middle-class and wealthy women have always had access to abortion, even when it was not legal. They are joined by social workers and others concerned that overturning *Roe* would create dangerous situations for poor women who are determined to end their pregnancies. In the end, the outcomes of abortion politics in the future may be determined not by the "usual suspects" of the prochoice and prolife groups, but rather by interests that are only tangentially touched by the issue.

The twenty-fifth anniversary of the U.S. Supreme Court decision in *Roe v. Wade*, on January 23, 1998, showcased the passionate politics that abortion triggers in our society. Dozens of interest group and religious leaders lamented or celebrated the decision that legalized abortion in America. Indeed, few issues are as contentious as abortion in contemporary American politics.[1]

Abortion seems omnipresent in post-*Roe* American politics—whether in party platforms, candidate selections, election campaigns, judicial nominations, funding for domestic and international programs, sex education, AIDs prevention programs, or debates over new reproductive technologies and cloning research, to name just some battlegrounds. It is no longer just the "usual suspects" who are involved in these struggles. In addition to the expected participants from prolife and prochoice interest groups are an array of groups representing religious, ethnic, medical, legal, scholarly, professional, social service, and partisan interests.

Even the first step in examining abortion politics, what to call the interest groups, gets engulfed in the irreconcilable differences, heartfelt passions, and opposing world views the issue includes. Many news organizations now try to use the mutually neutral sounding terms "prolegal abortion" and "antilegal abortion"; this is unsatisfactory to some because the term "anti" anything seems pejorative. Implicit in the new terminology is the acknowledgement that despite its legal status, abortion will still occur—whether it be legal or illegal. Whatever the labels settled on, the energy spent on these words show how abortion interest groups understand how important framing, language, and symbols are in winning citizens' support.[2]

Antilegal Abortion–Prolife Groups and Tactics

Abortion is a central issue in neoconservatism in America and the backlash against the women's movement and other progressive causes. The 1973 *Roe v. Wade* decision was met with outrage by prolife groups, and since then opponents of legal abortion have worked tirelessly to end these procedures and reverse what they see as a historic mistake by the Supreme Court. The most visible and powerful antilegal abortion groups include The National Right-to-Life Committee, The American Life League, Americans United for Life, and religious groups such as the U.S. Catholic Conference, the Moral Majority, and the Christian Coalition.

Prolife groups won a major post-*Roe* victory with the 1976 passage of the Hyde Amendment, which banned federal abortion funding. In the late 1970s, the specter of abortion being codified as a constitutional right (however inaccurate this designation might have been) by the proposed Equal Rights Amendment to the U.S. Constitution helped lead to its defeat.[3] The 1980 election of prolife President Ronald Reagan and a prolife platform for the Republican Party were also cast as victories for the antichoice forces. During the 1980s and early 1990s antiabortion activists engaged in single-issue candidate assessments for party nominations and general elections resulting in a concentrated presence of antiabortion politicians in the Republican Party and prochoice in the Democratic Party. In addition to partisan politics, antiabortion activists sought to restrict accessibility to abortions with actions including picketing clinics, doctors, and staff at their homes, harassing the children of doctors and staff when they were at school, blocking clinic entryways, jamming telephones, booking false appointments, calling in threats, videotaping and generally harassing people coming and going from the clinics, and much more.[4]

A group called Operation Rescue coordinated blockades at clinics around the country in the late 1980s and early 1990s, resulting in highly publicized showdowns in cities such as Wichita, Kansas, and Dallas, Texas, lasting for days or weeks, resulting in hundreds of arrests, and taxing the resources of the cities so targeted.[5]

Although displaying the commitment of prolife people and justified by activists in terms of civil disobedience for a just cause, to some observers these blockaders and sidewalk "counselors" were seen to be extremists and disruptive activists. Despite the official distancing of many national prolife group leaders from these tactics, collateral damage was done to the prolife cause by these confrontations and especially clinic murders.

In March 1993 and July 1994 in Pensacola, Florida, in separate events two clinic doctors and a security guard were murdered. At the end of December 1994, in Brookline, Massachusetts, two clinic receptionists were shot and killed. The men who shot and killed these people did not have "official" affiliations with prolife groups, but they were devoted to the cause, had received and studied literature from many prolife groups, and had participated in prolife meetings, demonstrations, and rallies of various sorts. Both men were impassioned prolife advocates. In late January 1998 a bomb explosion at an abortion clinic in Birmingham, Alabama, killed a security guard and severely injured a nurse.

In addition to national restrictions on abortion, such as the Hyde Amendment (limiting federal funding) and prolife dominance of Republican Party politics, antilegal abortion groups have been effective in winning policy victories in many state legislatures. Unable to make much more additional progress at the national level, targeting states has proved successful for prolife interest groups. Many state legislatures are more conservative than the national government and more vulnerable to single-issue group targeting. Especially at the beginning of this effort, prolegal abortion groups were not organized at the state level very well and had difficulty countering the antilegal abortion lobbying. Antilegal abortion groups also benefited from local church networks that could be mobilized to lobby on abortion as well as their larger religious agendas. Conservative churches were frequently successfully co-opted into abortion politics at the state and local level.

National groups working with state and local affiliates to write into law restrictive abortion policies hoped that subsequent litigation would maintain pressure on state and federal judges to accept restrictions on *Roe*, and eventually completely overturn it.[6] Although many states passed restrictions on abortion, a few such as Connecticut and New Jersey re-

jected antilegal abortion group efforts and affirmed their basic support for
the *Roe* framework.

As a result of these state reform efforts, in 1988 a very restrictive
Missouri abortion statute was accepted for review by the U.S. Supreme
Court. Attorneys at the Chicago-based group Americans United for Life
worked closely with Missouri officials to help bring the suit up to the
Supreme Court. *Webster v. Reproductive Health Services* was a clear showdown for abortion groups, some hoping to overturn *Roe*, and their opponents battling to retain at least parts of *Roe*.

When the Bush Justice Department announced it was going to advocate overturning *Roe* through its Solicitor General's brief to the *Webster*
case, it was a triumph for the antiabortion movement. This was the first
time the U.S. Justice Department sided with antilegal abortion interests
and urged overturning *Roe*. It represented the culmination of years of
hard work by antilegal abortion groups winning elections, ensuring prolife Republican appointments to the federal judiciary, and securing influence for antilegal abortion forces within the Republican Party.[7] It was also
linked to the neoconservative social movement in the country defining itself around "family values" and the related interpretations of the law.[8]

In the absence of abortion being recriminalized, antilegal abortion
forces have sought to restrict access to abortion. Stigmatizing and margin-
alizing doctors who perform abortions have reduced the number of physicians presenting themselves publicly as willing to perform abortions. This
has resulted in a decrease in the number of identifiable clinics and doctors who perform abortions. Many medical schools, either bowing to or an-
ticipating antilegal abortion outrage, now do not even teach how to safely
end a pregnancy. Many states have passed strict and expensive licensing
and monitoring requirements for clinics and practitioners, further discouraging public presentation of legal abortion choices to women. At the
local level, in addition, antilegal abortion groups try to block building and
licensing permits for new clinics, or revoke licenses or convince landlords
to cancel clinic leases. Some states do not have one abortion clinic or doctor so identified. Decreased access to abortion has become a central concern to many prochoice groups, and a triumph to prolife groups.

Prolegal Abortion–Prochoice Groups and Tactics

The 1973 *Roe v. Wade* decision was welcomed by many interest
groups, notably in the medical and legal communities. Doctors, nurses,
prosecutors, and police had witnessed the human misery the illegal abortion regime had reaped in hospital emergency rooms. Women's rights
groups were not the instigators in bringing the *Roe* case to the court. However, they welcomed the decision itself. When *Roe* was decided, many
prolegal abortion groups believed that would basically settle the issue politically and legally. They saw little need to defend *Roe*. In contrast, *Roe*

became, almost immediately, a catalyst for groups to mobilize against legalized abortion.

In addition, many interests with a stake in keeping abortion legal are multifaceted groups that have sought to advance large, demanding policy agendas; abortion politics was just one of many compelling issues. Moreover, some group leaders hoped others would defend abortion rights and that they would not have to engage this controversial and costly issue.

After the antilegal abortion groups won a series of victories, several organized interests stepped up their activities and became more visible in their defense of legal abortion. Under the leadership of Faye Wattleton, for instance, the Planned Parenthood Federation of America became a forceful voice for legal abortion.[9]

Antilegal abortion actions aimed at restricting and eventually over-turning *Roe* pushed prolegal abortion interests to respond with increased energy. The most visible and powerful prolegal abortion groups—the National Abortion Federation, the National Abortion Rights Action League (NARAL), the American Civil Liberties Union's Reproductive Freedom Project, the National Organization for Women (NOW), and the Planned Parenthood Federation of America—joined with other interests to coordinate their efforts into an information clearinghouse, the Abortion Information Exchange. The Exchange included medical groups, professional associations, organized labor, and environmental groups in addition to the usual suspects of the prochoice movement organizations from feminism, women's rights lobbies, and family planning groups.[10]

For prolegal abortion groups the 1989 *Webster* case served as a further catalyst, as they formed a cohesive national coalition to protect legal abortion.[11] The prochoice tactics emphasized the basic support for legal abortion in this country. NARAL, for instance, launched a "Who Decides?" public relations campaign asking the public who they wanted making their most private reproductive decisions for them: the government, the police, or themselves. The campaign included full-page magazine advertisements depicting couples being questioned about their birth control and reproductive decisions by government officials.

Both sides have always staged massive demonstrations and rallies marking *Roe's* anniversaries. For the prochoice camp the April 1989 "March for Women's Lives" in Washington, D.C., displayed the broad support for legal abortion choice, garnered widespread national media attention, and reminded politicians that abortion was more than a single-issue dispute. Rather, it was part of a large and powerful social movement concerned about women's health, agency, and power.[12] The march was intended to be a show of prochoice force in light of the then-pending *Webster* decision's importance to the future of legal abortion. Under the leadership of NOW's president, Eleanor Smeal, the march included a coalition of hundreds of women's, health, business, and civil rights organizations.

On a related, but distinct, front, given *Webster's* nature as a high-stakes case, a historic number of *amicus curia* briefs were filed in the case. More than 300 organizations, using more than 120 lawyers, drafted thirty-one separate briefs for the prochoice position in *Webster.* The prochoice briefs were coordinated by attorneys at the ACLU Reproductive Rights Project, Planned Parenthood, and the National Abortion Rights Action League (NARAL). In opposition, the prolife interests submitted forty-six *amici curiae* briefs that supported the restrictions in the Missouri statute.

Various peripheral interests were drawn into abortion politics by the *Webster* case. *Roe's* use of fetal viability as criteria for balances between doctors, women, and the state based on trimesters had been attacked by prolife forces using modern medical technologies to show the untenability of these trimester standards. Indeed, the U.S. Catholic Conference in their *Webster* brief described the fetus and the woman as "separate patients." To answer these doubts, 167 scientists and physicians signed a prolegal abortion brief to *Webster* maintaining that viability for a fetus was still about twenty-four weeks gestation.

The expanding coalitions of abortion groups was also evident in The Women's Equality Brief, signed by seventy-seven organizations including NOW, the American Association of University Women, the League of Women Voters, and the National Federation of Business and Professional Women's Clubs, among others. These groups stressed the need for legal abortion to achieve women's full rights as citizens. Similarly, a brief signed by 885 American law school professors asserted, "For women to achieve the full promise of 'equal protection,' it is necessary for them to control the childbearing decision." The National Coalition against Domestic Violence also spoke up in *Webster,* pointing out in its brief that given the gender-specific nature of the impact of abortion restrictions abortion should be protected by the courts using the Fourteenth Amendment's Equal Protection clause.

The Missouri statute at issue in *Webster* was so strict regarding prohibitions on state employees performing, advocating, discussing, even mentioning abortions, that even the American Library Association (ALA) and The Freedom to Read Foundation filed a joint brief warning the Court about the infringements on free speech such restrictions involved and their concern that public librarians would have to censor books. Their brief pointed out the information-access issues and potential chilling effects on public libraries raised by the Missouri statute.

In the *Webster* decision a splintered Supreme Court refused to overturn *Roe,* thus keeping abortion a legal option. But the Court did uphold many of the Missouri abortion restrictions. Several states subsequently considered and passed restrictive legislation, and a few states defeated restrictions. These state statutes were also subject to federal court injunctions, reviews, appeals, and decisions.

One piece of the prochoice strategy includes presenting the courts, on a continual basis, a vision of what legal abortion means to women. The first female U.S. Supreme Court Justice, Sandra Day O'Connor, has thus been a particular focus of prochoice lobbying. Justice O'Connor has proven a pivotal vote in defending the core holding of *Roe*, especially in the period before President Bill Clinton appointed two prochoice members of the Court.[13]

Moreover, Clinton campaigned for the presidency in 1992 (and 1996) with a clear and consistent prochoice position. To an extent his victory derived from a "gender gap" in which support for legal abortion was a key component.[14] President Clinton's 1992 election was very important to the prochoice cause on many levels. One of his first official acts was to remove abortion restrictions instituted during the Reagan and Bush administrations. And he has made prochoice appointments to the Supreme Court. In fact, his first appointment, Justice Ruth Bader Ginsburg, was one of the architects of much of the 1970s gender-based jurisprudence, including the relevant aspects of reproductive laws.

President Clinton and Attorney General Janet Reno also emphasized that they would use the power and resources of the Justice Department to stop violence at abortion clinics and to punish the perpetrators. In 1994 the FACE Act (Freedom of Access to Clinic Entrances Act) gave further ammunition to prochoice groups seeking to protect access to legal abortion, and was an important victory for prolegal abortion interests.

An Expanded Vision: Interests, Abortion, and Social Status

Whatever the constellation of laws and regulations regarding abortion in any country or period of history, women who want to terminate their pregnancies often do. Even if abortions are criminalized, stigmatized, and subject to severe punishments, some women, in their desperation, seek out illegal and sometimes dangerous means to terminate the pregnancy.

A woman's social class, race, and connections within a community shape her actual choices, even in periods when abortions are officially criminalized. Mark Graber demonstrated that criminalized abortion laws in the United States were selectively enforced, as many private doctors enjoyed great freedom to provide safe (yet illegal) abortions to their overwhelmingly middle- to upper-class white patients.[15] Such scholarship bolsters prolegal abortion group arguments that the option should remain legal and safe as established in *Roe*.

On this point, for instance, more than 281 American historians signed an *amicus* brief to *Webster*.[16] The history professors (certainly not the usual suspects in abortion politics) wanted the justices to understand the history of abortion laws and abortion practices in hopes of countering the antilegal abortion groups' stance that abortion has always been illegal and that *Roe* is an aberration that, on these grounds, deserved to be overturned. A separate *amicus* brief signed by hundreds of American law school deans corroborated the historians' points.

A Woman of Color Brief, sponsored by fifteen principal groups and supported by an additional 115 African American, Hispanic, Latina, American Indian, American Asian, and Puerto Rican women's rights and women's health organizations, pointed out that, prior to the *Roe* decision, poor women and many women of color had no safe options for terminating pregnancies. Therefore, they argued, restrictions on access to legal abortion will "disproportionately burden racial minority groups" and poor women. Not only are the terms of abortion in dispute, the entire history and background of abortion has come into play as its scope of conflict has been expanded into the politics of race and class.

A few antilegal abortion groups (Birthright, Covenant House, The Lutheran Church Missouri Synod) recognize the plight of women faced with an unwanted or unhealthy pregnancy, yet contend that abortion is not the answer. They argue that the community should help by providing increased social services and communal assistance for women and their children. This position is rare, however.

Some "liberal" prochoice groups have articulated an expanded vision of choice that incorporates the need for financial security, universal health care, safe housing, nonviolent domiciles, and complete funding for services for handicapped people to make women's decisions more freely chosen and less coerced by poverty, fear, and lack of community support. This may offer some *limited* common ground between groups on opposing sides of the abortion issue. Another issue forging some agreement among groups on both sides is the need to protect the choice to have children, no matter how handicapped or different they might be or how much in need of community assistance the family might be. Both prochoice and prolife groups are concerned with the eugenics potential in the future of reproductive politics.

An instance of this potential for common ground among the interest groups occurred during recent welfare reform discussions. When welfare reform was under debate in the U.S. Congress in 1995, an ad hoc, issue-specific coalition of both prochoice and prolife groups spoke out against one proposed provision, the "family or child cap." The proposal would have banned public assistance to unmarried teenage mothers and capped the cash assistance a welfare recipient could receive as additional children are born.[17] The Christian Coalition and other antilegal abortion groups did support the new Republican majority in the Congress, and welcomed many aspects of welfare reform, but the family cap gave them pause. The antilegal abortion groups, although not sanctioning out-of-wedlock teenage sexuality and births, worried that the family-cap proposal would push teenage girls and poor women to have abortions. The prolegal abortion groups opposed the family caps for similar reasons, and thus both sides opposed the caps because they would punish girls and women who chose to continue a pregnancy.[18]

Twenty-Five Years after *Roe:* The Abortion Wars Continue

Interest groups on both sides of the abortion debate continue to seek passage of national legislation to codify their positions and trump all contrary state laws or judicial decisions. The Freedom of Choice Act, an attempt by prochoice interests to codify into national law legal abortion, has little chance of getting anywhere in the Republican Congress of the late 1990s. At the same time, the Human Life Amendment to the Constitution, which would define human life and citizenship rights as beginning at the moment of conception, remains out of reach. The current Republican congressional leadership has proved cautious about appearing too extreme and triggering moderate Republican defections at the polls. Still, there have been real incremental victories for prolife forces both in the states and with congressional majorities that favor restricting access to abortions.

In 1996 Congress passed what supporters called a "partial birth abortion" ban and what opponents sought to frame more broadly by labeling it a ban on "late-term abortions." These abortions occur in the third trimester, sometimes very late in the gestation of the fetus. They are rare and are often linked to health issues for the pregnant woman or the fetus. In some of the most heart-wrenching and emotionally charged symbolic hearings and floor debates in recent congressional policy making, prolife representatives displayed large pictures of the procedures, and the results. Prochoice politicians tried to counter with testimony from women who had chosen this procedure to save their own lives, to abort fatally developing fetuses, and to save their fertility for future hoped-for pregnancies. President Clinton, as promised, vetoed the ban because no exception was made in the legislation for the health of the mother (the ban did include an exception for the *life* of the mother). Congress could not override Clinton's veto, and in 1997 it passed a similar bill, which Clinton again vetoed.

Given the relative infrequency with which partial birth abortions are performed, this issue has risen to the top of the prolife agenda for two related reasons. First, it offers political benefits in future elections when opponents of the ban can be portrayed as brutal "baby killers" by prolife interest groups. Second, the ban is part of an overall long-term, incremental prolife strategy to whittle away at *Roe*—in other words, to force politicians to vote on these difficult reproductive issues, bring lawsuits, and establish a legitimate government role in this policy domain that can then be expanded.

State by state attempts to restrict abortion choices and access will continue to be a major thrust of antilegal abortion interest groups. State bans on partial birth or late-term abortions continue to win passage in the states, although these restrictions will face lengthy court battles. In addition, abortion positions will remain a key candidate litmus test for political party nominations and an important factor in the general elections. State implementation of welfare reform might also engender some debate about the impact these policies are having on abortion rates per state.

National and Local Coordination

Increasingly, grassroots abortion interest group battles have witnessed national orchestration of seemingly spontaneous home-grown, citizen mobilizations.[19] As with many other interests, national prolife and prochoice organizations work closely with state affiliates on protests, legislation, lawsuits, and the provision of accurate, politically relevant information.

Most of the groups involved in abortion politics also participate in larger social movements with their strengths, networks, commitments, experiences, and shifting coalitions.[20] In particular, the main prolife groups have direct religious links, and religious leaders are prominent in their public activities and agenda setting.

In one forceful show of national interest group coordination with state affiliates, the National Right to Life Committee faxed copies of the national partial-birth abortion ban to several state affiliates. The South Carolina affiliate quickly found a legislative sponsor for the ban and had the national legislation edited to fit state law. The boilerplate ban passed through the South Carolina legislature in record time, with virtually no debate and only token opposition. The highly publicized national legislative debates over the ban helped the state affiliates win its passage in many states. State venues have been consistently more favorable to prolife interests than has the national political arena.

Expanding Coalitions

As E. E. Schattschneider noted, "The outcome of all conflict is determined by the scope of the contagion."[21] However reluctantly, health care professional associations and interest groups have been dragged into abortion politics. No longer is it just women's rights and single-issue prochoice groups versus single-issue prolife groups and the Catholic Church in these battles. Interest groups join coalitions for a variety of reasons, often bringing added strength and expertise to the lobbying effort at hand.[22] The range of groups participating has expanded and will continue to grow as abortion touches more and more other interests, especially in health care.

A recent fund-raising letter, for instance, from the Committee for the Separation of Church and State mentions abortion as a battleground where some people want to impose their religious views on others through the laws of the state. The Committee for the Separation of

Church and State is not a women's rights, prolife, or prochoice group, nor is it engaged in health care policy making. Its primary mission is to protect the "wall of separation between church and state" as central to the tradition of American religious freedom. Still, the group has submitted *amicus* briefs to the courts in abortion cases. As antilegal abortion interests succeed, albeit incrementally, in limiting access to abortions, groups like this will be drawn to lobby on abortion issues, based on their concern that the wall of church–state separation may be breached.

Legal or Illegal Tactics

Prolife interests continue to push the boundaries of when and where they can protest legal abortion and seek converts to their cause. One new tactic that has been met with some parental outrage is to target entryways to high schools in the morning before school starts, replete with huge color posters of aborted fetuses and brochures to hand the students.[23] The Reverend Flip Benham, of Operation Rescue, is now serving a jail sentence for trespass as a result of one such high school protest.

The specter of violence by a few antilegal abortion zealots also continues to shape the nation's abortion politics. Despite the distancing attempted by many antilegal abortion interest groups from these individuals, the groups suffer collateral damage thrown off from the shocking results of bombings, assaults, and murders at abortion clinics.[24]

Blurring Reproductive Politics Boundaries

New reproductive technologies have been used to strengthen prolife arguments that the fetus is an independent human being worthy of rights.[25] Paradoxically, however, many of these new reproductive technologies require the availability of legal abortion. Prenatal testing is often done so prospective parents can choose to abort a fetus with detected "defects." Fertility drugs and procedures that implant embryos into women are based on options for the woman to selectively reduce the often multiple embryos produced from the drugs and procedures.[26] Many doctors, clinics, and researchers, then, who are trying to help infertile people, have become involved in abortion politics because their practices are intertwined with the medical choices (including legal abortion) their patients might need. Associations of hospitals, doctors, nurses, public health officials, bioethicists, and medical school faculty have submitted briefs to the courts discussing their myriad concerns about legislative restrictions on abortion that affect the practice of medicine, doctor–patient relationships, and the ethical obligations of medical professionals in reproductive health. One prochoice *Webster* brief by the Association of Reproductive Health Professionals, for instance, discusses the problems of the overlaps and merging of abortion with many forms of birth control.

Medical innovations constantly reshape reproductive politics, thus raising questions about whether an action by health care providers and a woman is considered birth control or abortion. For example, abortion rights activists hope that eventual diffusion of new choices, such as RU-486 (the "abortion pill") or wider knowledge about the "emergency contraceptives" that prevent pregnancy will move attention away from the clinics as foci of antilegal abortion protests. Rather, pregnancy termination decisions and policy making would become more in the traditional, private province of relations between doctors and their female patients making individualized health care decisions.

At the same time, many prolife abortion groups label some common, popular, and seemingly noncontroversial birth control methods "abortifacents." Victories by prolife groups will possibly impinge on birth control options for many people.[27]

Americans are the most supportive of abortion at the early stages of pregnancy. New home pregnancy tests that can detect pregnancy very early, even before a woman misses her first menstrual period, combined with ultrasound to locate the embryonic sac, and smaller medical equipment to suction out the contents are new developments that blur the boundaries between birth control and abortion. These new early abortion procedures can occur eight or ten days after conception. Regarding this development, and its potential political impact, the vice president for medical affairs at the Planned Parenthood Federation of America stated, "For most women, the sooner they know they're pregnant and the sooner they decide what they're going to do, the better. With these very early abortions, we're talking about a whole gestational sac that's the size of a matchstick head. It's nobody's picture of a little baby sucking its thumb."[28]

In that the Roman Catholic Church and the National Right to Life Committee, among others, believe that human life begins with fertilization, opposition to this development was immediate. The media relations director for the National Right to Life Committee explained, "Scientifically speaking, there's no difference between a fertilized egg and what you have three weeks later. Saying it's OK to kill it in the early stages because you're more comfortable with that is completely arbitrary."[29] Whatever the outcome, the new procedure displays the role medical technologies play in abortion debates, and the increasingly confusing boundaries between contraception and abortion.

Conclusion

Continuous snipping and sniping, therefore, at all political levels seems guaranteed for abortion's future.[30] The penchant for rhetorical intensity and demonization of the opposition characterizes much of modern interest group politics.[31] Similarly, for the passionate interests involved in abortion politics there often seems "no neutral ground"[32] in this "clash of absolutes."[33]

New research on reproductive history, rights, and options ensure that many groups, not just the usual suspects, will find themselves pulled into abortion politics at various points in our continuous grappling with the issues. What is guaranteed is that interest group politics regarding abortion will be marked by the passions and interests discussed, displaying how important this policy domain has become in our politics and the powerful interest groups and surprising coalitions that come into play.

Notes

1. For further background see M. Margaret Conway, Gertrude A. Steuernagel, and David W. Ahern, *Women and Political Participation: Cultural Change in the Political Arena* (Washington, D.C.: CQ Press, 1997); Barbara Hinkson Craig and David H. O'Brien, *Abortion and American Politics* (Chatham, N.J.: Chatham House, 1993); David J. Garrow, *Liberty and Sexuality: The Right to Privacy and the Making of* Roe v. Wade (New York: McMillian, 1994); Kristin Luker, *Abortion and the Politics of Motherhood* (Berkeley: University of California Press, 1984); Eileen L. McDonagh, *Breaking the Abortion Deadlock: From Choice to Consent* (New York: Oxford University Press, 1996); James C. Mohr, *Abortion in America: The Origins and Evolution of National Policy, 1800–1900* (New York: Oxford University Press, 1978); Karen O'Connor, *No Neutral Ground? Abortion Politics in an Age of Absolutes* (Boulder, Colo.: Westview Press, 1996); Rosalind Pollack Petchesky, *Abortion and Woman's Choice: The State, Sexuality, and Reproductive Freedom,* rev. ed. (Boston: Northeastern University Press, 1990); Deborah L. Rhode and Annette Lawson, "Introduction," in *The Politics of Pregnancy: Adolescent Sexuality and Public Policy,* ed. Annette Lawson and Deborah L. Rhode (New Haven, Conn.: Yale University Press, 1993), 1–19; Raymond Tatalovich, *The Politics of Abortion in the United States and Canada: A Comparative Study* (Armonk, N.Y.: M. E. Sharpe, 1997); Laurence H. Tribe, *Abortion: The Clash of Absolutes* (New York: W. W. Norton, 1990).
2. D. A. Snow, E. B. Rochford, Jr., S. K. Worden, and R. D. Benford, "Frame Alignment Processes, Micromobilization, and Movement Participation," *American Sociological Review* 51 (1986): 464–481; see also Murray Edelman, *Constructing the Political Spectacle* (Chicago: University of Chicago Press, 1989); Laura R. Woliver, *From Outrage to Action: The Politics of Grass-Roots Dissent* (Urbana: University of Illinois Press, 1993).
3. Laura R. Woliver, "Review Essay: The Equal Rights Amendment and the Limits of Liberal Legal Reform," *Polity* 21 (Fall 1988): 183–200.
4. Marjorie Randon Hershey, "Direct Action and the Abortion Issue: The Political Participation of Single-Issue Groups," in *Interest Group Politics,* 2d ed., ed. Allan J. Cigler and Burdett A. Loomis (Washington, D.C.: CQ Press, 1986), 27–45; Marjorie Randon Hershey and Darrell West, "Single-Issue Politics: Prolife Groups and the 1980 Senate Campaign," in *Interest Group Politics,* ed. Allan J. Cigler and Burdett A. Loomis (Washington, D.C.: CQ Press, 1983), 31–59; Sue Hertz, *Caught in the Crossfire: A Year on Abortion's Front Line* (New York: Prentice-Hall, 1991); Mary Segers, "The Pro-Choice Movement Post-*Casey:* Preserving Access," in *Abortion Politics in American States,* ed. Mary C. Segers and Timothy A. Byrnes (Armonk, N.Y.: M. E. Sharpe, 1995), 225–245; Wendy Simonds, *Abortion at Work: Ideology and Practice in a Feminist Clinic* (New Brunswick, N.J.: Rutgers University Press, 1996).
5. James Aho, "Popular Christianity and Political Extremism," in *Disruptive Religion: The Force of Faith in Social Movement Activism,* ed. Christian Smith (New York: Routledge, 1996), 189–204; Dallas A. Blanchard, *The Anti-Abortion Movement and the Rise of the Religious Right: From Polite to Fiery Protest* (New York: Twayne, 1994);

John C. Green, James L. Guth, Corwin E. Smidt, and Lyman A. Kellstedt, *Religion and the Culture Wars: Dispatches from the Front* (Lanham, Md.: Rowman and Littlefield, 1996); Elaine Sharp, "A Comparative Anatomy of Urban Social Conflict," *Political Research Quarterly* (forthcoming); Elaine Sharp, "Culture Wars and City Politics: Local Government's Role in Social Conflict," *Urban Affairs Review* 31 (July 1996): 738–758; Rhys Williams and Jeffrey Blackburn, "Many Are Called but Few Obey: Ideological Commitment and Activism in Operation Rescue," in *Disruptive Religion: The Force of Faith in Social Movement Activism*, ed. Christian Smith (New York: Routledge, 1996), 167–185; Laura R. Woliver, "Abortion Conflicts, City Governments and Culture Wars: Continually Negotiating Coexistence in South Carolina," in *Culture Wars and Local Politics* (Lawrence: University of Kansas Press, forthcoming).

6. Dennis J. Horan, Edward R. Grant, and Paige C. Cunningham, eds., *Abortion and the Constitution: Reversing* Roe v. Wade *through the Courts* (Washington, D.C.: Georgetown University Press, 1987). The editors and most of the authors for this book are staff members or litigators for Americans United for Life.

7. See, for example, Greg D. Adams, "Abortion: Evidence of an Issue Evolution," *American Journal of Political Science* 41 (July 1997): 718–737; Oran P. Smith, *The Rise of Baptist Republicanism* (New York: New York University Press, 1997).

8. Jerome L. Himmelstein, *To the Right: The Transformation of American Conservatism* (Berkeley: University of California Press, 1990); Greg Ivers, "Please God, Save this Honorable Court: The Emergence of the Conservative Religious Bar," in *The Interest Group Connection: Electioneering, Lobbying, and Policymaking in Washington*, ed. Paul S. Herrnson, Ronald G. Shaiko, and Clyde Wilcox (Chatham, N.J.: Chatham House, 1998), 289–301; James R. Kelly, "Beyond Compromise: *Casey*, Common Ground, and the Pro-Life Movement," in *Abortion Politics in American States*, ed. Mary C. Segers and Timothy A. Byrnes (Armonk, N.Y.: M. E. Sharpe, 1995), 205–224.

9. Faye Wattleton, "A Champion for Choice: Adapted from *Life on the Line*," *Ms.* (September/October 1996): 45–53.

10. S. Staggenborg, *The Pro-Choice Movement: Organization and Activism in the Abortion Conflict* (New York: Oxford University Press, 1991), 83–84.

11. Alissa Rubin, "Interest Groups and Abortion Politics in the Post-*Webster* Era," in *Interest Group Politics*, 3d ed., ed. Allan J. Cigler and Burdett A. Loomis (Washington, D.C.: CQ Press, 1991), 239–255.

12. Laura R. Woliver, "Social Movements and Abortion Law," in *Social Movements and American Political Institutions*, ed. Anne N. Costain and Andrew S. McFarland (Lanham, Md.: Rowman and Littlefield, 1998), 233–247.

13. Karen O'Connor, "Lobbying the Justices or Lobbying for Justice?" in *The Interest Group Connection: Electioneering, Lobbying, and Policymaking in Washington*, ed. Paul S. Herrnson, Ronald G. Shaiko, and Clyde Wilcox (Chatham, N.J.: Chatham House, 1998), 267–288; Patricia A. Sullivan and Steven R. Goldzwig, "Abortion and Undue Burdens: Justice Sandra Day O'Connor and Judicial Decision-Making," *Women and Politics* 16 (1996): 27–54.

14. Alan I. Abramowitz, "It's Abortion, Stupid: Policy Voting in the 1992 Presidential Election," *Journal of Politics* 57 (February 1995): 176–186. On the impact of two prochoice Political Action Committees, EMILY'S List (a Democratic PAC) and WISH List (a Republican PAC) on the election see also Frank J. Sorauf, "Adaptation and Innovation in Political Action Committees," in *Interest Group Politics*, 4th ed., ed. Allan J. Cigler and Burdett A. Loomis (Washington, D.C.: CQ Press, 1995), 178–181.

15. An equal protection argument could be made, therefore, to protect legal abortion. "Equal justice under law" would strongly defend legal abortion because it is a deeply valued principle in American law. A weakness in abortion politics now,

Graber explained, is that many privileged people, given this history of abortion before *Roe*, do not believe they or their daughters would actually lose the choice of abortion if abortion were recriminalized. Abortion would be quickly relegalized if the criminal statutes were uniformly applied, even to people of privilege. Mark A. Graber, *Rethinking Abortion: Equal Choice, the Constitution, and Reproductive Politics* (Princeton, N.J.: Princeton University Press, 1996); and J. C. Mohr, *Abortion in America: The Origins and Evolution of National Policy* (New York: Oxford University Press, 1978).

16. Laura R. Woliver, "Rhetoric and Symbols in American Abortion Politics," in *Abortion Politics: Public Policy in Cross-Cultural Perspective*, ed. Marianne Githens and Dorothy McBride Stetson (New York: Routledge, 1996), 5–28.

17. Steve Daley and Carol Jouzalities, "House Votes to Ease Welfare Cuts," *Chicago Tribune*, March 23, 1995; Paul Richter and Elizabeth Shogren, "Clinton, Dole Announce Competing Welfare Plans," *Los Angeles Times*, August 1, 1995.

18. Elizabeth Shogren, "Senate Rejects Family Cap in Welfare Reform Debate," *Los Angeles Times*, September 14, 1995; Linda Feldmann, "Lawmakers Clash over 'Family Caps,'" *Christian Science Monitor*, August 9, 1995; Jill Zuckman, "House Committee Approves Core of GOP's Welfare Plan," *Boston Globe*, March 9, 1995.

19. See, for example, Burdett A. Loomis, "A New Era: Groups and the Grass Roots," in *Interest Group Politics*, ed. Allan J. Cigler and Burdett A. Loomis (Washington, D.C.: CQ Press, 1983), 169–191; and James G. Gimpel, "Grassroots Organizations and Equilibrium Cycles in Group Mobilization and Access," in *The Interest Group Connection: Electioneering, Lobbying, and Policymaking in Washington*, ed. Paul S. Herrnson, Ronald G. Shaiko, and Clyde Wilcox (Chatham, N.J.: Chatham House, 1998), 100–115.

20. D. Friedman and D. McAdam, "Collective Identity and Activism: Networks, Choices, and the Life of a Social Movement," in *Frontiers in Social Movement Theory*, ed. A. D. Morris and C. McC. Mueller (New Haven, Conn.: Yale University Press, 1992), 156–173; J. R. Gusfield, "Social Movements and Social Change: Perspectives of Linearity and Fluidity," in *Research in Social Movements, Conflict, and Change*, ed. L. Kriesberg (Greenwich, Conn.: JAI Press, 1981), 317–339; Hank Johnston, Enrique Larana, and Joseph R. Gusfield, "Identities, Grievances, and New Social Movements," in *New Social Movements: From Ideology to Identity*, ed. Enrique Larana, Hank Johnston, and Joseph R. Gusfield (Philadelphia: Temple University Press, 1994), 3–35; Doug McAdam, John D. McCarthy, and Mayer N. Zald, "Introduction: Opportunities, Mobilizing Structures, and Framing Processes—Toward a Synthetic, Comparative Perspective on Social Movements," in Doug McAdam, John D. McCarthy, and Mayer N. Zald, *Comparative Perspectives on Social Movements* (Cambridge: Cambridge University Press, 1996), 1–20; Carol Mueller, "Conflict Networks and the Origins of Women's Liberation," in *New Social Movements: From Ideology to Identity*, ed. Enrique Larana, Hank Johnston, and Joseph R. Gusfield (Philadelphia: Temple University Press, 1994), 234–263; Laura R. Woliver, "Mobilizing and Sustaining Grassroots Dissent," *The Journal of Social Issues* 52 (Spring 1996): 139–151.

21. E. E. Schattschneider, *The Semi-Sovereign People* (New York: Holt, Rinehart, and Winston, 1960), 2.

22. Kevin Hula, "Rounding up the Usual Suspects: Forging Interest Group Coalitions in Washington," in *Interest Group Politics*, 4th ed., ed. Allan J. Cigler and Burdett A. Loomis (Washington, D.C.: CQ Press, 1995), 239–258; and Anne N. Costain, "Representing Women: The Transition from Social Movement to Interest Group," in *Women, Power, and Policy*, ed. Ellen Boneparth (New York: Pergamon Press, 1982), 19–37; and Costain, "The Struggle for a National Women's Lobby: Organizing a Diffuse Interest," *Western Political Quarterly* 33 (December 1980): 476–491.

23. "God Is Going Back to School," Columbia [South Carolina] Sidewalk Counseling, Press Release, September 2, 1997.
24. See Jim Risen and Judy Thomas, *Wrath of Angels: The American Abortion War* (New York: HarperCollins, 1998).
25. The issue of the impact of new reproductive technologies, and the very new potential social impact of cloning, is a complex and lengthy topic. Regarding modern medicine and pregnancy, see Celeste M. Condit, *Decoding Abortion Rhetoric: The Communication of Social Change* (Urbana: University of Illinois Press, 1990); Janet Gallagher, "Fetus as Patient," in *Reproductive Laws for the 1990s*, ed. Nadine Taub and Sherrill Cohen (Clifton, N.J.: Humana Press, 1989), 185–235; Ann Oakley, "From Walking Wombs to Test-Tube Babies," in *Reproductive Technologies: Gender, Motherhood, and Medicine*, ed. Michelle Stanworth (Minneapolis: University of Minnesota Press, 1987), 36–56; Barbara Katz Rothman, *The Tentative Pregnancy: Prenatal Diagnosis and the Future of Motherhood* (New York: Viking, 1986); Laura R. Woliver, "The Deflective Power of New Reproductive Technologies: The Impact on Women," *Women and Politics* 9 (1989): 17–47; Laura R. Woliver, "The Influence of Technology on the Politics of Motherhood: An Overview of the United States," *Women's Studies International Forum* 14 (1991): 479–490; Laura R. Woliver, "Reproductive Technologies, Surrogacy Arrangements, and the Politics of Motherhood," in *Mothers in Law: Feminist Theory and the Legal Regulation of Motherhood*, ed. Martha Albertson Fineman and Isabel Karpin (New York: Columbia University Press, 1995), 346–359; Robert H. Blank, *Rationing Medicine* (New York: Columbia University Press, 1988), 148; see also Martha A. Field, "Controlling the Woman to Protect the Fetus," *Law, Medicine, and Health Care* 17 (1989): 114–129.
26. The recent birth of the McCaughey septuplets in Iowa highlights the given nature of legal abortion within the fertility clinics. This couple chose not to selectively reduce the many embryos resulting from the fertility drugs administered to the mother.
27. See, for instance, Patricia Bayer Richard, "Alternative Abortion Policies: What Are the Health Consequences?" *Social Science Quarterly* 70 (1989): 941–955.
28. Tamar Lewin, "New Procedure Makes Abortion Possible Days after Conception," *New York Times*, December 21, 1997.
29. Ibid.
30. For corroboration: Timothy A. Byrnes, "Conclusion: The Future of Abortion Politics in American States," in *Abortion Politics in American States*, ed. Mary C. Segers and Timothy A. Byrnes (Armonk, N.Y.: M. E. Sharpe, 1995), 246–264; Glen A. Halva-Neubauer, "The States after *Roe*—No 'Paper Tigers,' " in *Understanding the New Politics of Abortion*, ed. Malcolm L Goggin (Newbury Park, Calif.: Sage, 1993); Glen A. Halva-Neubauer, Raymond Tatalovich, and Byron W. Daynes, "Locating Abortion Clinics: Aggregate Data and Case Study Approaches to the Implementation Process" (Paper delivered at the Annual Meeting of the American Political Science Association, Washington, D.C., September 2–5, 1993); Mary C. Segers and Timothy A. Byrnes, "Introduction: Abortion Politics in American States," in *Abortion Politics in America States*, ed. Mary C. Segers and Timothy A. Byrnes (Armonk, N.Y.: M. E. Sharpe, 1995), 1–15.
31. Cigler and Loomis, "Contemporary Interest Group Politics: More Than 'More of the Same,' " in *Interest Group Politics*, 4th ed., Allan J. Cigler and Burdett A. Loomis (Washington, D.C.: CQ Press, 1995), 402–403.
32. Karen O'Connor, *Neutral Ground? Abortion Politics in an Age of Absolutes* (Boulder, Colo.: Westview Press, 1996).
33. Laurence Tribe, *Abortion: The Clash of Absolutes* (New York: Norton, 1990).

16

Lobbying the Public: All-Directional Advocacy
William P. Browne

The public has always been a target of lobbying efforts in American politics. Indeed, some of our most profound political theory—*The Federalist Papers*—first took shape as attempts to sway New Yorkers to support ratification of the Constitution. Yet lobbying the people is a difficult task. It is often very expensive, and it is an indirect route to influence. That is, an interest must convince the public (or a fair chunk of the public) that something needs to be done, and the public must then convince its representatives of the idea. Many are the obstacles waiting to upset that applecart. Still, when the public is aroused, or a part of it is articulate in approaching the government, it can be a most powerful force.

In this chapter William Browne examines some of the history of lobbying the public, along with its growing contemporary role in American politics. Browne develops the notion of *all-directional* lobbying. That is, many interests are not content just to play the inside game of private influence. Rather, they seek to define issues in the public arena and convince the public that they agree. Browne concludes that public interest groups and moralistic positions can benefit from such all-directional lobbying, and notes that corporate interests often have considerable resources to affect the debate. Whatever the outcome, lobbying has changed, moving far beyond the serpentine corridors of Capitol Hill.

T his chapter is about the hows and whys of lobbying the public. One reason for such lobbying should be apparent. Lobbyists target the public in order to reach policy makers, albeit indirectly: Messages beget messages, from lobbies to people to pols. Another reason is that organized interests seek to bypass policy makers by creating strong public sentiment. In the face of prevailing opinion, officials sometimes feel so compelled to act that legislation or regulation is bound to result, and with a certain content. Public opinion "messages" sometimes increase policy-maker deliberation, as citizens' voices are taken into account. Conversely, the creation of overwhelming public sentiment may reduce, even elimi-

Jane J. Mansbridge needs to be thanked for pushing for this revised title. Burdett Loomis needs to be thanked as well for his solid suggestions.

nate, deliberation among officials and between them and lobbyists. As a result, policy making looks more to be simple rubber stamping rather than thoughtful negotiating. As a member of Congress once explained, "You can frequently tell what the exact content of a yet unintroduced bill will be just by looking at a story in the news. If it's dramatically persuasive, Congress will bend over backwards."[1] And interests work hard to tell that kind of story.

This chapter also emphasizes the complexities of lobbying. Lobbying never was as simple as an advocate merely meeting with a public official and leaving her informed as to policy needs and consequences. That personalized "contact game" went on and still goes on, of course. It often just goes on in conjunction with other things, such as lobbying the public.[2] There have long been other lobbying tasks that also need to be used for an organized interest to gain attention, have influence, win on the desired issue, and achieve some position of permanence in politics. To lobby most successfully quite often means lobbying in all directions.[3] Or at least being able to engage in all-directional or multiple-target advocacy. That and the linkage between targeting the public and lobbying in its other forms will be explained in the following pages.

Why Lobbying Is So Difficult

Lobbying is difficult? Most will ask, "why"? What can be so difficult about taking a legislator to lunch and to a ball game? This is a typical reaction, and the reason for both the puzzled question and the often blank response is simple. As a job, lobbying is highly subject to stereotyping and misunderstanding. In addition, it is extremely difficult to explain. Lobbying includes many activities, and is far more than wining and dining a legislator.[4]

There are at least two reasons why lobbying is so difficult, both to do and to explain. The first reason is quite understandable. Lobbying is basically persuasion, and anyone who has tried being persuasive knows how tedious it can be and, especially, how hard it is to explain to others all that went into the process.

A second complication results from the structural, or institutional, features of American politics. As the Constitution's framers argued, American government was not designed to make quick decisions.[5] Quite the contrary. Ordinarily, public policy decisions were to be reached with great difficulty. Nobody who mattered and who won in the debate over the design of America's governmental structure wanted a president or a congressional majority to dictate policy to the rest of society.

This latter, structural problem is the emphasis in this chapter because it addresses why persuasion in American politics is so extremely trying. Public policy making was never easy; and it grew continually harder over time because American politics has been plagued by a complex and changing set of rules. The process is comparatively tedious as well, compared to other governments around the world. American policy makers have to contend with four related characteristics of U.S. politics: It is open, or permeable; it is democratic; it is representative; and it is republican. All of these conditions have affected lobbying and how it is best done.

Those characteristics mean that political participation in America has few boundaries. Any interest can petition any policy maker on nearly any concern, in nearly any way. In part, this openness depends on almost unrestricted constitutional guarantees of freedoms of speech and assembly, as well as the right to petition government. For all practical purposes, because of open entry, policy makers have to listen to any even halfway credible complainant. Because of representative values and electoral expectations officials listen especially to the ones with whom they find some degree of political kinship.

Republican forms of government set substantial voting rights for citizens, especially in electing policy makers. Democratic governments assign all participatory rights to nearly every citizen, regardless of social or economic status. And American government provides relatively small groups of people from distinct geographic regions, through states and districts, the chance to elect their own official representatives to legislatures. Separate governing powers with numerous checks and balances make that representative process even more permeable: American citizens have a wealth of options over whom to contact, persuade, and lobby. Legislators, chief executives, courts, and countless administrators are all fair game, and those in each of these institutions can be in one of several centers of decision making. Lobbyists can then select whomever is likely to listen and able to do something for a unique interest.

Why does this make policy making in American government so difficult? First, numerous decision makers each having their own responsibilities need to act in concert for public policy to emerge.[6] Any member of Congress can start an issue advancing, but eventually a majority of both houses have to agree, along with the president. Jumping through these legislative hoops entails exacting and time-consuming negotiation and compromise, often to no avail. Of course some lobbyists may well *desire* that result of no action. On other occasions and issues, they will not like it at all.

A second reason adds at least as much to the burden of governing. The complexity of American government encourages almost any interest from any part of the public to form.[7] No one will treat most organizers in harshly punitive ways. Almost any organized interest gets a hearing for two reasons. First, there are many policy-maker options available to lobby as targets. Second, there is nearly an assurance that public officials from different regions of the country and with different responsibilities have diverse policy values and preferences. So lobbies look for those who come from places most likely to support their ideas as well as they look for

merely iconoclastic individuals who may share their values. That can be
seen in the controversy over private property rights and environmental
protection. Members of Congress from the Southwest responded to interests who wished to protect private property use while legislators from
the rest of the country were still nearly all taking a proenvironmental position. The federal government already owned and controlled so much
western land that further limiting private land use was offensive, it was
believed by those from the West. There are all kinds of people who value
all kinds of things serving in policy-making positions. There may well be
within the Congress a potential champion for almost every interest.[8]

Few public officials want to offend or further arouse potential supporters, which might cut into their electoral base. With so many interests
freely coming to Washington and the state capitals, compromise and negotiation are far harder than they would be if only even a great many
politicians ruled together. But they do not. In the American political experience, the public in all its many sizes, shapes, and factions does much
of the ruling. Public officials frequently only sort out which interests will
get what, or otherwise determine what can be done with little public irri-
tation. With so many factions involved in the political process, keeping
conflicts to a minimum is no easy feat. In the end, lobbying in a crowded
political arena that includes lots of policy makers and organized interests
is definitely hard.

Using All-Directional Lobbying to Make Things Easier

To adequately answer the question of "What goes on and why?" in
the process of lobbying means to consider both the functions of lobbying
and the generic tasks of lobbying. It makes the greatest sense to consider
functions first, for they deal with the purposes of lobbying in a busy and
highly populated political arena. In discussing functional purpose, political scientists have long focused on gaining access to public officials as a
prelude to exercising influence. They tend to portray these components
of access and influence as a sequential process.[9]

Moreover, these scholars also tend to see winning access as an intimate dance between the seductive lobbyist and the seducible policy
maker. Campaign funds flow, as does information useful to pending policy
options. In return, public officials bring the temptress into the chamber.

What this chapter will do is debunk that notion of sequence by demonstrating through some extended examples that there is both more to lobbying and less to it than access followed by influence. This dichotomy of
first dancing and later following through on the just-established relationship is too neat and tidy to reflect actual lobbying activities. Sometimes a
web of interrelated tasks are created that needs to be pulled together by a
lobby. At other times, it is only necessary to let widespread public sentiment drive the policy process. The organized interest merely accepts the

positive results. Moreover, lobbying in America has always been this way. The major change over time is that lobbies have refined their techniques, made better use of communications technologies, and subsequently become more able to change public opinion. Volumes have been written about what tasks to engage in to reach public officials and quite a bit has been written about what to do in order to influence other interests.[10] Yet an inventory of the tasks for reaching the public fails to exist, as does an analysis of such lobbying over time. Because scholars do not fully recognize what lobbyists do to reach the public, and because reaching the public is one common route to reaching the other targets, some important gaps exist in understanding how lobbying proceeds.

Compiling an inventory of tasks for lobbying the public requires two lists. The first covers the meaning of the public, or who is being mobilized for what reasons. The public at the local, grassroots level can be seen in three ways. Obviously, members and joiners of the interest group are part of the public. So, too, are those who share a public identity with that membership. For example, some of the antiabortion public of the 1990s belongs to the Christian Coalition, whereas many who also oppose abortion do not. To be the most persuasive and to maximize the number of calls and letters to Congress, organized interests try to reach more than just those who have joined. They want to show that their members are representative of others who likely share their concerns. The Sierra Club does not merely mobilize its own rather upscale members, because doing so would demonstrate only what a small segment of the population thinks. Rather, it solicits calls and letters of support from everyone the group can target who may share an environmentalist self-identity.

The public, though, is never composed only of members and ready sympathizers. Within the general public, lobbyists also try to reach those who never give much thought to policy issues surrounding the environment or other issues. And that, of course, includes most Americans. Lobbyists want to plant the question in the body politics' collective mind: What will happen to all of us if the environment is badly degraded? What about food? What about quality of life? Scary thoughts. Fear motivates heartily, and organized interests get much more policy attention if a previously uninvolved segment of society forcefully expresses its supportive fears.[11] Recognizing this, interests target citizens in general as well as selectively among joiners or those who hold a related issue position, but lobbying the public does not stop there.[12]

Lobbyists pay great attention to the select groups of opinion leaders who in turn may influence others.[13] The media have always been primary opinion-leader targets in lobbying the public. As Ben Page argued, media coverage engages public deliberation.[14] However, so do community leaders, business and labor elites, as well as entertainment and sports celebrities. When a music star such as Willie Nelson goes to the public to complain of the plight of financially stressed farmers and blames government for their conditions, policy attention comes easily if and when the other targeted directions of lobbying reinforce his message. Actor Christopher Reeves did the same for paralyzed individuals by testifying before Congress, an event covered by what seemed most of the world's press.

This brings forward the second list, an inventory of the generic tasks of public lobbying. Because organized interests target the public for different reasons and through different types of proponents, the specific tasks performed are many and varied, they depend on whether a lobbyist targets rank-and-file group members, television viewers, or those who prepare the nightly television news. The only limit to the number of exact options is the imagination and creativity of the lobbyists and the professionals they hire to assist their work. So there cannot be an exhaustive list of specifics.

Nonetheless, there are four common tasks in lobbying the public, many of which members of the public and even some policy makers fail to recognize. One common, even mundane, method is to advertise the worth of a cause or a product, such as milk as consumed by the healthy celebrities who end up in magazine ads with milk "mustaches." Glamorizing helps establish importance, especially when public policy is pending as it has been for dairy producers. Another generic task is planting news stories, which serves the needs of a production-oriented media. Related to this is the task of designing the planted story to attract first the media and then those who read or view it. The idea is to get each story maximum publicity, not just coverage. Alluding to a pending or possible crisis is a particularly effective way to do that. Also used are recently released and startling opinion polls, anecdotes about some terrible event in the central city, or particularly chilling statistics. Such things get prominent coverage and are almost always picked up by other media sources, such as the wire services.

Finally, the tasks of lobbying the public include the preparation of stories, ads, and fears that will actually reach some public target and *then* be passed on to policy makers. One lobbyist said, "Not all planted items bubble up, go that is from the viewer to the halls of Congress. Why? Because they create only short-term concern and then are too quickly forgotten, usually by the next morning." The next task, as a result, is designing and often redesigning complex public messages that stay in front of people, retain a modestly lasting impact, and periodically recur. Getting policy attention thus merges with the function of keeping it, or with reinforcement. Another lobbyist went on, "It's not enough that some folks get poisoned by unsanitary ground beef. The idea is to show over time by several examples that this happens over and over." When recurrence happens, public officials respond as expected. Messages from lobbies to people to pols roll in, in droves. Lobbies also take advantage of existing news stories in much the same way. They add to them, highlight them, send them around, call attention to their meaning, put a particular spin of their

own on the story, and more generally keep the reference alive. The results are the same: Messages to policy makers flow in abundance and interest in the issue escalates. That is, if things go as the lobby intended.

The Farm Bureau Pioneers Modern Public Lobbying

It makes the greatest sense to begin the examples by looking at one
of the most venerable and referenced interest groups in the nation: the
American Farm Bureau Federation. The Farm Bureau became esteemed
not so much for its controversial issues but for the way it succeeded on
those issues. The group pioneered modern public lobbying through direct
mobilization of farmers. In doing so, the Farm Bureau demonstrated that
chasing access and securing influence go hand in hand, not in sequence.
An insightful case study showed most clearly the problems of distinguishing between winning access and having influence. Mark Hansen demonstrated how, as a mass membership group, the Farm Bureau broke new
ground by recruiting individual farmers for a national organization.[15]

The Farm Bureau both sought farmer opinions and kept its members knowledgeable about Washington politics. By 1921, members of
Congress were aware of this feat to the point of becoming uncomfortable
and even angry that those back home knew, in some detail, what individual officials were doing, or not doing, in addressing the looming economic depression in agriculture. Particularly grating were tales in which
legislative leaders ignored farm problems and in which rank-and-file congressional members followed those leaders rather than fought for constituent needs.

When some congressional members from farm states seemed unwilling to support Farm Bureau proposals, its lobbyists showered them
with public opinion polls. If they still remained reluctant, Farm Bureau
lobbyists acted as liaisons, arranging a plethora of nasty constituent messages from home. Telegraphs were the group's best friends. Personal visits by farmers were arranged as well. Throughout the lobbying process,
Farm Bureau lobbyists wandered in and out of legislative offices in what
initially seemed a vain attempt to win influence and more than a few relatively minor bills, including regulation of packers, controls placed on
grain exchanges, and introduction of federal agricultural loans. Access and
influence blended together.

The Farm Bureau helped shape two further conditions needed to
continue its success and move for major policy change. First, members of
Congress from midwestern farm states had to be freed, or at least protected, from potential reprisals from their legislative and party leaders.
The Farm Bureau could promise electoral support independent of political parties, which were increasingly seen as failing to grapple with the
problems of everyday Americans.[16] In that sense, the Farm Bureau was organizing in an era of progressive politics in a fashion that characterized sev-

eral popular, people-style interests of the 1920s, including labor.[17] It was not merely institutions being represented, as with business and finance.

The second need was for the Farm Bureau, with its quite small southern-state following, to lobby those farm cooperatives that actually did represent and have favor with the bulk of cotton farmers from that one-crop region. This took years, finally coming about successfully in the 1930s only when the cotton economy, like the corn and wheat economies in the Midwest, collapsed economically from too much supply and too little demand. Southern congressional representatives, at that point, finally were influenced by the already familiar and well-known Farm Bureau lobbyists as members from both the Midwest and South coalesced to get economic relief. A major reform bill, the Agricultural Adjustment Act of 1933, passed.

This example demonstrates the idiosyncratic nature of influence and how winning access and influence go together rather than in sequence. For an interest such as the Farm Bureau, winning does not just happen because a group's lobbyists can suddenly get in all the right doors. Access need not indicate that everyone's listening, or even *anyone*. An interest's cause must also be taken seriously by those in decision-making positions, and being taken seriously by some at any one time does not mean all that much. The Anti-Saloon League, a near contemporary of the early Farm Bureau, proved that point. Representatives were well known to Congress, but prohibition came only after the League mobilized its more than one-half million supporters within the public.[18] Not all showed up in street protests, but all of them became ardent and vocal opponents of "demon rum."

It may be best to put aside the elusive concept of access. Think instead of lobbyists simultaneously performing three representational functions: talking with public officials, actually getting their attention in the discussions, and continually reinforcing the importance of the issues and policy proposals that are being sold as essential. In the reality of daily lobbying, all three go together.[19] All of the directions covered by an all-directional lobbying strategy can be seen in the Farm Bureau example: aiming at public officials, aiming at other organized interests, and, of course, aiming at the grassroots public. The midwestern farm lobby needed captive legislators, the southern cooperatives, and also interested farmers nationally. Without the attention of any of the three, desired public policy was unattainable. In some circumstances, winning influence with all three types of targets is integral to success. That is what creates a lobbying web of interrelated tasks.

Lobbying the Public Was Not New

Some of the dynamics of targeting the public and weaving that web are new, especially as modern communications technology and science are used that were not even imaginable in the early days of the Farm Bureau. This section looks at these changes as well as historical constants.[20] The effects of changing technology can be seen in the major push by food industries in the past several years to gradually win the ability to employ irradiation in protecting their products, most recently beef, from bacterial contamination. Members of Congress have been hesitant to address the issue for three reasons. First, consumers, it is believed, tend to equate irradiation with things like nuclear fallout, which they certainly fear. No one wants to glow in the dark or develop a malignant disease. In addition, a few active consumer protection interests oppose this food safety method and threaten to take their position to an already reluctant public. Second, doing so would castigate public officials who approved irradiation. Third, as another consumer issue, irradiation expenses do raise food prices. Congressional reluctance, therefore, is understandable.

To overcome that reluctance, an ad hoc coalition of food industries have done several things. They have used telephone rooms with large numbers of stations and automatic dialers where calls can be made in volume to both trade association members and to other retailers. Beyond the normal complement of paid spokespersons, industry executives and scientists personally extolled the virtues of irradiation and argued how unfair it was that some products, such as poultry and even pork, could be legally irradiated and beef could not. Calls also emphasized that sales of these irradiated but labeled products were not dropping, that little public ire was actually evident, and that overall food safety—and not incidentally liability insurance rates—would improve. The calls carefully explained that approval did not mean that all processors would *have* to irradiate or that all consumers would have to buy only irradiated meats. Actually few of either opted for such foods. Those in the industry who were telephoned thus had several specific messages that they more or less agreed to that could be passed on to public officials, all of which were crafted by lobbyist employees and public relations experts. Retail businesses also were given messages about useful Internet and Web site information to follow. Beef associations cooperated with equipment manufacturers, food processing interests, and retail groups. But the major players were irradiation users and manufacturers.

At the same time, the media was bombarded with assistance on news stories, few of which at first glance appeared helpful to the irradiation industry or even to be coming from industry sources. Story lines emphasized that recent health standard and inspection changes failed to solve the bacterial problem, that outbreaks of illness were very serious and even deadly, and that such outbreaks would indeed continue under existing but still recent law. Lists of critical public officials and knowledgeable experts in health and science were provided to help reporters formulate stories. More Web site information was marketed.

In the end, all of this boiled down to one simple message: Irradiation is the best answer. Two things resulted. First, irradiation obtained positive media coverage, inspiring fear of food contamination often in the high-profile venues of the front page and 6:00 o'clock news. Not only did most major, politically thorough newspapers such as the *Washington Post* cover this ground, so did others. Although not noted for exhaustive analysis, the popular *USA Today* allocated nearly three pages of coverage. Second, the public learned, through substance and repetition, about the failure of government and the profound need for policy change. Something different was needed for the present meat inspection system. Beyond what members of Congress gleaned from the media, their staffs were responding to numerous calls and letters from all sorts of people. By targeting specific segments of the public, such as fast food burger buyers, and by seeing to each of the four generic tasks of lobbying the public, the industry made its central point that the long-known usefulness of irradiation was not going to go away. A secondary point was made as well: that the public could be at least somewhat managed on the irradiation issue. That, at least in part, is why in December of 1997 authorization to irradiate beef was won.

None of this lobbying of the public is truly new, except in scale and scope. Mobilizing the public has evolved since the days of Farm Bureau ascendance in the 1920s and 1930s. The functional purposes of expanding attention, reinforcing issue presence, and continuing to meet with policy makers have been the same for both food industries of the 1990s and the depression era farm lobby. The food industry was not, after all, selling an undiscussed method of bacterial protection to an uninformed government. Public officials knew about irradiation technology and had been extensively lobbied on it for years. They just were slow in listening, granting approval piece by piece. It was not unlike the Farm Bureau winning minor legislation in 1921 and finally capitalizing on a major reform bill in 1933.

Tedious response by American government is nothing new, however, not even in the face of an impressive lobbying effort. Mathew Carey had found the same slowness almost 200 years earlier than had beef irradiation interests. And his response to it was highly reminiscent of the behavior of the food industry on irradiation. Carey was a wealthy Philadelphia manufacturer with several factories and was also a zealous advocate for an active federal policy to develop commerce and industry in the early 1800s.[21] He was much like the present day Bill Gates of Microsoft. Both preached around the country about the need for a new political order to both change government structure and to rewrite federal statutes in the face of changing technology. Carey, like Gates, also was his own lobbyist for a "new industry"—manufacturing. The great disadvantages faced by Carey were easily seen. First, the early United States was essentially a laissez-faire republic, with government not expected to do much. Second, Carey wanted to do what was scarcely popular in what was then a largely agrarian nation whose social values emphasized farming and land ownership, not factory work.[22] Agrarianism was indeed its own widely held social myth.[23] U.S. leaders such as Thomas Jefferson espoused its virtues and decried the vices of cities and industrial conditions.

Carey responded by lobbying in all directions, recognizing—as did Gates and the Farm Bureau—that Congress and official Washington were not inclined to listen. So Carey preached around the country, wrote newspaper stories, and visited a wide range of other manufacturers and possible investors. He helped several types of industries such as forges to organize trade associations that could further mobilize industrial leaders and later work together in a larger political coalition. Contacts with public officials multiplied, including notable members of Congress and officials of the administration. Carey just failed to win, but his lobbying strategy was impressive. He moved on all three target types, yet his ideas were so alien to American social values that he won little public support and, therefore, next to none among policy makers. Agrarianism was too potent. Conditions and times for Carey were wrong.

Fifty years later a similar lobbying effort gained momentum and eventually achieved far more success in its all-directional advocacy. This one too wanted federal development policy, but of a very different sort than to assist manufacturing. Its advocates found favor by emphasizing agrarianism and championing efforts to develop the West and help people settle there. At least as far back as President William H. Harrison's administration in 1840, finance capitalists from Wall Street and industry wanted governmental assistance. Grover Cleveland's biographer later said it best about these people: "The pressure at times seemed intolerable."[24] And it had been for decades. Lobbyists were everywhere—from banks, law firms, railroads, timber, lumber, agriculture, mining, and even education. All clogged the halls of the Capitol, offering bribes as well as disseminating information about America's expansion and development needs. High-pressure politics became commonplace in a way that was never true of Carey's era, when neither organized interests nor "interested" ideas were all that common.[25] Lobbying in general had truly evolved since the turn of the century, but this was an instance of little more than imitation of Carey's strategy.

There were several reasons for the change. Most important were immediate and obtainable business opportunities in settling the West. These were not going to be met by magic, as some stories of adventure suggest, or by scores of people deciding on their own to pack up and leave the East. Businesses could build things and serve an expanding population, if that population was encouraged to participate. Similar opportunities later were evident in the reconstruction of the South after the Civil War. Yet underlying the developers' problem in both instances was the lack of capital to finance expansion. The economic collapses of the late 1850s had simply left financiers with no ability to develop or raise enough money on their own. Lobbyists from different segments of industry could work together in a loose coalition, formulate comprehensive plans for development and population settlement, and play the contact game among policy makers. But they could hardly win if the public failed to accept what they wanted, which was a great deal of support. Not only were public officials reluctant to invest without public acceptance, the developers themselves needed public participation—for labor, for consumers, for providing services, for moving to new places.[26] A comprehensive policy strategy was needed to develop what otherwise might stay empty places and provide no profits on investments.

As a consequence, finance capitalists spent as much energy in selling the frontier to the public as they did in lobbying federal officials. Even foreign immigrants were recruited. Those were far from easy feats.[27] Persuading people to leave the civilization of the eastern United States or their own foreign homelands in favor of a wild and isolated West, characterized by often terrible weather, many barely habitable climes such as mountains and deserts, and often unfriendly residents ranging from grizzly bears to hostile Native Americans was at best difficult. So development and settlement interests worked together and argued the patriotism of manifest destiny, or the predestined capture by Americans of the entire continent. And they played on the importance of furthering American agrarianism, property ownership, and Jeffersonian democracy.

Equally important, they marketed adventure, but not foolhardiness. No developer could have effectively used the slogan "Come West, lose your life." Rather, the story of the West became one of glamour and opportunity. And flyers, posters, stump speakers, and news stories were all created and planted to tell that story. Even dime-paper novelists, as the trash journalists of the nineteenth century were known, were recruited and even funded to write about popular themes such as beauty, independence in the West, and heroic frontier figures, such as predominately contrived western stars such as Wyatt Earp and Buffalo Bill: They were that era's Willie Nelson.

As lobbying simultaneously addressed policy-maker contacts, attention getting, and reinforcement of the importance of winning the West, public policy changed considerably. Much of the laissez-faire notion of federal government merely disappeared as policy makers were constantly pressed to do more. This was an institutional revolution. A plethora of odd policies passed, things that Americans of the time had not expected but came to easily cherish. Mining and lumbering were allowed on federally appropriated lands. The railroads were given other public lands and so were homesteaders. Agricultural and technical education was provided for rural areas. Technology to develop farming was established in what later in the century became the very active U.S. Department of Agriculture.[28] Why did policy makers respond so radically? At least in part they did so because favored treatment for development interests was combined with broad appeal as well as a bit of real largess for citizens. For better or worse, the public came to see western development as good for everyone, except perhaps for hostile Native Americans. And so too did public officials and multiple private interests.

The result was that all-directional lobbying and its public emphasis became thoroughly institutionalized in the policy process by at least the middle of the nineteenth century. What Carey had failed at became conventional politics, all because the new message was far better developed as consistent with American social values and social myths. Carey's had not been well tailored at all. What was going on with development and settlement policy also was setting the stage for the more pioneering public lobbying of interest groups such as the Farm Bureau in the 1920s. Although the Farm Bureau pioneered success for a peoples' lobby, it was only extending the tactical efforts of development and settlement interests and institutions. Only the technologies used by the Farm Bureau were truly new.

Continuing Evolution in Lobbying the Public

The evolution in the scale and scope of lobbying the public needs more attention. There have been numerous constants over time, but changes in both targeting the public and in influencing the public are important ones, even if not all that dramatic in comparison to the immensity of winning the West. Mathew Carey lost and development and settlement interests won at public policy despite similar strategies and a shared goal of nation building. Carey undoubtedly did less lobbying but, more important, he also worked the wrong side of strongly held public beliefs. The public could be persuaded when lobbyists played on their rather deeply held social values, as with agrarianism and Jeffersonian democracy. But to challenge these same values in favor of something else such as manufacturing and industrialization was hardly publicly marketable.

New techniques and technologies have changed lobbying, but the changes go beyond this. No question, there are better means today for reaching citizens: computer networks, more specialized magazines and news outlets, and far more sophisticated knowledge of winning at public relations. With the advent of personal computers and other technologies, organized interests are more capable and their staffs more skilled and more professional. The combined result has been that modern lobbying seems able to alter or create public beliefs rather than merely build on existing and often mythic ones. Carey could not change basic sentiments, nor did western business interests even try. The evolution of skills and technology now encourages nearly every modern interest, no matter its cause, to go to the public and engage in all-directional advocacy in order to win and keep policy makers' attention. And some feel that they can go to the public with ideas that people would otherwise not agree with. One member of Congress commented on this difference: "Everything about the public appears up for grabs: their likes, their dislikes, their cultural perspective, and even their religion. Personal values bounce dramatically." That member appears to be mostly correct, but not entirely so.

The ability to foster emerging public beliefs and values has been a fact of political life for the past quarter century. Several advocacy examples underscore how substantially this people-based politics now matters for public policy. The success of environmental lobbyists is a good place to begin because their public lobbying started to succeed quite early in this modern period. And environmental policy successes have been dramatic.[29]

How and why? Environmentalism and protection of the natural ecology were alien concepts at mid-century, and self-proclaimed environmentalists were far from mainstream in their values. Yet inroads to the public were nonetheless made as ecologists generated controversies by lobbying within other types of groups. Conservation groups were plentiful that championed interests in hiking, traveling, birding, shooting, hunting, fishing, and trapping. Such groups as the Audubon Society and the National Wildlife Federation (NWF) were quite prominent in society and certainly interested in long-term protection of the resources they used.[30] Their activists, moreover, were ready to read Rachel Carson's *Silent Spring*[31] and the books of other authors that traced habitat degradation.

Conservationists also began to acknowledge a flaw in their own policy recommendations, which were to release and plant more game and fish as well as develop more sites for recreation. Despite considerable and costly efforts by both federal and state governments, most natural resources still remained in decline as Carson demonstrated. Sportspeople became good public lobbying targets for environmentalists for that reason. And those are the people that environmentalists first lobbied and with whom they initially found some favor. It worked because ecologists always addressed the implications of their emerging science to sport and recreation issues. With continued cultivation over the years, conservation interests and environmental interests each gradually incorporated the goals of the other.

Public officials, though, ignored the shift even as old and friendly conservation lobbyists took them these recent and evolving messages.[32] Environmental protection was just too costly for policy makers for most to like it. Businesses were likely to be hurt, and jobs were likely to be lost. Compliance with regulations was excessively expensive in comparison to, for example, building fishing ponds and releasing fish. Those attitudes needed countering. Once again, although still lobbying Washington, environmental advocates targeted the public to do the countering, at least a second segment of it.

Although much of the environmental rhetoric seemed like scientific verbiage and so was boring to the general public, there was once again another likely starting point within the public. The emphasis was on schools.

Children were targeted through their elementary schoolteachers as part of a truly all-directional strategy. Teachers were better educated than the general public and they usually taught some science in elementary grades. Teachers also needed entertaining instructional materials, especially free or at least inexpensive ones. So the old-line conservation groups began to publish and distribute materials such as NWF's *Ranger Rick* magazine, that was a combination story book and informational newsletter. Of course these materials and the ensuing positive comments of children went home to parents. Kids got excited about saving the planet.

As attention and social recognition increased, such tactics were expanded. It became obvious to environmental interests that what they had discovered by floundering with public sentiment now should be more strategically focused. Teachers were provided materials for their own continuing educations, both academically and in professional association seminars. Issues were developed into projects to involve children. Films were made, with dramatic and often frightening footage of environmental degradation. Model curricula were designed and distributed. Requests for information were encouraged and quickly processed. Data was collected. Opinion polls were taken. Local activists were asked to go to schools and help teachers with special presentations. The media was encouraged to cover and report on environmental projects from their own local schools, which personalized what were otherwise "boring" science stories. As one former lobbyist laughed, "We wanted the public to concentrate on Johnny and Susie rather than on public horrors. Then the kids could tell the message to reporters and plant ideas."

In a steady progression, issue education moved from the elementary-school level, to secondary schools, to colleges and universities, even more to parents, and then to the general public. Along the line, as lobbying webs came together, the intense interests of the national media developed. In a sense the media followed the public's fears. As the contagion continued, regular people and reporters learned to talk in practical terms about environmental ideas and problems, about Rachel Carson. A diverse social movement of more than just organized groups resulted.[33] At the same time, intensively lobbied policy makers listened and most gradually began to accept the costs of environmental protection. Local governments, businesses, and eventually farming were regulated even as most policy makers continued to dislike the high costs of clean air, clean water, endangered species, and the like. But even hostile officials had little choice in the face of altered public beliefs.[34] Environmental and conservation interests continued to lobby the general public as well as media opinion leaders too intently for policy makers to neglect their wishes.

The specific approach of the environmentalists was idiosyncratic; but similarities were shared with other modern lobbying efforts that came together. Three of them gained substantial and widespread public attention in the late 1970s and early 1980s: the Religious Right, reformists who wanted limits on campaign contributions, and antitax advocates. Each of these interests in their own ways tapped into media coverage by issuing outrageous but believable charges of political abuse. Christians complained of moral decline, political reformists decried political corruption, and the antitax groups charged substantial waste in government operations. These were messages that large percentages of the public could easily comprehend, become familiar with, relate to, respect, and see as offering appropriate public policy responses. They had just not thought much about them before.

Until the Religious Right created its own very popular media outlets—particularly through television—politicians paid little or no attention.[35] The same neglect of political reformists was evident until interest groups such as Common Cause proved unusually astute at getting stories in print and then on the national airwaves.[36] Antitax groups tended to be small and far more local; it was widely believed that they were more politically isolated as well. Yet they generated noisy and contentious meetings throughout the nation. These meetings received considerable local media attention, then led to a spate of national stories, and finally convinced numerous more prestigious and mainstream political entrepreneurs to join the antitax movement.

Public attention on the part of all three types of interests was sustained through repeated charges. Of course public officials opened their doors and many even actively championed morality, reform, and tax limitation agendas. The groups then kept doors open using personal computer interaction and lots of continued grassroots mobilization. "In the cases you mentioned," one very prominent policy maker said, "I discounted their importance because they weren't typical bread-and-butter matters. Boy was I wrong, but I've since jumped on board on all three."

As with the environment, these three sets of interests once again represented issues that were quite believable, even socially nice. But each nonetheless was still thought to be more than what would grab and hold political attention. Those who held that opinion were wrong in the extreme as each set of advocates converted its own large segments of the public. In the process, all three interests changed American politics considerably by adding newly significant issues. Taxes are now bad, abortion is a moral and political dilemma, and campaign financing reform will not go away.

Was all this issue education or was it merely putting a familiar and favorable face—or a spin—on things that the public understood quite well and valued? It appears to be a little of both, which is why that earlier mentioned congressional member who saw all public values as "up for grabs" was not entirely correct. As for whether public relations education or existing public familiarity matters most, veteran Washington lobbyists frequently brought up the unexpected but hard-won prominence of gay and lesbian advocates. "Now that's really a bad cause," said one, "but they won massive public attention by the spin placed on their demands." How? Very simply these activists did not try to sell the public on homosexuality.

Rather, by using elaborate electronic and person-to-person communications networks, they marketed human rights—a familiar and time-honored American theme. The lobbyist went on, "Homosexuals boldly grabbed the public's focus by talking about and planting stories about violations of simple human decency. When they did that they became of undeniable political significance, both to the public and at the same time to the pols."

The use of existing public values by lobbyists rather than the creation of new public wants can be seen in a mid-1990s effort to reduce the size of several state deer herds. Farm interest groups and insurance companies undertook what was potentially a very messy and controversial cause. After all, conservation groups had for years worked diligently to see deer herds expand. Moreover, the general public had been conditioned to see plentiful deer herds as both aesthetically and environmentally pleasing.

In the face of such obstacles, advocates took their case directly to the public. Farm and insurance industries sought to redefine what they wanted, and in so doing neutralize hostile reactions. Laid out was a carefully articulated policy goal: reduction of deer herds in selected areas where the animals exceeded ideal populations and led to high farm and insurance losses. Only some states with high deer populations were targeted. Then, with equal care, the economic and personal damages of too many deer were emphasized. Automobile accidents and repair costs were soaring, it was reported. Insurance costs were greatly increasing as a result. Human lives and limbs were being lost in more and more driving accidents. All that was presented very directly as news with dramatic footage. Farm financial losses were shown as staggering. Some farmers told on camera how they loved deer but had such high losses that family futures were threatened. Almost anyone could relate to these problems.

And plentiful opportunities were carefully crafted to most effectively bring these arguments forward. First, farm and insurance lobbyists sought to get high-profile editorial coverage from major state radio, television, and newspaper sources. Second, these advocates then sought headline coverage in the same places. When public opinion leaders were already talking about the well-publicized problems, only then were local and regional media targeted. Even in prime hunting locations, coverage was abundant, one-sided, and well spun. Few citizens were angered. Suddenly, once reluctant state legislators were more than happy to discuss herd reduction plans. The difference between this web and the one spun twenty years earlier by environmental interests was that deer-herd reduction was developed with great attention to strategic planning. At the onset and deep into the policy process, environmentalists groped for attention more than they planned for it in exact ways. The difference reflects increasing confidence by various interests in now making lobbying the public pay off. It is now more conventional strategy.

Lobbying the public, then, is not a last-ditch struggle of desperate interests. Any organized interest can do it and most will try. Such lobbying has become a means for an ever-widening range of organized interests to take their demands and place them in the context of what the public already values, such as plentiful food and safe highways. Certainly there exists considerable room for simple public manipulation, even in promoting inaccuracies.[37] For much of the public, however, lobbying brings forward policy alternatives to people that they otherwise would not have considered. Yet they find these alternatives understandable if presented persuasively.[38] Public lobbying creates believability by highlighting the prospects for what seems sensible social and political change.[39] That seems to be a constant over the years that has not changed as radically as has the technology, the public relations skills, and the scale and the scope of public advocacy. As another lobbyist concluded, "Yeah, but you can't sell just anything. And really you never could."

Conclusion

The point of this chapter is simple. Normal, everyday Americans are part of the lobbying process. From business executives to small-town fundamentalist Christians, people both lobby themselves and are targets of lobbying. Often they lobby themselves after being targeted. Lobbying in America has always been too difficult and the political process too crowded for organized interests to give policy makers in smoke-filled rooms their total attention. American governments are politically open, democratic, and have a representative structure that encourages popular participation. There always is someone who occupies a political office who will eventually listen to nearly any interest.

To better control these crowded conditions, lobbyists have long sought to cover multiple targets from citizens to other organized interests. Such all-directional lobbying wins public supporters and works to get and keep lobbyists into the doors of those making decisions. Carey recognized that fundamental notion, and so did western developers, the Farm Bureau, and prohibition interests. Nearly 200 years after Carey, almost every lobby at least considers addressing the public as one of its advocacy tasks.

Despite this constant over time, there are some important changes in lobbying the public. Although one of the constants has been use of whatever media was most available in each political era, the vehicles for communication have evolved dramatically. Carey spoke personally to often small crowds; so did development interests that also sponsored dime novelists in the West. The latter, however, got larger crowds than did Carey. The Farm Bureau mobilized telegraphs to Congress, and multiple interests have lately became prominent by using television, the Internet, and e-mail.

An evolving revolution in electronic communications makes winning media attention and successfully using its appeal far more commonplace. Only a rare contemporary lobby fails to use available technology for mobilization purposes.

Yet, it is *not* simply more lobbying of the public in far better efficient and direct ways that has evolved. In the nineteenth century, lobbyists who were most successful only identified and manipulated widely held social myths such as agrarianism. Those who really wanted to change basic social values lost. Today's lobbyists rarely stop there. True, they nearly always look for favorable public values that they can use. Moreover, they link their own specific policy demands to those public values wherever they can, using new technology and new public relations skills to do so. Doing that creates what lobbyists like to call "good issues."

And that is precisely where the biggest change has entered into lobbying the public. More organized interests enthusiastically try to build a public recognition of policy options and alternatives that were previously not considered by everyday people or by media sources. Prestigious Washington lobbyists insist, accurately or not, that more than half of the daily news stories in the national media were planted by organized interests. Lobbyists tell people, as one veteran Washington advocate said, "See, here's what you believe. We do too. See what you actually face as problems? We can and will help you address them."

Has the shift toward influencing a broader range of public values changed anything about the distribution of American political power? Do new interests such as environmentalists matter more today? Or have business interests used their financial advantages to monopolize high-tech communications? Contrary positions exist on these questions.

One view is that businesses have regained the political upper hand because they can afford the best technologies and pay for the most public advocacy.[40] There is obviously some truth in that assertion. Businesses do buy great equipment and hire those with considerable skills. Yet, at the same time, other scholars as well as examples in this chapter emphasize that good government, moralistic, and public interest lobbies all have recently won considerable influence.[41] Their victories make sense because these are not poor and resourceless interests. Moreover, lobbying the public need not be tremendously expensive.

In the end, these contrasting views cannot be resolved without further study of lobbying the public and all-directional advocacy. For now, however, one explanation seems to hold: Whether business or reformist, no interest will likely win if it champions a bad issue that the public will not come to value because of existing citizen sentiments.[42] Businesses will lose on bad issues. Environmentalists and antiabortion advocates will win on inherently believable and persuasive issues that reflect social values. Technological superiority probably matters less than does the issue an organized interest wants to pursue.

Notes

1. Quotes in this chapter come from personal interviews by the author. The sources for these interviews were assured anonymity, and thus no names are used. Those interviewed serve as the basis for this chapter.

2. Kay Lehman Schlozman and John T. Tierney explain that most surveyed interests (75 percent) do most things (twenty of twenty-seven tasks). See their *Organized Interests and American Democracy* (New York: Harper and Row, 1986), 149–152.

3. William P. Browne, *Groups, Interests, and U.S. Public Policy* (Washington, D.C.: Georgetown University Press, 1998). The ideas in this chapter are taken from that research.

4. Alan Rosenthal, *The Third House: Lobbyists and Lobbying in the States* (Washington D.C.: CQ Press, 1993).

5. James Madison, *The Federalist Papers*.

6. Kenneth J. Shepsle, "The Changing Textbook Congress," in *Can the Government Govern?* ed. John E. Chubb and Paul E. Peterson (Washington, D.C.: Brookings Institution, 1989), 238–266.

7. James T. Bonnen, William P. Browne, and David B. Schweikhardt, "Further Observations on the Changing Nature of National Agricultural Decision Processes, 1946–95," *Agricultural History* 70 (Spring 1996): 130–152.

8. Susan Webb Hammond, "Congressional Caucuses in the Policy Process," in *Congress Reconsidered*, 4th ed., ed. Lawrence C. Dodd and Bruce I. Oppenheimer (Washington, D.C.: CQ Press, 1989), 351–371; Christine A. DeGregorio, *Networks of Champions: Leadership, Access, and Advocacy in the U.S. House of Representatives* (Ann Arbor: University of Michigan Press, 1997).

9. Lester W. Milbrath epitomizes this view; see his *The Washington Lobbyists* (Chicago: Rand McNally, 1963), 297–304.

10. An excellent compendium is Rosenthal, *The Third House*.

11. Stephen E. Frantzich, *Write Your Congressman: Constituent Communications and Representation* (New York: Praeger, 1986), 66.

12. L. Harmon Zeigler and G. Wayne Peak realized this early on in *Interest Group Politics in American Society*, 2d ed. (Englewood Cliffs, N.J.: Prentice-Hall, 1972), 125.

13. Elihu Katz and Paul F. Lazarsfeld, *Personal Influence* (Glencoe, Ill.: Free Press, 1955).

14. Benjamin I. Page, *Who Deliberates? Mass Media in Modern Democracy* (Chicago: University of Chicago Press, 1996).

15. John Mark Hansen, *Gaining Access: Congress and the Farm Lobby, 1919–1981* (Chicago: University of Chicago Press, 1991).

16. Elisabeth S. Clemens, *The People's Lobby: Organizational Innovations and the Rise of Interest Group Politics in the United States, 1890–1925* (Chicago: University of Chicago Press, 1997).

17. Hansen, *Gaining Access*, 27.

18. Peter H. Odegard, *Pressure Politics: The Story of the Anti-Saloon League* (New York: Columbia University Press, 1928).

19. Frank R. Baumgartner and Beth L. Leech reinforce this view. See *Basic Interests: The Importance of Groups in Politics and in Political Science* (Princeton, N.J.: Princeton University Press, 1998).

20. Allan J. Cigler and Burdett A. Loomis, "Contemporary Interest Group Politics: More Than 'More of the Same,'" in *Interest Group Politics*, 4th ed., ed. Allan J. Cigler and Burdett A. Loomis (Washington, D.C.: CQ Press, 1995), 394–398.

21. Kenneth W. Rowe, *Mathew Carey: A Study in American Economic Development* (Baltimore: John Hopkins University Press, 1993).
22. Ross B. Talbot and Don F. Hadwiger, *The Policy Process in American Agriculture* (San Francisco: Chandler, 1968), 31–32.
23. John M. Brewster, "The Relevance of the Jeffersonian Dream Today," in *Land Use Policy and Problems in the United States*, ed. H. W. Ottoson (Lincoln: University of Nebraska Press, 1963), 86–136.
24. Matthew Josephson, *The Politicos: 1865–1896* (New York: Harcourt, Brace and World, 1963), 531.
25. James Sterling Young, *The Washington Community, 1800–1828* (New York: Harcourt, Brace and World, 1966). Government was seen as sterile without lobbyists.
26. Willard W. Cochrane, *The Development of American Agriculture: A Historical Analysis* (Minneapolis: University of Minnesota Press, 1979), 78–89.
27. Murray R. Benedict, *Farm Policies of the United States, 1790–1950* (New York: Twentieth Century Fund, 1950).
28. Ibid.
29. Robert C. Paehlke, *Environmentalism and the Future of Progressive Politics* (New Haven, Conn.: Yale University Press, 1989), 14–22; Christopher J. Bosso, "Adaptation and Change in the Environmental Movement," in *Interest Group Politics*, 3d ed., ed. Allan J. Cigler and Burdett A. Loomis (Washington, D.C.: CQ Press, 1991), 151–176.
30. Carroll Pursell, ed., *From Conservation to Ecology: The Development of Environmental Concern* (New York: Crowell, 1973); Bob Pepperman Taylor, *Our Limits Transgressed: Environmental Political Thought in America* (Lawrence: University Press of Kansas, 1992), 51–80.
31. Rachel Carson, *Silent Spring* (Boston: Houghton-Mifflin, 1962).
32. J. Clarence Davies, III, and Barbara S. Davies, *The Politics of Pollution*, 2d ed. (Indianapolis: Pegasus, 1975).
33. Taylor, *Our Limits Transgressed.*
34. Michael E. Kraft and Norman J. Vig, "Environmental Policy from the 1970s to the 1990s: Continuity and Change," in *Environmental Policy in the 1990s*, 2d ed. (Washington, D.C.: CQ Press, 1994), 3–29.
35. Allen D. Hertzke, *Representing God in Washington: The Role of Religious Lobbies in the American Polity* (Knoxville: University of Tennessee Press, 1988), 44–93.
36. Andrew S. McFarland, *Common Cause: Lobbying in the Public Interest* (Chatham, N.J.: Chatham House, 1984); Lawrence S. Rothenburg, *Linking Citizens to Government: Interest Group Politics at Common Cause* (New York: Cambridge University Press, 1992).
37. It seems unlikely that lobbyists would lie to the public more than to policy makers. Credibility is still at stake. Getting caught is probable. John R. Wright, *Interest Groups and Congress: Lobbying Contributions and Influence* (Boston: Allyn and Bacon, 1996).
38. Jane J. Mansbridge, *Beyond Adversary Democracy* (Chicago: University of Chicago Press, 1983); and her "A Deliberative Theory of Interest Representation," in *The Politics of Interests: Interest Groups Transformed*, ed. Mark P. Petracca (Boulder, Colo.: Westview, 1992), 32–57.
39. Doris A. Graber, *Mass Media and American Politics* (Washington, D.C.: CQ Press, 1980), 148–150.
40. Darrell M. West and Burdett A. Loomis, *The Sound of Money: Voices of Influence in a High-Tech Age* (New York: W. W. Norton, 1998).
41. Jeffrey M. Berry, *The Interest Group Society*, 3d ed. (New York: Longman, 1997), 233–236.
42. Browne, *Groups, Interests, and U.S. Public Policy*, chaps. 7 and 8.

17

All in the Family? Interest Groups and Foreign Policy

Eric M. Uslaner

The 1996 election and its aftermath produced a host of allegations of foreign donations to the Clinton campaign and a high-profile congressional investigation into possible abuses. Although the investigation eventually fizzled, foreign interests' intervention into American politics had become a widely acknowledged possibility. Although the public might have been surprised by such special interest activities, veteran observers of Washington politics were shocked only by the brazen nature of some of the financial schemes, such as the laundering of contributions through Buddhist nuns. The intervention of foreign interests into American political life has existed as long as has our constitutional system—from the French and English in the eighteenth century to the Israelis and Greeks in more recent times.

Eric Uslaner uses ethnic groupings as one set of lenses to examine the attempts to bring foreign issues (and foreign policy issues) into American politics and policy making. Although he notes the continuing strength of pro-Israel groups, Uslaner notes the growing difficulty in separating "foreign" from "domestic" policy making and the declining possibility of making clear "moral" arguments on foreign policy decisions. Rather, the world has grown more complex, and with this complexity, lobbying by ethnic groups and foreign lobbies (and their American surrogates) has come to resemble most other attempts to exert influence. Unity among ethnic interests still counts, but generating that unity in a complex, interdependent world is no mean feat.

When we think of interest group politics, we generally focus on domestic policy. On foreign policy, the entire country is supposed to speak with a single voice. Policy is supposed to reflect a national interest

Support of the General Research Board, University of Maryland—College Park, is gratefully acknowledged, as is the assistance of Nalini Verma, Fred Augustyn, Rodger Payne, and Galen Wilkenson. The comments of Allan J. Cigler, Burdett A. Loomis, and George H. Quester are greatly appreciated, as is the assistance of Jeffrey H. Birnbaum of *Fortune* and Ted Clark of National Public Radio. Some of the data employed come from the Inter-University Consortium for Political and Social Research, which has no responsibility for any interpretations herein.

that has its roots in moral principles. After Iraq invaded Kuwait in 1990, Americans had a sustained argument about whether to get involved in the Gulf War. Some opponents said that the real reason the administration wanted to send troops to the Persian Gulf was to guarantee that Kuwaiti oil would continue to flow to American refineries. Was this somehow wrong? Would a debate over oil supplies be considered illegitimate if we were discussing the state of the economy?

Because the stakes of foreign policy are higher than those of domestic policy—the wrong decision in foreign policy could lead to a nuclear confrontation—we expect foreign policy decisions to be less subject to the whims of group pressure. Instead, we as a nation make decisions based on a common interest, which is more than the sum of the interests of different groups in the society. And it is an *American* interest that is primary. To most Americans, an interconnected world does not mean that we all have the same interests or values. So foreign policy should be made on the basis of principles—American principles. Americans should be primarily concerned with domestic issues and put American interests first when looking beyond our borders. American firms, even if they compete in the international marketplace, should also put the interests of their fellow citizens first. And outsiders—foreign firms and especially foreign governments—should keep their proper distance.

However, in recent years, there has been an explosion of lobbying by groups concerned with foreign policy, especially ethnic groups supporting their "mother countries." American Jews have long lobbied successfully on behalf of Israel and many groups have tried to copy the Jewish model. But this traditional model, relying on the moral claims that Jews made for Israel, no longer is the dominant one for ethnic groups. Supporters of Israel took the high ground as long as they could rest assured that they had a monopoly on moral arguments. Once they lost that monopoly, they began to act like any other interest group—rewarding their friends and punishing their enemies. They took an increasingly active role in raising money to back candidates for office. And the clear lines of distinction between American supporters of Israel and the Israeli government vanished. Foreign interests were now trying to affect American policy directly. In the case of Israel, they were not "buying influence." They did not need to, because American Jews had more money to spend than did Israelis. But, as other groups copied the model of pro-Israel lobbies, the nature of the debate changed.

Foreign policy interest groups began to look more and more like domestic groups, with one key difference: The fights among domestic interest groups were still all in the family of Americans. Now, it was unclear whether some groups were more loyal to their "mother country" than to the United States. And in some cases, especially where constituency groups were weak politically, foreign countries took a direct role in American domestic politics. In the 1996 presidential election, foreign interests allegedly made direct campaign contributions to the reelection campaign of President Bill Clinton. Some of these funds may have even come from the government of China, which was seeking to protect its favored trading status with the United States.

Many people worried that decisions that ought to be made on the basis of moral concerns—what should the role of America be in the world, especially when it is the only superpower—instead are now made through group conflict and campaign contributions. When does it become illegitimate for Jewish Americans to lobby on behalf of Israel or Cuban Americans *against* the Castro regime in Cuba or Chinese Americans to take sides between the "two Chinas" (the People's Republic and Taiwan)? If it is acceptable for Chinese Americans to lobby for China, why is it not acceptable for the Chinese to lobby for themselves? If the Chinese (or others) can appropriately exert pressure in Washington, should they be prohibited from influencing who gets sent to Washington?

And here is the dilemma underlying group conflict in American foreign policy. When an ethnic group is united, it can take the high ground. When American Jews were single-minded in their support for Israel and when Cuban Americans were united in their opposition to the Castro regime, both groups could make moral arguments. Israel was the beacon of light in the Middle East and Castro was the devil in Latin America. Neither group had substantial opposition. Arab Americans were decidedly weaker than American Jews and had fewer domestic allies and very little public support. The Castro regime had no supporters at all with any degree of political clout. Yet as divisions grew within both communities, it was more difficult to gain support outside one's own group for the cause. When you cannot be sure everyone is with you, you may feel compelled to use more confrontational strategies to win support. But how legitimate do others view these tactics and how successful can they be? In an April 1997 *New York Times*/CBS News survey, 45 percent of Americans said that they were bothered most by foreign government contributions to "buy influence," compared to 25 percent for American special interest groups and 21 percent for "wealthy people."[1]

Ethnic Groups in Foreign Policy

Among the most prominent—and long-standing—lobbies on foreign policy are those representing ethnic groups in the United States and their ties to the home country. Mohammed E. Ahrari has suggested four conditions for ethnic group success on foreign policy. First, the group must press for a policy in line with American strategic interests. Second, the group must be assimilated into American society, yet retain enough identification with the "old country" so that this foreign policy issue motivates people to take some political action. Groups that stand outside the mainstream of American life, Arab Americans for a complex of reasons discussed later and Mexicans because many are not citizens, cannot mobilize for political action. Third, a high level of political activity is required. Fourth, groups should be politically unified.[2] To Ahrari's list we add several additional criteria. The group's policies should be backed by the larger public. The group should be sufficiently numerous to wield political influence. Finally, the group must be seen as pursuing a legitimate interest. Speaking on behalf of one's ethnic group is acceptable so long as others do not think you have divided loyalties or somehow will profit from your lobbying efforts.

American Jews are distinctive in their ability to affect foreign policy. They have established the most prominent and best-endowed lobby in Washington by fulfilling each of the conditions for an influential group. In recent years, some conditions have not been met and the pro-Israel lobby is no longer the dominant force it once was. Its rival in Washington, the pro-Arab lobby, has remained weak because it has failed to meet any of the conditions.

The Israel and Arab Lobbies

The best organized, best funded, and most successful of the ethnic lobbies represents the interests of Israel. Jews, who dominate the pro-Israel lobby, make up 2.7 percent of the American population. Yet they are strongly motivated and highly organized in support of Israel. They seek to provide U.S. financial aid (both economic and military) to Israel and to deny it to those Arab nations in a state of war with Israel. Since its inception in 1951, the lobby has rarely lost an important battle. In recent years, Israel's policies have become more controversial in the United States—and within Israel itself. The splits within Israel have been mirrored in the American Jewish community, which has weakened the traditional pro-Israel lobby.

Israel receives by far the largest share of American foreign aid, more than $3 billion a year. Only Egypt even approaches the Israeli aid figure. In 1985 Israel and the United States signed a free-trade pact that eliminated all tariff barriers between them in 1995. Israel benefits from large tax-exempt contributions from the American Jewish community, including some $500 million in direct charitable grants and a similar amount from the sale of Israel government bonds.[3] No other foreign nation is so favored.

The pro-Israel lobby traditionally combined one organization devoted entirely to the cause of that country and a wide-ranging support network. The American Israel Public Affairs Committee (AIPAC), founded in 1951, has a staff of 150, an annual budget of $15 million, and 55,000 members. It operates out of offices one block away from Capitol Hill,[4] with considerable political acumen: "In a moment of perceived crisis, it can put a carefully researched, well-documented statement of its views on the desk of every Senator and Congressman and appropriate committee staff within four hours of a decision to do so."[5]

The organization's close ties to many congressional staffers keep it well informed about issues affecting Israel on Capitol Hill. Its lobbying connections are so thorough that one observer maintained, "A mystique has grown up around the lobby to the point where it is viewed with admiration, envy, and sometimes, anger."[6] Activists can readily mobilize the network of Jewish organizations across the country to put pro-Israel pressure on members of Congress in their constituencies, even in areas with small Jewish populations. In 1991 the lobby organized 1,500 "citizen lobbyists," armed with individualized computer printouts of their legislators' backgrounds. They pressed for additional aid to Israel because of the damage it incurred in the Gulf War.[7] AIPAC works together with other interest groups, particularly organized labor.[8]

The Arab lobbying effort has been far less successful. There were no major Arab organizations operating at all before 1972, and a Washington presence did not begin until 1978. The oldest Arab group, the National Association of Arab Americans (NAAA) claims 13,000 members, a mailing list of 80,000 names, most of whom are inactive, and $500,000 annual budget funding a staff of twenty-five.[9] Unlike most Arab nations, the NAAA long recognized Israel's right to exist. A rival organization, the American Lebanese League, is harshly critical of the NAAA and views it as essentially anti-American.[10] Two newer organizations are the Arab-American Anti-Discrimination Committee (AADC), with 25,000 members, which fights negative stereotypes of Arab Americans, and the Arab-American Committee (AAC). Only the NAAA lobbies in Washington; the AADC and the AAC are split by the personal animosities between the groups' founders.[11] Unlike AIPAC, the NAAA makes no pretense of being free from the direct influence of the "mother country."

The Arab uprising in the West Bank and Gaza that began in 1987 has energized the Arab American community. NAAA now maintains a grassroots network organized by congressional district, patterned directly after AIPAC.[12] The Arab-American Anti-Discrimination Committee was founded in 1980 on the model of the B'nai B'rith Anti-Defamation League, established some fifty years ago to combat discrimination against Jews. It does not lobby on legislation.

There have been some efforts to get American businesses with interests in the Middle East, especially oil companies, to do more lobbying and fund-raising for the Arab cause, but they have not yielded much success to date. One analysis concluded, "Most Arab embassies throw impressive parties, but have little day-to-day contact with Congress, according to lawmakers and aides. Israel, by comparison, has a staff of congressional relations counselors who keep in touch with Capitol Hill."[13]

The heart of the difficulty of Arab American lobbying efforts is found in the existence of another group, the American Lebanese League, which claims 10,000 members and seeks a democratic and pro-Western Lebanon. It represents Christian forces in Lebanon, which have little in common with the Muslims and Druze of that country. Even a past president of NAAA admitted the central hindrance to Arab lobbying in the United States:

> We can't represent the Arabs the way the Jewish lobby can represent Israel. The Israeli government has one policy to state, whereas we couldn't represent "the Arabs" even if we wanted to. They're as different as the Libyans and the Saudis are different, or as divided as the Christian and Moslem Lebanese.[14]

Inter-Arab divisiveness thus accounts for some, but not all, of the difficulties that these lobbying organizations confront.

Public opinion plays a much larger role. Americans have for a long time taken a much more sympathetic view toward Israel than toward the Arabs. Most polls show that Americans favor the Israeli position by between a three to one margin and a five to one divide. Occasionally, as during the Israeli invasion of Lebanon, the 1985 TWA hostage crisis, or perceived Israeli intransigence in negotiating peace, public support for Israel drops sharply, but it has generally rebounded. Even as the Arab uprising in the Israeli-occupied territories has sapped public support for Israel, there has been little appreciable increase in support for the Arab cause.

The roots of the friendship between the United States and Israel include factors such as (1) a common biblical heritage (most Arabs are Muslim, an unfamiliar religion to most Americans); (2) a shared European value system (most Arabs take their values from Islam, which is often sharply critical of what they perceive to be the amoral tenor of the West); (3) the democratic nature of Israel's political system (most Arab nations are monarchies or dictatorships); (4) Israel's role as an ally of the United States (most Arab countries have been seen as either unreliable friends or as hostile to American interests); and (5) the sympathy Americans extend toward Jews as victims (Arabs are portrayed as terrorists or exploiters of the American economy through their oil weapon).[15]

Jews benefit from a high rate of participation in politics, and Arab Americans are not as great a political force. Jews are among the most generous campaign contributors in American politics: 60 percent of individual contributions to President Clinton's 1992 campaign came from Jewish donors. In 1996, 27 percent of American Jews said that they contributed to a presidential candidate. Fewer than 5 percent of non-Jews gave money to *any* candidate for office.[16] Arab Americans have not been very active in politics. Only 100,000 belong to any Arab American organization compared to two million Jews who are active in Jewish causes.

Many Arab Americans, especially the older, native-born, shun politics. They are divided politically, with younger and more liberal Arab Americans voting Democratic and raising $750,000 for Jesse Jackson's 1988 race for the presidency, for example. Older, more conservative Arab Americans identify with Republicans for their support for traditional social values. Overall Arab Americans are split in their party identification: 42 percent call themselves Republicans and 37 percent Democrats. Democratic identifiers sometimes find their support unrequited: Arab Americans complained that the 1984 Democratic nominee Walter Mondale returned their campaign contributions and Michael Dukakis, the 1988 nominee, told Arab Americans he did not want their endorsement. But Arab Americans were becoming more active. Two NAAA leaders report that Arab Americans were the only ethnic group to provide Republican volunteers in every state for Reagan and that no ethnic group provided more volunteers than Arab Americans for President Clinton's reelection campaign.[17] By 1996, Arab Americans had become more active in politics in both parties and they have become a prominent swing group in the politics of at least one state—Michigan.[18]

Although Arab groups are divided among themselves and have no common frame of reference, American Jews have traditionally been united behind support of Israel. A 1982 survey of American Jews showed that 94 percent considered themselves either pro-Israel or very pro-Israel. Two-thirds often discuss Israel with friends and, by a three to one margin, reject the notion that support for Israel conflicts with one's attachment to the United States. Three-quarters of American Jews argue that they should not vote for a candidate who is unfriendly to Israel, and one-third would be willing to contribute money to political candidates who support Israel. Jewish commitments to Israel declined by the 1990s. Nevertheless, 70 percent still felt very close or close to Israel in 1996 and 83 percent say that they follow news about Israel at least "somewhat closely." Ninety-seven percent said that they consider Israel's security to be at least "very important" and 76 percent said that caring about Israel is "a very important part of my being a Jew."[19]

Overall, the pro-Israel lobby prior to the late 1980s met all of the conditions identified as critical for a group to be successful. The Arab American lobby met none (see Table 17-1). Jews were well assimilated, had a high level of political activity, were homogenous in their support of Israel, and had the support of public opinion. Israel was seen as a strategic asset by the American public and particularly by decision makers. Activity on behalf of Israel was perceived as legitimate by the American public; backers of AIPAC and other organizations did not stand to gain from their lobbying. They had to contribute their own money to participate. Although not numerous in comparison to many other groups, American Jews and other supporters of Israel were concentrated in key states that were important to presidential candidates (New York, California, Pennsylvania).

Arab Americans met none of the conditions. Americans have generally not seen Arab nations as strategic allies. Many Arab Americans are not well assimilated into American society and politics; the community is neither homogenous with respect to Middle East politics nor politically active. American public opinion has never been favorable to the Arab

Table 17-1 Conditions for Success by Ethnic Interest Groups for
Pro-Israel and Arab Americans

	Pre-1987		Post-1987	
	Pro-Israel groups	Arab Americans	Pro-Israel groups	Arab Americans
Conditions				
Conforms to U.S. strategic interests	+	−	•	−
Group well assimilated	+	−	+	−
High level of political activity	+	−	+	−
Group internally homogenous	+	−	−	−
Group has support of public opinion	+	−	•	−
Group numerous with political clout	+	−	+	−
Group tactics legitimate	+	−	•	−

+ Condition met positively
− Condition not met (met negatively)
• Condition partially met

(or Palestinian) cause. The financing of Arab American organizations by Middle Eastern interests and the active pursuit of changes in U.S. policy by economic interests have served to weaken the legitimacy of the Arab American cause.

In 1987 the pro-Israel groups began to lose some of their clout. The Palestinian uprising against Israeli control of the West Bank and Gaza (the *intifada)* raised international consciousness about the Palestinian cause and led to a lessening of American public support for the Jewish state. They also led to conflicts within the Jewish community as to what Israel ought to do. When Israel and the Palestine Liberation Organization signed their peace accord at the White House in September 1993, a deeper schism arose among American (and Israeli) Jews. It is always difficult to deal with former enemies. Moreover, the conflict over the peace process reflected tensions within Israel over religious issues.

American Judaism is divided into three major blocs—Orthodox, Conservative, and Reform. These divisions reflect disagreements over which religious laws one must follow. Seven percent of American Jews call themselves Orthodox, 38 percent Conservative, and 42 percent Reform.[20] In Israel, the Orthodox have a monopoly on organized religious practice. Religious parties have been prominent actors in right-wing coalition governments in Israel. They have pressured these governments to deny recognition to Conservative and Reform conversions conducted in the United States. The Orthodox have been among the most critical of the peace process as well, with Reform and Conservative Jews being more strongly in favor of movements toward reconciliation with the Palestinians.

American Jews have been split in recent years over both religious issues and peace. Seventy-five percent of Reform and Conservative Jews support the peace process, with just 12 percent opposed. Almost 60 percent of Orthodox Jews *oppose* the peace process. A majority of Reform and Conservative Jews support the decision of most Jewish organizations (and the Israeli government) to back American foreign aid to Israel, and almost two-thirds of the Orthodox oppose such assistance. And a majority of Reform Jews say that Orthodox and non-Orthodox Jews have little in common.[21] The conflicts within American Jewry reflect similar disputes in Israel.

The power of the pro-Israel lobby rested on unity within the Jewish community and achieving widespread support beyond this small group. Yet conflicts over religion and peace led to the fractionalization of the Jewish lobby. AIPAC became increasingly linked to the more hawkish right-wing government in Israel in the 1980s. In turn, Labor Party Prime Minister Yitzhak Rabin, in a highly unusual move, intervened in "domestic" American Jewish politics, urging rabbis to support the peace process. The prodding was an explicit warning to AIPAC, which long had worked with whatever Israeli government was in power. An internal power struggle within AIPAC ousted the conservative leadership and restored the liberal tilt to the organization. In turn, the (then) opposition Likud party stepped up its efforts to discredit the peace process. The Likud supported the hawkish Zionist Organization of America, which directly competed with AIPAC for legislative support and which covertly sent its own former Cabinet members to lobby on Capitol Hill.[22]

Jewish American politicians have long been a bulwark of Israel's support on Capitol Hill. Most Jews are Democrats and so are most Jewish elected officials: forty-two of the forty-five Jewish House members and nine of the ten Jewish Senators (as of 1998) are Democrats. They have long been a united bloc in favor of any Israeli government, but especially supportive of Labor administrations that have pursued peace. And they have sought out positions where they could be of help to Israel. Almost 20 percent of the Senate Foreign Relations Committee and the House International Relations Committee are Jewish. The lone Arab Americans in the House and Senate do not serve on these committees. The current chair of the House International Relations Committee, Rep. Benjamin Gilman (R-N.Y.), has cast his lot with some of the most vociferous opponents of peace with the Palestinians.

On religious issues, one group of Orthodox rabbis declared that the Reform and Conservative movements are "not Judaism." In turn, the chancellor of the largest Conservative seminary demanded the dismantling of the office of Chief Rabbi in Israel, because it was perpetuating the Orthodox monopoly on religious practice.[23] The conflicts over religion pitted the same groups against each other as did the arguments over peace. The pro-Israeli lobby had prevailed in the past because it did not have to worry about strong Arab American interest groups. It still did not. Its new enemy was itself.

Public opinion had become less supportive of Israel, though not much more friendly to the Arabs. The pro-Israel lobby was wounded, but not mortally. Yet Arab Americans still failed to meet any of the conditions in Table 17-1. Even after 1987 the "worst" pro-Israel groups scored was a single negative rating. One senator who called AIPAC "ruthless" nevertheless admitted that "there's no countervailing sentiment." And James Zogby, head of the Arab-American Anti-Discrimination Committee, admitted, "We don't make policy."[24]

Most American Jews are Reform or Conservative—and most support the peace process and even favor American pressure on Israel.[25] And this leads to an irony: The divisions in Jewish opinion are not as great as the public fights might suggest. So behind the scenes, where it counts, the group with the greater unity and greater organization and participation can still prevail most of the time. A survey by *Fortune* magazine of 2,200 Washington insiders ranked AIPAC as the second most powerful lobbying group in Washington in 1997.[26] The pro-Israel lobby is no longer the overpowering force it once was, but it still fares quite well.

Other Ethnic Interest Groups

No foreign policy interest group, and certainly no ethnic group, has the reputation for influence that the pro-Israel forces have. Even a weakened AIPAC still sets the pace—for two reasons. First, AIPAC is the model for most other successful groups. Second, like the Jewish community, other ethnic groups have been divided over the best course of action for their countries of concern. The ethnic lobby that was poised to capture the role of "king of the Hill" from AIPAC, the Cuban American National Foundation, has been wrought with its own conflicts.

Latinos

Latinos now constitute about 10 percent of all Americans, up from 6.4 percent in 1980. Yet they have little unity. The largest groups of Latinos are Mexicans and Puerto Ricans, who are relatively poor and who are likely to back liberal Democratic candidates in elections. The third largest—and best organized—group is Cuban Americans, who are much more affluent and generally support conservative Republicans.[27]

Mexican Americans constitute 60 percent of all Latinos, but many are not American citizens and even those who are have ambivalent feelings toward Mexico. Until recently Mexican leaders did not encourage intervention on behalf of Mexico by Mexican Americans. Now they do. And Mexicans and other Latinos from Central America have become more active in political life. Latinos now hold fourteen of eighty seats as well as top leadership positions in the California legislature's lower house.[28]

The next largest group is Puerto Ricans. Yet they too are divided over the status of Puerto Rico, some favoring statehood, others continuation of the commonwealth status, and some independence. A 1985 meeting of the National Congress for Puerto Rican Rights could not reach a resolution over the issue of coordinating strategies with other Hispanic groups. Some Puerto Ricans resent other Latinos because on average Puerto Ricans earn less although they have had American citizenship longer.[29] For countries such as El Salvador and Nicaragua, where American policy is more controversial, foreign policy lobbies are dominated by religious organizations, such as the Washington Office on Latin America, with few ties to the indigenous communities. These organizations largely focus on human rights issues. Some have influence on Capitol Hill, but their lobbying activities tend to concentrate more on legislators who are already committed to their cause.[30]

The third largest group, Cuban Americans, are much better off financially and vote heavily for Republican candidates. Cubans represent just 5.3 percent of Latinos in this country. Yet, they have established the second most potent ethnic lobby in the country, the Cuban American National Foundation (CANF). Cuban Americans are generally strongly anti-Communist. They helped fund Lieutenant Colonel Oliver North's legal expenses during the investigations into the Iran-Contra affair and a lobbying effort to force Cuban troops from the African nation of Angola.[31]

The Cuban American National Foundation's founder, Jorge Mas Canosa (who died in late 1997), was called "the most significant individual lobbyist in the country."[32] The foundation lobbied successfully in 1985 for Radio Marti and in 1990 for TV Marti, direct broadcast stations aimed at Cuba from the United States. In 1996 Canosa and the CANF were the major movers in the Helms-Burton Act that tightened the American economic embargo against Cuba. The federal government funds a resettlement program for Cuban refugees that the CANF runs. The CANF has one hundred directors, each of whom contribute $10,000. It claims 50,000 donors. CANF contributed to fifty-six congressional campaigns in 1988 and to forty-eight in 1990, focusing largely on members of the House Foreign Affairs Committee. Overall, its Free Cuba Political Action Committee has contributed $670,000 to congressional candidates from 1982 to 1992 and more than $1 million to presidential candidates in 1992 alone.[33] Two of the three Cuban American representatives—two Republicans from Florida and a New Jersey Democrat—serve on the House International Relations Committee, compared to just one other Latino member. Mas established close personal ties to former president George Bush, as well as anti-Communist leaders of other countries, such as Russian president Boris Yeltsin, Argentinean president Carlos Menem, and Angolan rebel leader Jonas Savimbi.[34]

Yet the CANF may have been proven too partisan for its own good. Although it has backed some Democrats in Congress, its partisanship has been overwhelmingly Republican. In early 1993 it blocked a Black Cuban American nominee of the Clinton administration for the post of chief policy maker on Latin America. That tilted the administration toward a more moderate line on Cuba. Clinton invited one hundred Cuban Americans to the White House for Cuban Independence Day, slighting CANF officeholders. A new more moderate Cuban American group, Cambio Cubana (Cuban Change), was founded and the administration appeared more sympathetic to it when it did little to stop Congress from slashing funding in half for Radio Marti and from abolishing TV Marti.[35]

Fearing that it might lose influence, the CANF moved to establish closer relations with the Democratic Clinton. In 1994 Mas helped persuade Clinton to take a harder line against Castro when the Cuban leader put refugees on boats headed toward the United States. Clinton, at Mas's urging and with his explicit support, took a tough line against the refugees, putting them in detention and sending them back to Cuba. Clinton also put further restrictions on funds that Cuban Americans could send to relatives living in Cuba.

The CANF was patterned after AIPAC and, ironically, it is facing some of the same strains that the pro-Israel lobby has encountered. Like AIPAC, it has gone through an internal power struggle. In 1994, an employee at the Spanish-language network of Music Television (MTV) charged that CANF pressured MTV to fire her. She had organized a private tour to Havana to see a Cuban singer in concert. The next year a federal investigation into Radio Marti charged that Mas improperly intervened in the daily operations of the station, trying to dismiss his critics. The radio station also was charged with deliberately distorting American policy toward Cuba, undermining negotiations with the Castro regime. And in 1997, popular singer Gloria Estefan came under sharp attack by CANF supporters when she supported a Miami concert by Cuban musicians.[36]

Clinton's hard line toward Castro also revealed fissures in the Cuban American community. Many Cuban Americans, including conservative members of Congress and moderate Cuban American groups, were angry over the president's decision not to admit Cuban refugees into the United States.[37] Cuban Americans are no longer singularly preoccupied with Castro. A survey of Cuban Americans in 1995 found that 68 percent favor negotiating with the Castro regime over the future of Cuba, with even larger majorities of higher income and younger Cuban Americans taking this position. Like American Jews, most Cuban Americans (73 percent) said that a candidate's position on Cuba is important in determining their vote in local elections. But 64 percent believed that all points of view on Cuba deserved to be heard; just 34 percent said that returning refugees to Cuba was the right policy.[38] Cuban Americans are, like Jewish Americans, less united than they once were. Cuban government representatives now can address audiences in Florida without being harassed and a Spanish-language radio station in Miami now airs a talk show with a host who regularly attacks the CANF and other hard-liners. The head of Cambio Cubana even went so far as to meet with Castro in 1995.[39]

The fragmentation of the Latino community traditionally has limited the unity and effectiveness (especially on foreign policy issues) of the Hispanic Caucus in the House of Representatives. But a new issue has united Latinos—and the Hispanic caucus. The Republican congressional majority enacted restrictive immigration legislation in 1996. Latinos from every nationality and from both parties banded together to protest this legislation. The House Hispanic Caucus took a strong stand against the legislation.[40] The restrictive clauses in the legislation led to a surge in naturalization rates, especially among Latinos. Latino voter registration rolls grew by almost 30 percent in 1996, both because of naturalization and because of increased interest in politics. Every immigrant group reported a surge in both turnout and in the share of the vote they gave to Democratic candidates. Clinton's margin among Latinos rose from 60 percent in 1992 to 72 percent in 1996. The surge in Latino votes for Democrats allowed Clinton to carry two states he lost in 1992 that have large Hispanic populations: Arizona and Florida. Although Cuban Americans in Florida still gave a plurality of their votes to Republican nominee Bob Dole, Clinton fared better than any recent Democratic nominee.[41] Many immigrant communities felt under attack from the new legislation, and, at least for a time, this overarching issue may overtake more particularistic concerns of each nationality group. With the death of Mas, divisions in the Cuban American community are likely to become more pronounced.

Greeks and Turks

Greek Americans were long considered second in power to the pro-Israel lobby. The American Hellenic Institute Public Affairs Committee (AHIPAC) is consciously modeled after AIPAC; the two groups have often worked together. AHIPAC lobbied successfully for an arms embargo on Turkey after its 1974 invasion of Cyprus and has pressed for a balance in foreign aid between the two states. The two million Greek Americans are very politically active and loyal to the Democratic Party: In 1988 they raised more than 15 percent of Greek American Michael Dukakis's early campaign funds. In contrast, the Turkish American community of 180,000 is not well organized. Recently it has employed a Washington public relations firm to lobby the government, but it has no ethnic lobby and maintains a low profile. As one member of Congress stated, "I don't have any Turkish restaurants in my district."[42]

Overall, Greek Americans are advantaged over Turkish Americans on virtually every condition. They are more assimilated into American life, are more active politically, are more homogenous and numerous, and—to the extent they are Christian rather than Muslim—have public opinion on their side. Each group claims strategic importance. Because the demands of each can be met through foreign aid, there is no fundamental clash. Greek American influence has waned as American foreign policy has shifted emphasis from Greece and Turkey to other trouble spots, especially after the fall of the Soviet Union limited the strategic value of both Greece and Turkey to the United States.

The Greek lobby made a brief comeback in the public eye when it successfully pressured the Clinton administration in 1994 to deny diplomatic recognition to the new nation of Macedonia. Macedonia was part of the former Yugoslavia, but Greece charged that the new country was provocative in taking the same name as a province in northern Greece. Until Macedonia changed its name, Greece would impose an economic blockade and press others not to recognize the new country.[43] Ultimately the United States was able to pressure both sides into a compromise that averted a possible war. The Greek lobby was widely criticized for supporting a policy that many other groups could not understand. Outsiders could not comprehend why two countries could consider war because of a name.

Turkish groups have been buffeted by the strong alliances between pro-Israeli forces and Turkey's historic antagonists, the Greeks and the Armenians. But recently Turkey, even though its population is 99 percent Muslim, has forged its own links with American Jews. Turkey and Israel have military links, because both fear Syria (a common neighbor), Iraq, and Iran. In 1997 the B'nai B'rith Anti-Defamation League presented Turkish Prime Minister Mesut Yilmaz with its Distinguished Statesman Award. Yilmaz also met with leaders of AIPAC and the American Jewish Committee.[44]

Eastern Europeans

The Eastern Europeans have a long history of political activism. There are eight million Polish Americans and almost a million Lithuanians, Latvians, and Estonians. For many years these groups pressed the United States to pressure the Soviet Union to withdraw from Eastern Europe. These ethnic groups had little impact on foreign policy. They pressed the government to sacrifice détente with the Soviet Union, a policy at odds with that of presidents of both parties. After the Soviet Union disbanded and Lithuania, Latvia, and Estonia gained independence in 1991, the long-time alliances in the Baltic American community threatened to come apart as each ethnic group fought for a share of the decreasing American foreign aid pie.[45]

In the late 1990s, lobbies representing the interests of the formerly Communist nations came back together to support a common mission:

membership in the North Atlantic Treaty Organization (NATO), the Western alliance. A multiethnic bloc, Central and East European Coalition, supported the entry of Poland, the Czech Republic, Slovakia, and Hungary into NATO. Eastern European ethnics represent 10 percent or more of the population in fourteen states. The different nationality groups banded together, believing that unity would benefit all of them (which it eventually did). Lobbying groups for nations not included in the initial round of NATO expansion—such as Latvia, Lithuania, and Estonia—supported others' early entry. They hoped that the initial success of some countries would lead to their own admission to NATO. The linchpin of the coalition is the Polish American community, who is "next to Jews and Greeks . . . probably the country's best organized ethnic coalition."[46]

African Americans

African Americans, like Latinos, traditionally have been more concerned with domestic economic issues than with foreign policy concerns. Most African Americans cannot trace their roots to a specific African country. Until the 1960s, black participation in politics was restricted, both by law and by socioeconomic status. There were few African Americans in Congress, especially on the foreign policy committees, or in the Foreign Service. African Americans contribute little money to campaigns and electorally they have been strongly tied to the Democratic Party, thus cutting off lobbying activities to Republican presidents and legislators. African American activity on foreign policy heightened over the issue of the ending of the apartheid system of racial separation in South Africa. The Congressional Black Caucus and TransAfrica, a lobbying organization, in 1993 expanded its role to become a think tank dealing with foreign policy issues.

The South African issue united African Americans. President Ronald Reagan ultimately agreed in 1985 to accept sanctions against the South African government, pushed in that direction by the weight of public opinion, a mobilized African American community, and a supportive Congress. The Congressional Black Caucus has also taken firm stands on sending U.S. troops to Somalia, lifting the ban on Haitian immigrants infected with the AIDS virus, and pushing the United States to restore ousted Haitian President Jean-Bertrand Aristede to office. With the demise of the apartheid regime in South Africa, the Congressional Black Caucus has turned its attention to Haiti. Together with TransAfrica, it has also strongly protested human rights abuses in Nigeria.[47]

Four of the forty-eight members of the House Foreign Affairs Committee are black; African Americans increasingly have held key positions on foreign policy in the executive branch and they are now more united on wider issues of Africa than ever before.[48]

Asian Americans

Asian Americans are the fastest growing ethnic group in the United States. Their population doubled in the 1970s and again in the 1980s. Asian Americans now constitute 3 percent of the population and their population is expected to triple (from 7.2 million in the 1990 census to 20 million) by 2020.[49] Yet Asian Americans have not been prominent in political life. Because most immigrants have not become citizens, their participation rate is substantially lower than that of other ethnic groups. Only two members of the 120-member California General Assembly are Asian Americans and there is only one Asian American governor, Gary Locke (D-Wash.).

Many recent immigrants are preoccupied with economic issues and eschew politics. They came from cultures without democratic traditions and have not placed adaptation at the top of their agenda. The Asian American community is diverse and there are few common bonds among Koreans, Indochinese, Japanese, and Chinese. There are tensions between Japanese Americans and Chinese Americans stemming from Japan's occupation of China during World War II. Vietnamese immigrants bear grudges against Cambodians, and Hindus and Moslems from South Asia have long-standing quarrels. One writer called the idea of a Pan-Asian identity "ludicrous."[50]

Many recent Asian American immigrants still see themselves as "guests" in a strange land and are reluctant to get involved in politics. Others simply want to be left alone by the government, believing that self-reliance is the best course. When they do vote, Asian Americans have mostly cast ballots for Republicans. They are attracted by the strong anti-Communist positions of the GOP, as well as the party's emphasis on family values. Even in 1996, when virtually all immigrant groups increased their support for Democratic candidates, Asian Americans still gave a plurality of their votes to the Republican candidate (48 percent to 43 percent).[51] Japanese Americans are an exception. They are overwhelmingly Democratic and have high rates of participation. In 1998 only two Asian Americans, a nonvoting delegate from American Samoa and Rep. Jay Kim (R-Calif.), served on the House International Relations Committee. Kim, the first Korean American elected to Congress, nevertheless said, "I have no special agenda for Asian-Americans."[52]

There are nine Asian Americans in Congress, all but one (Kim) of whom are Democrats. Most of the Asian Americans come from California and Hawaii. In 1994, they formed the Asian Pacific Caucus, admitting members without regard to race or ethnicity. Two non-Asian members from California and one from Hawaii joined. The founding of the caucus mirrors increased activity by Asian Americans. Asian Americans, as we shall see, were important campaign contributors, especially to Democrats that year.

The Electoral Connection in Foreign Policy

Most lobbyists concentrate on legislation in Washington, but tactics have been shifting increasingly toward the electoral arena. Interest groups use political action committees to channel contributions to candidates for Congress. If a sound presentation does not convince a legislator to accede to one's cause, the argument runs, perhaps a campaign contribution might. Former senator Charles McC. Mathias, Jr. (R-Md.), worried that such tactics might make it difficult for the nation to speak with one voice on foreign policy:

> Factions among us lead the nation toward excessive foreign attachments or animosities. Even if the groups were balanced—if Turkish-Americans equaled Greek-Americans or Arab-Americans equaled Jewish-Americans—the result would not necessarily be a sound, cohesive foreign policy because the national interest is not simply the sum of our special interest and attachments . . . ethnic politics, carried as they often have been to excess, have proven harmful to the national interest.[53]

The strategies of pro-Israel groups usually have focused on placing intense constituency pressure on legislators who make either anti-Israel or pro-Arab statements. The most notable efforts occurred in Illinois in 1982 and 1984. Rep. Paul Findley (R-Ill.) and Sen. Charles Percy (R-Ill.), who chaired the Foreign Relations Committee, were strong critics of Israel. Jewish sources raised $685,000 to defeat Findley in 1982 and $322,000 to beat Percy two years later; a California donor contributed more than $1 million in "uncoordinated expenditures" against Percy.

Pro-Israel political action committee contributions rose from $2,450 in 1976 to $8.7 million in 1990—a higher figure than that for the largest domestic political action committee (PAC), the realtors. Virtually every senator and most members of the House have received support from the more than eighty pro-Israel PACs. Senate Foreign Relations Committee members received $1.2 million from pro-Israel groups in 1990, more than twice as much from the second largest ideological PAC and representing 40 percent of all ideological political action committee contributions. Pro-Israel PACs have, like others, concentrated on incumbents; they also favor Democrats by more than two to one. Arab Americans are far behind: In 1986, they contributed just $70,000 to congressional candidates compared to $4.6 million for pro-Israel groups.[54]

What should the role of money in American politics be? Is political support to be given to the highest bidder? Even though ethnic lobbies do not stand to benefit financially from a foreign policy that suits their preferences, many Americans are simply so skeptical of the role of money in politics that they will worry that something is not right. Support for foreign policy initiatives might be seen as open to influence to campaign contributions. The victorious group might be viewed with suspicion by the larger public, much as large corporations are. The strategy of influencing policy by shaping the membership of Congress could backfire.

Although 61 percent of Americans believe it is acceptable for American Jews to contribute money to Israel, almost 40 percent of Americans believe that Israel has too much power in America. Forty percent also believe that American Jews would side with Israel rather than the United States should there be a conflict between them.[55] When a group applies electoral pressure, especially through financial clout, it may lose credibility with the larger public. The moral claims that American Jews and other supporters of Israel make may appear suspect when foreign policy lobbying comes to resemble the rough and tumble of domestic politics. Other PACs financed by foreign money, including American subsidiaries of Japanese firms and foreign car dealers, have more direct economic stakes and have used their clout to shape tax law in at least one state. As long as the money is raised exclusively in the United States, such practices are legal. As such strategies prove effective, they will become more widespread.

Campaign contributions by another ethnic group, Asian Americans, became a source of contention in the 1996 elections. Where did the money come from—from Asian Americans or from Asians? What did campaign contributors want? Were the funds donated to promote good government or to buy influence for foreign interests?

Asian Americans may not yet be a big presence in domestic politics. But they have contributed large amounts of money—more than $10 million—to presidential campaigns in 1988 and 1992, second only to Jews.[56] Asian Americans reportedly gave $10 million or more in 1996, mostly to Democrats and especially to President Clinton. Asian American contributions came under scrutiny when it was revealed after the 1996 elections that at least $1.2 million of the donations to the Democratic National Committee (DNC) were improper, as will be discussed.

The National Asian Pacific American Campaign Plan sought to raise $7 million from Asian Americans and promised, in return, special access to the White House. The DNC's chief fund-raiser among Asian Americans, John Huang, appeared to have promised face-to-face meetings with the president for large contributors. And many of the contributions came not from Asian Americans but from Asians: individuals from Indonesia, Japan, Taiwan, South Korea, Vietnam, and China. Contributions from foreigners are illegal. The DNC ultimately returned $3 million in improper contributions. The Republicans also received large contributions from Chinese, Taiwanese, and Hong Kong interests, though they were less widely publicized.[57]

The Asian American campaign contributions raised a host of legal and ethical questions. It looked unseemly for the president to meet with large campaign contributors, although Clinton argued that recent Republican presidents had pursued the same strategy. But the Democratic presidential campaign of 1996 seemed different. Many of Clinton's contributors were not just business executives but foreign businesses—and other foreigners. James Riady, of the Indonesian conglomerate the Lippo Group, made substantial contributions to the DNC and met with the president in the Oval Office six times. DNC official Huang was previously U.S. chief of the Lippo Group. Other contributors included Buddhist nuns from a Taiwan-based order who wrote checks for $140,000 at a luncheon with Vice President Al Gore. And it was alleged, though not documented, that the Chinese government tried to funnel contributions to the DNC in 1996. The Chinese reportedly wanted to put pressure on the administration to renew China's preferred trade status, which was under attack because of the nation's questionable human rights record. Such direct intervention in American politics would not be unusual for China (or for many other countries). Major American companies doing business in China—including Boeing, General Electric, General Motors, Nike, and IBM—lobbied on behalf of the Beijing government's trade status.[58]

Conclusion

Americans worry about foreign influence in domestic politics. We have distinguished between campaign contributions and lobbying by foreign agents and governments and donations and pressures from American companies with interests abroad. Our laws reflect this distinction. Yet could we have drawn the line too sharply? Are we encouraging foreign interests to secure friends in the United States whose motives are less suspect simply because they are Americans?

One test of what constitutes an American interest, though hardly an ethical one, is what works. Perhaps there is no moral resolution to the problem of money in politics, but only a recognition that tactics that prove too heavy-handed may backfire. Pro-Israel groups were buffeted by charges that they had inappropriately mixed lobbying with fund-raising. In 1996, their PACs raised "only" $2 million, less than half of what they had spent in some recent contests.[59] Perhaps this reflects a realization that money may buy an election or two, but it cannot swing a large bloc of votes. Perhaps it is a reaction to criticism from other groups that this tactic was not in Israel's best interest. And perhaps Asian Americans may become more reluctant to contribute to campaigns in the future, given the negative press they have received.[60] Even so, there is little reason to believe that the interests in foreign policy will be restricted to moral pleadings and ethnic groups as we enter the twenty-first century. Foreign policy now resembles domestic policy more than ever. The consensus on what American policy should be has evaporated and with it went the argument that there was a distinctive moral foundation to our international relations.

Notes

1. Francis X. Clines, "Most Doubt a Resolve to Change Campaign Financing, Poll Finds," *New York Times*, April 8, 1997, A1, A10.
2. Mohammed E. Ahrari, "Conclusion," in *Ethnic Groups and Foreign Policy*, ed. Mohammed E. Ahrari (New York: Greenwood Press, 1987), 155–158.
3. Cheryl A. Rubenberg, "The Middle East Lobbies," *The Link* 17 (January–March 1984): 4.
4. Thomas L. Friedman, "A Pro-Israel Lobby Gives Itself a Headache," *New York Times*, November 8, 1992, E18.
5. Sanford Ungar, "Washington: Jewish and Arab Lobbyists," *Atlantic*, March 1978, 10.
6. Ben Bradlee, Jr., "Israel's Lobby," *Boston Globe Magazine*, April 29, 1984, 64.
7. Lloyd Grove, "On the March for Israel," *Washington Post*, June 13, 1991, D10.
8. Robert H. Trice, "Congress and the Arab-Israeli Conflict: Support for Israel in the U.S. Senate, 1970–1973," *Political Science Quarterly* 92 (Fall 1977): 443–463; and Robert Pear with Richard L. Berke, "Pro-Israel Group Exerts Quiet Might As It Rallies Supporters in Congress," *New York Times*, July 7, 1987, A8.
9. Bill Keller, "Supporters of Israel, Arabs Vie for Friends in Congress, at White House," *Congressional Quarterly Weekly Report*, August 25, 1981, 1527–1528; and David A. Dickson, "Pressure Politics and the Congressional Foreign Policy Process" (Paper delivered at the Annual Meeting of the American Political Science Association, San Francisco, August–September 1990).
10. Keller, "Supporters of Israel," 1528.
11. Nora Boustany, "Arab-American Lobby Is Struggling," *Washington Post*, April 6, 1990, A10.
12. Rubenberg, "The Middle East Lobbies"; Keller, "Supporters Vie"; Steven L. Spiegel, *The Other Arab-Israeli Conflict* (Chicago: University of Chicago Press, 1985), 8; and David J. Saad and G. Neal Lendenmann, "Arab American Grievances," *Foreign Policy* (Fall 1985): 22.
13. Keller, "Supporters of Israel," 1528.
14. Quoted in Spiegel, *The Other Arab-Israeli Conflict*, 8.
15. John Spanier and Eric Uslaner, *American Foreign Policy Making and the Democratic Dilemmas*, chap. 7; Andrew Kohut, *America's Place in the World II* (Washington, D.C.: Pew Research Center for The People and The Press, 1997), 99.
16. Thomas L. Friedman, "Jewish Criticism on Clinton Picks," *New York Times*, January 5, 1993, A11. The data on Jewish contributors come from the executive summary of a survey of 1,198 American Jews for the Israel Policy Forum, September 1997, by Penn, Schoen, and Berland and Associates. The data on other contributors come from the 1996 American National Election Study.
17. "Arab Americans Take an Increased Political Role," *New York Times*, November 4, 1984, 74.
18. Religious News Service, "Muslims Overwhelmingly Favor Clinton, According to Poll," *Washington Post*, November 2, 1996, B7; Steven A. Holmes, "Influx of Immigrants Is Changing Electorate," *New York Times*, October 30, 1996, A16.
19. Leon Hadar, "What Israel Means to U.S. Jewry," *Jerusalem Post International Edition*, June 19–25, 1982, 11; Bradlee, "Israel's Lobby," 8; American Jewish Committee, *In the Aftermath of the Rabin Assassination* (New York: American Jewish Committee, 1996).
20. Executive summary of a survey of 1,198 American Jews for the Israel Policy Forum, September 1997, by Penn, Schoen, and Berland and Associates.
21. American Jewish Committee, *In the Aftermath of the Rabin Assassination*.
22. Laurie Goodstein, "Rabin Urges U.S. Rabbis to Push Peace," *Washington Post*, September 6, 1994, A1, A4; J. J. Goldstein, "Only in America: Likud vs. Labor," *New York Times*, July 2, 1994, 19; Rowland Evans and Robert Novak, "Likud's

'Gang of Three,'" *Washington Post*, November 17, 1994, A23; Jonathan Broder, "Maverick," *Jerusalem Report*, June 16, 1994, 32–33.

23. Gustav Neibuhr, "Rabbi Group Is Preparing to Denounce Non-Orthodox," *New York Times*, March 24, 1997, A11; Neibuhr, "U.S. Jewish Leader Enters Fray over Religious Control in Israel," *New York Times*, April 17, 1997, A1, A20.

24. Saad and Lendenmann, "Arab American Grievances," 22; Boustany, "Arab-American Lobby Is Struggling."

25. Executive summary of Israel Policy Forum survey.

26. Jeffrey H. Birnbaum, "Washington's Power 25," *Fortune*, December 8, 1997, 144–158.

27. Tomas Rivera Center, *The Latino Vote at Mid-Decade* (Claremont, Calif., 1996).

28. Robert Reinhold, "Mexico Leaders Look North of the Border," *New York Times*, December 8, 1989, A1, A28; Lou Cannon, "Southern California's Boom Is Latino-Led," *Washington Post*, July 12, 1997, A3.

29. Rodolfo O. de la Garza, "Chicanos and U.S. Foreign Policy: The Future of Chicano-Mexican Relations," *Western Political Quarterly* 23 (December 1980): 571–572; and Jesus Rangel, "Puerto Rican Need Discussed at Home," *New York Times*, June 3, 1985, B18.

30. Bill Keller, "Interest Groups Focus on El Salvador Policy," *Congressional Quarterly Weekly Report*, April 24, 1982, 895–900.

31. Robert S. Greenberger, "Right-Wing Groups Join in Capitol Hill Crusade to Help Savimbi's Anti-Communists in Angola," *Wall Street Journal*, November 25, 1985, 58.

32. John Newhouse, "Socialism or Death," *The New Yorker*, April 27, 1992, 77.

33. Newhouse, "Socialism or Death," 76–81; Lee Hockstadter and William Booth, "Cuban Exiles Split on Life after Castro," *Washington Post*, March 10, 1992, A1, A14; Peter H. Stone, "Cuban Clout," *National Journal*, February 20, 1993, 449; and Larry Rohter, "A Rising Cuban-American Leader: Statesman to Some, Bully to Others," *New York Times*, October 29, 1992, A18.

34. Larry Rohter, "Jorge Mas Canosa, 58, Dies; Exile Who Led Movement against Castro," *New York Times*, November 24, 1997, A27.

35. John M. Goshko, "Controversy Erupts on Latin America Post," *Washington Post*, January 23, 1993, A4; and Larry Rohter, "Moderate Cuban Voices Rise in U.S.," *New York Times*, June 27, 1993, A16.

36. Larry Rohter, "MTV Worker Ousted over Cuba Concert," *New York Times*, June 9, 1994, A12; Steven Greenhouse, "U.S. Reportedly Finds That Head of Radio Marti Tried to Dismiss His Critics," *New York Times*, July 27, 1995, A10; Guy Gugliotta, "USIA Probes Activist's Role at Radio Marti," *Washington Post*, July 22, 1995, A1, A12; Donald P. Baker, "Miami's Cuban American Generations Split over Anti-Castro Rule," *Washington Post*, October 18, 1997, A3.

37. Mireya Navarro, "In Crisis over Cuba, Moderates and Castro Supporters Cry out to Be Heard," *New York Times*, August 31, 1994, A11; Navarro, "Cuban-Americans Dismayed by U.S. Policy Shift," *New York Times*, May 3, 1995, A15.

38. Guillermo J. Grenier, Hugh Gladwin, and Douglas McLaughen, *The 1995 FIU Cuba Poll* (Miami: Florida International University, 1995).

39. Mireya Navarro, "New Tolerance Sprouts among Cuban Exiles," *New York Times*, August 25, 1995, A14; Navarro, "Castro Confers with Exiled Foe," *New York Times*, June 28, 1995, A1, A8.

40. David Rampe, "Power Panel in the Making: The Hispanic Caucus," *New York Times*, September 30, 1988, B5; Lizette Alvarez, "For Hispanic Lawmakers, Time to Take the Offensive," *New York Times*, August 25, 1997, A14.

41. Dan Carney, "Immigrant Vote Swings Democratic . . . As Issues Move Front and Center," *Congressional Quarterly Weekly Report*, May 17, 1997, 1132–1133.

42. Thomas M. Franck and Edward Weisband, *Foreign Policy by Congress* (New York: Oxford University Press, 1979), 191–193.

43. Jim Hoagland, "Caving in to the Greek Lobby," *Washington Post*, March 30, 1994, A19.
44. Ted Clark, "Report on Turkey and Jewish-American Organizations" on National Public Radio's "Morning Edition" (December 23, 1997), unofficial transcript.
45. Isabel Wilkerson, "A Battle Is over for Baltic-Americans," *New York Times*, September 3, 1991, A9.
46. Michael Dobbs, "Domestic Political Costs Will Mount after the Rhetoric Is Spent," *Washington Post*, July 7, 1995, A1, A24.
47. Karen DeWitt, "Black Group Begins Protest against Nigeria," *New York Times*, March 17, 1995, A10.
48. Milton D. Morris, "African-Americans and the New World Order," *The Washington Quarterly* 15 (Autumn 1992): 19; and Keith B. Richburg, "Americans Bring an Agenda out of Africa," *Washington Post*, May 30, 1993, A39; Steven A. Holmes, "With Persuasion and Muscle, Black Caucus Reshapes Haiti Policy," *New York Times*, July 14, 1994, A10.
49. James Sterngold, "For Asian-Americans, Political Power Can Lead to Harsh Scrutiny," *New York Times*, November 3, 1996, A36.
50. Stanley Karnow, "Apathetic Asian-Americans?" *Washington Post*, November 29, 1992, C2; Sterngold, "For Asian-Americans, Political Power Can Lead to Harsh Scrutiny."
51. Carney, "Immigrant Vote Swings Democratic."
52. Sonal Gandhi, "Asian American Political Behavior," seminar paper for Government and Politics 399U/Honors 378J, The 1992 Elections, Fall, 1992; Karnow, "Apathetic Asian-Americans?"; and "Asian-Americans in Politics? Rarely," *New York Times*, June 3, 1993, A16. Kim pleaded guilty to campaign finance violations and was defeated in a Republican primary in 1998.
53. Charles McC. Mathias, Jr., "Ethnic Groups and Foreign Policy," *Foreign Affairs* 59 (Summer 1981): 981.
54. Charles R. Babcock, "Israel's Backers Maximize Political Clout," *Washington Post*, September 26, 1991, A21; Barbara Levick-Segnatelli, "The Washington Political Action Committee: One Man Can Make a Difference," in *Risky Business*, ed. Robert Biersack, Paul Herrnson, and Clyde Wilcox (Armonk, N.Y.: M. E. Sharpe, 1994); Edward Roeder, "Pro-Israel Groups Know Money Talks in Congress," *Washington Times*, September 18, 1991, A7; and Richard H. Curtiss, *Stealth PACs* (Washington, D.C.: American Educational Trust, 1990).
55. Hyer, "Tolerance Shows in Voter Poll"; and CBS News press release, October 23, 1988; Lipset and Raab, *Jews and the New American Scene*, 126.
56. Sterngold, "For Asian-Americans, Political Power Can Lead to Harsh Scrutiny."
57. Terry M. Neal, "Asian American Donors Feel Stigmatized," *Washington Post*, September 8, 1997, A1, A8; Tim Weiner and David E. Sanger, "Democrats Hoped to Raise $7 Million from Asians in U.S.," *New York Times*, December 28, 1996, A1, A5; and Michael Weisskopf and Michael Duffy, "The G.O.P.'s Own China Connection," *Time*, May 5, 1997, 45–46.
58. Ruth Marcus, "Oval Office Meeting Set DNC Asian Funds Network in Motion," *Washington Post*, December 29, 1996, A1, A6; Terry M. Neal, "Asian American Donors Feel Stigmatized," *Washington Post*, September 8, 1997, A1, A8; Bob Woodward and Brian Duffy, "Chinese Embassy Role in Contributions Probed," *Washington Post*, February 13, 1997, A1, A9; Charles R. Babcock, "'Grass-Roots' Lobbying Credited with Saving China's Trade Status," *Washington Post*, April 27, 1997, A11.
59. Vince Beiser, "Are Pro-Israel PACs Packing It in Prematurely?" *Jerusalem Report*, October 31, 1996, 10.
60. Neal, "Asian-American Donors Feel Stigmatized."

IV. CONCLUSION

18

From Big Bird to Bill Gates: Organized Interests and the Emergence of Hyperpolitics

Allan J. Cigler and Burdett A. Loomis

It was a wonderful lesson in democracy. Here was "evil Newt" trying to kill Big Bird. There was a public outcry and we were inundated with calls from viewers. We told them if they cared about [cutting funds for public broadcasting], they should let their elected representatives know.

—Paula Kerger, WNET vice president for governmental relations

[PBS] had a letter-writing campaign. They organized grass-roots lobbying.

—Lawrence Jarvik, author and PBS critic

In 1995–1996, after gaining control of Congress, members of the new Republican majority set their sights on cutting all funds for television's Public Broadcasting Service (PBS), which they saw as representing both an inappropriate use of federal funds and a bastion of liberal thought. Given that federal spending on public broadcasting had been declining since the 1980s and that it could not lobby (at least formally) on its own behalf, PBS looked vulnerable, given the House Republicans' early success in 1995 in passing its Contract with America. But PBS did have an important, latent resource: the support of millions of individuals who watched public television, and especially those whose children had grown up with *Sesame Street*'s endearing characters.

PBS and its member stations were prohibited from lobbying, yet they did find ways to mobilize their viewers and subscribers to communicate with their representatives in Congress. In that PBS supporters are widely distributed across the country and disproportionately well-educated, this group responded quickly and effectively to the congressional threats, as framed by PBS executives such as Paula Kerger of New York's WNET.[1] Once the political conflict was defined in terms of increasingly unpopular Speaker Newt Gingrich (R-Ga.) against the always popular Big Bird, the battle was essentially over—and PBS survived, more or less intact. Indeed, in 1997 the Congress voted to appropriate $300 million for PBS in fiscal year 2000, an increase of $50 million above the 1999 spending level.

In 1988 Microsoft had no meaningful Washington presence, and Democrats controlled both houses of Congress. Ten years later Microsoft was discovered planning a huge (and surreptitious) public relations offensive to counter federal antitrust initiatives, to say nothing of burnishing the image of CEO Bill Gates. And Republicans were seeking to extend their four years of control on Capitol Hill, which might allow them to mount another attack on public broadcasting. Even more important than these major changes to the political landscape, however, has been the broad trend toward the politicization of almost all communication—ranging from television's *Ellen*'s conversion from a situation comedy to an advocacy program for gay rights to the exponential increase in Internet usage.

In the past two editions of *Interest Group Politics*, our concluding chapter has emphasized how interest groups have sought certainty within political and policy contexts that have grown more uncertain. Although some interests continue to find protection within small policy niches (for example, a modest weapons procurement program or a specific tax break), the stakes of policy decisions have grown larger, even as federal spending has consistently declined as a share of the overall economy. The key governmental decisions often do not flow from appropriations but from regulations that set the ground rules for private sector competition.[2] High-stakes decisions in how firms can compete in such fields as telecommunication, banking, and health care dictate that interests make sizeable investments in the political process—from congressional campaigning to regulation-writing—even if they cannot demonstrate that their spending makes a difference. The stakes are so high—billions of dollars, in fact—that spending several millions (or tens of millions, in Microsoft's case) seems to make good sense. In addition, those who benefit most directly—the political class of lobbyists, pollsters, public relations firms, and campaign consultants—have few incentives to reverse the process.

In this concluding chapter we will broach the argument that interests—especially moneyed interests—increasingly have come to dominate political communication in the United States. Both on the electoral and policy-making sides of American politics, information is shaped by expensive campaigns that seek to dominate the discourse on the major issues of the day. This does not mean that traditional electoral politics is unimportant, nor that honored lobbying tactics of access and personal relationships are insignificant. Far from it. Still, in a post-Cold War–post-civil rights era, the absence of overarching societal issues (with abortion as something of an exception) means that interests will compete aggressively in selling their version of public policy problems and solutions—solutions that may, as with telecommunications reform, greatly enrich specific private groups.

Politics more than ever has become an offshoot of marketing. In such a context, most information is "interested." That is, the information reflects, sometimes subtley, sometimes not, the underlying views of the interests who sponsor and disseminate it. Even science becomes adversarial, because, it seems, every side on an issue can purchase a study to support its point of view. Indeed, the tobacco discourse of the late 1990s is noteworthy because the industry finally retreated from some of its most ludicrous "scientific" claims that denied the carcinogenic and addictive elements of smoking. Most lessons of the past thirty years have schooled interests to construct a coherent story line and stick to it, on policies ranging from teenage pregnancy to international trade.[3]

We will examine the changing roles of organized interests in electoral politics and policy making. If not offering a complete picture, our vision does integrate the findings of many of this volume's chapters with a few major trends in American politics.

Groups, Parties, and Campaigns: A Blurring of Roles

The long-standing relationship between political parties and interest groups in elections has changed in recent decades. Rather than aggregating various mass interests, parties have developed some of the policy-advocating characteristics typically associated with more narrow interests. At the same time parties have become less important to mobilizing voters and running campaigns. Although the vast majority of interest groups still refrain from direct electoral involvement, more and more of them have assumed some of the activities usually associated with parties, such as recruiting candidates, organizing campaigns, and running advertisements. In some tight races, interest group voices have even drowned out those of the candidates.

The decline of parties in elections represents a long-term trend that began around the turn of the century, but a series of party and campaign reforms in the early 1970s were responsible for drastically altering party–interest group relations in the electoral process. The party reforms broke the state and local organizational control over party business, including the nomination process, and thus created opportunities for organized interest influence.[4] The campaign finance changes of the early 1970s also offered advantages to interest groups. The growth of political action committees (PACs), the limitations on party spending, and the requirements that the individual campaign organization be the legal agent of the candidate all had the effect of decreasing an already diminished party role in providing campaign resources to candidates.[5]

The parties did adapt to the interest group threat. By the mid-1980s the national parties were increasingly becoming service vendors to party candidates, successfully coping with the realities of modern, candidate-centered campaigns. PAC–party relations became less conflictual and more cooperative. Both parties embraced their emerging role as brokers by forming loose fund-raising alliances with many PACs and beginning to offer them regular assistance in directing contributions to particular campaigns, as well as aiding candidates in soliciting funds from potential donor PACs.[6] The fear of some that organized interests (through PACs) would supplant parties in the electoral process never materialized.

The 1990s have witnessed another benchmark in relations between parties and organized interests, one that may presage an even more prominent role for *both* parties and organized interests in the electoral process, perhaps at the expense of candidate domination of campaign agendas. If Paul Herrnson (Chapter 7) is correct, the candidate-centered system that has characterized electoral politics for more than half a century may face its most serious challenge to date.

There are a number of prominent features of the emerging system. Foremost is the huge escalation of organized interest money found in our most recent elections, much of it raised and spent outside of the controlling provisions of the Federal Election Campaign Act (FECA). Although some of the growth has been in PAC and independent spending (see Chapter 9), as Herrnson points out the most startling development has come in extensive soft money contributions by organized interests to the national political parties—money creatively spent by the parties beyond FECA restrictions. These contributions, in some instances more than $1 million, do not typically come from interest groups per se but most notably from individual corporations. The rise in importance of soft money to the parties may increase organized interest leverage on individual campaigns, as well as on the parties. In 1996, for example, the major parties succeeded in raising $285 million in soft money,[7] but this achievement rendered them highly dependent on large contributions from affluent interests.

The overall number of organized interests offering financial support has expanded as well, with many new groups entering the fray. For example, the American Cancer Society, a venerable nonprofit organization, recently contributed $30,000 to the Democratic and Republican parties in order to gain "the same access" as others, according to its national vice president for federal and state affairs, who said, "We wanted to look like players and be players."[8] Although this action is subject to a court challenge, the tax-exempt society sees such gifts as appropriate because the funds were targeted to party annual conferences and dinners, not campaign activity.

Beyond soft money contributions, the direct campaign efforts mustered by some organized interests in the mid-1990s were of historical proportions. Organized labor spent $35 million in 1996 to reverse the 1994 Democratic loss of Congress; some of these funds went to train union activists to organize targeted congressional districts and to increase voter registration, but the bulk of the funds went to buy air time for 27,000 television commercials in forty congressional districts—almost 800 spots per district.[9] In 1996 the National Rifle Association became active in more than 10,000 political races at local, state, and national levels (see Chapter 6), despite running a deficit and cutting its staff.

Another distinguishing feature of the emerging system is the blurring of traditional party and interest group roles in campaigns. In 1996, for example, both national parties became *group patrons*, as they used some of their soft money to fund group electoral activity such as registration drives and telephone banks (see Chapter 7). Republicans contributed to a number of antitax and prolife groups, and Democrats channeled some of their funds to a variety of groups they believed would mobilize minority voters. In a very real sense, the parties were contracting out their voter mobilization function to various organized interests. Both parties, but the Republicans in particular, have also "created a dazzling galaxy of policy institutes, foundations and think tanks, each of which can raise money from private interests and which can aid the party and party candidates in a variety of ways."[10]

A number of organized interests have been increasing the level of their activities in what traditionally has been thought of as party arena. As James Guth and his associates (Chapter 8) put it, "In an era when party organizations have either atrophied or find it difficult to activate sympathetic voters, religious interest groups are an important new force. . . . Such groups have become significant electoral competitors (and often adjuncts) to party committees, candidate organizations, and other traditional interest groups." Thus, in 1996 religious grassroots contacts of potential voters compared "quite favorably" with voters' contacts by party organizations, political candidates, and business or labor groups. More than 54 million voter guides were distributed using church-based networks in 1996. In a number of states, Christian Right adherents have captured the formal Republican Party organization, and one estimate counted roughly 200,000 movement activists as involved in the 1996 elections at various levels.[11]

Although many of the efforts of organized labor and the Christian Right have been coordinated with party or candidate efforts (most often unofficially, so campaign finance laws would not be violated), a lot of interest group electoral activity in the 1990s has been independent of candidate or party efforts. It is difficult at times to discern which organized interests were involved, because expenditures and disclosure are not regulated by current campaign finance laws. For example, at least $150 million was spent on issue advocacy campaigns in 1996.[12] As long as the ads did not advocate voting for or defeating a specific candidate, interests could express their issue-based concerns in a thinly veiled attempt to support or oppose a given candidate.[13] Well-known groups such as the AFL-CIO, the Sierra Club, the National Education Association, the National Abortion Rights Action League, and the National Federation of Independent Businesses were especially prominent. Some entities operated in the shadows. Triad Management, a political consulting firm, apparently channeled at least $3 million from conservative donors to purchase television ads in support of competitive-seat Republican candidates. Approximately twenty-five groups sponsored $100 million in issue advocacy ads in 1996, and they concentrated their efforts in fifty-four competitive House and Senate races.[14] In some cases the amount spent on issue advocacy in a race has exceeded that spent by the candidates, raising concerns that the candidates themselves had lost control over the discourse of the campaign.[15] That is precisely the point for some interest group leaders. As Paul Jacob, executive director of U.S. Term Limits, observed, "If politicians get to control the campaign, these issues [such as term limits] won't be talked about."[16]

Existing campaign finance laws have lost much of their meaning, and prospects for meaningful change are remote (see Chapters 6 and 9). As a consequence, neither parties nor interest groups are much constrained in their fund-raising and spending behavior. Parties have more money than ever before and can be expected to expand their efforts as well. Court rulings now permit parties to engage in independent spending in the same manner as interest groups, and using soft money for issue advocacy advertisements is in vogue.

The meaning of all this for American representative democracy is unclear. In many ways party–interest group relations have been functionally altered, especially in that the party now has an enhanced electoral role as a fund-raiser. But in the process of becoming a vendor engaged in modern candidate-centered elections, the party has surrendered some of its traditional functions of grassroots activism and voter mobilization, which have been largely left to those organized interests with adequate resources to perform them.

National parties look suspiciously like special interests themselves, with their primary concern being to raise campaign resources for their parties' officeholders seeking reelection (the party of the incumbents), with little advice from party activists.[17] When incumbents are threatened, both national parties may even cooperate with each other, as they did in 1987 in the face of a public outcry over congressional pay raises (the party chairs agreed not to offer financial support to challengers of those incumbents who had made the pay raise a campaign issue).[18]

An electoral system based largely on the ability of parties and their candidates to raise funds from organized interests, especially through large contributions, inevitably clashes with the dominant notion of parties as representatives of mass interests and potential counterweights to the excessive demands of particular interests. Rather, the parties may well have become, as political scientist Thomas Ferguson has theorized, not much more than investment vehicles for wealthy interests who can choose to invest directly in candidates, or broadly in parties, or specifically in issue advocacy advertisements.[19]

Interests, Information, and Policies: Many Voices, Whose Tune?

If organized interests have changed their approaches to electoral politics, so too have they altered their strategies to affect governmental decisions. Although organized interests continue to lobby in time-honored ways within the corridors of Washington institutions, such as Congress and bureaucratic agencies, they have begun to spend more time shaping perceptions of problems and political agendas. In addition, they are devoting more and more attention to earlier stages of policy formulation, especially the fundamental defining and redefining of issues. Indeed, successfully defining conditions as problems (such as smog, learning disabilities, or global warming) often represents the single most important step in changing policies.[20]

In the politics of problem definition, everyone can play by calling a press conference, releasing a study, going on a talk show, commissioning a poll, or buying an advertisement. There is no shortage in Washington either of well-defined problems or potential solutions, as the capital is awash in arguments and evidence that seek to define problems and set agendas. What is more difficult to understand very well is how certain definitions come to prevail within the context of political institutions that often, though not always, resist the consideration of new—or newly packaged—ideas.

As problem definition and agenda status become increasingly important elements of policy making, organized interests have stepped up their attempts to expand, restrict, or redirect conflict on given issues. The public interest and environmental movements of the 1960s often led the way in understanding these elements of political life, leaving business to catch up in the 1970s and 1980s.[21] Jeffrey Berry, a long-time student of public interest groups, has concluded that citizen groups have driven the policy agenda since the 1960s, thus forcing business interests to respond to sets of issues developed by groups such as Common Cause and environmental organizations.[22]

Following on the heels of these agenda successes has been the institutionalization of interests within the government, especially when broad public concerns are at stake.[23] For instance, many of the 1995 battles over the Contract with America placed legislators in sharp conflict with programs supported by members of government agencies, such as the Environmental Protection Agency. Moreover, many interests have found homes *within* the Congress in the form of caucuses composed of sitting legislators.[24]

And there's the rub. *As more interests seek to define problems and push agenda items, more messages emanate from more sources.* For threatened interests, whether corporate, environmental, or professional, the decision to socialize a conflict (and to expand the attentive audience) has no meaning unless it can be accomplished. Even Ralph Nader, the past master of using the press to expand the scope of conflict, has recently found it difficult to attract media attention.[25] Some interests can cut through the cacophony of voices; in particular, those in E. E. Schattschneider's "heavenly chorus" of affluent groups can—at a price—get their message across by spending lavishly on public relations campaigns or by buying advertising time and space.[26] In addition, if such messages are directed toward legislators who have received substantial campaign contributions from these same interests, they typically reach an audience already inclined toward receptivity.

The emphasis on problem definition looms large when major public policy issues are on the table and tremendous uncertainty exists. Lots of substantive interests are in play, many competing scenarios are put forward, legislative decisions are always contingent, and public policy outcomes are often filled with unanticipated consequences. As cozy policy-making triangles have been replaced by loose, ill-defined policy communities, decision making under conditions of great uncertainty has become the rule, not the exception.[27]

In policy battles, the capacity to obtain information and control its dissemination is the most important political power of all. Political scientist James Thurber echoes Schattschneider in arguing that if participants cannot resolve conflict on their own turf, "'outsiders' from other committees, agencies, bureaus, groups, the media, or the general public will take the issue away from them."[28] This scope-of-conflict perspective is extremely important to the dynamics of policy formulation, and it is also a source of the greatest type of uncertainty of all—conflict redefinition, as in changing a simple agricultural issue into a more complex environmental problem. The possibility of redefinition is exacerbated by the high stakes—often incredibly high—of policy decisions that may reshape entire sectors of the economy, such as health care and telecommunications.

The high stakes of recent policy controversies and the uncertainty under which those battles have taken place have generated huge amounts of spending on lobbying public officials. Any estimate of the funds expended to affect the outcomes of these broad sets of prospective policy changes—as with the $100 million estimates for health care in 1993–1994—is likely to be too low, largely because many corporate interests and trade associations informally devoted substantial resources (overhead, salaries) to defeating the Clinton plan. Although neither health care reform nor telecommunications deregulation fell into the category of pure winner-take-all decisions,[29] both did propose to affect about one-seventh of the national economy (roughly speaking, $1 trillion). The stakes were extremely high and perceived as such by virtually all involved. And in some instances, the policy stakes reflected an actual winner-take-all choice, especially for specific industries such as medium-sized health insurers, some of whom viewed their very survival at stake in the health care debate. Nor were these policy changes especially unusual; recent trade policies, tort reform, and securities and banking legislation all fall into the category of high-stakes policy decisions, as do continuing efforts at electric utility deregulation.

Although some corporate interests (such as Microsoft, until the 1990s) have resisted involvement in Washington politics, there has been a surge of activity since the late 1970s.[30] As Jeffrey Birnbaum has observed, the growth of corporate (and trade association) lobbying makes good economic sense: "[Even] in relatively small changes to larger pieces of legislation . . . big money is made and lost. Careful *investment* in a Washington lobbyist can yield enormous returns in the form of taxes avoided or regulations curbed—an odd negative sort of calculation, but one that forms the basis of the economics of lobbying."[31]

The nature of high-stakes decisions makes such investment almost mandatory, given the potential for tremendous gains and losses. In addition, the usual cost-benefit logic that applies to most managerial decisions—lobbying extensively versus building a new plant or embarking on an ambitious new research project—does not apply in high-stakes circumstances, because the potential benefits or costs are so great that virtually any expenditure can be justified, even if its chance to affect the outcome is minuscule. Indeed, spending on a host of tactics—from election contributions to insider access to public relations campaigns—may represent a strategy designed as much to protect lobbyists from criticism by their corporate or trade associations as to influence a given decision.

It may be a mistake to make too much of a distinction between an organized interest spending money in investing in candidates through contributions and providing information to elected officials with lobbying, advertising, or public relations campaigns. Interests employ a wide array of tools in pressing for advantage. Nevertheless, information exchanges between interest groups and legislators are distinct from the seeking of influence through contributions or favors. One scholar, Jack Wright, has noted that interests

> achieve influence in the legislative process not by applying electoral or financial pressure, but by developing expertise about politics and policy and by strategically sharing this expertise with legislators through normal lobbying activities. . . . [Organized interests] can and do exercise substantial influence even without making campaign contributions and . . . contributions and other material gifts or favors are not the primary sources of interest group influence in the legislative process.[32]

Even if information, and not favors or contributions, reflects the basis for interest group influence, does that mean that money is unimportant? Or that all information is equal? Hardly. Inevitably, some interests have much greater resources to develop information that shapes policy debates. For this reason, a disproportionate share of the policy and political information that is collected reflects the views of well-heeled interests that subsidize think tanks (see Chapter 11), pay for surveys, and engage public relations firms.

Interests, Hyperpolitics, and the Permanent Campaign

At the turn of the twenty-first century, the outward appearance of the Washington lobbying community remains true to its manifestations in

1975 or 1985; the Gucci culture continues apace, with expensive suits and the constant buzz of the telephone call (cellular these days). In many ways, this appearance of stability is not deceptive at all. The big dogs of capital lobbying are still there—a Tommy Boggs or a Tom Korologos[33]— trading on personal ties, political acuity, and the ability to raise a quick $10,000 (maybe even $100,000) with a word in the right ear at the right time.[34] Favors are granted, favors are returned, and the quality of their political intelligence remains top flight.

At the same time, things are not the same. Some of the changes are obvious: the ability to create all varieties of grassroots pressure, a tactic raised to art form by Jack Bonner's firm;[35] the promise and uncertainty of the Internet (a recent survey reported that 97 percent of all legislative staff used the Internet to gather information);[36] and the rash of policy-oriented television advertisements that have followed in the wake of the series of "Harry and Louise" commercials used in the health care debate. Moreover, the assault of issue-advocacy advertising in the 1996 congressional campaigns (in the wake of liberating court decisions that weakened restrictions on spending for such ads) may have ushered in an era of interest group-dominated electioneering. In addition, the entry of highly sophisticated information industry players into the political process (for example, Microsoft, a host of Silicon Valley firms, to say nothing of content providers such as Disney, which now owns ABC) may well lead to the politicization of many decisions over both the channels and the content of communication.

In general, we see three major trends taking shape and complementing each other. First, more interests are engaged in more kinds of behaviors to influence policy outcomes. Interests monitor more actions than they once did, and stand ready to swing into action more quickly when a red flag is raised (often by a lobbyist on retainer). Given the high stakes of governmental decisions, whether in a House committee or an EPA bureau, the monitoring–action combination is a worthwhile investment.

Second, there is little distinction, for most practical purposes, between "outside" and "inside" lobbying. Most effective influence relies on both. To be sure, a key provision can still find its way into a omnibus bill without a ripple, but battles over most major issues are fought simultaneously on multiple fronts. A call or fax from a House member's most important banker or editor or university president can be prompted by a lobbyist at the first sign of a problem in a committee hearing or, more likely, a casual conversation. Jack Bonner and a dozen other constituent-lobbying experts can construct a set of grassroots (or elite "grasstops") entreaties within a few days, if not a few hours. And a media buyer can target any sample of legislators for advertisements that run in their districts, thus ensuring that they know that their constituents and key Washington interests are watching their every action on an important bill.

Related to the diminished distinction between Washington and constituency-based lobbying is the increasing joint emphases on lobbying in state capitals and Washington. In particular, the tobacco settlement activity and the intensive campaigns of Microsoft to ward off antitrust actions in the states demonstrate how national and state politics are linked in an age of devolution.[37] (See Chapter 4.)

Third, and perhaps most dramatic, is the declining distinction between the politics of elections and the politics of policy making. Of course, in a democracy these are inextricably linked, and PACs may have solidified these ties since the 1970s. But these linkages have become much stronger—in many ways reflecting the "permanent campaign" of presidential elections–politics that emerged in the 1970s and 1980s. Blumenthal sees this as combining "image-making with strategic calculation. Under the permanent campaign government is turned into the perpetual campaign."[38] In the 1990s, many interests have come to see the combination of electoral and policy politics in much the same light, with the issue advocacy ads of 1996 serving as the initial demonstration of this new era. In addition, many interests are now viewing the "campaign" idea as one that defines their broader lobbying strategies and blurring the lines between electoral campaigns and public relations efforts.

All three of these trends—a move toward more activities, a lessened distinction between inside and outside lobbying, and the adoption of campaign-based strategies—come together in a 1998 business community initiative on international trade. Based on an initiative from the Commerce Department (and the tacit backing of a cautious White House), corporate advocates of free trade have embarked on a series of campaigns to argue publicly on behalf of free trade. As the *National Journal* reported, "The patrons of these pro-trade campaigns are typically multinational businesses, trade associations, lobbying groups and Washington think tanks, all called to action by Congress's declining support for . . . trade liberalization."[39] Responding to the growing strength of the much less well-funded loose coalition of labor, human rights, consumers, and environmental groups, the protrade interests, although not abandoning their insider initiatives, have reacted to their opponents' success in expanding the scope of the conflict over trade to issues such as domestic jobs, human rights, and environmental quality. Consider, for example, the actions of Cargill, the huge, privately held agriculture and financial services conglomerate. Historically, the firm has sought influence in the quiet ways, scarcely causing a ripple in public perceptions. But in 1998 the corporation sent 750 sets of videotapes, fact sheets, and sample speeches to its domestic plants and offices, so that its employees could make public pitches in community after community about the domestic impact of trade, especially in rural areas.[40]

At the same time, one thirty-year-old trade coalition (the less than aptly named Emergency Committee for American Trade) is sponsoring a campaign based on Cargill's efforts, while the Business Roundtable, another veteran group of top corporate leaders, "is spending a million dollars [in 1998] to shore up support of free trade in the districts of a dozen congressmen."[41] The Chamber of Commerce and the National Association of Manufacturers have initiated similar efforts to offer their members information and analyses to buttress free trade arguments beyond the Beltway.

In addition, a host of think tanks, from the moderate Brookings Institution to the libertarian Cato Institute, have developed initiatives to provide higher quality information on the benefits of trade. On a related tack, the Washington-based Center for Strategic and International Studies has embarked on a pilot project in Tennessee to educate public officials, corporate leaders, academics, and students on the strategic importance of enhanced international trade.[42]

The combination of many business organizations, the Commerce Department, a variety of think tanks, and congressional supporters illustrates the "campaign" nature of large-scale lobbying. The direction of influence is not clear, as business leaders respond to administration entreaties, but also hope to pressure the White House to support free trade aggressively. The lobbying is directed at community leaders and the public at large, but there is little capacity to measure its effectiveness. It does not seek, at least in 1998, to influence a particular piece of legislation. Rather, the campaign emphasizes an entire set of narratives on free trade that can be used by the executive branch, legislators, lobbyists, or grassroots advocates.

If we multiply this trade initiative by dozens of other campaigns, sponsored by dozens of other coalitions (usually Washington-based), we get the sense of what Browne calls "all-directional" lobbying (Chapter 16), where specific targets are less important than the capacity of the rhetoric to shape the issue, whether on western lands (Chapter 14) or long-distance telephone communication. We may well end up with less-than-coherent policy outcomes, because so many groups have their say.

Take foreign policy, once the bastion of bipartisanship and executive-branch dominance. As Eric Uslaner points out in Chapter 17, foreign policy lobbying reflects both the interests of Americans with ties to their "home" countries and the increasing globalization of the American economy. As journalist R. C. Longworth concluded in a 1998 series of articles:

> A fragmented, hyphenated nation plagued by interest group politics is projecting a fragmented, hyphenated foreign policy dominated by so many lobbies and interest groups that, on any given day, there seem to be hundreds of policies out there, baffling the rest of the world.
>
> The Irish lobby has pushed the Northern Ireland settlement. The Jewish lobby has propelled the U.S. actions against Iran and Iraq. . . . The Cuban lobby dictated the Helms–Burton Act, which infuriated America's best friends. The Armenian lobby has organized American

restrictions on aid to Azerbaijan, which sits on the top of some of the world's biggest oil deposits, and in cooperation with the Greek lobby works daily to humiliate Turkey, one of America's best allies in the eastern Mediterranean.[43]

Given such cacophony, coupled to high-stakes decisions, it is no wonder that those cultural icons Bill Gates and Big Bird have entered the political fray. Their respective interests, both economic and cultural, are great, and the costs of investing in lobbying, although substantial, pale before the potential benefits. But there is a cost to this extension of politics to much of our communication, what we choose to call *hyperpolitics*. If all information is seen as interested, as just one more story, then how do decision makers sort it all out? What voices cut through the "data smog"[44] of a society that can cough up studies and stories at a moment's notice, and communicate them broadly or narrowly, as tactics suggest? Although some students of interest groups, such as William Browne (Chapter 16) and Jeffrey Berry, see hopeful signs for a vigorous pluralism that accords major roles to consumers, public interest advocates, and environmentalists, we remain skeptical.[45] The costs of lobbying in a hyperpolitics state are great, and the stakes are high. Money surely does not guarantee success, but the capacity to spend keeps well-heeled interests in the game, able to play the range of games that have come to define the politics of influence as we move further into the age of information.

Notes

1. Irvin Molotsky, "How One Tough Bird Survived the Attacks on Public Broadcasting," *The New York Times*, November 27, 1997, B1.
2. Pietro Nivola, "Regulation: The New Pork Barrel," *The Brookings Review* (Winter 1998): 6–9.
3. See Darrell West and Burdett Loomis, *The Sound of Money* (New York: W. W. Norton, in press).
4. See, for example, Byron Shafer, *Quiet Revolution* (New York: Russell Sage Foundation, 1983).
5. See Paul Herrnson, *Party Campaigning in the 1980s* (Cambridge: Harvard University Press, 1988); Xandra Kayden, "Alive and Well and Living in Washington: The American Political Parties," in Michael Maragolis and Gary Mauser, eds., *Manipulating Public Opinion* (Pacific Grove, Calif.: Brooks/Cole, 1989).
6. Larry Sabato, *PAC Power* (New York: Norton, 1984).
7. Jill Abramson, "Parties Press Hunt for Cash Despite the Calls for Reform," *New York Times*, May 12, 1998, A20.
8. Jonathan D. Salant, "Cancer Group Gave to GOP, Democrats," *Kansas City Star*, March 30, 1998, A12.
9. Paul Herrnson, *Congressional Elections: Campaigning at Home and in Washington* (Washington, D.C.: CQ Press, 1998), 123–124.
10. Clyde Wilcox and Wesley Joe, "Dead Law: The Federal Election Finance Regulations, 1974–1996," *PS* 31 (March 1998): 15.
11. John C. Green, "The Christian Right and the 1996 Elections: An Overview," in *God at the Grass Roots*, ed. Mark J. Rozell and Clyde Wilcox (Lanham, Md.: Rowman and Littlefield, 1997), 1–14.

12. Annenberg Public Policy Center (University of Pennsylvania) estimate, cited in Donna Cassata, "Independent Groups' Ads Increasingly Steer Campaigns," *CQ Weekly*, May 2, 1998, 1114.
13. See, for example, Robert Dreyfuss, "Harder Than Soft Money," *The American Prospect* 36 (January/February 1998): 30–37.
14. Dreyfuss, "Harder than Soft Money," 30.
15. Richard Berke, "Interest Groups Plan to Create Their Own Ads for Campaigns," *New York Times*, January 11, 1998, A16.
16. Cassata, "Independent Groups' Ads Increasingly Steer Campaigns," 1114.
17. For a provocative discussion of who is represented by today's parties, see Frank J. Sorauf, "Political Parties and Campaign Finance," in L. Sandy Maisel, ed., *The Parties Respond,* 3d ed. (Boulder, Colo.: Westview Press, 1998), 225–242.
18. Allan J. Cigler, "Political Parties and Interest Groups: Competitors, Collaborators, and Uneasy Allies," in Eric M. Uslaner, ed., *American Political Parties: A Reader* (Itasca, Ill.: F. E. Peacock, 1995), 426.
19. Thomas Ferguson, *Golden Rule* (Chicago: University of Chicago Press, 1995), and West and Loomis, *The Sound of Money,* chap. 2.
20. See, among others, many of the articles in David Rochefort and Roger Cobb, eds., *The Politics of Problem Definition* (Lawrence: University Press of Kansas, 1994), and Frank Baumgartner and Bryan Jones, *Agendas and Instability in American Politics* (Chicago: University of Chicago Press, 1993).
21. David Vogel, *Fluctuating Fortunes* (New York: Basic Books, 1989), 295–297.
22. Jeffery Berry, *The Power of Citizen Groups* (Washington, D.C.: Brookings Institution, forthcoming).
23. See Gary Mucciaroni, *Reversals of Fortune* (Washington, D.C.: Brookings Institution, 1995).
24. Susan Webb Hammond, *Congressional Caucuses in National Policy Making* (Baltimore: Johns Hopkins University Press, 1998).
25. Ralph Nader, "Minimal Media Coverage of Auto Safety Initiative," *Liberal Opinion*, March 27, 1995, 26.
26. E. E. Schattschneider, *The Semi-Sovereign People* (New York: Holt, Rinehart, and Winston, 1960), and West and Loomis, *The Sound of Money.*
27. See William E. Browne, *Cultivating Congress* (Lawrence: University Press of Kansas, 1995), and John Wright, *Interest Groups and Congress* (Boston: Allyn and Bacon, 1996).
28. James Thurber, *Divided Democracy* (Washington: D.C.: CQ Press), 336.
29. Robert H. Frank and Philip J. Cook, *The Winner-Take-All-Society* (New York: Basic Books, 1995).
30. See Hanna Rosin, "Mining Microsoft," *The New Republic*, June 8, 1998, 13.
31. Jeffrey Birnbaum, *The Lobbyists* (New York: Times Books, 1993), 4, emphasis added.
32. Wright, *Interest Groups and Congress,* 88.
33. Thomas Hale Boggs is the well-connected son of former Democratic House leader Hale Boggs and brother of ABC commentator Cokie Roberts. A nominal Democrat, Boggs has been a major presence in Washington politics since the 1970s, and his firm grosses more than $10 million per year in lobbying fees. Korologos is similar to Boggs, save with a Republican spin; working as a partner of Timmons and Company, he represents such powerful interests as the NRA, Anheuser-Busch, and Major League Baseball.
34. A 1998 *Washingtonian* article that lists the alleged top fifty lobbyists in Washington is filled with many of the usual suspects, although it does contain a disproportionate number of former legislators, who have cemented their personal ties with decision makers during their days in the Congress and thus do not have to

contend with stricter ethics rules on entertainment. See Kim I. Eisler, "Show Me the Money," *Washingtonian* on-line (http://www.washingtonian.com).

35. Jack Bonner and his firm have changed the face of Washington lobbying to the extent that grassroots campaigns have become commonplace and available for purchase. More than most lobbyists, Bonner works to target grassroots efforts on key members of Congress.

36. James A. Thurber, *Congress and the Internet* (Washington, D.C.: Center for Congressional and Presidential Studies, The American University, 1998).

37. On Microsoft, see Greg Miller and Leslie Helm, "Microsoft Plans Stealth Blitz to Mend Its Image," *Los Angeles Times*, April 10, 1998, 1.

38. Sidney Blumenthal, *The Permanent Campaign* (New York: Touchstone, 1982), 23.

39. Julie Kosterlitz, "Trade Crusade," *National Journal*, May 9, 1998, 1054. In addition to the specific citations noted here and later, the following paragraphs draw generally on this story.

40. Ibid., 1055.

41. Ibid.

42. Ibid., 1056.

43. R. C. Longworth, quoted in Georgie Anne Geyer, "Politics Dominates U.S. Policy," *Lawrence Journal-World*, May 9, 1998.

44. The term was coined by David Shenk, *Data Smog* (New York: HarperSanFrancisco, 1997).

45. Berry, *The Power of Citizen Groups*.

Index

Republican Party (*continued*)
  campaign committees, 151–152, 158
  campaign finance, 151–152, 154, 158,
    161–162
  campaign finance reform, 164, 210
  Christian Right and, 169
  environmental issues, 322
  ethnic groups, 370–371, 376, 380, 382
  federal land management, 308
  fundraising, 277
  immigration legislation, 377
  interest group access, 278
  Latinos, 374, 375
  National Endowment for the Arts, 291,
    296
  National Rifle Association and, 136, 138
  religious interest groups, 172, 180, 182–189
  reverse lobbying, 259
  soft money, 207
Research, 102–103, 106, 236, 237, 390–391.
  See also Science Coalition
Research America, 110
Research studies
  corporate giving, 67–75
  environmental organizations, 41–42, 61*n*18
  higher education, 98–99, 115*n*14
  lobbyists, 222–223, 233*n*11
  methodologies, 42, 68, 98–99, 115*n*14,
    171, 222–223, 233*n*11
  organization and structure, 88–95
  religious interest groups, 171–189
Revenue Act of 1971, 195
Riady, James, 383
Rifle, 132
Riker, William, 286
Rimsza, Skip, 124
RNC. *See* Republican National Committee
Rockefeller, John D., Jr., 237
Rockefeller, Nelson, 289
Rockford Institute, 241
Rock the Vote campaign, 108
Rocky Mountain Oil and Gas Association,
  308
Roe, Emery, 312
Roe v. Wade (1973), 15, 327, 329–331, 332,
  333–334, 335. *See also* Abortion
Roll Call, 103
Roosevelt, Franklin D., 238
Rosin, Hanna, 269
Rothenberg, Larry, 41, 44, 285
Russell Sage Foundation, 237, 240

Sabato, Larry, 151
Sage, Margaret Olivia, 237
Salisbury, Robert H., 6–7, 16, 27, 40–41, 121
Sarbanes, Paul (D-Md.), 203, 212*n*36
Save the Manatee Club, 36, 46, 54–55
Savimbi, Jonas, 375
Savings and loan scandal, 27, 28
SBREFA. *See* Small Business Regulatory
  Enforcement Fairness Act of 1996

Scaife, Richard, 239
Schattschneider, E.E., 336, 395–396
Schick, Allen, 236
Schlafly, Phyllis, 296
Schlozman, Kay Lehman, 100, 101, 112, 175,
  285
Schmidt, John, 264
Science Coalition, 102, 107, 109, 110, 112
Scott, David, 42
Scott Paper Company, 65
Scott, Ray, 15–17
Second Amendment Foundation, 131
Second Amendment issues. *See* National
  Rifle Association
Selway-Bitterroot Wilderness, 322
Senate. *See* Congress
Serrano, Andres, 291–292, 293
Sesame Street, 389
SHEEOs. *See* State Higher Education
  Executive Officers
Sierra Club, 224
  campaigns and elections, 161
  ecosystem model, 314
  federal lands, 304, 310
  growth of, 311
  issue advocacy, 393
  litigation department, 37
  lobbying by, 347
  membership, 36, 37, 311
  web site, 46
Silent Spring (Carson), 356
Slovakia, 379
Small Business Regulatory Enforcement
  Fairness Act of 1996 (SBREFA), 276
Smeal, Eleanor, 331
Snow, Donald, 45
Social issues. *See also* Cultural issues; Interest
  groups, religious
  abortion, 330, 331, 333–335
  civic gospel, 180
  class structure, 18–19, 23
  corporate giving, 65
  cultural conflict, 305
  environmentalism, 356–357
  ethnicity, 19
  federal lands, 309, 312
  foreign policy, 365–366
  gun control, 124
  interest group development, 20–21
  interest group politics, 27–28
  lobbying, 232
  National Endowment for the Arts, 292,
    293, 295–296
  postindustrial society, 18
  religious regions, 180–181
  valence issues, 19
Social Security, 12, 28, 102
Society for Professional Journalists, 223
Soft money. *See* Campaign finance, soft
  money
Somalia, 379